RE-ENVISIONING PSYCHOLOGY

RE-ENVISIONING PSYCHOLOGY

Moral Dimensions of Theory and Practice

Frank C. Richardson
Blaine J. Fowers
Charles B. Guignon

Jossey-Bass Publishers
San Francisco

Jossey-Bass books and products are available through most bookstores. To contact Jossey-Bass directly, call (888) 378-2537, fax to (800) 605-2665, or visit our website at www.josseybass.com.

Substantial discounts on bulk quantities of Jossey-Bass books are available to corporations, professional associations, and other organizations. For details and discount information, contact the special sales department at Jossey-Bass.

TCF Manufactured in the United States of America on Lyons Falls Turin Book. This paper is acid-free and 100 percent totally chlorine-free.

Excerpt from "The Rock" in *Collected Poems 1909–1962* by T. S. Eliot, copyright 1936 by Harcourt Brace & Company, copyright © 1964, 1963 by T. S. Eliot, reprinted by permission of the publisher.

Library of Congress Cataloging-in-Publication Data

Richardson, Frank C.

  Re-envisioning psychology : moral dimensions of theory and practice / Frank C. Richardson, Blaine J. Fowers, and Charles B. Guignon. — 1st ed.

    p. cm.

  Includes bibliographical references and index.

  ISBN 0-7879-4384-3 (hardcover)

  1. Psychology—Philosophy. 2. Psychotherapy—Philosophy. I. Fowers, Blaine J., 1956– II. Guignon, Charles B., 1944– III. Title.

  BF38 .R524 1999

  150'.1—ddc21

                       98-40146

FIRST EDITION

HB Printing 10 9 8 7 6 5 4 3 2 1

Contents

*This book is dedicated to Betsy Aylin, Susan
Green, Sally Marie Guignon, and our children.*

ACKNOWLEDGMENTS

FRANK RICHARDSON AND BLAINE FOWERS would like to express their gratitude to a group of friends and colleagues associated with the Division of Theoretical and Philosophical Psychology of the American Psychological Association, for their stimulating company and support in recent years. In addition to our dear friend Philip Cushman, our thanks go to Isaac Prilleltensky, Suzanne Kirschner, Rachel Hare-Mustin, Jeanne Marecek, Hank Stam, Rob Woolfolk, Brent Slife, Richard Williams, Jack Martin, and Jeff Sugarman.

Frank Richardson and Blaine Fowers would also like to thank a most remarkable crew of graduate students in recent years—intelligent, high-minded, willing to take risks—who have shared in and contributed much to this adventure of ideas: Kevin Groves, Linda Ridge Wolszon, John Christopher, Greg Lambeth, Rob Teply, Vince River, Tony Rogers, Tim Zeddies, Jennifer McCarroll, Amy Hemp Monagle, Alan Keston, Michael Tredinnick, Lynne Harkless, and Andrew Wenger. Greg Lambeth and John Christopher contributed significantly to papers that turned into Chapters Four and Eight and should be considered coauthors of these chapters.

Finally, we would like to thank our editor, Leslie Berriman, for key ideas, enthusiastic encouragement, and invaluable practical advice.

RE-ENVISIONING PSYCHOLOGY

INTRODUCTION

Where is the wisdom we have lost in knowledge?
Where is the knowledge we have lost in information?

—T. S. Eliot

AS TEACHERS, WE SEE at first hand the cracks in the foundations of academic and professional psychology. We find that thoughtful undergraduates, committed graduate students, and many of our colleagues have serious doubts at times about the intellectual value or social significance of the theories and research findings of modern psychology. They are often genuinely fascinated with the topics under discussion, including such things as self-esteem, human development, gender differences, group dynamics, human psychopathology, and schools of psychotherapy. But they often worry whether research reported on these topics really sheds much light on them or comes up with more than what one philosopher of social science calls "wordy elaborations of the obvious" (Taylor, 1985a, p. 1). They may be uncomfortable with mainstream psychology's claim to be a value-neutral science of human behavior. If it is strictly neutral, they wonder, how can it be relevant to human affairs except as some sort of manipulative behavioral technology? Moreover, they see few signs that the social disciplines will ever even approach the natural sciences in explanatory or predictive power. If that is not discouraging enough, it may strike them that even if we had more raw predictive and technological prowess, we might only compound some of our biggest problems. After all, influential critics and commentators throughout the twentieth century have been saying that we seem to diminish in

I

wisdom as we grow in technological capacity. The more we dedicate ourselves to gaining control over nature and some social processes, the less
we seem able to meaningfully reflect about the *ends* or goals we should
be pursuing or that are really worth pursuing (Habermas, 1973;
Horkheimer, 1974).

Our society may accord professional psychologists and psychotherapists too much respect. It is not clear how much we understand about
human behavior. It is uncertain how often we can make a significant difference in people's lives. And it is unclear how essential a contribution
we make to the search for some deeper wisdom about living or a better
society. No doubt we do some good and make some contributions. However, both inside and outside the professional psychology arena, many
doubts are surfacing. Some of them are touched on in a recent book by
James Hillman and Michael Ventura (1992) titled *We've Had a Hundred
Years of Psychotherapy and the World's Getting Worse*. Critics worry
that the theories and actual practice of modern psychotherapy may subtly encourage individuals to think of themselves in too narrow a way. Psychotherapy may encourage them to view not just the overcoming of
psychic wounds and deficits but life itself as a matter of breaking free
from the past in order to engage in an endless pursuit of "self-realization." Over the long run, however, this attitude may be self-defeating. It
may be difficult for men and women to meet life's difficulties and find a
measure of happiness without some sense of tradition, belonging, or
wider loyalties. Modern psychology tends to ignore such factors of loyalty and belonging, however, or even to treat them as impediments to
"self-actualization."

Academic and professional psychology became tremendously prominent and influential in American life in a very short time during the last
half of the twentieth century, leading Philip Rieff (1966) to speak of a
"triumph of the therapeutic" in our time. Perhaps because modern psychology is both so recent and so imposing a phenomenon, it tends to
breed either true believers or sharp detractors rather than thoughtful critics who are willing and able to sort out the wheat from the chaff in this
world of ideas, to discriminate the truly insightful from the merely fashionable or trivial. However, it may be just such criticism that students,
thinking practitioners, and citizens of our psychology-saturated culture
need most. In this book, we explore some of the reasons why modern
psychology, so energetic and productive in many ways, is peculiarly deficient in examining its own basic assumptions and questioning its entanglement with some of the less admirable features of the society of which
it is an integral part.

Two of the authors of this book, Frank Richardson and Blaine Fowers, were trained as practicing psychologists and social scientists. For a time we pursued our careers with a sense of real purpose and satisfaction. However, we soon began to raise the aforementioned questions for ourselves with a great deal of interest and a certain amount of personal urgency. After all, these questions challenged our careers and some of our deepest beliefs and commitments. This book reflects our journey into and (for us, anyway) part of the way out of a wilderness of confusion about these matters. We have found the hermeneutic philosophy of Hans-Georg Gadamer, Paul Ricoeur, and Charles Taylor, along with the writings on moral philosophy of Alasdair MacIntyre, to be our best guides in this undertaking. Our main and best instruction in these matters has come from the book's third author, Charles Guignon, a philosopher long interested in the interface of psychology and philosophy.

In this introduction, we outline the main themes and critical questions we discuss at greater length throughout the book. The chapters that follow are grouped in three parts. Part One deals with the cultural and moral underpinnings of modern psychotherapy and its entanglement with modern ideologies. Part Two discusses similar issues at the core of social science inquiry. Part Three explores how we might move toward a re-envisioned, more interpretive psychology.

Ethical Underpinnings of Modern Psychotherapy

Our journey began when certain troubling questions about the social meaning of modern psychotherapy arose in our practice and reflection. As we began to ponder these matters, it soon became clear that questions and worries of this general sort have been raised a number of times over the years, from Freud's day to our own. We will review in the following pages several of the critiques that emerged from within the therapy tradition itself. One of the most notable of them is Erich Fromm's discussion, a half-century ago, of the "ambiguity" of modern freedom. Fromm worried that modern psychology might actually compound many of the dilemmas of a modern existence focused on liberation without providing any compelling purposes that might make a liberated way of life worth living.

These earlier critiques are remarkably insightful, even if their authors did not propose entirely satisfactory solutions to the problems they identified. Also remarkable is how unaware most teachers and students of psychology are today of these past expressions of apprehension about their field. Such naïveté perpetuates a shallow view of psychology's own stormy intellectual traditions, a luxury we can no longer afford.

Most of the caviling and criticism raised over the years concerning modern psychotherapy clusters around a basic issue we might frame in this way: To what degree does twentieth-century psychotherapy represent a significant contribution to human welfare and the struggle for a good society? Is it possible that the modern therapy enterprise to some extent subtly reinforces a shallow, one-sided individualism in our kind of society? Does it help perpetuate such modern social ills as the loss of community, the decay of any sense of individual purpose beyond shallow and self-serving ends in living, emotional isolation, alienation, and emptiness?

It seems undeniable that the myriad forms of counseling and psychotherapy in our society often benefit individuals and families. Moreover, few would disagree that modern psychology has shed light on basic human struggles, especially on the ways people defensively distort their experiences and truncate their living in response to the threats and uncertainties of an often precarious existence, and has illumined how these self-inflicted wounds result from and play themselves out in distorted human relationships. But all modern psychotherapy theories tend to operate with certain basic assumptions that call for reflection. For example, most of them portray people in a highly individualistic manner as hampered by untoward early life experiences from moving along a life path often described in terms of "separation and individuation."

Philip Cushman (1990) reminds us that a great deal of contemporary theory and research in psychology confirms the great extent to which a relatively happy and flexible life depends on "a nurturing early environment that provides a great deal of empathy, attention, and mirroring" (p. 604). But he wonders if these conclusions might, in part, reflect the unacknowledged influence of our historical situation. Contemporary parents seem to be saddled with the responsibility for providing a kind and degree of nurturance that is rare in human history, perhaps because today we live in a "less communal and certain world" in which "more traditional sources of guidance have been lost" (p. 605). Whatever the reason, we seem to believe that children need a great deal of acknowledgment and empathy from their caregivers. Nevertheless, Cushman argues, the picture of the good life to which many adults aspire in our society actually tends to undermine our ability to meet this pressing need.

Generally speaking, according to Cushman (1990, p. 604), the "bounded, masterful self" of our time "is expected to function in a highly autonomous, isolated way" and "to be self-soothing, self-loving, and self-sufficient." Unfortunately, he thinks there is evidence that the inflated, would-be autonomous self of modernity almost inevitably collapses into an "empty self," whose characteristics of fragility, sense of emptiness, and proneness to fluctuation between feelings of worthlessness and grandiosity are often said to be the hallmarks of neurotic psychopathology in our day (Kohut, 1977). Cushman (1990, p. 604) defines emptiness as, "in part, an absence of communal forms and beliefs," which leaves individuals quite vulnerable to influence from cultural forms such as advertising and psychology, both professional and "pop," which emanate authority and certainty. So it is telling that the goals of psychotherapy are usually rendered in terms of more effective individual behavior, enhanced self-realization, or a kind of personal authenticity in which one chooses one's own values and directions in splendid isolation from the pull of tradition or society. Little is said about ethical qualities of character or commitment that many feel are essential to a worthwhile or fulfilled life. The absence of such qualities may be a virtual recipe for personal shallowness and social fragmentation. Moreover, in their absence it is unclear why such autonomous, self-interested individuals would ever "choose to undergo the self-sacrifice and suffering necessary" to raise flourishing children in modern America (p. 605). One danger of all this, Cushman believes, is that academic and professional psychology may reinforce a one-sided "preoccupation with the inner self" that "causes the social world to be devalued or ignored except to the degree that it mirrors and thus becomes appropriated by the self." As a result, the social and cultural milieu "loses its impact as a material force, and social problems lose their relation to political action" (p. 605).

The phrase *Me Decade* or *Me Generation* has been so widely bandied about and has become such a cliché that it is easy to forget its origin in Tom Wolfe's astute and often hilarious essay (1983), "The Me Decade and the Third Great Awakening," first published in 1976. Wolfe expresses worries about American individualism similar to those of Cushman. He wonders if he is not seeing the culmination of a dangerous trend in American culture identified by Alexis de Tocqueville in the early part of the nineteenth century. Using a recently coined word, Tocqueville (1835/1969) observed in the 1830s a new kind of "individualism," less extreme than what was traditionally called egoism but with similar results. He defined individualism as "a calm and considered feeling which disposes each citizen to isolate himself from the mass of his fellows and withdraw into the circle of family and friends; with this little society formed to his taste, he gladly leaves the greater society to look after itself." In American democracy, Tocqueville finds, there are more and more people who are not rich or powerful but have enough in the way of wealth and skills to "look after their own needs." They "owe no man anything and hardly expect anything from anybody." They "form the habit of thinking of themselves in isolation and imagine that their whole destiny is in their hands. Unfortunately, such a way of life not only makes "each man forget his ancestors, it hides his descendants from him, and divides him from his contemporaries; it continually turns him back on himself alone, and threatens, at last, to enclose him entirely in the solitude of his own heart" (p. 506).

Wolfe's "Third Great Awakening" refers to the outbreak of a new quasi-religious worship of the self in the Me Decade of the 1960s that parallels in intensity Jonathan Edwards's era in the 1740s and what historians call the Second Great Awakening of religious enthusiasm in many sectors of American life from about 1825 to 1850. Wolfe thinks that much of the appeal of such 1960s phenomena as encounter groups and est training came from their ability to focus, at least momentarily, enormous amounts of attention and energy on "the most fascinating subject on earth: Me. . . . Just imagine . . . my life becoming a drama with universal significance . . . analyzed, like Hamlet's, for what it signifies for the rest of mankind." This movement is not simply vulgar egoism, Wolfe suggests. It responds to a real need to be somebody in the anonymous sea of contemporary humanity and is no less admirable than the pursuits of many of the cultural elite of modern times. Wolfe writes: "[Tocqueville's idea of the modern individual] lost 'in the solitude of his own heart' has been brought forward into our time in such terminology as *alienation* (Marx), *anomie* (Durkheim), the *mass man* (Ortega y Gasset), and *the lonely crowd* (Riesman). The picture is always of a creature uprooted by industrialism, packed together in cities with people he doesn't know, helpless against massive economic and political shifts—in short, a creature like Charlie Chaplin in *Modern Times,* a helpless, bewildered, and dispirited slave of the machinery." This "victim of modern times," according to Wolfe, has always been "a most appealing figure to intellectuals, artists, and architects." They have eagerly devised many schemes for improving the minds of these poor lost souls or socially re-engineering the world they live in. However, once these ordinary individuals "started getting money in the 1940s, they did an astonishing thing—they took their money and ran! They did something only aristocrats (and intellectuals and artists) were supposed to do—they discovered and started doting on *Me!* They've created the greatest age of individualism in American history!" (Wolfe, 1983, p. 279).

Most psychotherapy and counseling over the last few decades, to be sure, has been concerned not with the relative frivolities of 1960s encounter groups and est weekends but with individuals who are painfully depressed or crippled by anxiety, or with "dysfunctional" families that destroy some of their members and pass their miseries on to another generation. Still, if critics like Cushman and Wolfe are right, psychotherapy and counseling may tend, along with the good they do, to promote a "preoccupation with the inner self" that by itself does little to restore a sense of wider purpose within some community of shared values, without which the conditions for personal insecurity and directionlessness may only be reinforced, promoting yet more preoccupation with inner distress.

Wolfe concludes his discussion by putting the new movements he satirizes into historical perspective. Most people, he contends, "have *not* lived their lives as if thinking, 'I have only one life to live.'" Rather, they have lived "as if they are living their ancestors' lives and their offsprings' lives and perhaps their neighbors' lives as well." Whether or not they believed in personal survival after death, they have embraced some version of "serial immortality." They have seen themselves as "inseparable from the great tide of chromosomes of which they are created and which they pass on." They did not feel that the "mere fact that you were only going to be here for a short time" gave one "the license to try to climb out of the stream and change the natural order of things" (1983, p. 292).

When he toured the United States, Robert Coles (1987) found, no matter where he went, many such attempts to "climb out of the stream." People were all too ready to speak in a psychologically charged vocabulary of their "problems" and "issues." "The hallmark of our time," he writes, is "lots of psychological chatter, lots of self-consciousness, lots of 'interpretation.'" Psychology here means "a concentration, persistent, if not feverish, upon one's thoughts, feelings, wishes, worries—bordering on, if not embracing, solipsism: the self as the only or main form of (existential) reality" (p. 189). Robert Bellah and his colleagues (Bellah, Madsen, Sullivan, Swindler, & Tipton, 1985, p. 143) term this intense concentration on the self as a self-contained unit *ontological individualism* and doubt "whether an individualism in which the self has become the main form of reality can really be sustained."

Jerome Frank (1978), the distinguished psychotherapy researcher and interpreter of therapy as a cultural phenomenon, summarizes many of the concerns that have been raised over the years about the implicit values of modern psychotherapy. He observes that as "institutions of American society, all psychotherapies . . . share a value system that accords primacy to individual self-fulfillment," including "maximum self-awareness, unlimited access to one's own feelings, increased autonomy and creativity." The individual is seen as "the center of his moral universe, and concern for others is believed to follow from his own self-realization." In Frank's view and ours, these values are admirable in many ways. One cannot help but admire the passionate intensity and devotion with which so many modern therapists have sought to free individuals from debilitating conflicts and unnecessary constraints, in order that they might live fuller lives. Nevertheless, concerns grow that the results of these activities and therefore the practices of therapy themselves are somewhat morally ambiguous. For example, Frank notes, the implicit value system of modern psychotherapy "can easily become a source of misery in itself" because of its unrealistic expectations for personal happiness and the burden of resentment it imposes when inevitable disappointments occur. In his opinion, the literature of psychotherapy gives little attention to such traditional, possibly worthwhile values or virtues as "the redemptive power of suffering, acceptance of one's lot in life, adherence to tradition, self-restraint and moderation" (pp. 6–7).

Recently, Robert Fancher (1995) has made similar observations. He argues that modern therapy systems assert unsubstantiated claims about being based on some sort of science of psychopathology. According to Fancher, however, behind the facade of an objective theory of "mental health" or neutral science of human behavior, each of these systems promotes a view of the good life, a value system, or a "culture." These "cultures of healing" may have real virtues, but they seem to have many questionable features or values as well. Concerning one of these cultures, psychoanalysis, Fancher writes (pp. 124–125) that psychoanalysts often

> do not seem to recognize that there is no inherent reason why the satisfaction of instinctual needs and inclinations must necessarily be the measure of truth. There is no inherent reason why internal dynamics, rather that one's place in society, must be the principle source of health or illness. For most of history, in most civilized cultures, the kind of internal fulfillment that psychoanalysis values has been suspect, and fidelity to "one's station and its duties" has generally been a higher value. [These] psychoanalysts may offer a superior way to live, or a way of living that makes more sense in a highly mobile, modern society. What they are also doing, though, is promulgating a set of values that they rarely defend on moral or social grounds—though the moral and social ramifications of these values are immense. Their justification, instead—and this is one of the main problems with all mental health care—is that this is what "health" is.

It is high time, Fancher contends, to own up to these cultural and moral value commitments, subject them to thoughtful analysis, and let them be thoroughly discussed in democratic debate.

Unfortunately, Frank's and Fancher's thoughtful critiques also illustrate how difficult it is to get around the impasse—assuming it is an impasse—that they have identified. Fancher gives us no clues as to how we might envision a cultural universe in which it would make sense once again, or in some new way, to practice "fidelity to one's station and duties" as opposed to keeping up with the Joneses or grabbing all the gusto while we go around (presumably) once. Frank gives few suggestions as to how we might synthesize, let us say, self-restraint or finding meaning in suffering with the aggressive modern pursuit of health, success, and "individual self-fulfillment." As a matter of fact, regrettably or not, the ideals of individual self-fulfillment and the neglected values Frank and Fancher mention seem like mutually exclusive alternatives.

Perhaps this should not come as a surprise to us. After all, modern psychology and psychotherapy likely came into existence in large part as ways of dealing with problems of living engendered by the breakdown of supporting institutions and the dissolution of linkages of shared purpose and obligation that characterize modern cultural life (Progoff, 1956; Sarason, 1986). They were designed to help individuals break free from the past, not find a way to reconnect with it—to help them make do with much less community, not restore or renew it. Surely, the thinking goes, any community worth having would only be strengthened by having more truly liberated and self-reliant members. But suppose the available patterns of work, intimacy, and meaning in the wider society are deficient or confused in ways that make it difficult to sustain individual integrity and purposefulness, or even achieve it in the first place. Then more "liberation" is beside the point, or just makes matters worse.

Critics like Cushman, Frank, and Fancher are suggesting that we are presently in such a situation to some degree and so need to rethink what modern psychotherapy has to contribute to human welfare. What are its enduring insights? How could some of its resources be recast or redirected? What errors or excesses need to be permanently discarded? We hope to take a few additional steps toward answering such questions. Such progress will only come from taking a longer historical view of the problem than we usually do in the social sciences, and from digging deeper into what Slife and Williams (1995) term *implicit assumptions*—which often have far-reaching consequences—about social science, psychotherapy, and the good life. In Chapter One, we look at what we consider to be some of the main dilemmas of modern culture and attempt to put them in a wider historical and critical perspective. The rest of the chapters in Part One explore how these dilemmas show up at the heart of therapy theory and practice.

Beyond Scientism and Constructionism

For more than half a century, most mainstream psychology has held fast to the idea that critical questions about the effectiveness and social contribution of psychotherapy can be answered properly only by empirical research into whether different approaches to behavior change "work"— that is, whether they work efficiently in bringing about desired results. However, there have always been a few dissenters who objected that the complexity and subtlety of human interactions elude the grasp of standard research approaches. Other critics have argued that there are many crucial questions empirical research simply cannot answer. For example, such research might shed light on whether particular approaches are conducive to achieving particular ends, but it can give us no insight into whether such ends are worth pursuing in the first place.

In recent years, doubts about the value of psychotherapy research have intensified questions about whether the methods of mainstream social science in general are appropriate to their subject matter. Many people inside and outside the field are asking whether psychology can or should model itself on the natural sciences or whether it should try to be a science at all. They ask, Has the attempt of mainstream academic psychology to produce a genuine science of human behavior been successful, or even promising? Or has it mainly produced findings of only limited value or yielded merely commonsensical or even trivial results? When we investigated these questions, we were surprised to discover how much the same kind of one-sided individualism that has created vexatious dilemmas concerning freedom and moral values in the modern psychotherapy enterprise seems also to be an important factor in ongoing debates about the status of psychology as a field of inquiry.

Slife and Williams (1995, 1997) clearly identify one of the major stumbling blocks for a would-be scientific social science. Such scientific approaches have generally treated theorizing as distinct from, and subordinate to, the use of scientific methods to uncover knowledge. The claim is that our theories or conjectures are valid or acceptable only to the extent that they are tested and confirmed by methods that have been determined in advance quite apart from any particular theoretical beliefs. On such a view, one might wonder if one should be a behaviorist, a true believer in psychoanalytic theory, or a transpersonal psychologist and expect to find out which position to adopt through the use of the proper method!

The problem with such a view, however, is that methods are adopted on the *basis* of some theoretical or philosophical beliefs about the nature

of things and how we come to know the world. We would have no idea
about what sorts of methods might be useful—or even that we needed
methods in the first place—except on the basis of preconceived beliefs
about the human realm, beliefs that are inseparable from social and moral
ideals. Thus, as Slife and Williams (1997) argue, "method itself is a theory—a philosophy. Similar to any other theory or philosophy, it makes
assumptions about the world, and important implications arise from those
assumptions." These presupposed theoretical or philosophical ideas rule
out some kinds of explanations and evaluations and support others. So,
in unreflective scientistic approaches, "some psychological ideas are ruled
out in a very unscientific manner—by philosophical fiat in the guise of
'scientific method'" (p. 120).

These days, it is becoming increasingly clear that theory and method
are intimately intertwined; they profoundly influence each other and are
different facets of the particular stance toward the world we have adopted
or different aspects of the language games (the philosopher Wittgenstein's
term for ways of talking about and constructing the world governed by
social norms and conventions) or practices in which we are engaged.
Acknowledging this interdependence of theory and method, however,
pulls a number of major props out from under the edifice of the mainstream social sciences, and basic changes in these disciplines seem
inevitable.

Increasingly, critics (Bellah, 1983; Taylor, 1985b) are suggesting that
the distinctive moral tenor and commitments of modern times have played
a central role in fashioning the kind of social science that has been so
prominent in our society. In Chapter One, we describe that tenor as emancipatory and liberationist. But we have already discussed some of the ways
various critics think this moral and political outlook colors the theory and
practice of modern therapy. It has led to a one-sided individualism in our
way of life that perpetuates a permanent stance of resistance against the
abridgement of our dignity or rights by arbitrary authority or by forces
of dogmatism or domination rationalized by such claims to authority. One
of the reasons that the ideal of a value-neutral social science has been so
congenial to us is that it fits well with and reinforces modern individualism as an ethical program for living.

The natural sciences have been so successful in modern times in part
because their practitioners have cultivated the ability to abstract out the
meanings and values that normally present themselves in our dealings
with the life-world in order to look at nature as if it were an aggregate
of brute, material objects and processes in mechanistic, law-governed
relations. Too often, modern thinkers have assumed that because this

"objectified" picture of the world gives us a fruitful way of looking at things for certain purposes, it must depict reality as it is at the most basic level. This objectified world is not the only world, however. There remains the messy, changeable, emotionally charged and morally and existentially engaged world of everyday life. This is a world where "ignorant armies clash by night," where there is no life without risk, where ventures often fail, where everyone dies, and where there is no final or certain truth about anything, though one senses that one must *live* some truth or other or one has not really lived at all. That world is, in Nietzsche's words, the "human, all too human" realm of which social science tries to make sense. Mainstream social science may collude in our all-too-human attempts to keep the messy everyday world at a distance or to gain more direct control over it than is either possible or desirable.

Taylor (1995) describes the modern outlook on the nature of knowledge and the relation of the knower to the world. Knowledge consists in the correspondence of our beliefs to an external reality that has determinate properties independent of our beliefs and practices. Ideally, we possess reliable methods that allow us to be sure that our knowledge of reality is entirely "objective," that is, uncontaminated by our wishes, fears, or evaluations. It is because our knowledge is anchored in objective fact that it can serve as the basis for accurate predictions that enable us to re-engineer things in some desired way. Correlated with this modern representational view of knowledge is an unprecedented view of the human person as essentially a knowing subject. A human being, in this view, appears as a kind of isolated point of consciousness and will standing entirely apart from the world of brute objects. This kind of dimensionless point of conscious activity, what Taylor (p. 7) calls the modern *punctual self,* is "ideally disengaged, that is . . . free and rational to the extent that he has fully distinguished himself from the natural and social worlds, so that his identity is no longer to be defined in terms of what lies outside him in these worlds." Also, the punctual self is seen as "free and rational to treat these worlds—and even some of the features of his own character—instrumentally, as subject to change and reorganizing in order the better to secure the welfare of himself and others" (p. 7).

The conception of the self as a detached knower goes hand in hand with a profound aspiration to individuality and separateness, Taylor suggests; reflecting the antiauthoritarian temper of modernity, it is as much a *moral* ideal as a scientific one. Our modern ideal of freedom as self-autonomy dictates that any dependency of the self on the world will compromise the individual's autonomy and dignity. This helps explain why the primary goal of mainstream social science has been to work out strictly value-neutral explanations or descriptions of human dynamics. It also helps explain why social scientists insist on treating cultural and moral values as purely subjective and feel the need to distance themselves from such subjective elements in order to concentrate on finding causal laws of human behavior.

This view of knowledge as certified representations of fully independent objects has been questioned by recent philosophers of science (Bernstein, 1983; Kuhn, 1970b). Such critics encourage us to view natural science inquiry as a creative, interpretive endeavor in which even "objective facts" depend in part on the theories we "hammer out" (Rorty, 1979) and in which theory selection depends on such "values" as parsimony or fruitfulness. Nevertheless, the representational view still has a great deal of appeal for us. It seems consistent with the way we detach ourselves, in natural science inquiry, from the concerns and commitments of everyday life to examine and experiment with the world in a specialized manner— even if it exaggerates that detachment and too hastily generalizes it to all forms of knowing. The representational outlook also resonates with the modern individualistic ideal of disengaging from custom and tradition to make up our own minds and chart our own path.

In Part Two of this book, we argue that in the realm of everyday life, knowledge and understanding are different from the form they take in the natural sciences. In studying humans, we are often concerned not with impersonal explanation or even with producing certain reliable results but with grasping the *meaning* of people's actions and the *quality* of their motives and aims. Understanding meanings is an essential part of being who we are in carrying out our aims and projects and relating to one another and is at the very heart of our social existence. According to Taylor (1985a), in many cases we have to understand an individual's "vision of things" to make sense of what he or she is doing. In fact, it appears to be the case that individuals' "thoughts and perceptions" or the "meanings things have" for them shape their action and define important emotions like pride or shame. But this means that "personal interpretations can enter into the definition of the phenomenon under study" (pp. 120–121). Moreover, as we shall see later in this book, these interpretations or meanings are an intensely social affair, for the most part held in common by a community, hammered out through dialogue in a morally and existentially engaged life-world.

Our aim in this book is to employ hermeneutic ontology to elucidate this engaged human realm as a basis for reinterpreting psychology. In the account of the human sciences we propose, it seems best to view social theory as a "form of practice" (Richardson & Christopher, 1993; Taylor,

1985b). For such a hermeneutic practice, the kind of understanding sought and obtained in many areas of the social sciences should be thought of not as objective findings arrived at by a special scientific methodology but as a reflective and systematic continuation of our dynamic human existence, of the human struggle itself.

This is not to say that we cannot apply experimental and correlational methods to the subject matter of social life in ways that produce valuable information about the makeup and dynamics of human phenomena. There is no reason to accept the claim of some humanists and phenomenologists that such methods should be confined to specialized areas of psychology such as physiological psychology or studies in perception, areas that are generally seen as under the purview of natural science. Surely these methods have a place in the kind of social inquiry that studies what is variously called the whole person, lived experience, or fully motivated agency in familiar cultural contexts. In these forms of inquiry, we can employ experimental and correlational methods to detect significant patterns and regularities that might otherwise be difficult or impossible to ascertain. One might argue, however, that such information only has meaning for us when it is integrated into a richer account of human dynamics, an account that brings to light the meanings and goals that shape and define people's actions in particular contexts (Slife & Williams, 1995; Taylor, 1985a).

For example, we now have a large amount of research concerning the causes and correlates of "self-esteem" in individuals in our kind of society. Research and theory of this sort seem to be intended to help us better understand and bolster the kind of durable self-approval that can be attained by distinct, autonomous, self-reliant individuals. Such self-esteem, we believe, enables us to participate in a mobile, pluralistic, highly competitive, consumer society like ours without being undone by its many challenges, disappointments, and rejections. Thus, research and theory of this sort seem to be shaped at the core by a certain faith: that our kind of mobile, competitive society is a viable and worthwhile enterprise. In other words, it is animated and shaped in part by a certain vision of the good life or good society. Of course, social scientists do not usually acknowledge that such an ethical vision is an essential part of empirical research programs. The constitutive role of this article of faith will be apparent, however, if we recall that the very social universe assumed and tacitly affirmed by self-esteem theorizing was characterized in the 1930s and 1940s by Erich Fromm, Karen Horney, and others as a virtual recipe for severe personal fragmentation and emotional malaise. Fromm and Horney may not have described a clear alternative for us, but they argued persuasively that our rather shallow and overly competitive way of life, oriented so much toward individual popularity and success, was in fact the source of many modern emotional problems in living.

What is important to grasp here is that proponents of different ethical visions would tend to disagree about the interpretation of particular research findings and often would recommend quite different directions for inquiry. Thus, findings of a positive correlation between self-esteem and some type of achievement might be celebrated by one researcher but criticized by another on the grounds that the personality characteristics or the kind of achievement measured are of questionable value or even reflect unworthy qualities. What is at issue here is not what correlations can be identified but what has intrinsic worth or deserves our admiration. Yet another critic might argue that although the self-esteem assessed by the research has some positive aspects, this trait actually arises less from autonomous self-regard than from shared cultural or moral values, or from some other factor. In this critic's view, these findings would have very different implications than are commonly assumed.

Do feelings of emptiness and purposelessness reflect a need for greater individual autonomy or a lack of a healthy sense of limits and wider purpose? Should we encourage self-esteem training or community service for the schoolchildren of America? William Damon (1995) has argued recently that our society suffers in many ways from a lack of sufficiently high standards of achievement and virtue for children. Suppose research showed that raising such standards in certain situations produced a certain amount of emotional stress and turmoil in young people. Should this be interpreted as indicating that raising standards is a healthy or unhealthy approach to socialization or education? These examples are exaggerated a bit to make a point, and they obviously do not necessarily represent mutually exclusive alternatives. But in each case, the conclusion one draws will depend partly on the ethical vision that guides the research. Nor can the matter be decided by considering longer-term outcomes, for our understanding of what such outcomes *mean* will be influenced by the values held by the researcher or by the community of which he or she is a part.

In Chapters Six and Seven, we analyze two domains of contemporary research in psychology to illustrate how social science research findings—even those that are methodologically sound, cautiously interpreted, and illuminating about human dynamics—do not amount to strictly neutral accounts of objective states of affairs. On the contrary, these findings comprise interpretations of the meaning of some aspect of the wider social and historical life-world that envelops us and shapes our commitments and activities. Moreover, because these interpretations often become social influences in their own right, altering the reality they seek to make sense of or evaluate, the ideal of austere objectivity becomes even more questionable.

How then are we to discriminate among the manifold, constantly shifting interpretations of human life that guide and shape our investigations? That is the question of the day. Taylor (1985b) notes that we today live in a society that celebrates and pursues a wide "diversity of goods." We endorse a range of moral, political, aesthetic, and religious values that may embody sharp tensions, such as those between self-interest and altruism, humility and assertiveness, or quiet acceptance and a lust for life. Somehow we have to fit these diverse goods into roughly coherent patterns that make some sense and allow us a measure of coherence and integrity in our lives. There would seem to be no honest way that the social sciences could be made simpler or less ambiguous than everyday human existence itself, including, for that matter, the lives of social scientists.

In Chapters Eight and Nine we outline a hermeneutic approach to these thorny issues. We argue that such an approach allows us to move beyond scientism in social inquiry. By *scientism* we mean not legitimate science but the dogmatic insistence that the subject matter of our science, in this case human action and social life, must be approached by way of methods that are treated as being beyond question. This commitment to a particular conception of method is so rigid that if you question whether experimental and correlational methods are the main or exclusive road to understanding, some mainstream social scientists will respond that they cannot take your arguments seriously because the only alternative is intellectual chaos or rampant subjectivism. To be sure, many individual social scientists balance their belief in the sanctity of their methods with a certain amount of open-mindedness or even humility in the face of the difficulties of achieving trustworthy knowledge of human events. But their dogmatic adherence to method excludes from consideration the idea that methods should be determined by the subject matter as much as the subject matter be approached in terms of available or preferred methods.

We are well served by many of the ideals of modern social science. At times, nothing is more important than an accurate and comprehensive reporting of events and experiences. That our interpretations always color our accounts of what happens, and may even help shape the events themselves, does not mean that we should not try to be objective in a number of ways. But much of the insight or understanding we achieve in ordinary life and social science comes only by way of participating in the search for understanding in an authentic and sometimes personally demanding manner. In studying human phenomena, the distance or detachment we achieve in order to critically examine our way of life is always partial and provisional, in contrast to the scientific aspiration to complete objectivity that has informed so much modern social science.

In the chapters of Part Two, we analyze several of the main alternatives to conventional, scientific social science that have been proposed in this century. A significant minority of psychological investigators over the years has felt that some kind of descriptive or phenomenological approach to understanding human action, including many varieties of increasingly popular "qualitative" research strategies, represents a more appropriate and promising path to follow. There certainly is great value in these approaches. In some form, they may represent the way of the future for some branches of human science inquiry. However, as we shall see, they fail to clarify the nature of understanding in social science. In fact, they commonly preserve a key element of the scientistic outlook they reject. These approaches, too, typically aspire to an impossible objectivity; instead of seeking timelessly true, value-neutral explanations of human behavior, they seek timelessly true, value-neutral descriptions of meaningful human events. They are of limited help in clarifying how to discriminate better from worse interpretations in an imperfect world.

We also examine the viewpoint of what are sometimes called critical social scientists (for example, Fox & Prilleltensky, 1997), whose ideas also have much to recommend them. These thinkers argue that the ideal of pristine objectivity claimed by mainstream social scientists is an illusion that masks a concealed ideological commitment to the status quo of modern, technological society and serves to rationalize its many depersonalizing and oppressive aspects. This is an illuminating critique. But one is bound to wonder if these thinkers' particular ideals and priorities concerning expanding democratic opportunity and achieving greater distributive justice—the ones they feel should inspire and direct social inquiry—are the correct ones, or the most important ones, for a decent society. Among the circle of friends and acquaintances most of us have there can be found intelligent and sincere dyed-in-the-wool liberals, political or cultural conservatives, new age thinkers, confirmed existentialists, quiet religious souls, principled atheists, and resolute postmodernists. Their more or less friendly contestations will go on forever. How could we possibly determine which overall philosophy of human life and living should guide our inquiries and interventions?

In the face of this disagreement and confusion, it is tempting to accept some sort of postmodern or social constructionist doctrine according to which these different views are not actual or even possible "truths" about the human situation but, in Foucault's words, merely "truth effects" produced by the forces at play in specific cultures and eras. The different views are all radically contingent, utterly relative, and that is that. In Chapter Ten, we argue that contemporary postmodern and social constructionist theorists (Gergen, 1985; Rorty, 1982) help release us from the idea that the social disciplines must fit the mold of the natural sciences, and help restore a sense of how much human action is embedded in history and culture. They help us both to appreciate the limits of what we can understand and control in the human sphere and to take greater responsibility for the inescapable moral dimension of social inquiry. In other words, these thinkers help both contract and expand our horizons in beneficial ways.

Nevertheless, the acute moral relativism inherent in this position seems both implausible and rather destructive to many of us. We cannot help but be struck by the absolute certainty with which postmodern or social constructionist thinkers deny the very possibility of absolutes or of any settled moral convictions. In fact, it turns out to be quite difficult to maintain that peculiar conviction. The details of the argument will have to wait until later. For now, we might note that our actual situation seems quite different from the way postmodern theorists usually portray it. In our actual lives, it seems, we neither can achieve certainty about the uncertainty of our condition nor simply relax and go with the flow of uncertainty. Instead, we find ourselves in a situation where we always do take some beliefs and ideals very seriously *even though* we are often beset by doubt and can never find a final intellectual resting place. To be caught in such a tension seems like a definition of what it means to be human.

Postmodern and social constructionist viewpoints have a growing influence in both academic and professional psychology today. We argue, however, that they represent a somewhat hasty overreaction to the quandaries and shortcomings of mainstream social science. We invite you to consider whether our version of a hermeneutic alternative points to a better path for human science inquiry. The spirit of this alternative is reflected in the words of Heidegger (1977, p. 129): "Truth is not a feature of correct propositions which are asserted of an 'object' by a human 'subject' and then 'are valid' somewhere, in what sphere we know not; rather, truth is disclosure of things through which an openness essentially unfolds." In Chapter Nine, we spell this idea out in a less cryptic and more down-to-earth fashion. But Heidegger's words point us in what we take to be the right direction. What we are looking for is not a new or better way to certify beliefs about an independent reality but a way of moving down the path toward greater understanding.

Conceiving of truth or understanding less in terms of correct propositions and more as an appropriate, authentic, or truthful way of being involved with life (Williams, 1994) has certain advantages. For one thing, this approach seems congruent with the wisdom conveyed, however crudely and haltingly at times, by modern psychotherapies. For another, it can help make the wide diversity of goods and the plethora of cultural and moral outlooks we confront in a shrinking world and a pluralistic society seem less overwhelming. In this view, we don't need Archimedean points or demonstrable timeless truths in order to have genuine understanding or credible moral convictions. Filling out this view is a tall order. However, we argue that hermeneutic notions of understanding and dialogue have much to contribute to this undertaking. They portray us as more connected to the meaningful pursuits and shared purposes of an historical culture than modern individualism suggests and, at the same time, as fully capable of the kind of sharp-eyed criticism of dogmatism and domination that is the special genius of modern ethical and political thought. Therefore, the hermeneutic outlook might serve us well as a wider philosophical framework for re-envisioning psychology.

Toward an Interpretive Psychology

The hermeneutic approach outlined in this book has much in common with what Jerome Bruner (1990) calls *cultural psychology*, whose basic subject matter is "acts of meaning." Bruner describes how, during what has come to be known as psychology's Cognitive Revolution of the late 1950s and 1960s, he and some of his colleagues "intended to bring 'mind' back into the human sciences after a long cold winter of objectivism." Unfortunately, in his view, the "new cognitive science" that has emerged has gained "its technical successes at the price of dehumanizing the very concept of mind it had sought to reestablish," with the result that it has "estranged much of psychology from other human sciences and the humanities" (p. 1).

Bruner (1990, pp. 2–5) advocates a "renewed cognitive revolution—a more interpretive approach to cognition concerned with 'meaning-making.'" This approach would focus on the "symbolic activities that human beings employ in constructing and in making sense not only of the world but of themselves." Regrettably, in Bruner's view, much cognitive psychology today tends to reduce the "construction of meaning" to the "processing of information." There is a place, of course, for the properly scientific investigation of human cognitive capacities. But the kind of "meaning and the processes that create everyday [human action are] surprisingly remote from what is conventionally called 'information processing.'" The notion of *information* employed by many cognitive psychologists is quite narrow and limited. As a rule, they adopt an approach according to which "computability [is] a necessary criterion of a good theoretical model." Such an approach, however, precludes such important but, in their view, "ill-formed questions as 'How is the world organized in the mind of a Muslim fundamentalist?' or 'How does the concept of Self differ in Homeric Greece and in the postindustrial world?'"

It seems to us that this miscarried cognitive revolution presupposes that a human being is, at its core, what Cushman (1990) calls a *bounded, masterful self*. This view of human cognition thereby reinforces the assumptions that meaning is something found strictly within and that a narrowly instrumental or manipulative stance toward the outer world is the only sensible one. Bruner's notion (1990) of human behavior as consisting most basically of "acts of meaning" points to an alternative view. According to Bruner (pp. 12–13), human beings

> do not terminate at their own skins; they are expressions of culture. To treat the world as an indifferent flow of information to be processed by individuals each on his or her own terms is to lose sight of how individuals are formed and how they function . . . Given that psychology is so immersed in culture, it must be organized around those meaning-making and meaning-using processes that connect [humans] to culture. This does *not* commit us to more subjectivity in psychology; it is just the reverse. By virtue of participation in culture, meaning is rendered *public* and *shared*. Our culturally adapted way of life depends upon shared meanings and shared concepts and depends as well upon shared modes of discourse for negotiating differences in meaning and interpretation.

The hermeneutic approach elaborates and applies ideas like Bruner's in the service of transforming psychology. Chapter Ten addresses the fundamental problem of a wide gulf between formal theory and actual practice in the modern psychotherapy arena. This gulf is likely the main reason for the proliferation of so many diverse schools of therapy and the lack of success in harmonizing them in any theoretically coherent and practically useful manner. This gap, and therefore the endless dissatisfaction about the adequacy of any particular theory, seems to be rooted not in the much ballyhooed differences among the theories but in the hidden assumptions about human agency and the good life they actually share. We use a detailed analysis of the widely influential, contemporary revisionist psychoanalytic theories of Heinz Kohut and Roy Schafer to detect these hidden assumptions and tacit values. In the light of this analysis, we discuss how, from a hermeneutic vantage point, we might begin to respond to a thorny problem: much of modern psychotherapy theory and practice seems to perpetuate cultural confusions and deficiencies that contribute significantly to the emotional difficulties these theories seek to clarify and cure.

Chapter Eleven discusses, as specifically as we can at the moment, what it might mean to move beyond scientism and constructionism in social inquiry. We try to sketch at least some of the elements of an approach and some of its principles that would allow us to preserve the best methods and virtues of mainstream social science while acknowledging that we will have to abandon the role of what Foucault calls *universal intellectuals*, who aspire to timeless truths about the social realm. Instead, in the hermeneutic view, we need to see ourselves as something resembling what Foucault calls *specific intellectuals*, those who, as citizens and members of particular traditions and communities, understand that their theories and findings are part and parcel of their search for the good life and a more decent society.

These suggestions of ours about how to rethink psychology do not amount to hard-and-fast conclusions but are meant to keep the conversation going and, as much as possible, add to its quality and depth. We hope that you find some merit in these ideas and are inspired to join in this kind of theoretical and philosophical discussion—indeed that you come to see it as an essential part of psychological inquiry.

PART ONE

ETHICAL UNDERPINNINGS OF MODERN PSYCHOTHERAPY

I

DILEMMAS OF
MODERN CULTURE

IN THIS BOOK, WE DESCRIBE ways in which modern psychology and psychotherapy reflect many of the persistent dilemmas and confused aims of modern culture. Psychology and psychotherapy arose partly as a creative response to the strains and perplexities of the modern way of life. But they also incorporate and perpetuate some of the problematic assumptions of modernity, or so we argue. Many of the much-discussed dilemmas of modern culture seem to be variations on the theme of expanding personal autonomy, which is often purchased at the price of considerable alienation.

Although we argue that modern psychology and psychotherapy tend to perpetuate questionable features of our way of life, we do not intend to cast either psychology or that way of life in a mainly negative light. Modern society offers many of its members precious benefits: increased longevity, respect for human rights and dignity, and the opportunity to develop one's own unique talents and proclivities. Moreover, it would seem foolish to unduly deprecate modern society, even if it has often exploded in violence or declined into shallow consumerism, simply because in the course of a few centuries we moderns have not perfectly understood our complex existence and have failed in some respects to help people come to terms with the enduring perplexities and tragic dimensions of the human situation. Nevertheless, psychology does seem to be intimately entangled with many of the questionable ideologies and some of the downright foolishness of the current culture.

Modern Dilemmas

Peter Berger (1973, 1977) provides a particularly insightful analysis of certain dilemmas of modernity. In using the word *dilemma,* he refers to

25

certain features of modern life that expand human powers and enhance individual uniqueness but also undercut the matrix of reliable social ties and shared meanings needed to support them. The most basic dilemma Berger identifies is abstraction. *Abstraction* refers to our ability to detach ourselves or to abstract away from the everyday experience of reality as "an ongoing flux of juncture and disjunction of unique entities," a flow of events and experiences that is often marked by unexpected turns of events and emotional surprises. Through the power of abstraction, we come to view events and even our own experiences and actions as separate components of formal, impersonal systems in which they are "continuously interdependent in a rational, controllable, predictable way" (1973, p. 27).

Abstraction is part and parcel of the pervasively influential processes of the "capitalist market" and the "bureaucratized state" as well as the experience of life in large cities and exposure to the media of mass communication (Berger, 1977). On the level of consciousness, abstraction establishes particular forms of thought, especially a "quantifying and atomizing cognitive style, originally at home in the calculations of entrepreneurs and engineers," which leads to ignoring and even "repressing" other kinds of spontaneous, passionate, numinous, or contemplative experiences and emotions. On the level of social life, such abstraction entails the "progressive weakening, if not destruction, of the concrete and relatively cohesive communities in which human beings have found solidarity and meaning throughout most of history" (p. 71).

The second main dilemma is *futurity*, which Berger (1977) describes as a "profound change in the temporal structure of human experience, in which the future becomes a primary orientation for both imagination and activity." Time is conceived as "precise, measurable, and, at least in principle, subject to human control. In short, time is to be mastered." Futurity means "endless striving, restlessness, and a mounting incapacity for repose." In premodern China, Berger points out, the clock was a harmless toy. But in Europe it became what Baudelaire called a sinister Deity. The notion of one's life as an actively planned career reflects this conception of temporality, as do the long-range plans of large-scale institutions and entire societies. Human life becomes greatly dominated by the calendar and the clock. To an amazing extent, we "have become engineers and functionaries even in the most intimate aspects of our lives" (pp. 73–74).

Berger sees a third dilemma in the process of *individuation*. He calls our attention to how modernization entails a "progressive separation of the individual from collective entities," which has both dramatically enhanced individual autonomy and brought about an "historically unprecedented counterposition of individual and society" (1977, p. 75). Individuation involves a painful paradox. At the same time that traditional, concrete communities "have been replaced by the abstract megastructures of modern society, the individual self has come to be experienced as both distinct and greatly complicated—and, by that very fact, in greater need of the personal belonging which is difficult in abstract institutions." According to Berger, as institutions grow more abstract and the people in them more individuated, the threat of anomie increases significantly.

In identifying these dilemmas, Berger aims not to reject modernity but to contribute to a needed "critique of modernity" that necessarily touches on both "fundamental philosophical and highly concrete practical-political questions" (1977, p. 80).

Alan Wolfe (1989) builds on insights like Berger's and expands our understanding of what he terms "modernity and its discontents." Wolfe notes that many citizens of modern Western societies enjoy unique gifts of freedom from everyday struggles for economic survival and the possibility of living unaware of political battles taking place around them. Yet many people feel that something is missing in their social world. Recalling "Max Weber's image of a society without a soul," Wolfe notes that for such people, "economic growth and political freedom do not seem enough." We appear to have the "basis for the good life, but its actual attainment seems just beyond the possible" (p. 1).

Wolfe (1989) argues that at the center of this discontent lies a profound confusion about obligation. In one sense, people today are remarkably free and unencumbered by obligations. But in another sense, "economic growth, democratic government, and therefore freedom itself are produced through extensive, and quite encumbered, dependence on others" (p. 2). The "sheer complexity of modern forms of social organization creates an ever-widening circle of newer obligations beyond those of family and locality." Even as "modernity expands the scope of moral obligations, it also thins their specificity" (p. 3), because many of the ties moderns have are to abstract, generalized others, in contrast to the more restricted, specific ties of family or locality in traditional societies. In this situation, it is impossible to rely simply on traditional authoritative moral codes, leaving us unclear about how to resolve our differences and reach agreement about important matters of conduct and obligation.

Modern societies, Wolfe argues, have generally sought to manage their complexity through one of two large-scale, impersonal mechanisms: the market or the state. Economic approaches to social and moral regulation rely on prices and other market instruments to allocate limited resources, restrain individuals' desires, and coordinate their actions. But such systems tend to place a price on everything and turn individuals into cogs in the economic machinery. People have little opportunity to renegotiate the constraints placed on them or their obligations to others so long as they are governed by unseen forces or an "invisible hand." In contrast, political approaches to moral regulation emphasize "collective obligation over individual freedom." But they tend to undermine individual initiative and responsibility in another way. "When, for example, government collects my taxes and distributes the money to others," it "assumes responsibilities that would otherwise be mine." I am "not obligated to real people living real lives around me; instead my obligation is to follow rules, the moral purpose of which is often lost to me," tempting me to avoid such "abstract and impersonal" obligations if I can (1989, pp. 9–10). In Wolfe's words, "Unlike Rousseau's natural man, who was born free but was everywhere in chains, modern social individuals are born into chains of interdependence but yearn, most of the time, to be free" (p. 2).

Wolfe (1989) argues that there is an alternative to allowing the impersonal mechanisms of the market or state to organize the codes of moral obligation we live by. We can cultivate and take responsibility for a third realm, namely "civil society," which we have allowed to "wither away" somewhat. Civil society consists of "families, communities, friendship networks, solidaristic workplace ties, voluntarism, spontaneous groups and movements," and the like. In this realm, "no abstract and formal rules exist specifying what we owe others and others owe us." Instead, "moral obligation ought to be viewed as a socially constructed practice, as something we learn through the actual experience of trying to live together with other people" (p. 20). We need to view ourselves more as "rule makers" than as "rule followers" (p. 22) who mainly conform to the laws of the state or the law of supply and demand. In the realm of civil society, we are less free than the individual aspiring to autonomy who wants mainly to do his or her own thing, but we are genuinely free and responsible to fashion or reshape the moral rules that govern the practices of intertwined lives.

Psychological theory infrequently considers seriously the possibility that human development and fulfillment are directly hindered by this kind of confusion about one's interdependence and obligations in a modern context. Mainstream psychology tends to focus on the more or less successful coping of separate individuals making their way in the sort of social universe Wolfe describes, where civil society has significantly withered away. From a psychological point of view, one might predict that individuals in this situation would oscillate between an exaggerated sense of personal autonomy and a sense of being the victim of forces beyond their control. In fact, just such an oscillation may lie at the heart of emotional disorders involving intense shame that seem to be on the increase and are a very "hot" topic in current discussions of psychopathology and in the popular psychology literature. Michael Lewis (1992), an exception to the general neglect of the cultural context in analyzing such phenomena, describes the difference between pathological shame and guilt—which, if not excessive, is a socially and morally valuable emotion—in the following way. Guilt can serve to alert the person that they have violated a standard or rule and focuses their attention on possibly altering their behavior. Shame floods the person with a sense of being fundamentally inadequate and unworthy and an intense desire to hide or disappear.

Lewis argues persuasively that pathological shame as we know it is partly a symptom of a way of life that encourages individuals to "seek complete freedom" (p. 233). He writes, "Our culture has become more shame-driven as we have turned toward personal freedom, and beyond it to narcissism" (p. 230). In both everyday life and much social science, we tend to ignore the fact that individuals are defined "within a context or a group of contexts" (p. 233). As a result, individuals tend to feel that they must attain an almost impregnable autonomy or are inadequate, vulnerable, or ashamed. Any solution to this predicament, Lewis argues, must include "commitment," which "by its nature, frees us from ourselves and, while it stands us in opposition to some . . . joins us with others similarly committed. Commitment moves us from the mirror trap of the self absorbed with the self to the freedom of a community of shared values" (p. 235).

The ideas of Berger, Wolfe, and Lewis illumine current cultural quandaries and suggest helpful responses to them. But these writers leave important questions unanswered, especially concerning what might serve as the *basis* of a restored sense of community or individual purpose in the highly individualistic, intensely skeptical world of today. Wolfe wants us to take back some of the territory occupied by market and state and assume active, shared responsibility for fashioning "moral rules" in a revitalized civil society. Presumably the content of those rules would depend on the particular traditions of the society in question and the challenges it currently faces. But Wolfe is quite vague about what the basis or justification for these rules would be. In a post-traditional world, what sort of authority or conviction would these rules and obligations have for us that would allow us to resist the pressures to sell out to the distractions of a consumer society and abandon our responsibilities to the encroaching agencies of market or state?

Lewis's notion of commitment is hazy as well. It is almost impossible for modern souls not to feel a great deal of antagonism between "freedom" and a "community of shared values," and it is therefore quite hard for them to sustain a sense of purpose beyond clearly self-interested pursuits. To many, this notion of commitment will seem to be either an illusion or a matter of sheer dogmatism, even fanaticism. To get to the bottom of these questions, we will have to take a longer historical view of the erosion of community and common purpose in modern times and dig deeper into its philosophical origins.

Premodern Outlooks

Charles Taylor (1985b) helps us to gain perspective on our own age by contrasting the modern Western sense of the self with that belonging to earlier times and other cultures. He begins with the premise that for humans in general, "to define my identity is to define what I must be in contact with in order to function fully as a human agent and specifically to be able to judge, discriminate and recognize what is really of worth or importance, both in general and for me" (p. 258). This premise is true even in a modern context in which the reality a person may seek to be in contact with is her own deeply personal inclinations or her capacity to choose her own values apart from custom or tradition. In premodern or traditional societies, people apprehend themselves, in what Berger (1979) terms a "pretheoretical" or taken-for-granted manner, as being in contact with and defined by a hierarchical and meaningful order of being. In such a way of life, as Clifford Geertz (1973, p. 90) puts it, myth or ritual tunes "human action to an envisioned cosmic order and projects images of order onto the plane of human existence." As a result, men and women acquire meaningful roles to play on the mundane as well as the cosmic plane. They acquire what Anton Antonovsky (1979) calls a *sense of coherence* that helps make "affectively comprehensible" the uncontrollable and tragic aspects of human life.

In classical Western civilization, before the advent of modern viewpoints, there was a shared view of human life as part of a meaningful cosmic drama. Both Greek and biblical perspectives, despite many differences, have a similar conceptual structure (MacIntyre, 1981). Human life is seen as moving toward a certain end, or *telos,* such as life as a citizen in the *polis,* citizenship in the Kingdom of God, or contemplation of higher levels of truth or reality. Such a *telos* pictures the aim of human life as existence in harmony or fellowship with nature or God. The good or proper life is an achievement of character and community. It is characterized by acquired human qualities or virtues such as courage, justice, or love. Within such a teleological vision of life, there is no characteristic modern gap between *is* and *ought,* or between fact and value. Questions about how we ought to live are answered through insight into the meaningful current of existence itself, a current directed toward a shared human Good that we all have an essential purpose to realize and enjoy.

Premodern outlooks permit us to resolve our moral dilemmas in the context of a larger understanding of cosmic justice. Cicero asserts that no one is able to "judge truly of things good and evil, save by knowledge of the whole plan of nature and also of the life of the gods" (De Finibus III, 73). The premodern sense of human existence is perhaps best stated by Plato: "The ruler of the universe has ordered all things with a view to the excellence and preservation of the whole. . . . And one of these portions of the universe is thine own, unhappy man, which, however little, contributes to the whole; and you do not seem to be aware that this and every other creation is for the sake of the whole, and in order that the life of the whole may be blessed; and that you are created for the sake of the whole, and not the whole for the sake of you" (Laws 903c). We moderns tend to react to such words with considerable ambivalence, with both aversion and yearning. We may find the attitude toward life they convey comforting, and perhaps even life-enhancing, at the same time that they arouse deep suspicion and incredulity in us.

The writings of Václav Havel (1995) echo these traditional insights. From his unique perspective as an artist, writer, and president of the Czech Republic, he writes about a profound need, as he sees it, to recapture today an appreciation for "the experience of transcendence in the broadest sense of the word." Havel comments, "I know that to my own detriment I am too suspicious of many things." He argues that in the wake of the collapse of twentieth-century totalitarian utopias, a "rapid dissemination of the basic values of the West" is desirable, specifically the ideas of "democracy, human rights, the civil society, and the free market" (p. 48). However, he notes that many people today in non-Western societies, although drawn to these values, also object to what seem to be their common by-products, such as "moral relativism, materialism . . . a profound crisis of authority . . . frenzied consumerism . . . the selfish cult of material success" and the "dreary standardization and rationalism of a technical civilization." Havel attributes these conditions to "forgetting that we are not God." But such materialism and superficiality are not the inevitable fruit of liberal democracy. It is possible to take cognizance of the "missing side of the democratic solution," rediscover "democracy's own transcendental origins," and renew its "respect for that non-material order which is not only above us but also in us and among us," the "only possible and reliable source of man's respect for himself, for others, for the order of nature . . . and thus for secular authority as well" (p. 49).

Still, even one who is attracted to Havel's proposal has to deal with the fact that these insights come down to us in a form that may be impossible for a modern mind to accept in a literal way. Robert Kane (1994) reminds us that people in premodern societies "often identified a sacred mountain or some other place near their home as the center of the universe." Thus the "axis of the world went through that point," providing the "spiritual center of their world" and "access to the divine." But one of the main stories of modern civilization is a "gradual undermining of this sense of spiritual centering." One major consequence is a "loss of roots, or a sense of cultural continuity that makes of the past a source of meaning" (p. 4). Another is the loss of the sense that our own and our society's deepest beliefs and aspirations have universal significance and therefore command lasting respect or devotion. The source of this loss, Kane points out, is not just modern pluralism but "pluralism plus uncertainty about how to resolve disagreements between conflicting points of view" (p. 13). Together they erode our convictions to the point where, in Nietzsche's image, we recognize "a thousand different tribes beating to a thousand different drums" and become the "first people in history who are not convinced we own the truth" (Kane, 1994, p. 13).

Modern Consciousness

The modern outlook and sense of life differs from the premodern in a number of striking ways. The moral temper of the modern age has always been antiauthoritarian and emancipatory. Modern consciousness was fashioned by a kind of progressive desacralizing of the universe to eliminate any impediment to the full exercise of human freedom in intellectual and scientific spheres and in practical affairs. One crucial influence in the advent of modern consciousness was the thought of the Protestant reformers. Their reaction was directed against prevailing religious practices that promised salvation as the result of merely mechanical actions or magical rituals that failed to engage in a sincere manner the heart and mind of the believer. Thus Luther insisted that salvation is achieved not by works but by faith alone. He carried forward the tendency toward inwardness that had been developing since the Renaissance by distinguishing sharply between the inner condition of the individual in relation to God and the outward roles one enacts in society. The action of grace in the inward realm is necessary if we are to break out of the vicious circle of self-love, but the everyday affairs of individuals and the secular responsibilities of princes and magistrates are left for the most part in their own hands, beyond the influence of the church.

The rise of modern science, accompanied by what Weber called the "disenchantment of the world," furthered the collapse of the traditional vision of a hierarchical and teleological cosmic order. Galileo first clearly defined scientific method in contrast to magic and religious belief. What is crucial in understanding natural phenomena, he claimed, is the ability to distinguish what really exists in nature, nature as it is in itself, from what exists only in our experience of nature, that is, mere appearance. Thus it seems that modern science developed by cultivating a special form of abstraction that we will call *objectification*. To adopt an objectifying stance toward things is to bracket or ignore all the rich, subjective appearances of the things we encounter in everyday life, that is, to abstract out all the values and meaningful relationships that show up within our ordinary experience so as to be able to regard the world as made up of brute, inherently meaningless objects with no intrinsic or defining relations to one another.

The classical example of this objectifying point of view is found in the seventeenth-century distinction between primary and secondary qualities. An ordinary table might strike me as ugly, brown, hard, cool to the touch, and useful for my purposes. But *in itself* the table does not have these characteristics (although its charged particles reflect light waves and have kinetic properties that can *cause* me to experience it in these ways). Scientific objectification calls for the ability to see such apparent features, or *secondary qualities*—color, hardness, usefulness, and so on—as existing only in the mind of the beholder. They are the products of my own subjective attitudes, interpretations, and interactions with the table. The real table as it is in itself, stripped of all such observer-relative, merely subjective qualities, must be understood as a brute material object with a spatio-temporal position and quantifiable physical properties but with none of the value-laden web of connections to a meaningful life-world that my table has in my everyday experience.

This objectifying outlook of modern science profoundly affects our modern view of reality. It leads to the conviction that only those properties of nature that can be precisely quantified are real and that nature itself is a totality of brute material objects in mechanistic, law-governed relations—an aggregate of physical things that can be mastered through a cool, disengaged methodology. Thus, experienced features of things—beauty, usability, goodness, and the like—are not really in the things we find around us. They are human fabrications, products of our interpretations and aims, not features of reality as it is in itself. As a consequence, from the standpoint of the naturalistic outlook of modern science, the traditional belief that the world is an arena of meanings with inbuilt values and purposes is no longer tenable.

Taylor (1975) points out that the new picture of a thoroughly disenchanted cosmos leads to a quite new understanding of the human person or self. The objectifying outlook on the world is essentially correlated with a view of the person as having a "self-defining identity" (p. 8). Winning through to this new sense of identity "was accompanied by the sense of exhilaration and power, that the subject need no longer define his perfection or vice, his equilibrium or disharmony, in relation to an external order" (p. 9). The horizon of human identity is now to a great extent found *within,* as critics like Wolfe (1989) and Cushman (1990) have noted. The resulting view of a fundamental gulf between individuals and their world is an essential ingredient of much twentieth-century social science. Without this view, our theory, research, and practice would be quite different from what they are today. Bellah (1983, p. 377) writes that "social science is itself the product of a particular kind of social crisis, the crisis of the transformation of traditional society into modern society." At the core of the modern outlook is a Promethean impulse that makes us willing to sacrifice the consolations of membership in any larger moral order or spiritual community for the full measure of what it takes to achieve human freedom and dignity.

Modern consciousness gives a central place to an objectified picture of reality to be mapped by empirical observation and explained by natural science. In late modern times, this confident, scientific, materialist picture of things often gives way to an existentialist view of a solitary self freely choosing its own values over and against a meaningless void and in opposition to a conformist society. Or it may be replaced by a postmodern sense of detached irony and insouciant play with historical meanings that present themselves as ephemeral and entirely relative, abandoning even the kind of moral seriousness that existentialists still allow. In fact, both existentialist and so-called postmodern viewpoints are still quite modern in the sense that they incorporate modernity's sharp disjunction and diminution of meaningful ties between self and world or person and society.

The Modern Scientific Outlook: Problems and Consequences

Today, many would argue that this view of reality and knowledge is more scientism (the worship or deification of science) than true science. There seem to be no good grounds for insisting that reality must be understood as nothing other than that which is captured or illuminated by the approach to understanding of abstraction and objectification. From the perspective of influential "postempiricist" philosophies of science, scientific theories and models are *interpretations* of the workings of the natural world. The scientistic claim that reality is ultimately quantifiable physical stuff simply cannot be established through methods that restrict themselves in advance to acknowledging only physical properties.

Questioning the assumptions of metaphysical materialism both enhances our appreciation of the creative and ingenious nature of scientific inquiry and undermines modern scientism. There seems no good reason to deny outright the validity of other *kinds* of interpretations of our experience and events, reflecting different ways of being involved with society and the world. Interpretations of this sort may turn out to play an important role in the best forms of social science. There is no good reason to assume in advance that these interpretations and meanings are merely subjective glosses on neutral, objective states of affairs. There is no justification for universalizing this detached standpoint and petrifying it in an ontology of self-encapsulated subjects confronting a world of hard, cold fact on hand for their observation and manipulation.

When the method of objectification is taken as the very definition of an epistemically mature stance toward life, trouble ensues. This view rather dogmatically absolutizes a certain detached, dispassionate, spectator view of knowing and relating to the world. Such abstraction and detachment may be necessary and appropriate for certain purposes, but in many situations, they will only hamper us or have harmful consequences. Many postmodern and hermeneutic thinkers argue that "the language of science, when applied to the study of human beings, is a relatively impoverished language. Using traditional scientific investigations, we force ourselves to study human beings at a distance" (Slife & Williams, 1995, p. 195). More generally, Taylor (1985a, p. 160) argues that in many circumstances there should be no question of "abstracting from the significance for us of what we are examining." In many of life's important "situations of involvement," trying to step back from things by way of something like the method of objectification would be counterproductive, to say the least. In those situations, we need to do almost the opposite. We need to get closer to our feelings, motives, or attachments to others, get past the defensiveness that distorts them or keeps us at a distance from them, and engage them more fully, in order to better appreciate what they are all about. Doing this often changes us in irreversible ways. Perhaps one of the functions of modern psychotherapy is to help people re-engage in these sorts of ways in a civilization gone slightly mad for objectification and technical prowess at the expense of all else.

A one-sided stress on the objectifying point of view may be an important source of some of the peculiar irrationalities and pathologies of modern life. Many of these seem to involve circumstances where a valuable
kind of impersonal stance toward certain events or issues becomes
overused, eventuating in a damaging depersonalization of some part of
personal or social life. Taylor (1985b) summarizes a number of these puz-
zling and disturbing features of modern social existence. One is a tendency
toward "meaninglessness and subordination of work." We come to feel
like cogs in the machinery of private or public bureaucratic organizations,
cut off from meaningful ties to our fellow workers, from the end-products
of our work, and from the good of the larger society. Second, there is the
"mindless lack of control of priorities" resulting from a "definition of
the good life as continuing escalation in living standards" and little else.
The inability to discriminate priorities or set healthy limits is no doubt a
major source of uncontrolled growth and damage to the environment. It
also contributes to the high-stress lifestyles and diminished ability to
appreciate or live in the moment about which so many of us complain
nowadays. Third, Taylor suggests, "commodities become 'fetishized' in a
non-Marxist sense, endowed magically with the properties of life they sub-
serve, as though a faster car might actually make my family life more
intense and harmonious." All these features of our way of life deliver a
painful body blow to "our image of ourselves as realized moderns, determining our purposes out of ourselves, dominating and not being dominated by things" (p. 281).

Moral Values: Objective or Subjective?

Should we wish to rethink our priorities in today's society, perhaps seeking to temper our overweening commitment to mastery and control, we
would immediately encounter a major obstacle. Apart from the magni-
tude of the undertaking, we are at best highly ambivalent about whether
it is even proper to reason together about the kind of cultural and moral
ideals that set our priorities and define our way of life. We are comfortable with technical solutions, individual preferences, and democratic decision making, but not with moral reasoning about the inherent goodness
or worth of our own or anyone else's conception of the good life.

We have lived with this ambivalence for several centuries. In the eighteenth and nineteenth centuries, it fell to certain thinkers to try to make
sense of the place of moral values or ideals of the good life within a new
objectified and disenchanted picture of the world and to clarify the nature
of moral obligation in a new kind of society dedicated to the freedom of

the individual. MacIntyre (1981) suggests that during this era, philosophy constituted a "central form of social activity," very different from the tucked-away academic specialties of the present, which rarely claim for themselves any larger social relevance that they would care to defend in the marketplace of ideas. We take seriously MacIntyre's contention that the failure of that earlier culture and its philosophical high priests to solve our modern confusion about freedom and authority determines the "form both of our academic philosophical and of our practical social problems" today (p. 36). Moreover, it seems that in the twentieth century, the public charge to provide moral wisdom and guidance to individuals in our brave new modern world has passed, for better or worse, from such philosophers to social scientists and psychotherapists (Rieff, 1966; Wolfe, 1989).

Anyone concerned with making sense out of human values or ideals of the good life in modern culture faces an excruciating "either-or." One possibility is to locate such values or ideals in the "objective" realm. This would fit with our experience of them as something authoritative that stand over against us and command our respect, obedience, or even a certain amount of reverence or awe. Nevertheless, to a modern sensibility, regarding these values or ideals as objective can seem illusory, a mere projection of our wishes and ideals onto things, inauthentic, and perhaps a convenient rationalization in the service of one's own selfish interests. It may also seem outright dogmatic, authoritarian, or imperialistic, the inevitable precursor of the sort of discrimination and domination we have learned to despise and do battle against in modern times.

Another possibility is to locate moral values and ideals of the good life in the inward or "subjective" realm. This approach would fit with our profound modern sense of the relativity of morals and customs across societies and eras. It would also fit with our deep commitment to respecting the right of every individual or group to define the good life for themselves. Often we are quite comfortable with viewing our own and others' cultural and moral values as ultimately merely subjective products of custom and habit that could be revised without impropriety should they no longer serve our long-term interests.

Bellah et al. (1985) argue that contemporary U.S. society by and large confines moral ideals to the realm of private choice but tries to do this in a way that preserves a degree of ethical seriousness. We are constrained to think of moral values in a way that clashes as little as possible with our culture's primary commitment to the ideal of individual freedom or autonomy. For us, culture itself exists mainly "for the liberation and fulfillment of the individual." At the same time, Americans are in many ways a very moral people who do not wish to dispense entirely with moral commitment. The "genius" of this society's moral outlook, according to these authors, is that it "enables the individual to think of commitments—from marriage and work to political and religious involvement—as enhancements of the sense of individual well-being rather than as moral imperatives" (p. 47). So we take these values seriously, but we protect our perception of autonomy by conceiving of them as largely subjective, as values that serve individual well-being but neither have any implacable objective reality nor issue from an outside authority.

In the end, however, neither the objectivist nor the subjectivist alternative seems plausible or acceptable. The first seems morally offensive, and the second appears to undermine most people's very conception of morality. It seems unacceptable to treat our moral values and commitments as simply given and objective in the way that certain kinds of moral absolutism and religious fundamentalism do, even if we appreciate that they are responding to a very real and frightening kind of anomie. The objectivist approach makes it very difficult to rethink our moral outlook and commitments when that is needed. Many times, in a complicated and changing world, we come to feel that something we took to be a moral issue is really largely a matter of personal preference, or vice versa. And events often compel us to refine or recalibrate our moral sensibility concerning such matters as child rearing, family obligations, social issues like welfare and affirmative action, conflicts between ethical principle and personal advantage, and overall ideas of what amounts to a worthwhile or successful life. The notion of moral values as simply objective naively equates questioning authority with defying authority or rejecting it altogether. Paradoxically, this approach gives moral values a status that is just as arbitrary as when they are reduced to matters of mere personal taste or preference.

The second alternative—embracing subjectivism—may seem like a safe retreat from dogmatism and domination, but it also presents great difficulties. For one thing, there seems to be a contradiction in first claiming to take moral values seriously and then going on to explain or justify them as something that serves our interests or enhances our well-being. On the one hand, if we are free to define our interests or well-being any way we wish, then we are not taking these ideals or commitments seriously in the sense that most of us mean when we talk about *moral* values. They are not serious moral values in the ordinary sense but only more or less useful means to whatever ends in living we happen to entertain. On the other hand, if what we mean by our interests or well-being *includes* certain moral values or commitments, then we are not justifying them merely on the basis that they produce some desired effect or work to our advantage. Rather we are assenting to them because they seem intrinsically right or have some genuine authority for us, including the authority to define our direction or ends in living. Thinking of our commitments as enhancements of personal well-being may seem like a workable compromise between autonomy and authority. But in the long run, either the commitments will erode or our sense of autonomy will seem compromised, or both.

Moreover, we suggest that thinkers who defend a strong moral relativism usually seem, ironically, to have a pronounced moral reason for doing so. They defend it because in the end they feel it undermines dogmatism and domination, or advances the cause of human freedom, or represents a more honest and mature response to the human situation than does believing that our commitments or hopes have any sort of support or foundation in the nature of things. But *why* should we oppose dogmatism, care about freedom, or be stoically mature in that way? Why not brutalize others, sell ourselves into slavery, or immerse ourselves in comforting illusions? Sincere relativists seem to have no good answer to these questions, even though they suggest we should act as if we did. They seem to harbor serious moral commitments for which there is no place in their official philosophy. Surely many of these ideals are worthy ones. But rather than undermine our own best values, it might be wise to try to find a philosophy that makes better sense of them. Thus, in Chapter Ten we outline the sort of hermeneutic philosophy we feel gives a better account of the "inescapable" commitments (Taylor, 1989) that shape human action.

Of course, it is always possible to bite the bullet and proclaim a more complete and in a sense more honest moral relativism. To a great extent, Freud did just that at the beginning of the twentieth-century romance with psychology and psychotherapy. Most of the therapy tradition has been uncomfortable with such a thoroughgoing relativism and has tried, earnestly if unsuccessfully, to wiggle off the hook. More recently, certain existentialist (Yalom, 1980) and social constructionist (Gergen, 1985) thinkers have tried to explain how a consistent relativism makes the most sense and—rather paradoxically, we think—better advances human welfare. However, we will argue that this sort of moral relativism is ultimately not a plausible view. It really does not describe our experience of things at the deepest level and presupposes an impossible detachment from the passions and purposes of the human struggle.

Modern consciousness has found it difficult to make sense of moral values. Treating them as subjective or as objective, in the usual modern sense of those terms, seems inadequate. Nevertheless, the modern understanding of our selves as self-defining individuals confronting an objectified, neutral universe does not seem to admit of any alternative. What Ricoeur (1973) calls the *antinomy of value,* the "central antinomy of [modern] moral philosophy," begins to take shape. The question is, Are values created or discovered? In Ricoeur's words, "If values are not our work but precede us, why do they not suppress our freedom? And if they are our work, why are they not arbitrary choices?" (p. 156). Throughout this book we try to show that struggles with this dilemma and a lack of success in resolving it have shaped at their core social science and psychotherapy as we know them.

The Modern Problem of Justifying Morality

Alasdair MacIntyre (1981) in *After Virtue* gives us a profound diagnosis of our confusion and ambivalence concerning the place of moral values in the scheme of things and the place of ethical deliberation in the conduct of human affairs. MacIntyre tells a compelling story about how, in his view, leading philosophers from Hume through the nineteenth century struggled to explain the modern world to itself. Each of these thinkers, so the story goes, inherited and gave genuine credence to some fundamental moral notions that in earlier times reflected criteria of good and evil thought to be embedded in the order of things. However, these older values and virtues only make the sense they do in the context of a meaningful cosmic order. They represent achievements of character and community whose intelligibility rests on their connection with the roles humans are thought to play in this wider story. But each of these early modern thinkers also lived on this side of the "break with the continuity of meaning in tradition occasioned by the Enlightenment" (Gadamer, 1987, p. 244). Because they adopted a new and unprecedented kind of modern consciousness, they were deeply wedded to a conception of humans as moral agents free from the automatic and built-in constraints of traditional hierarchies and teleologies and in a very real sense sovereign in their moral authority. Human beings belong to themselves and not to their traditions.

Yet, paradoxically, these thinkers assented to at least modified or somewhat abridged versions of values and virtues that came from those traditions. They acknowledged such things as honesty, promise keeping, benevolence toward those in need, and some conception of justice. The problem for moral philosophy is how to preserve *both* a strong sense of personal autonomy *and* the authority of fundamental moral commitments. These post-Enlightenment thinkers were not simply seeking some sort of compromise under duress. On the contrary, they and their culture genuinely wanted to honor both freedom and responsibility as they understood them. Their problem, then, was figuring out how to construe moral values so that they (1) do not violate the hard-won ideal of autonomy but (2) still retain enough authority to keep such values from appearing arbitrary and irrational, not just to others but to themselves as well.

Although efforts to resolve this dilemma of freedom and authority took a number of different forms, MacIntyre discerns a pattern running through them all. They were all different versions of "the Enlightenment project of justifying morality" (1981, p. 35). This project attempted to ground morality on facts about some familiar aspect of human nature, such as reason, feeling, or will. Given the outlook of these thinkers, such features of human nature are morally neutral—brute facts about humans with no evaluative dimension or bonds to a wider cosmic context. It should be evident that such a view of human nature contrasts strongly with premodern views. For Plato, for example, reason is more than a dexterity at solving problems; it is the capacity to see the order of things and to see how this order reflects an order of Ideas itself aimed at achieving the Good. But for these post-Enlightenment thinkers, reason "discerns no essential natures and no teleological features in the objective universe available for study by physics" (MacIntyre, 1981, p. 52).

According to MacIntyre, these Enlightenment thinkers tried to justify morality by arguing that moral values grow naturally out of the full and proper exercise of the particular capacity or tendency taken as crucial to humans (reason, feeling, will, and so on). Using this approach to justification, one need not appeal to a transcendent order of things in order to justify morality or make sense of the claim it makes on us. Instead, moral values spring naturally from these facts about our human nature. Interestingly, even our contemporary propensity to think of ethical commitments as "enhancements of the sense of individual well-being rather than as moral imperatives" (Bellah et al., 1985, p. 47) reflects this approach. According to the pervasive view of morality in the United States today, if we exercise our inherently human capacity for wholeness, happiness, or fulfillment, then we will naturally want to include certain moral commitments as part of the package.

MacIntyre (1981) shows how this Enlightenment project of justifying morality worked in influential types of modern moral philosophy. For example, Kant's ethics tried to justify morality by treating it as a product of our own inherent rationality. According to Kant, moral deliberation enjoins us to act only on maxims that can be consistently universalized or, in another formulation, to treat others as ends in themselves and not merely as means to our own personal ends. A second example is utilitarian moral theory, which holds that individual and social good will follow from improved calculations in the service of our natural propensity to obtain pleasure and avoid pain. We will also discuss a third attempt to justify morality: the moral outlook of Romanticism, which has proved to be so influential in psychology and psychotherapy. Romanticism encourages us to eschew false social masks and deceits and follow the "voice of nature" revealed in our unspoiled feelings and spontaneous impulses. This Romantic ideal is the source of the many influential theories of self-realization and self-actualization in contemporary thought.

Kantian Ethics

Kant's view is that rationality itself dictates a rational test for evaluating the rules or maxims that guide our choices and actions in situations that demand moral deliberation. In Kant's view, the deciding factor cannot be whether the action chosen will lead to greater happiness for oneself or others, for it is the defining mark of a *moral* decision that issues of inclination and personal preference are set aside. Moreover, our conception of happiness is too vague, people differ too greatly in their views of happiness, and those views may be too contaminated with self-interest to guide moral reasoning. In the same way, the test of a maxim or precept can never be that it is commanded by God. To conclude reasonably and justifiably that we should do something commanded by God, we "would also have to know that we always ought to do what God commands. But this last we could not know unless we ourselves possessed a standard of moral judgment independent of God's commandments" (MacIntyre, 1981, p. 43).

So morality is neither a means to the end of happiness nor blind obedience to the dictates of a higher power. Fortunately, Kant believes, there is a third possibility. His famous categorical imperative, to act only on maxims that can be consistently universalized, provides a principle of practical or moral reason that "employs no criterion external to itself" (MacIntyre, 1981, p. 43). Kant argues that the application of this test of consistent universalizability yields a genuine morality that depends neither on securing worldly benefits nor on sacrificing one's moral autonomy to an outside, arbitrary authority. Applying this principle we find, for example, that "Always keep promises" passes the test, whereas "Only keep promises when it is convenient" does not.

The categorical imperative is part of a larger Kantian ethical theory that expresses values many of us accept and cherish, such as regard for human rights, respect for the dignity of the individual, and the ideal of ethical discussion as offering good reasons for moral decisions rather than simply relying on unquestioned authority or current preferences. But it is important to realize that the categorical imperative must be purely *formal* in order to accomplish its aims. We are enjoined to act in a way that is logically consistent with the abstract principle of the categorical imperative, not to seek any particular outcome or results. If the categorical imperative were not purely formal, then morality would be based on producing nonmoral or merely desired outcomes, such as security or happiness, or on conforming to the prejudices of tradition or the dictates of some authority—in other words, on factors that have nothing to do with genuine moral decisions.

As Hegel and many other critics point out, however, the extreme formalism of Kant's categorical imperative is not really independent of substantive moral commitments; instead, it merely conceals those commitments under the guise of neutrality. For example, Kant suggests that a maxim endorsing the keeping of promises only when it is convenient fails to satisfy the categorical imperative or pass the test of consistent universalizability. If this flawed maxim were adopted universally, then promises would not be taken seriously and promising would become meaningless. But this line of thought is ultimately not convincing. For one thing, this worry about the consequences of maintaining or not maintaining the institution of promise making seems to slip into the very "consequentialist" concerns Kant wanted to extrude from ethical thinking. As Norman (1983) points out, the mere fact of undermining the practice of keeping promises can be deplored only if one adopts additional, evaluative presuppositions affirming that this practice *ought* to exist in the first place. To put it another way, we have to presuppose that there is something inherently *good* about a way of life in which people keep their promises before we can agree that it is the *right* thing for them to do even when it does not serve their selfish interests.

It should be obvious that bringing in specific moral viewpoints about a good or worthwhile way of life that is either supported or undermined by the keeping of promises violates Kant's cardinal principle that practical or moral reason be obedient only to commands it gives itself. A morality that is tied to nurturing a particular kind of character or community life, according to this approach, is *heteronomous,* no longer genuine moral thinking because it does not flow from the exercise of our inherent rationality. Thus, Kant holds that the only principle for evaluating norms or maxims is in terms of purely formal, rational consistency or universalizability. The problem is that there does not seem to be any purely rational inconsistency in willing a world of pure egoists who strictly follow maxims of only "looking out for number one" or who only keep promises when it suits them. Of course, this is just the sort of situation that Kant wants to preclude. According to MacIntyre, Kant's version of the Enlightenment project turns out not to *establish* but to *presuppose* a way of distinguishing between right and wrong or of specifying what is a good life. Kant's noble purpose was to harmonize full human rationality and autonomy with genuine moral conviction. But his program seems to dissolve into either uncritically obeying an outside authority or following principles based merely on achieving results one happens to desire.

Utilitarian Moral Theory

Utilitarian ethics seeks to provide an enlightened morality and program for social reform based on a solid psychological foundation. This foundation is supplied by Jeremy Bentham's thesis that humans act from only two basic motives: to maximize pleasure and to avoid pain. From this naturalistic orientation, Bentham concludes that, in making moral decisions, one must (1) calculate the pleasure and pain an action will cause for all of those involved and then (2) pursue actions and policies that produce the greatest pleasure and the least pain for the greatest number of individuals. Because this calculation is solely concerned with the greatest good for the greatest number, individuals who make the calculation must think of themselves and their loved ones as only units in a totality and so not privileged in any sense.

The utilitarian approach to ethics has had enormous appeal for obvious reasons: it seems to place a hard-nosed concern for human welfare on a no-nonsense scientific basis. We don't have to saddle ourselves or others with unrealistically saintly ideals or formal principles. We can just roll up our sleeves and get down to work to improve the human situation in tangible ways. A great deal of twentieth-century psychology and psychotherapy has been formulated in a utilitarian spirit. The moral emphasis in most therapy theories derives not from the ethical quality of the individuals or society the therapy tends to promote but from removing barriers to individuals' pursuing success and happiness in whatever way they wish. The science of psychology is supposedly not obedient to any particular vision of the good life. Its research and theory provide means for re-engineering personal and social life in whatever way the citizenry happens to prefer.

Nevertheless, critics point out a number of problems with the utilitarian view. One serious problem relates to the fact that there are an enormous variety of human satisfactions, from culinary delight to religious feeling, that defy direct comparison on a single scale of quality or quantity (Adler, 1985; MacIntyre, 1981). As a result, it is difficult to imagine how one could calculate the units of pleasure and pain needed for the utilitarian approach.

Kant and Kantian liberals point out another difficulty with utilitarianism: it fails to take seriously the distinction between persons. It treats society as a whole as if it were a single person and tries to maximize the overall sum of such pleasures or satisfactions. Thus, utilitarians would be unable to come up with a good reason why the pleasure of thousands of Roman spectators would not outweigh the pain of a handful of Christians eaten by lions, so far as the greatest good for the greatest number is concerned. Kant felt that the utilitarian calculus failed to respect the inherent dignity of persons and tended to treat some people as means to the happiness of all, thus failing to respect each person as an end in himself or herself.

Recently, Bernard Williams (1986) has pointed out a central failure of utilitarianism. Utilitarians portray human beings as engaged in a kind of direct pursuit of happiness. But according to "an exceedingly ancient platitude" (p. 101) this pursuit may be impossible or at least self-defeating. Happiness may come only as a by-product of seeking the good or doing the right thing, not when sought as an end in itself. Utilitarianism does involve a kind of morally serious commitment to adhere to the results of calculations concerning both one's own and others' happiness. But a strong case can be made, Williams argues, that a moral agent does not act from such calculations but is "identified with his actions as flowing from projects and attitudes which in some cases he takes seriously at the deepest level, as what life is all about." To demand that a person be ready to set these aside if calculations of utility require is "to alienate him in a real sense from his actions and the source of his action in his own convictions." This would really amount to "an attack on his integrity" (p. 102).

Because of these deep-seated problems in utilitarianism, it seems that Kantian liberalism, with its emphasis on individual dignity and rights, formal ethical principles, procedural justice, and the priority of the right over the good, best captures the moral ideals of the modern age. Despite its limitations, however, utilitarian thought continues to exert a great deal of influence, especially among those skeptics and tough-minded naturalists who hesitate to assert any universal or objectively valid ethical ideals but still desire some sort of moral orientation or direction. Utilitarian thinking has had immense appeal to social scientists who wish to remain rigorously scientific and unsentimental while still presenting themselves as concerned with improving human welfare.

As a matter of fact, it is evident that utilitarian thinkers and most social scientists do not wish to tether our moral decision making to the whims of the moment or to whatever any one individual happens to find pleasurable or diverting. They are not saying that anything goes. Rather, they assume that people will opt for decent, civilized satisfactions and, like themselves, be dedicated to relieving needless suffering and working for justice in human affairs. The problem is that utilitarian thought, like Kantian liberalism, really does not *establish* but rather *presupposes* a way of distinguishing between right and wrong or of specifying the good life. It represents a sincere attempt to give us a moral sense of direction while banning all unscientific and morally suspect traditional ideals. In the end, however, it fails to accomplish either of these aims.

The Romantic Moral Outlook

As we mentioned earlier, a third attempt to justify morality, Romantic thought, might be added to MacIntyre's list (1981). Romantic thought of the late eighteenth and early nineteenth century has had an enormous effect on ideas about human freedom and fulfillment in modern times, and they influence twentieth-century psychology and psychotherapy profoundly. The Romantic sensibility reacts strongly to the alienation from nature and the one-sided emphasis on rational control in the conduct of life encouraged by Enlightenment thought. Romanticism eschews the disengagement from and disenchantment of the universe so central to the rationalist and scientific enterprises; instead, it celebrates closeness to nature, following instinct, mythical consciousness, and beauty and art. The most influential figure in the formation of Romantic thought, Rousseau, believed in a "natural morality" that is corrupted in high society with its falsified human relations. For Rousseau (cited in Solomon, 1985, pp. 494–497), "the first impulses of nature are always right" and should be trusted, because "the cause of our being . . . has provided for our preservation by giving us feelings suited to our nature." As "man is by nature a social animal," chief among our innate impulses is a "social feeling" that manifests itself as conscience, "the infallible judge of good and evil." According to Romantic views, we should strive to recover the pristine source of our moral sensibilities by recapturing the original sense of life's purpose that is embodied in myth, artistic imagination, and childlike responses deep within us. It is not reason that guides us to the good life but the "voice of nature" revealed in our unspoiled feelings and spontaneous impulses.

The Romantic image of the natural as a healing power and source of goodness defines a great deal of what life is all about for many contemporary people and has shaped much thinking about the goals of psychotherapy, often framed in terms of self-realization or self-actualization. Yet despite the evident worthiness of an emphasis on inner self-exploration and creative activity, the belief that it will by itself lead to an understanding of what constitutes the morally good life is highly questionable. There seem to be a multitude of "natural" and spontaneous feelings within us, including a capacity for cruelty and ruthless cravings for power. How are we to sort out impulses that are worthy from those that are not? No clear answer is provided. So it appears that the Romantic vision, too, presupposes rather than grounds genuine distinctions between good and evil. In the end, it seems that Romanticism, Kantian, and utilitarian approaches are all more successful in identifying what they are *against*, such as arbitrary authority or lack of spontaneity, than what they are *for* in terms of the shape of the good life.

o

John Dewey (1960, p. 255) wrote that "integration and cooperation between man's beliefs about the world in which he lives (is's) and his beliefs about the values and purposes that should direct his conduct (ought's) is the deepest problem of modern life. It is the problem of any philosophy that is not isolated from that life." Perhaps a lot of philosophy and social science has been unduly isolated from practical life. But even those who have faced the problems of modern life squarely, such as Kantian liberals, utilitarians, and Romantic thinkers, seem to have encountered daunting obstacles in fashioning a coherent moral outlook for modern times. In subsequent chapters, we suggest that newer, twentieth-century philosophical viewpoints like existentialism and postmodernism or social constructionism share in many of the same difficulties incurred by these earlier versions of the Enlightenment project. All these views represent different attempts to seal off the possibility of reverting to what are seen as traditional dogmatisms and mystifications while still holding out a way of finding a sense of integrity, authenticity, or moral direction in modern circumstances. Their differences notwithstanding, they all struggle with finding a way to balance freedom and responsibility in our brave new world.

However, each of these approaches appears to founder in similar ways. They each presuppose certain values or moral commitments that they try to justify on the basis of some fundamental facts about human nature. As we have seen, they reason in a vicious circle and ultimately fail to convince. Nietzsche saw that the claims of these modern moralists to have this sort of solid foundation turn out to be unsubstantiated, leading to a certain kind of "nihilism" (MacIntyre, 1981; Solomon, 1973). We argue in this book that the moral presuppositions of various forms of thinking in modern psychology and psychotherapy incorporate one or another of these problematic modern approaches to ethics.

Liberal Individualism

These philosophical attempts to justify morality have not been limited to the rarefied regions of academic discourse. Various forms of Kantian, utilitarian, and Romantic thought provide the basis for some of the most pronounced features of contemporary American culture. The need for justifying morality was occasioned by the growing attachment Enlightenment thinkers developed toward individual autonomy. This preoccupation with the individual is found in both Locke's utilitarian and Rousseau's Romantic formulations of the social contract. They assume that the basic unit of human reality is the individual person, who is assumed to exist and have determinate characteristics prior to and independent of his or her social existence. It follows, then, that social systems must be understood as artificial aggregates of individuals which are set up to satisfy the needs of those individuals. As this individualist outlook evolved, people came to be seen as possessors of inherent dignity and bearers of inalienable rights, as their own source of meaning and purpose in living, and individual fulfillment came to be seen as the definitive aim of life.

The influence of individualism is powerful in both psychotherapy and contemporary social science. Modern social scientists generally intend—even when claiming to be value-free or value-neutral—to aid in the active re-engineering of human society in directions indicated by fundamental Western ideals of freedom, dignity, and inalienable rights for all individuals. In later chapters we argue that the modern social science enterprise is thus commonly underpinned by one or another version of a certain disguised ideology, best described as philosophic liberalism or liberal individualism (Sandel, 1996; Sullivan, 1986). *Some* set of social and moral commitments, usually unacknowledged, underpin all psychological theories and interpretations of research findings. *Most* of these theories and interpretations appear to be decisively colored by a variant of liberal individualism. This ideology or moral outlook is an indelible dimension of much modern social science as an intellectual enterprise and historical movement. Bringing its specific moral beliefs to light and critically scrutinizing them should be a high priority for us.

Bellah et al. (1985) suggest that modern individualism takes two main forms, centered on two competing but interwoven ideals for living. They call the first *utilitarian individualism*, which "takes as given certain basic human appetites and fears . . . and sees human life as an effort by individuals to maximize their self-interest relative to these given ends" (p. 336). From the beginning of the modern age, critics have objected to this view of life and living as excessively detached, calculating, emotionally isolating, and overly preoccupied with instrumental control over events to the neglect of other important concerns and purposes in living.

The second kind of individualism came mainly from writers associated with the Romantic movement. Bellah et al. (1985) term it *expressive individualism*. It arose in opposition to utilitarian individualism and holds that "each person has a unique core of feeling and intuition that should unfold or be expressed if individuality is to be realized." This unique core is "not necessarily alien to other persons or to nature," with which the person may be able to merge under certain conditions (p. 334).

However, we must emphasize that the modern outlook has usually counterbalanced the heavy stress on self-interest and self-realization found in utilitarian and expressivist forms of individualism with a strong ethical emphasis on regarding human agents as imbued with dignity and inherent worth and as possessed of natural rights. In this view, albeit paradoxically, individuals are seen as both radically self-interested *and* obligated to respect and advance the freedom and rights of all people. There never has been agreement as to precisely what freedom means or exactly what rights individuals possess and should seek to ensure (Sandel, 1996). But we continue to refine our understanding of these ideals and further their implementation, obviously an unfinished task, in the present day.

Liberal individualism is a mold of thought and way of life that is synonymous with much modern consciousness, and it appears to be built into the assumptions of much social and psychological theory. Nevertheless, like the forms of the Enlightenment project of justifying morality described by MacIntyre, it embodies a number of severe inner tensions or contradictions that lead to its progressively unraveling in practice. One of the essential features of the utilitarian version of liberal individualism is that it limits human reason to judgments about more or less efficient means-ends relations and leaves the choice of ends to innate promptings or individual preference. The focus on procedural or means-ends rationality is aimed at expanding our instrumental prowess and protecting our freedom from deceptive dogma or authoritarian control. If we cannot reason validly about the ends we seek because they are left to individual or subjective preference, then no one is entitled to impose their values or way of life on anyone else.

Of course, this situation runs a high risk of deteriorating into an amoral clash of power against power. In order to prevent such a calamity from occurring, this approach supplements an uncompromising instrumentalism with a view of individuals as possessing natural rights or as imbued with inherent dignity and worth. This combination of an instrumental view of action and respect for human dignity and rights finds expression in an ethical outlook centered on formal principles of procedural justice or fairness (Neal, 1990; Rawls, 1971). Supposedly, this approach avoids designating any particular ends or ways of life as superior while also assuring respect for individuals and their choices. Such principles "constitute a fair framework within which individuals and groups can choose their own values and ends, consistent with a similar liberty for others" (Sandel, 1996, p. 11).

The worthy ideals of liberal individualism underwrite our enhanced modern sensitivity to overt or psychological abuses of power and to their rationalization in theory or precept. Nevertheless, this outlook harbors some deep internal inconsistencies that lead it to be significantly self-undermining on a practical level. For example, this approach tries to strike a balance between self-interest and a moral sense by incorporating in the same human agent both an ordinary, strictly "desire-controlled personality" and a superordinate "free, rational self" capable of entirely subordinating desire to principle (Sullivan, 1986, p. 87). This split is dramatically evident in the functions of the id and the ego in Freud's metapsychology, but we can also find parallels in most other theories of personality or psychotherapy. However, the existence of such a profound gulf between one aspect of the self dominated by self-interest and another capable of rational mastery over all such inclinations seems both logically and psychologically implausible.

Liberal individualism conveys a heavily one-sided, self-centered view of human thought and action. Even the permutations of this view that stress self-expression and self-realization or the radical existential choice of one's fundamental values and projects retain this instrumental cast. Inbuilt inclinations, authentic inner promptings, or existential choice give individuals their ends in living. Much of human agency is focused on determining how best to pursue these pregiven or separately determined goals in everyday life. Such an approach advocates thinking of basic human values as subjective or arbitrary. Thus Mill's famous remark in *On*

Liberty: "Mankind are greater gainers by suffering each other to live as seems good to themselves, than by compelling each to live as seems good to the rest" (1860/1956, p. 17). Such a view, needless to say, affords human reason no resources to explain or defend the worth of ends.

Oddly enough, this truncating of the scope of human reason and responsibility appears to take place for sincere moral reasons. Liberal individualism seems to be embroiled in the paradox of advocating a thoroughgoing neutrality toward all values as a way of *promoting* certain basic values of liberty, tolerance, and human rights. Justice is strictly procedural, which means that no one can define the good life for anyone else. However, this strategy throws the baby out with the bath. If reason cannot defend the worth of ends, it also cannot defend liberal individualism's vision of a way of life characterized by dignity and respect (Sullivan, 1986). A serious commitment to human dignity and rights clearly sketches out a way of life that is taken to be morally superior or *good in itself.* But what is to prevent a principled neutrality toward all notions of the good life from extending to those basic values of liberty and human dignity as well, undermining their convincingness and stripping them of any possibility of rational defense (Kolakowski, 1986; Sarason, 1986)?

On a practical level, liberal individualism's insistent characterization of human action and motivation as exclusively self-interested may become a self-fulfilling prophecy. The direct pursuit of security and happiness, when it defines what life is all about, seems to increasingly dissolve the capacity to respect and cherish others (Bell, 1978) It erodes our capacity for devotion to the best modern ideals of freedom and justice. This erosion is perhaps a key facet of a process described by Selznick (1992). He aptly summarizes how the modern moral sensibility brings benefits of greater individual freedom, increased equality of opportunity, efficiency and accountability, and the rule of law, but does so at the price of what he calls *cultural attenuation,* the diminishing of "symbolic experiences that create and sustain the organic unities of social life." In his view, there has been a "movement away from densely textured structures of meaning to less concrete, more abstract forms of expression and relatedness." This movement "may contribute to civilization—to technical excellence and an impersonal morality—but not to the mainsprings of culture and identity" (p. 6). The price to be paid for cultural attenuation becomes clearer with the passage of time. Selznick argues that "modernity, especially in its early stages, is marked by an enlargement of individual autonomy, competence, and self-assertion. In time, however, a strong, resourceful self confronts a weakened cultural context; still later, selfhood itself becomes problematic" (p. 8).

Our contention is that liberal individualism in some form is the disguised ideology of much modern psychology and psychotherapy. As a result, psychology and psychotherapy theory and practice incorporate many of the conceptual and practical insufficiencies of this pervasive modern moral outlook. This leads them to harbor at least partial blind spots concerning some of the most pressing modern dilemmas in living and therefore to perpetuate some of the very difficulties in living for which they proffer a cure. This is a large claim. As always, the devil is in the details. In the remaining chapters of Part One we try to show more specifically how a number of representative modern therapy theories share in this predicament.

2

FREEDOM AND COMMITMENT
IN MODERN PSYCHOTHERAPY

MODERN PSYCHOTHERAPY IS deeply embroiled in the dilemmas of modern culture discussed in the previous chapter. It is difficult to know where to start in sorting out the genuine insights of the therapy enterprise from its more questionable features. It may be helpful to begin with a remarkable feature of that enterprise; namely, modern psychotherapy presents a somewhat anomalous situation: quite different-appearing types of therapy question one another's theoretical and practical value, even though most of them seem to have something illuminating to say about human life and emotional problems and many can claim some support from empirical research for their effectiveness. Anyone teaching a course in theories of counseling or psychotherapy confronts this confusing situation in attempting to compare those theories in a meaningful way. It also can be discouraging to students in these classes who hope to discriminate on some rational basis between better and worse theories of therapy. They often find that they can neither comfortably settle in with just one or two of the bewildering array of theories available nor find a way to harmonize these different perspectives to any great extent.

One very sensible proposal in response to this situation has been for theorists and therapists to work toward a truly eclectic psychotherapy that includes what is worthwhile and eschews what is deleterious in the various therapies, relying as much as possible on demonstrated effectiveness through empirical research (Norcross, 1986). One difficulty with this project, however, is that different therapies may have partly different goals for clients, perhaps based on different understandings or visions of what life is all about (Messer, 1986). Different, value-laden criteria of effectiveness may be internal to each therapy system, thus eliminating any common standard for evaluating the soundness of these therapies. A less obvious but more troubling problem is the possibility that all the major systems of modern therapy may incorporate values or under-standings of life that are distorted or inauthentic in some manner. An eclectic approach, far from dealing with this problem, would preserve it and hide it from view! Westerman (1986) specifically encourages eclec-tic theorists to take the underlying philosophical perspectives and ethi-cal positions of psychotherapy systems seriously. In this spirit, this chapter attempts to examine the important and, it turns out, somewhat confused ethical underpinnings of several representative modern therapy theories.

Ira Progoff (1956) wisely observed that "psychology began as an unconscious search for meaning in a civilization whose traditional mean-ings had been destroyed" (p. 14). Progoff and others (for example, Sara-son, 1986) have suggested that modern psychology and psychotherapy came into existence, in part, as ways of dealing with problems in living engendered by the breakdown of supporting institutions and the dissolu-tion of linkages of shared purpose and obligation that characterize mod-ern cultural life. The chapters of Part One try to illustrate how the theories and practice of modern psychotherapy are deeply implicated in a search for meaning and direction in modern circumstances. In general, theories of psychotherapy seem to be caught in the tension between, on one side, our need for some kind of authoritative guidelines for living and some basis for genuine community and, on the other, the privileged status accorded to our understanding of freedom or autonomy, with its pro-found distrust of authority. In this chapter, we examine several represen-tative perspectives on therapy and suggest that each of them incurs similar difficulties in reaching an accommodation between this ideal of freedom and a commitment to some sort of life-guiding values. For this reason, they risk perpetuating some of the conditions that give rise to the prob-lems in living they were devised to cure.

Freud and the "Analytic Attitude"

So far as its moral or ideological underpinnings are concerned, modern psychotherapy begins, with psychoanalysis, on a profoundly ambiguous note. On the one hand, "the Freudian analysis of morality appears to be a traumatic negation of traditional moral beliefs" (Ricoeur, 1974, p. 976). On the other hand, Freud may properly be viewed as a "moralist [who] derives lessons on the right conduct of life from the misery of living it" (Rieff, 1959, p. ix).

Philip Rieff (1966) makes a useful distinction between pre-Freudian "therapies of commitment" and an historically novel "analytic attitude" that emerges with psychoanalysis. In Rieff's view, all traditional forms of psychological healing prescribe a certain amount of "repression" or self-denial. They do so in exchange for building a sense of meaning in life around the affirmation of ethical or religious values that only make sense when the self is conceived as part of a meaningful cosmic order with which the self tries to get in touch or in harmony. One is compensated for these losses or self-denials by "pleasures higher and more realizable than instinctual gratification" (p. 10). In contrast, Freud's view of healing is based on an "analytic attitude" that explicitly rejects all objective moral laws, perceived cosmic purposes or divine will, or numinous religious experiences, which support such compensation. They are at best illusions, at worst symptoms of illness. Such beliefs or values exact a greater or lesser price of repression in return for no real psychic gain. It is an ironic mark of the moral seriousness of psychoanalysis that it allows no compromise whatsoever on this point.

In the Freudian scheme, the ego seeks to "reduce the forces and influences which work in it and upon it to some kind of harmony" (Freud, 1933, p. 104). Rieff (1959, p. 61) terms this the "formal and integrative task" of managing conflicting forces or claims originating outside the ego in the id, superego, and external reality. The ego is the seat of "reason," but such reason is in no way the source of moral judgment, as in traditional views. Rather, it is a pragmatic, controlling reason, whose slightest consent to the authority of traditional moral beliefs would undermine the ego's ability to gain accurate insight into the true causes of neurotic suffering or strike even a tenuous balance among the warring influences in everyday life.

The "analytic attitude" not only reflects the now familiar idea that we live in a thoroughly disenchanted cosmos but also represents a rigorous application of that idea to basic problems of human suffering and fulfillment following the many failures to refurbish or replace traditional moral views. The core of Freud's recommended outlook in a world devoid of larger purposes and traditional consolations is unbending realism about these losses, and adoption of a stringent "doctrine of maturity . . . with its acceptance of meaninglessness as the end product of therapeutic wisdom" (Rieff, 1966, p. 43). But Rieff points out that in an age of science, this stark view implies something quite different from the quasi-religious submission to fate as understood in earlier tragedy. It puts a uniquely modern emphasis on "the control and manipulation of everyday life, the care and development of one's psychological forces. The undertone of tragedy in [Freud's] doctrine of immutable conflict has superimposed upon it the comic solvent, therapy" (p. 63). So the negative of meaninglessness is balanced off by the positive of successful instrumental action, perhaps enhanced by therapy, which gains what limited quantities of gratification may be procured in a very imperfect world.

It is no wonder that Rieff (1966) suggests that after psychoanalysis has lowered one's compulsions and increased one's options in living, one may face the dilemma of "being freed to choose and then having no choice worth making" (p. 93). The Freudian psychoanalytic vision of a relatively sane existence appears to walk a very thin line indeed between illusion and despair. In any case, this vision might be thought to represent the original psychoanalytic solution to the problem of easing the tension between a modern distrust of authority and the need for some kind of life-guiding values, albeit trying to keep those values at bare minimum. However, we have serious reason to doubt the adequacy of this solution, considering that Freud himself strayed significantly from this narrow path and gave voice to deeply held moral and philosophical prejudices that are disallowed by the strictly analytic attitude.

In *Sincerity and Authenticity,* Lionel Trilling (1971) speculates as to why Freud seemed reluctant to envision the mere possibility, even under conditions of increased material abundance, of more gratification and less "discontent" in culture. Trilling attributes this reluctance to a Nietzschean fear of "the 'weightlessness of all things,' the inauthenticity of experience which [Nietzsche] foresaw would be the consequence of the death of God" (p. 156). So Freud may have held to his particular kind of pessimism about human possibilities because "from religion as it vanished [he] was intent on rescuing one element, the imperative actuality which religion attributed to life" (p. 157). The trouble is that there is no way to defend this particular feeling toward life from within the Freudian scheme. It does not follow from the rejection of traditional beliefs—in fact it is a version of one of them—or from the assertion of the ego's purely managerial role in the psyche. This means that Freud's sense of the gravity or tragic worth of life may appear quite arbitrary and dispensable to those who do not happen to share Nietzsche's or Freud's particular predilections concerning the good life. That seems to be the reason why Rieff (1966) suggests that the somewhat heroic analytic attitude helps pave the way for a new "therapeutic age" marked by the quite different, much less high-minded values of "psychological man," who "has no higher purpose than the maintenance of a durable sense of well-being" (p. 13).

For the most part, Freud thinks "it is the interminable task of analysis to break the strangleholds of authority on the psyche" (Rieff, 1966, p. 46). It is regrettable that this morally serious enterprise should encourage the slide into something like what Lasch (1978) terms a morally shallow culture of narcissism. It would be even more painfully ironic if, over the long run, the analytic attitude tended to produce a condition similar to that it set out to cure. Lasch attempts to summarize some recent psychoanalytic insights and put them in a broader social context: "The decline of authority in an ostensibly permissive society does not . . . lead to a 'decline of the superego' in individuals. It encourages instead the development of a harsh, punitive superego. . . . As authority figures in modern society lose their 'credibility,' the superego in individuals increasingly derives from the child's primitive fantasies about his parents—fantasies charged with sadistic rage—rather than from internalized ego ideals formed by later experience with loved and respected models of conduct" (p. 12).

Freud's thought also gives evidence of a more specific moral prejudice that, strictly speaking, should be excluded by the analytic attitude. He was expressly opposed to any hierarchical division of human nature into "higher" versus "lower" purposes or goods. Instead, he proposed a radically egalitarian view of human nature as made up of "a democracy of opposing predispositions, deposited throughout every nature in roughly equal intensities" (Rieff, 1966, p. 17). For a moral agent, this imposes the demanding task of somehow "reserv[ing] the capacity for neutrality between choices even while making them" (p. 13). However, Freud violated that neutrality. In Rieff's view he hoped that "reason, the most aristocratic" of those predispositions, would, "despite its congenital weakness, cleverly manage to reassert itself . . . in a modest, even sly way that would alternatively dazzle and lull the more powerful emotions into submission" (p. 18). So Freud reasserted the positive value of prudent rational control over the emotions and circumstances of life endorsed by Enlightenment humanists, such control itself a descendant of the ancient virtue of *sophrosyne* or balance among bodily appetites imposed by reason. But in the absence of anything like the ancient order of Platonic Ideas or more modern schemes of natural law, the endorsement of this value, although an essential constituent of Freud's outlook, seems quite arbitrary.

Jung and Individuation

The outcome of Freud's thought leaves subsequent psychotherapy theorists in an awkward position. A case could be made that major theoretical innovations in the therapy field have been motivated in part by a concern (1) to preserve Freud's profound critique of moralistic or otherwise inauthentic restrictions on human autonomy while (2) circumventing the drift toward nihilism that his views either encourage or fail to deter. These attempts at reconciliation have not been entirely successful, however.

If the Freudian ego represents a relatively pure form of the ideal of the modern disengaged self—a self that achieves such freedom as is possible by objectifying its world—then the Jungian ego seems to signify at least a partial return to the idea of a self that can be defined only in relation to an encompassing meaningful order. For Jung (1966) the unconscious is not the essentially negative *unconscious repressed* but a more positive locus of suprapersonal, nonrepressed patterns of meaning, or *archetypes,* that express themselves in the length and breadth of human life. The ego or ordinary conscious self is no longer a morally isolated mediator among alien energies. Rather, the ego, along with the shadow, archetypes, and other characters, may play constructive roles in the drama of a complex larger Self.

The notion of this larger Self, grounded in the archetypes, is the key to the original Jungian synthesis of traditional meanings with a modern sense of freedom from intellectual dogma and arbitrary moral constraints. The Self is both the raw material and goal of human life. That raw material includes a rich panoply of archetypal possibilities for action, both good and evil, light and dark. The course of life is the teleological unfolding and integration of the Self through the master psychological process of *individuation.* The goal of that process is *wholeness,* a condition of balance and harmony between conscious and unconscious, ego and shadow, even good and evil as conventionally defined, resulting in a "wider, more comprehensive consciousness" (Jung, 1966, p. 178). The contrast with Freud is great. Neurosis no longer means the embrace of meanings and values that only serve to rationalize oedipal guilt and hamper effective instrumental activity by the ego. Rather, for Jung, the person is "called" by a "voice of nature" to a "vocation" within the larger arena of the Self. And neurosis is a "defense against the objective, inner activity of the psyche . . . which, independently of conscious volition, is trying to speak to the conscious mind through the inner voice and lead him towards wholeness" (1954, p. 183).

Jung describes the archetypes as impersonal and transpersonal. In Scott's words (1977, p. 30), the archetypes provide a "nonsubjective, ontological grounding for individuality *and* for human subjectivity in general." Their nonhistorical, universal status secures the right of their symbolic manifestations in experience—of which they are the source and "original pattern"—to be interpreted on their own terms and not reduced to veiled expressions of libido or Thanatos. What difference does this make in the concrete business of living? According to Scott (1977, p. 37), Jung believes that "a person becomes a responsible participant in the world only to the extent that he becomes conscious of the world-forming processes which work through him and which control him willy-nilly (unconsciously) as long as he 'projects' on objects without being aware of the source of his projections."

Thus, Jung replaces the stoic and unbelieving analytic attitude with "a psychological discipline that seeks to work with the inherently integrative processes of the unconscious psyche in order to achieve a realization of the Self" (Progoff, 1956, p. 181). But of what specifically does that task consist? It turns out that the archetypes only partly define a credible moral universe for the human agent. Unlike traditional virtues or the idea of personal salvation, they do not outline a shared human good which it is our essential purpose to realize and enjoy. Archetypal meanings are, to be sure, discovered rather than created. But their authority to define the good is distinctly abridged by the fact that once manifested in experience, they are demoted to serve as raw material for the faintly Nietzschean, largely self-defining enterprise of achieving self-realization or "wholeness."

Jung (1954, p. 239) wrote that "mankind is . . . psychologically still in a state of childhood—a stage that cannot be skipped. . . . The vast majority needs authority, guidance, law. . . . The Pauline overcoming of the law falls only to the man who knows how to put his soul in the place of conscience. Very few are capable of this." Archetypal meanings are a cacophony of diverse and inconsistent voices, which call us to many possibilities of evil and good, sickening and healing, illusion and truth. Wholeness does not consist in discerning which of these voices seem authentic and articulating them as guidelines for the good life. Rather, the values they represent must be relativized, embraced, transcended, and fused into what Jung called a "complexio oppositorum," a balance or union of opposites. Perhaps the most distinctive feature of Jung's approach to ethics is his notion that we should "partially" but "not completely" succumb to the evil that an inner voice brings before us. For "if by self-assertion the ego can save itself from being completely swallowed, then it can assimilate the voice, and we realize that the evil was, after all, only a semblance of evil, but in reality a bringer of healing and illumination" (Jung, 1954, p. 185).

Let us risk oversimplification for the sake of an example. To affirm the value of, say, moral seriousness or heroic self-assertion is necessarily to suppress or deny their opposite numbers, namely spontaneous play or appropriate submission to fate. In Jung's view just this polarization of opposites, the cutting of one of them off from conscious assimilation, causes emotional illness. Now Jung might have construed the overcoming of such polarization as a reinterpretation of what these values are really all about. For example, the opposition between acting on impulse and rigid moralizing might be overcome through articulating an ideal of flexible responsibility that incorporates both spontaneity and acting on principle in a more coherent understanding of the good life. Surely the idea of a union of opposites takes much of its meaning from such a familiar process. In the last analysis, however, self-realization for Jung seems to consist of something different than such a clarification of what our values are all about. Given meanings or values seem to serve in a quasi-instrumental manner as means to the end of a different *kind* of outcome than moral clarification, namely wholeness or individuation. That is part of what it means to put one's "soul in the place of conscience."

The notion of individuation seems to be the vehicle for striking a certain balance or compromise between authority and freedom. Archetypal meanings cannot be reduced to Freudian or other alien terms. But the authority of the archetypes is severely qualified by the fact that neither their implicit conceptions of good and evil nor fresh reinterpretations of their true meaning for us define the human good. Rather, these meanings are transformed and integrated in some unique manner in order to achieve "wholeness." This approach avoids arbitrary authority by justifying values as serving a kind of psychic health or well-being that is "beyond good and evil." But it also makes choosing and integrating these values a radically free or self-defining process, one unguided by any criteria that might distinguish the process from arbitrary preference. Thus the individuated ego has really lost any sense of a genuine "vocation" within the meaningful ambit of a larger Self.

Of course, Jung is quite serious about restoring a dimension of transcendent meaning to human life. Thus he writes of a "life-will that is born with the individual" and asserts that "'growth' is the objective activity of the psyche, which, *independently of conscious volition,* is trying to speak to the conscious mind through the inner voice and lead him toward wholeness" (1954, p. 183). A voice or will from the deep unconscious speaks to us with authority, and we either defend ourselves against it neurotically, at a price, or follow its direction to our "vocation" and "destiny."

But how are we to harmonize the activity of this unconscious center of volition with the activity of the individuated ego that seems to pursue wholeness via a kind of radically free choice? The authoritative voice of nature that calls us to wholeness cannot be simply the voice of archetypes. Their meanings are not so much to be followed or obeyed as to serve as the raw material for a more self-defined individuation process. The nature of the autonomous choices made by the individuated ego effectively sever any genuine moral links to the unconscious and isolate the ego from any such deeper call. It seems that the unconscious, then, can influence the conscious realm only by overriding it, in either a brute causal or a psychologically domineering manner and not through some gentler form of persuasion or tutelage. It may well be that a sense of genuine authority and uncompromised freedom can work together *somehow* for good in human affairs. But Jung's portrayal of how this actually takes place apparently comes close to attributing *both* authoritarian submission *and* amoral choice to the individuated ego, rather than finding a clear and convincing way beyond the opposition between them.

Fromm and Self-Realization

For better or worse, few therapy theorists since Jung have so seriously invoked such a dimension of cosmic or quasi-religious meaning in their analysis of psychological illness and its cure. Most have taken a more humanistic and pragmatic tack. But most also continue to struggle with integrating a concern for human autonomy with some sort of intrinsic values. Erich Fromm's writings represent an interesting and influential attempt to think through difficult questions about the moral dimensions of modern psychotherapy that most writers slight or evade.

In his perhaps most famous book, *Escape from Freedom,* Fromm (1941/1965) discusses what he calls the ambiguity of freedom. He writes that human existence begins "when the lack of fixation of action by instincts exceeds a certain point." It begins to dawn on humans that theirs "is a tragic fate; to be part of nature, and yet to transcend it." Individuals in traditional societies are protected somewhat from this awareness by an "identity with nature, clan, religion." They may "suffer from hunger or suppression," but they do not "suffer the worst of all pains—complete aloneness and doubt." The unprecedented advance of freedom and individuation in modern times has severed the connection with nature, community, and tradition to a much greater extent, with decidedly "ambiguous" results. There is "on the one hand the growing independence . . . from external authorities, on the other hand . . . growing isolation and the resulting feeling of individual insignificance and powerlessness." This situation greatly tempts individuals to "escape from . . . freedom into submission or some kind of relationship to man and the world which promises relief from uncertainty," be it submission to authoritarian regimes, psychological masochism, or mindless consumerism (pp. 48–53).

Fromm (1941/1965) argues that our current situation often "makes freedom an unbearable burden" because we suffer from a "lag between 'freedom from' and 'freedom to.'" This results in a "disproportion between freedom *from* any tie and the lack of possibilities for the positive realization of freedom and individuality" (p. 53). In a similar vein, Taylor (1989) discusses what he calls the modern problem of "situating freedom." Most modern conceptions of freedom see it as something individuals "win through to by setting aside obstacles or breaking loose from external impediments, ties, or entanglements. To be free is to be untrammeled, to depend in one's action only on oneself." Freedom understood as "self-dependence" contrasts with older definitions of it as "order or right relation," which is inseparable from carrying out one's obligations and finding one's fulfillment within some larger ethical or spiritual drama. In Taylor's view, modern conceptions of freedom tend to be "negative" in the sense that they define it mainly as "liberation," be it liberation from political oppression or from inner barriers to self-expression or self-creation (pp. 155–156).

Fromm brilliantly spells out the consequences of this one-sided individualism for psychological well-being and human relationships. He builds on Marx's ideas about how modern capitalism relentlessly destroys precapitalist institutions and values necessary for social and political stability. Many non-Marxist thinkers have made a similar point, however. For example, Sullivan (1986, p. 33) discusses the relevance of the civic humanist tradition of moral and political thought stemming from Aristotle to the "contemporary crisis of liberal society." Sullivan contends that the "paradoxical effect of the growth of liberal capitalist society has been to undermine those social relations which have historically restrained and modified self-interested competition," thus undermining the honesty and trust necessary for the stable functioning of a market economy itself!

As a psychologist, Fromm takes this kind of analysis further into the realm of emotional dynamics and interpersonal relationships. He describes the rise in late modern times of a certain "marketing orientation." It is one of his main categories of emotional pathology, but Fromm emphasizes that it affects nearly everyone to some degree. According to Fromm (1947/1975), the "modern market is no longer a meeting place but a mechanism characterized by abstract and impersonal demand." Unlike the traditional local market, commodities do not have "use value" defined by the shared standards of a community but "exchange value" determined by impersonal market demand and sometimes quite shallow or transient desires (p. 76). This pervasive modern market has a profound effect on social character and emotional well-being over time. A widespread "personality market" develops in which both professionals and laborers greatly depend for their material survival and success on a capricious kind of personal acceptance rather than on traditional use value or ethical qualities. More and more, a person experiences himself as a commodity. More precisely, he experiences himself simultaneously as the seller *and* the commodity to be sold (p. 77). Increasingly, a person's "self-esteem depends on conditions beyond [one's] control." The result is "shaky self-esteem," a constant "need of confirmation by others," and feelings of "helplessness, insecurity, and inferiority." One "encounters one's own powers as commodities alienated from oneself." What matters is "not . . . self-realization in the process of using [one's powers or attributes] but . . . success in the process of selling them" (p. 80). Also, one comes to experience others in a similar way, as commodities. Thus equality no longer means the basic right of humans "to be considered as ends in themselves and not as means" so much as "interchangeability," the very negation of individuality (p. 81). Hans-Georg Gadamer (1981, pp. 73–74) made a similar point: "The individual in society who feels dependent and helpless in the face of its technically mediated life forms becomes incapable of establishing an identity. . . . In a technological civilization . . . in the long run the adaptive power of the individual is rewarded more than his creative power. Put in terms of a slogan, the society of experts is simultaneously a society of functionaries . . . inserted for the sake of the smooth functioning of the apparatus."

Finally, Fromm (1947/1975) notes that in such a society, relationships among people become "superficial" because it is not really the people themselves but those people viewed as interchangeable commodities that are related. Many hope that they can find a cure for this superficiality and alienation in the "depth and intensity of individual love." Unfortunately, however, "love for one person and love for one's neighbor are indivisible; in any given culture, love relationships are only a more intense expression of the relatedness to [others] prevalent in that culture. In the marketing orientation, one's self-esteem is never secure. One cannot ever get enough acceptance from others. As a result, lasting, satisfying ties of love and friendship become enormously difficult. The consequences are "depersonalization, emptiness, and meaninglessness" (p. 82). Thus Fromm astutely anticipates more contemporary discussions of our "culture of narcissism" (Cushman, 1990; Lasch, 1978).

What does Fromm recommend to moderns caught in the throes of the unfortunate freedom of a market-oriented culture? How can we orient ourselves to that freedom in a meaningful way? How do we determine to what ends our freedom ought to be exercised? Fromm wrote, "My experience as a practicing psychoanalyst has confirmed my conviction that problems of ethics cannot be omitted from the study of personality, either theoretically or therapeutically. The value judgments we make determine our actions, and upon their validity rests our mental health and happiness" (1975, p. 258). In *Man for Himself* and elsewhere, Fromm argues that Freud's narrow scientism prevents him from addressing "man in his totality, which includes his need to find an answer to the question of the meaning of his existence and to discover norms according to which he ought to live" (p. 17). What Ricoeur (1973, p. 998) called Freud's *suspension of ethics* appears not to have worked. Fromm (1975) takes the bull by the horns and tries to define an affirmative middle ground between (1) heteronomous, "authoritarian" sources of moral insight such as "revelation [and] the authority of the church" and (2) a "relativistic position which proposes that value judgments and ethical norms are exclusively matters of taste or arbitrary preference." The latter view is unacceptable: "since man cannot live without values and norms . . . relativism makes him an easy prey for irrational value systems" that supply norms based on the "demands of the State, the enthusiasm for magic qualities of powerful leaders, powerful machines, and material success" (p. 15).

For Fromm this middle ground is occupied by "humanistic ethics," a version of Enlightenment belief enriched by psychological insight, according to which autonomous human reason is capable of discerning valid ethical norms based on a solid and obtainable "knowledge of human nature." Fromm advocates an ethically serious version of self-realization that must be carefully distinguished from "ethical hedonism." The goal of the former is not the mere "satisfactions" or "irrational pleasures" that result from the removal of tension. It is a more positive sort of fulfillment requiring "emotional effort," and it only accompanies genuinely "productive activity" (1975, pp. 191–192). But what exactly is self-realization or the character of a self-realized life?

Fromm argues that a close look at human nature reveals that "mental health, like physical health, is not an aim to which the individual must be forced from the outside but one the incentive for which is in the individual and the suppression of which requires strong environmental forces operating against him" (1975, p. 220). Human "destructiveness is a secondary potentiality in man which becomes manifested only if he fails to realize his primary potentialities." Evil will result "only if the proper conditions for . . . growth and development are lacking, just as too moist soil will cause a seed to rot rather than develop into a proper tree" (pp. 219–220). Unfortunately, however, this analogy between the normal growth of a tree and the achievement of historically conditioned, socially situated human goods is strained and suspect on many grounds. Many shallow or insensitive forms of living do not appear to be the result of a stunted naturalistic process but to be just as "developed" as courageous and loving ones in terms of the exercise of human powers and skills. Fromm's argument seems to *presuppose* rather than identify the criteria of worth by which he distinguishes "primary" (that is, good) from "secondary" (that is, unworthy) human potential.

One way to explain Fromm's dilemma is in terms of the difficulty of formulating a convincing ethical outlook in a disenchanted universe peopled by modern, self-defining individuals. Fromm takes on that task. He asserts, in effect, two basic conditions for a valid ethics, which perhaps no single, consistent approach could ever satisfy. On the one hand, he asserts that "man, indeed, is the 'measure of all things.' . . . There is nothing higher and more dignified than human existence" (1975, p. 23). There is no need for "ethical behavior to be related to something *transcending* man" to keep it from being merely the expression of an "isolated, egotistical individual" (p. 23). Indeed, any adequate response to existential dilemmas begins with the ability to "face the truth, to acknowledge his fundamental aloneness . . . in a universe indifferent to his fate" (p. 53). On the other hand, just in order to address creatively our existential dilemmas, we must rise above "ethical hedonism" and "establish norms of conduct and value judgments which are objectively valid for all men," without which "desire is the test of value and not value the test of desire" (p. 24).

What sort of norms, one wonders, can so easily achieve universality without a hint of moral realities transcending individual human nature, and escape subjectivism without risking dogmatism in any way? Fromm (1947/1975) outlined a certain "productive orientation" or "productive character" built around ideals of nonpossessive love and nonexploitative, productive work that contributes to the general welfare. Although such a proposal is laudable in many ways, it seems to be either crucially vague or morally insufficient. First of all, one might question why designating these particular ideals of love and productiveness as "objectively valid norms" does not amount to a subtle new form of dogmatism that seals them off from scrutiny and revision in the light of new experience. In fact, many sharp concerns have been raised over the years about his particular formulation of these values (Friedman, 1984; Held, 1980). Are they really sufficient, as Fromm implies, to sustain lasting commitments beyond mutual self-interest, a sense of existential meaning in the face of tragedy, or social ties beyond cooperation to attain ultimately individual satisfactions? It is easy to doubt that they are. Or, if these norms or ideals are understood as just referring to the way of life that Fromm and others happen to prefer, why are they morally compelling and able to rescue us from "radical subjectivism," as Fromm urgently wishes them to do?

Fromm's most subtle effort to reconcile the claims of freedom and authority lies in his doctrine of self-realization as an overarching ideal for human life. "The aim of man's life . . . [is] the unfolding of his powers according to the laws of his nature" (1947/1975, p. 29). Thus, "the sole criterion of ethical value [is] man's welfare" (p. 22), and aims and activities are good or worthwhile if they serve the end of self-realization. The difficulty is this: it is hard to see how self-realization could be defined except in terms of the values implicit in these aims and activities, such as nonpossessive love and productiveness. Yet if we ask just *why* we should adopt these seemingly attractive values, we are in effect told that we should do so because they are means to the end of self-realization. Fromm cannot have it both ways. Self-realization may be the *same thing* as productive living and nonpossessive loving, which Fromm deems the most worthwhile way to live. But then why are these values anything more than someone's dogma dressed up as psychological theory? Or self-realization may be something different from this kind of living and loving, making it an *extrinsic effect* of this kind of life. But then what would distinguish it from the arbitrary preferences or payoffs of the kind of hedonistic or subjectivistic ethics that Fromm wants to surpass? What is more, "objective norms" would then be justified by their desirable effects rather than being genuine "tests of desire."

Looking back, we see a striking contrast between Fromm's profound diagnosis of the dilemmas of modern freedom and the rather weak solutions he proposes for addressing them. Fromm (1941/1965, p. 52) writes that there is "only one possible, productive solution" in relating to the world for "individualized" people who courageously embrace their freedom and refuse to sell out to authoritarian or escapist options. That solution is "active solidarity" with all people and "spontaneous activity, love and work," which unite us with the world not by instinctual or unquestioned practices of our way of life but as "free and independent individual[s]." However, it is not clear how a program of "productive work contributing to the general welfare" (p. 53), by itself, could provide a sense of individual or social purpose with which to counter the sort of one-sided individualism and merely negative "freedom from," tending toward emptiness, that he himself so well documents. What ends should we cultivate and enjoy *after* we have broken the bonds of paternalism and oppression, either collectively through social reform or individually via psychotherapy? What positive sort of "freedom to" would really help confront the threats of meaninglessness and death that are an indelible part of the human situation? What kinds of convictions or goals in living could plausibly stem the tide of the "marketing orientation" in this brave new world? Fromm seems to have no good answer to these questions. He fails to offer us a compelling "freedom to."

Rational-Emotive Psychotherapy

Rational-emotive psychotherapy and the writings of Albert Ellis (1962, 1977) also give evidence of an honest struggle to reconcile freedom with some other values, albeit with quite different results. Ellis forthrightly states, "All psychotherapy is, at bottom, a value system" (1973, p. 28). He also tries to be explicit about his own values. Although he asserts repeatedly (for example, 1973, p. 161) that his main goal as a therapist is to minimize irrational anxiety and hostility, he does not stop with that merely negative definition of psychological well-being. Rather, he states positively that clients should be encouraged to decide that "it is good for me to live and enjoy myself" and to decide "to strive for more pleasure than pain" (p. 23). He also contends that clients can discover that these values are attractive and correct through evaluations "entirely within the empirical realm" (p. 23).

These remarks may make it seem as if Ellis is a straightforward advocate of what he has called "long-range hedonism," with the undoing of certain "irrational beliefs" being the chief means to the end of attaining a "maximally satisfying existence" (1973, p. 23). But such is not the case. As a serious clinician Ellis reckons more profoundly than that with life's dark side. He seems to fret continually about what he calls our inborn biological tendency to think irrationally or magically, leading to self-blame, blame of others, and emotional disturbance. Indeed, it seems at times in his writings as if the struggle against this tendency, rather than striving for pleasure, becomes the main business of living! Ellis appreciates the paradoxical stubbornness of human masochism and self-defeat.

Moreover, he may be interpreted as proposing a cure for this misery that goes beyond ordinary therapy technique, namely his own recommended philosophical outlook.

This outlook appears to have two distinct elements. One element is an apparently thoroughgoing, explicitly antireligious *hedonism* generally consistent with Rieff's "analytic attitude." The second is less obvious but crucial to Ellis's approach. It is a strong emphasis on a kind of *detachment*—a detachment from the lottery of love and fortune that bears some resemblance to traditional philosophical or religious stances toward life, such as the Stoic ideal of freedom from destructive passions in a life lived in accordance with nature, or St. Paul's understanding of the Christian life lived "in but not of the world." Though far from advocating an otherworldly philosophy, Ellis seems to appreciate that simple hedonism is insufficient for human beings remorselessly exposed to many disappointments, evils, tragedies, and death. "Irrational beliefs," after all, are irrational because they make an individual's equanimity or sense of self-worth dependent on external circumstances, such as achievement, approval of others, or the absence of frustration or discomfort. Successful therapy severs this rationally indefensible connection between attitude and circumstance. It often means questioning and rejecting many common cultural beliefs and values. Indeed, according to Ellis, the "elegant" rational-emotive therapy solution to fundamental human dilemmas has been achieved when people finally arrive at the point where "practically under all conditions for the rest of their lives [they] would not upset themselves about anything" (quoted in Weinrach, 1980, p. 156).

However, this ideal of detachment and the good life is confusing and questionable. The original Stoic notion of detachment from irrational attachments and destructive passions only made sense in the context of belief in a kind of living, rational cosmic order that afforded a consoling sense of community with the universe and acceptance of one's place in it. But Ellis's version of detachment, unlike this or other traditional schemes of life, does not function to orient persons toward "higher" ethical or religious realities. Could it mean complete detachment from all cares or feelings of any sort? That could be accomplished equally well by catatonia or suicide. Is it just pretending to oneself that pleasures do not mean so much or disappointments wound so sharply as they otherwise would? That would hardly be possible when seeking pleasure and avoiding pain are the main substantive goals in living.

Of course, Ellis is not recommending stupefaction or self-deception as the alternative to emotional distress. Rather, he seems to interrelate these two values of hedonism and detachment in a certain manner in order to attain effective wisdom about meeting life's difficulties. Thoroughgoing hedonism is significantly diluted and qualified by detachment so that it is no longer simply the calculated pursuit of self-defined satisfactions. In a parallel way, detachment becomes more than an end in itself by functioning as a means to the end of a better hedonism, of greater pleasure and less distress. Detachment is somehow supposed to function to keep us from becoming too invested in the only thing there is to be invested in. It helps us play, but not too seriously, the only game there is to play.

No doubt the rational-emotive framework can assist individuals in reconsidering their strategies in living and putting their all-too-human concerns in some larger perspective. This therapy theory has taken a serious stab at a kind of wisdom that may be the object of perennial search: how to become and stay involved in life in a nondefensive and meaningful way in spite of its great uncertainty and inevitable, deep pain. But its vision of life remains critically vague concerning how to steer some middle path between meaninglessness and self-destructive naïveté. It is not at all clear how detachment can function to meliorate hedonism without the individual's transforming his or her goals. As a matter of fact, this approach seems to bear some resemblance to the attempt—many would consider it inauthentic—to become emotionally involved with a person or committed to some enterprise while somehow remaining invulnerable to pain or despair.

Dilemmas of Freedom and Responsibility

Each of these modern therapy theories appears to be shaped in part by an effort to resolve an acute tension between (1) a desire to hold on to some sort of intrinsic values and (2) a commitment to preconceived notions of human freedom in a posttraditional world that makes it difficult to embrace those values without seeming to court dogmatism or violate legitimate human autonomy. Interestingly, each of these theories, their differences notwithstanding, seems to adopt a variation of the same general strategy for harmonizing freedom and authority under modern circumstances. They first introduce or assume a few intrinsic values from one or another of our moral or religious traditions, though usually in a disguised and diluted form. In that way, they at least partially escape the threat of directionlessness and what Max Weber termed a loss of meaning in modernity. Then, however, they conform to the radical pragmatism of the modern age (which is uncomfortable with any given authority) by putting these values to work in an instrumental manner. The theories represent these values as means to the end of a kind of naturalistic or morally neutral "well-being," usually thought of as either an inbuilt end of the human organism or simply whatever the individual chooses or prefers.

This approach may seem to eschew any arbitrary authority while incorporating some intrinsic values. The wholeness, self-realization, or mere gratification we pursue is not dictated by any given tradition or arbitrary authority, yet certain worthy or attractive values are endorsed as indispensable means to attaining those ends. But the approach cannot succeed. On the one hand, we might claim that we affirm these values solely because they serve ends we just happen to pursue. But then the values clearly lack any real authority to evaluate or shape those ends. There would be no reason not to discard those values should we decide to seek different and incompatible goals in living. It is still the case that anything goes, or might go. On the other hand, we might stress that these values really do define a particular theory's understanding of the good or right kind of life by defining part of what that theory *means* by human health or well-being in the first place. Then, however, any defense of these values as contributing to this outcome is circular and specious. Any authority that attaches to these values still seems quite arbitrary, and our characteristic modern sense of moral freedom is compromised.

This same analysis could be extended to other therapy theories and discussion of values in therapy. For example, client-centered theory in effect defends its master value of self-actualization as fostering expression of the purely naturalistic promptings of an "organismic valuing process" (Rogers, 1951). But it clearly *selects* certain human potentialities to nurture over others on a basis that is never clarified. Similarly, Allen Bergin (1980) recommends that clinical psychology return to certain healthy traditional moral and religious values, but then seeks to defend those values as contributing to "lower rates of emotional and social pathology and physical disease" (p. 102).

In response to contemporary dilemmas of freedom and responsibility, a great many people have turned to such psychological notions as therapy, communication, and personal growth, not just for aids in restoring individuals to a common life but for fundamental definitions as to what life is all about. Rieff (1966) dubbed this phenomenon the "triumph of the therapeutic" in modern life. But the foregoing analysis strongly suggests that modern therapeutic wisdom does not represent a clear alternative to traditional belief or rootless modern freedom so much as an enticing but ultimately confused and unsatisfactory blend of the two. Bellah et al. (1985) suggest that "the belief that personal growth goes on endlessly and in any direction points up the ultimately aimless nature of the organic metaphor in . . . post-Freudian therapeutic hands" (p. 126). The problem, however, is not so much that American individualism ignores other values that might leaven or guide individual freedom as that it encourages us, to paraphrase Fromm, to see desire as the test of our commitments rather than to see these commitments as the test of our desires. We don't want to dispense with moral values but are uncomfortable evaluating them other than in terms of what "works" or "feels good."

No doubt modern psychotherapy has afforded many penetrating insights into personal and social dynamics that deepen our understanding of the conditions for genuine freedom and could assist us in fashioning more viable forms of community. But therapy cannot serve as both horse and rider. Therapeutic work presupposes shared cultural allegiances and a shared moral outlook derived from tradition or other sources. It is beginning to look as though our modern liberal and individualistic outlook by itself presents an ultimately confusing backdrop for the therapeutic endeavor. Its assumptions about the world prestructure our outlook in such a way that our only alternatives are empty freedom, ungrounded authority, or an inconsistent mix of the two.

What is the source of this antagonism between freedom and authority in twentieth-century therapy theories? Looked at one way, the conflict seems to arise straight out of an uncritical assumption of what Bellah et al. (1985) term *ontological individualism*. We tacitly view human beings atomistically as discrete centers of experience and action concatenated in various ways into social groups, struggling to reduce inevitable conflicts with others through negotiations and temporary alliances. This viewpoint seems to explain why values and ideals confront the self with claims that either seem weak and morally insufficient—really just an expression or rationalization of self-interest—or else seem a harsh imposition, a curtailment or violation of our hard-won autonomy.

The fact that these theories are so imbued with ontological individualism lends support to our argument that modern psychotherapy is deeply embroiled in the dilemmas of modern culture and modern consciousness described in Chapter One. Where do we go from here? For one thing, we need a continuing effort to sort out modern psychotherapy's genuine insights from those portions of therapy theories that merely uncritically endorse questionable modern ideologies. That will surely take a long time and involve a careful weighing and sifting of the assumptions and tacit values underlying our ideas and practices, a kind of critical reflection that generally seems quite alien or irrelevant to most social scientists and therapy theorists. We will try to take further steps down that road in the following chapters. Later on, we will explore ways in which hermeneutic thinkers like Gadamer (1975) and Taylor (1985a, 1989) seek to dissolve and fundamentally recast ontological individualism. The hermeneutic approach attempts to recapture something of a premodern sense of belonging and indebtedness to larger realities while preserving undiminished our modern critique of arbitrary authority. At least this approach has the merit of attacking at the root our modern confusions about values. Psychotherapy theory and practice will have to do the same if they want to be "part of the solution" in a time of cultural transition and crisis.

3

INDIVIDUALISM, FAMILY IDEOLOGY, AND FAMILY THERAPY

IN THE PREVIOUS TWO CHAPTERS, we touched on some of the ways that a variety of individual therapy approaches rather unreflectively incorporate contemporary cultural values related to individualism. Some theorists (for example, Doherty & Boss, 1991) have asserted that because family therapy focuses primarily on patterns of relationships, it is not reliant on individualistic presuppositions. On its face, the focus of family systems theory on relationship patterns, and the approaches to family therapy that follow from that focus, appear to present a *relational* rather than an *individualistic* view of humans. On closer examination, however, we will see that although family therapy theorists overtly reject certain facets of individualism, family therapists incorporate a cultural ideal of family life that was developed as part of the societal accommodation to and support of modern individualism. In general terms, family therapy theorists assume that healthy nuclear families are marriage centered, intimate, adaptable, quite autonomous, and intent on maintaining privacy. If our assessment of the connection between family therapy and individualism is correct, then family therapy theorists are in the awkward position of perpetuating a potent ideology that seems to bear some of the responsibility for the very distress that family therapists seek to remedy.

In order to clarify the affinity between family therapy and individualism, we will recall the helpful distinction Bellah et al. (1985) make between utilitarian and expressive individualism. The utilitarian strand of individualism assumes that humans have certain basic appetites and fears and sees human life as an effort to attain one's desires and reduce aversive experiences through rational and strategic action. From this perspective, social relationships are seen in contractual terms, and individuals form relationships in order to advance their self-interest.

The expressive strand of individualism is critical of the utilitarian emphasis on instrumental control, and instead advocates following the "voice of nature" revealed in our unspoiled feelings and the spontaneous purposes that naturally emanate from within.

Both the utilitarian and expressive forms of individualism take as fundamental the individual's autonomy in her choice of goals. Taylor (1985b) points out two consequences of this for moderns. First, if each individual determines her own aims in life, individual feelings become central in knowing which goals to pursue. From the utilitarian outlook, we should pursue those things that bring us pleasurable feelings, and the expressive perspective encourages us to be engaged in pursuits that help us to feel more fully alive and more in touch with ourselves, with others, and with nature. Because fulfillment is no longer tied to matching a social or cosmic pattern or conforming to the ethical imperatives of that pattern as it was in premodern times (see Chapter One), the attainment of one's aims becomes evident mainly in whether one feels pleasure, fulfillment, or connection with sources of meaning in oneself or nature.

Because purposes have become the province of individuals, a retreat from the intense community life characteristic of previous centuries was necessary. From the individualistic point of view, the premodern scheme of divine or cosmic meaning into which the individual must fit herself involved social requirements and evaluations that illegitimately constrained and distorted the individual's decision making and action. The fulfillment of autonomous individuals cannot be subject to the scrutiny or evaluation of the community, nor can it be expected to conform to a set pattern. As privacy became necessary to support the emerging autonomy of individuals, communal life withered. Nevertheless, even emancipated individuals are seen as "needing" some social connections for their fulfillment. Involvement with like-minded others helps support the individual's choices and aims. Experiencing love and nurturance have become keys to fulfillment in modern life. Over the past two centuries, individuals have increasingly chosen their friendship, family, and community ties in accordance with their preferences and goals (Mintz & Kellogg, 1988).

The Evolution of the Intimate Family

The contemporary nuclear family has inevitably become the center of modern living because it offers both the privacy required by autonomous individuals and the emotional satisfaction found in relationships based on the affinity and love needed to sustain the emancipated individual (Bellah et al., 1985; Mintz & Kellogg, 1988). Hareven (1987), the family historian, highlights the shift from the sociability and community-centeredness of the premodern family to the privatized modern family. She states that in contemporary family life, "the home is viewed increasingly as a retreat from the outside world. The family has turned inward, assuming domesticity, intimacy, and privacy as its major characteristics as well as ideals. The privacy of the home and its separation from the work place have been guarded jealously as an essential feature of family life" (p. 53).

The historical rise of individualism has both altered and been influenced by the evolving nuclear family. The premium placed on autonomy requires freedom from social constraints, and privacy within which individual aims can be nurtured and satisfied. Privacy does not necessarily entail isolation but is attained through relationships that are based on affinity and are pursued in relatively self-contained families and friendship networks. The growing importance of individual fulfillment receives further definition as we increasingly find many of our primary satisfactions in the experiences of love with a chosen partner, in devoted parenting of planned children, and in friendships based on mutual affinity and similarity. Marriage and child rearing have become increasingly voluntary; they are seen more and more in terms of self-fulfillment and are based on mutual affection and relational harmony rather than obligation (Popenoe, 1990). Furthermore, over the last century and a half, the family as an institution has changed from an interdependent unit of production to a group focused on consumption and the nurturance of children (Hareven, 1987; Mintz & Kellogg, 1988). The changes in the family both accommodate to the requirements of individualism and give the family a distinct shape in the contemporary United States.

Thus contemporary family life is characterized increasingly by its emotional self-containment, an emphasis on affectionate marriage, devoted concern for children, and a general idealization of intimacy. In a recent national survey, respondents identified emotional nurturance, open communication, mutual respect, respect for parental authority, and a happy marriage as the most important values in family life (Mellman, Lazarus, & Rivlin, 1990). Bellah et al. (1985) point out how this inward focus has removed the family from its role as "an integral part of a larger moral ecology tying the individual to community, church and nation" and placed it at "the core of the private sphere, whose aim is not to link individuals to the public world but to avoid it as far as possible" (p. 112).

Recognizing this sharp division of modern life into private and public domains is crucial to our understanding of the modern identity and the part the nuclear family plays in supporting it. The public realm has come to be seen as increasingly impersonal, contractual, and hostile as it has become more industrialized and bureaucratized. Thus public life has become more and more problematic as an arena in which the meaning and satisfaction of one's life can be cultivated. This change complements the increasing importance of the private realm (with the nuclear family as its centerpiece) as the source of emotional satisfaction and purposeful living.

The separation of public and private life into often antagonistic yet indispensable realms has forced us to somehow blend or accommodate utilitarian and expressive outlooks in modern life. Taylor (1985a) suggests that, in general, the expressive sensibility is supposed to tune people in to unique personal desires and goals while various instrumental activities permit these desires to be satisfied. In this view, the maintenance of the material basis for the private space and emotional satisfaction of the family provides the incentive for a great deal of instrumental activity in the "external" world. Thus the public domain tends to be dominated by actions designed primarily to enhance private fulfillment within the family. The family is therefore often seen as "a haven in a heartless world" (Hareven, 1987; Lasch, 1977).

The Problematic Centrality of Families

Yet the idea of the family as a haven from the self-serving activity of the public realm is something of a myth. An important corresponding shift has occurred in the last century in how the relationships between individuals and families are enacted, one that increasingly undermines the solidarity of modern families. In the nineteenth century, a corporate understanding of the family was dominant, with a much firmer commitment to the collective well-being of the family even where this required significant sacrifices on the part of individual family members. In contrast, the modern family is seen as the arena in which the most significant and personal aspects of the individual's choice and emotional satisfaction are to be fostered. Indeed, the family is increasingly seen as the sphere within which individual needs and desires are to be satisfied. As Hareven (1987, p. 44) puts it, "the overall pattern of historical change over the past century has been one of an increasing shift from a commitment to family collectivity to individual goals and aspirations." This shift in emphasis to the primacy of the individual's aims may, in many cases, escape notice due to a happy coincidence of the requirements of individual and collective well-being. However, when there is a conflict in these areas, it has become increasingly common for the family as a collectivity to be overlooked. This neglect itself may not be apparent because the other family members, to the extent that they are able, are busily pursuing their own private purposes.

As we have seen, the current ideal of the family is intimately tied to the development of the modern identity, which combines utilitarian and expressive individualism. Yet in placing the family at the very center of modern society, the current ideology of the family has paradoxically tended to undermine its stability and well-being. This is a result of the incompatible and insupportable demands made on marriages and families by expressive and utilitarian individualist ideals. The expressive ideal represents an insupportable burden because it calls on the family and in particular the marriage to be the primary locus of emotional satisfaction, belonging, and purpose in modern living (Bellah et al., 1985; Mintz & Kellogg, 1988). This, as we know, has proven to be more of a burden than the institutions of marriage and the family can bear. For example, we find ourselves in the conundrum of having an unprecedented divorce rate at the same time that marriage is our single most popular voluntary institution (Schoen, Urton, Woodrow, & Baj, 1985) and is seen as the prime source of happiness in life (Lee, Seccombe, & Shehan, 1991; Weingarten, 1985).

Another indicator of the burdens this ideology places on the family are the persistent calls for strengthening the family as a means for dealing with the many ills of our society. In surveys about social problems such as crime, moral decay, and so on, respondents see the family as principally responsible—as though families, by simply "shaping up," could resolve these long-standing social difficulties (Fineman, 1994; Mellman et al., 1990).

The instrumentalism (a utilitarian emphasis) that characterizes much of modern living is invading the nuclear family as well and is incompatible with expressive ideals such as belonging and harmony. The problem here is that even the cherished relationships of the family are all too easily relativized to the appetites and desires of its individual members, leading to more fragile, less committed relationships (Fowers & Wenger, 1997). In other words, we are increasingly viewing the family as another arena within which individual needs can be met. To the extent that the business of life is really about finding authentic fulfillment as an individual, family relationships become secondary to this end. The fragility of affinity-based marriages is one effect of modern individualism. If the treasured affection of a marriage withers, then the spouses will find it quite natural to end the marriage in favor of seeking a more emotionally satisfying relationship. This is exactly what a great many individuals do.

Another example of the incompatibility of expressive and utilitarian ideals in contemporary families is found in a major national survey of families (Mellman et al., 1990). Although respondents identify spending time with family as the most effective way to strengthen families, a very large majority say they would take a new job that offered more money, prestige, or both, even if this meant less time with their families. This growing trend toward voluntarism in family activity leads to family members' seeing family ties more in terms of choices than obligations. Thus, in sharp contrast to the early modern vision of a commitment-based involvement that emphasized the inherent value and intersection of family and community life, the modern ideology of the family tends to emphasize voluntary participation in families contingent on emotional attachment, individual satisfaction, and compatibility with other individual pursuits.

The difficulties encountered in living as private, intimate families have led family researchers, policymakers, and mental health professionals to view the family as fragile and in need of support and assistance (Donzelot, 1977; Lasch, 1978). The so-called assistance offered to the "struggling" institution of the family has, according to some critics, amounted to a powerful form of social control. Donzelot termed it a policing of the family, and Lasch decried the interventionism that made it appear that families could not function without the direction of professionals. Moreover, if those interventions perpetuate the problem in the cure, such efforts to shore up the "fragile" family may actually accelerate the trends leading to its current difficulties. This professional attention has tended to intensify the parent-child bond and unrealistically raise the expectations for emotional satisfaction within the family. (One might, by the way, agree with Donzelot and Lasch in questioning the degree of social control our society and government exercises over families without endorsing these authors' implied solution of simply increasing autonomy for families. By itself, this emphasis on the reduction of external control may represent an expansion of utilitarian individualism and the public-private split rather than a cure for current social ills.)

One of the important consequences of this interventionism is that when difficulties arise, the focus of attention is usually on the difficulties *within* families, particularly on their interpersonal aspects. This has the effect of reifying this model of the family by focusing attention on interpersonal difficulties within families and away from scrutinizing this ideal of the family itself or the ways that society contributes to current family dilemmas (Bernal & Ysern, 1986; Hare-Mustin, 1986; James & McIntyre, 1983). Therefore, the contemporary ideal of the family seems to perform the ideological function of supporting the political and social status quo by strictly separating the public and private worlds and focusing intervention and concern on internal family transactions.

There is much to appreciate in the idyllic vision of the happy nuclear family founded on ongoing voluntary participation and motivated by individual fulfillment within the family. At the same time, the difficulties that ordinary families have had in managing the extraordinary and overwhelming burdens placed on them have led to widespread social intervention and control. It is no coincidence that family therapy came on the scene in the postwar era just as these pressures were becoming full-blown. A therapeutic modality that promised relief to overburdened families now appears to have been an inevitability and often seems to be the eminently sensible approach to the problem.

By gaining an understanding of the modern family and its therapy in their sociohistorical context, we can begin to bring into focus the evident danger of perpetuating and perhaps even exacerbating contemporary strains on families through well-meaning therapeutic efforts. To the extent that family therapists endorse this modern ideology of the family and intervene with families in ways that assume the values of familial self-containment, affinity-based relationships, the centrality of marriage, and the adaptability of families, they can be said to perpetuate the burdens of modern families and the individualism that is inextricably bound up with the current ideal of the family. Ironically, family therapists would then be perpetuating the individualism at the societal level that was so wisely questioned at the familial level. If this is true, it calls for intense reflection on the conceptual and value bases of family therapy. Let us begin with an examination of some foundational family therapists' writings in order to explore the extent to which the field of family therapy has adopted the utilitarian-expressive individualistic ethic of the larger culture.

Family Therapy and the Modern Ideology of the Family

Family therapy is based on the foundational insight that a connection exists between individual difficulties and familial interactional patterns. This premise has led family therapists to direct their therapeutic efforts toward changing interpersonal patterns in order to relieve the presented symptoms. It is generally argued in the literature that clients choose the goals (that is, the symptoms to be resolved) and that the therapist responds by assisting the family in reaching these goals. This assertion is somewhat misleading, however. In fact, the therapist sees the problem not as the symptom itself (for example, little Johnny's truancy) but as the family's interaction pattern (for example, the patterned interaction of an ineffectual mother, an authoritarian father, and an uncontrollable child). As Minuchin (1974), a major family therapy theorist, puts it, "Family structure is not an entity immediately available to the observer. . . . The therapist analyzes the transactional field in which he and the family are meeting in order to make a structural diagnosis" (p. 89; compare to Colapinto, 1991, pp. 433–444). Similarly, Madanes (1991) points out, "What makes a therapist choose a particular strategy is how he or she conceptualizes a problem as well as the particular characteristics of the problem. . . . These characteristics are mostly in the head of the therapist" (p. 397). Although the end result may be the reduction of the presenting symptom, family therapists accomplish this through theoretically based formulations of family structure and process. Thus, the most profound change in the family is not actually determined by the family but follows directly from the therapist's interpretations of the family's "transactional field."

The family therapist's interpretation of the family's patterns of interaction is important because it leads directly to decisions about what to change. This can be seen most clearly in Minuchin's (1974) pioneering Structural Family Therapy. As Hoffman (1981) points out, "Minuchin's normative model for a family that is functioning well is especially useful. . . . [T]he therapist then has the task of noting the angle of deviance between [the model] and the family that comes in the door. Therapy, from a structural point of view, consists of redesigning family organization so that it will approximate this normative model more closely" (pp. 262–263). Although Minuchin's approach to family therapy has perhaps the most explicitly normative model, he is far from alone in prescribing a standard for normal family functioning.

As Doherty and Boss (1991) note, there is relatively little explicit expression of the values underlying different approaches to family therapy; this necessitates inferring value positions. Our reading of the family therapy literature suggests that it is suffused with the family ideology discussed earlier. To support our conclusion, we include illustrative quotations from classic family therapy theorists. We do not suggest that this analysis invalidates their insights or therapies, nor do we pretend to give full coverage of any of these theories. We wish only to document the specific cultural and moral values embedded in a wide variety of family therapy theories in the hope that this will promote a more open, self-reflective discussion of the moral foundations of family therapy.

The Emotionally Private Family

Family therapists generally place a great deal of importance on a clear and firm boundary between the family and its environment. This therapeutic stance is particularly prominent among structural and strategic family therapists. This focus in and of itself powerfully underwrites the idea of the primacy of nuclear families. Structuralists (Minuchin, 1974; Minuchin & Fishman, 1981) emphasize that the decision regarding who should be included in the family therapeutic unit is a powerful strategy through which boundaries can be established. Selvini-Palazzoli, Cirillo, Selvini, and Sorrentino (1989) characterize dismissing extended family members from therapy as an essential aspect of one of their most recent intervention strategies. They explain its importance in providing "an irrevocably fixed demarcation line around the nuclear family" (p. 19) in order "to deal with the universally pathogenic phenomenon of blurred intergenerational boundaries" (p. 23). Although Minuchin (1974) explicitly recognizes the value of the extended family in adverse (but not optimal) conditions, he asserts that the involvement of the extended family may create difficulties in clearly allocating responsibility, thereby increasing confusion and stress in the nuclear family.

In one of the most frequently read books on family therapy, Minuchin (1974) emphasizes the importance of separating from the family of origin in order to form a new family. He states that "[a] marriage must replace certain social arrangements that have been given up for the formation of the new unit. Creation of the new social system means the creation or strengthening of a boundary around the couple. The investment in the marriage is made at the expense of other relationships" (p. 30). Bowen (1978, p. 108) concurs in saying, "Once differentiated from their parental families, [spouses] can be close to members of their own [nuclear] families or to any other person without fusing into emotional oneness."

These authors seem to be promoting an ideal of a nuclear family that endeavors to minimize interference from the extended family and larger community. Thus family therapy tends to privatize both therapy and family life. There is the sense that relations with the kinship network need to be carefully monitored so that the nuclear family is not disturbed in its central tasks of providing emotional closeness and rearing children. Until very recently, relationships with the community were seldom discussed by family therapists except as arenas in which symptoms show themselves or in terms of the need for the therapist to take the family's ethnicity or socioeconomic status into account when devising interventions.

There have been a number of recent counterpoints to this overfocus on nuclear families. Feminists (Balcom & Healey, 1990; Bograd, 1990; Hare-Mustin, 1986) have pointed out that by endorsing familial privacy, family therapists help obscure intrafamilial sex-role inequities and their connection to social conditions that disadvantage women. Others have highlighted the broader social embeddedness of families. For example, Elizur and Minuchin (1989) discuss how "dysfunctional family patterns" are often replicated within and exacerbated by the treatment systems designed to help troubled family members. However, the more intrusive the treatment program (that is, the more it violates nuclear family boundaries), the more negatively it is portrayed. Thus, the concept of nuclear family boundaries is central to their critique of these institutions. Elizur and Minuchin do discuss a more community-based approach to mental illness that can be developed within Israeli kibbutzim. Their description of community-based therapy in a kibbutz is enlightening and potentially useful. In two important respects its usefulness is limited, however. First, Elizur and Minuchin did not discuss the differences between the social contexts of the kibbutzim and mainstream Western culture in a way that might allow therapists to adapt to other contexts the type of broad, innovative therapeutic focus the authors discuss. Second, their critique is directed at other mental health institutions and does not attend to the barriers to their proposals within the field of family therapy itself.

Several recent books have examined the importance of the broader social and political context of families (Imber-Black, 1988; Mirkin, 1990; Schwartzman & Kneifel, 1985). These works take a wider view in investigating the asymmetry of the relationship between larger systems and families, the perpetuation of gender inequality, spouse abuse, and the importance of culture in therapy. This represents an important step toward reclaiming the broader implications of systems theory and showing how family therapists can view families in a relevant and meaningful context. Although space does not permit a thorough discussion, we would caution, however, that the solutions offered or implied by these authors seem to be mainly based on expanding individual rights and family empowerment. For all their merit, they may exemplify a subtle, uncritical version of contemporary family ideology with its endorsement of the emotionally private family empowered for the purpose of promoting individual well-being. These authors focus primarily on societal conditions or specific family problems and do not illuminate how completely family therapy has itself incorporated the current ideology of the family.

Thus, with some recent exceptions, family therapy seems to have rather single-mindedly promoted the privacy of the nuclear family, as much through inattention to the embeddedness of the family in a larger social network as through the negative evaluation of extended family and community meddling. This conceptual neglect of the *healthy* social embeddedness of families is curiously contrary to systems theory and may well indicate the power of the contemporary ideology of the family in shaping family therapy theory.

The Centrality of Marriage

The health of the family is seen by many family therapy theorists as a reflection of the well-being of the marital and parenting dyad. Papero (1990) considers defining and clarifying the relationship between the spouses to be the first of four priorities of the therapist (the other three do not involve any *particular* relationship within the family; for example, the therapist must avoid becoming triangulated). Whitaker and Blumberry (1988) describe marriage as "the foundation of the family" and remark that "significant investment elsewhere can drain the vitality from the marriage" (p. 23). The centrality of the marriage in family therapy is also emphasized by Minuchin (1974, p. 57): "In simple human terms, husbands and wives need each other as a refuge from the multiple demands of life. In therapy, this need dictates that the therapist protect the boundaries around the spouse subsystem. . . . The spouse subsystem must achieve a boundary that protects it from interference by the demands and needs of other systems. The adults must have a territory of their own—a haven in which they can give each other emotional support."

It is generally assumed that symptoms will arise in the family when this boundary is not maintained. Thus Haley (1976) said, "It is useful to assume that a child problem reflects, or is a performance of, a marital problem" (p. 31). This dictum is part of the conventional wisdom of family therapists (Framo, 1965; Selvini-Palazzoli et al., 1989). Therefore, Hoffman (1981, p. 215) could say, "Most family therapy with a child includes an attempt to uncover this disagreement [between the parents] and to refocus it as an issue between the parents." Of course, there is much truth in such dicta, which are often useful in analyzing and intervening in troubled family interactions. But it is not necessarily true that child problems simply or exclusively reflect spousal difficulties.

Thus marriage has been accorded a double significance among family therapists. First, it is seen as an essential element in the well-being of the adult partners in the nuclear family and must be jealously guarded against intrusion. Second, when there is a symptom in one of the children, it is assumed to be secondary to some unresolved marital problem. Thus the marriage is pivotal for the mental health of the parents and indirectly so for the children as well. This view of marriage places it at the very fulcrum of society, because the nuclear family is one of the central points of access for the primary emotional rewards of modern society. It is hardly

surprising that this heroic burden proves overwhelming for many ordinary marital relationships. The continuing high rate of divorce is no doubt
one symptom of this pressure. A progressive, general decrease in marital
satisfaction over the past three decades may be another (Glenn, 1991).
This difficulty can only be exacerbated when family therapy theory and
practice place the responsibility for the well-being of both parents and
children so firmly on the marital relationship.

The Primacy of Intense Affective Relationships

The individualistic notion that human action is directed primarily toward
the satisfaction of personal desires and appetites is reflected in the idealization of intimacy in modern families. Emotional intimacy is seen both
as essential to the individual's ability to pursue other ends and as gratify-
ing in itself. In this vein, Bowen (1978) asserts that the improvements in
the symptomatic behavior of the children are due to the parents' becoming more "emotionally close, more interested in each other than in the
patient" (p. 68). Similarly, we have noted how Minuchin (1974) also
emphasizes the emotionally supportive function of the spousal subsystem.

The focus on intimacy is not limited to the marriage. Whitaker and
Blumberry (1988) emphasize that "[a]nother indicator of family health is
room for the intimacy of loving, as well as for the upset of hating. All are
free to engage in *intense interchange*" (p. 201, italics added). Hoffman
(1981, p. 191) also identifies intimacy as crucial to individual and family
well-being in her assertion that "the family does . . . have a 'product'
which no other institution can replace. There is probably only one invisible but important task which few other institutions can perform as well.
This has to do with an orderly access to intimacy." As Kempler (1981,
p. 28) describes it, the family is "a resource, a place for emotional development and refueling, and a sanctuary where each can safely be."

In his exposition of Bowen's Family Systems Theory, Papero (1990)
takes the intense affective bonds of families in the contemporary United
States as normative not only for this society but for the *species*. This leads
him to compare the current highly emotional experiences of falling in love
and the contemporary intensity of the parent-child bond to the mating
cycle of ring doves, which is genetically coded and is carried out in rigid
sequences.

The emphasis on intimate intrafamilial relationships turns out to be
quite consistent with the division of social relations into public and private realms; the family, as the center of the private realm, provides emotional gratification through "intense interchange" and "emotional

refueling." This focus on intimacy within the family is distinctively modern in three ways. First, the very idea that emotional intimacy is one of the primary goods in human living is a rather recent development and is part of the modern "affirmation of ordinary life" (Taylor, 1989, p. 211). This emphasis on the goodness and worth of ordinary life is an outgrowth of a post-Reformation Judeo-Christian spirituality that rejected conventional hierarchies of power and worth and viewed the ordinary in sacred terms and as an object of grace. Taylor points out that the modern derivative of the affirmation of ordinary life tends to dispense with any higher tier of value altogether. This leaves us with a kind of terminal anti-elitism or anti-authoritarianism that tells us only what it is *against* and not what it is *for*. In the absence of any positive standards of value, ordinary life is reduced to a simple hedonism or subjectivism without any way to explain *why* that life is good or on what basis we *should* respect it.

Second, the assumption that the closest ties are to be found within the nuclear family developed along with contemporary individualism and its version of the family. Third, emotional intimacy is valued primarily because it is beneficial to individual family members. Thus Hoffman (1981) sees intimacy primarily as a "product" to which individuals need access, Kempler (1981) emphasizes the family as a resource for individuals who "extract" what they need, and Whitaker and Blumberry (1988) view the primary importance of the security and caring within the nuclear family in terms of promoting the ultimate independence of the offspring.

Family Adaptability

The fourth major assumption of family therapists is that healthy families are characterized by their ability to adapt to changing circumstances. Minuchin (1974) exemplifies the valuing of both emotional inwardness and adaptability to society in saying that "family functions serve two different ends. One is internal—the psychosocial protection of its members; the other is external—the accommodation to a culture and the transmission of that culture" (p. 46). He goes on to say, "The more flexibility and adaptability that society requires from its members, the more significant the family will become" (p. 50). In describing the aims of family therapists, Haley (1976, p. 168) also affirms the importance of adaptability: "The goal should be to allow room for change, negotiation and flexible alternatives." Similarly, Hoffman (1981, p. 91) extols familial malleability in this way: "Flexibility about both the degree of internal connectedness and connection with the outside world seems to be the distinguishing mark of the family that does best." The emphasis placed by experiential family therapists on spontaneity, growth, and flexibility as indicators of familial well-being is consistent with the contemporary model of the adaptive family as well (Roberto, 1991; Whitaker & Blumberry, 1988).

Family therapy theorists widely affirm flexibility, reflecting what appears to be an unquestioned acceptance of the current societal structure and demands on the family, whatever they may be. By tacitly accepting the separation of public and private realms, family therapy theorists encourage families to adapt in their private lives to political and normative demands of the public realm without questioning at all the political, cultural, or moral values embodied by that realm. Family therapy theorists seem largely to have ingested the modern ideal of the family in toto and therefore uncritically promote the cultural status quo and its questionable view of the good life.

Promoting the ideal of the flexible nuclear family is thus likely to increase the already considerable pressures families experience. The expectation that the family will absorb the impact of societal changes and protect the well-being of its members is rather overwhelming, particularly in a rapidly changing world characterized by a lack of a firm institutional support structure for families. Further, this flexibility requires that each family meet these demands without any established guidelines, traditions, or rules. Adaptability means, after all, the ability to alter rules and structures according to current demands. The goals of maximum adaptability and the intense private fulfillment of individuals are presented as a smooth program for family well-being. In actual practice, they often clash and, unless modified by other value commitments, are a recipe for increased difficulty.

Expanding Family Theory

Our main conclusion is that family therapy's unacknowledged acceptance of contemporary family ideology calls for some rethinking of this therapeutic modality. Although family therapists are undoubtedly often helpful, they, for the most part, uncritically endorse the ideal of the emotionally private, intimate, and adaptable family which is an outgrowth of modern individualism. This standpoint seems to presuppose the desirability of the contemporary view of the family and its role in supporting the unique sort of modern individualism that encourages individuals to expect a great deal from the social universe while sharply attenuating any ties of belonging or obligation they have to it. Unfortunately, the very success of family therapy in bringing the locus of dysfunction to the family and defining well-being in familial terms has reinforced the notion that families are best seen as insulated safe havens that provide the center of meaningful living in an otherwise indifferent and unassailable society. Many authors (Bellah et al., 1985; MacIntyre, 1981; Sullivan, 1986) see this fragmentation and loss of community as a primary problem facing U.S. society, with particularly negative consequences for families. Therefore family therapists run the risk of perpetuating the orientation to the nuclear family in the U.S. that seems to have resulted in enormous strains and moral confusion for contemporary individuals and families.

Family therapy must come to terms with its moral dimension rather than assume it operates only or primarily on a transactional level (Boszormenyi-Nagy & Krasner, 1986; Fowers & Wenger, 1997). To do this requires a greater appreciation of the values and ideals that animate family life within extended families, communities, societies, and historical traditions. Although family therapy theory has gone beyond conceiving of extended families and the larger community as either pathogenic or irrelevant, it has almost completely failed to acknowledge their importance in providing a context of meaning and purpose in family life.

The inescapability of promoting some ideal of family life in family therapy leads us to advocate the expansion of family therapy's systemic notion of social embeddedness beyond the transactional level to explicitly include the cultural and moral sphere. We need somehow to balance the invaluable modern emphasis on individual dignity and rights with a renewed appreciation of the extent to which human beings are intrinsically social. Our personal and family identities all develop within social practices and institutions that direct and orient us to act and feel in certain ways. They are not mere tools external to the individual; rather, they constitute the moral context that shapes us at the core (Sullivan, 1986). Therefore, we must acknowledge that our very definitions of familial well-being, dysfunction, and therapeutic action are inescapably formed within a field of cultural and ethical meanings and values.

This means that individuals and families cannot independently create their own context and values but rather are necessarily a part of a larger cultural pattern. We simply cannot expect to find sufficient meaning and purpose within the affective attachments of the family. Family therapists who understand this will not promote the narrow ideal of mutual emotional grooming within the family as a sufficient end in itself. Rather than place so much emphasis on familial intimacy, family therapists could help open connections to the community and to ongoing traditions that provide a broader, deeper sense of what life is all about. Families may find guidance, support, and a more complete sense of belonging by coming into contact with these traditions. These resources can help reduce some of the burdens currently placed on the nuclear family.

These recommendations have implications for three of the major trends in contemporary family therapy. First, there are a great many pragmatic or problem-focused family therapists who claim to value only efficient techniques for attaining client goals. The dominant utilitarian-expressive individualistic perspective in our society makes it easy for family therapists to reinforce the sort of extreme separation of individual and social, fact and value, means and ends, and technique from cultural and moral values that some critics feel is a major blind spot of modern Western society (Bernstein, 1976; MacIntyre, 1981). These related splits or dichotomies have allowed most modern therapies, including most family therapy, to maintain the illusion that it employs value-neutral "techniques" that are not organically linked to one or another view of the good life in the contest of ideologies in which humans define themselves. If our analysis is correct, we will have to dispense with that illusion. Such "techniques" are not morally neutral but are, in part, forms of communication, acculturation, and influence that steer both therapists and families in the direction of one or another ethical outlook and particular way of life. In other words, our therapeutic theories and methods help construct families that are consistent with our premises. Therefore, an unexamined emphasis on technique and effectiveness constitutes a serious form of moral blindness.

The second major trend involves recent work on larger systems (for example, Imber-Black, 1988; Schwartzman, 1985), ethnicity in family therapy (McGoldrick, Preto, Hines, & Lee, 1991), and the social and political contexts of family therapy (Mirkin, 1990). This growing literature represents a promising beginning in expanding family therapy's vision beyond nuclear families. However, it seems to us that these authors are subject to much the same critique as classical family therapy unless their perspective is deepened to explicitly discuss contemporary social and therapeutic ideals regarding the nature of healthy families and how extended families, communities, and society contribute to the self-understanding of families and to their well-being. Moreover, like the classic family therapy writings, this work fails to explicitly recognize that family therapy itself participates in the contemporary value matrix within which families are defined and shaped.

The third trend is the increasing attention in contemporary family therapy to the moral concerns raised by two groups of family therapists who have placed the ethical dimension at the core of their work. Contextual family therapy (Boszormenyi-Nagy & Krasner, 1986) is based on the idea that there is an essential moral dimension in human interaction. Contextualists have suggested an ethical model that emphasizes individuals' accepting responsibility for interpersonal consequences of their actions and a balance of give and take between family members. Feminists (Bograd, 1990; Hare-Mustin, 1986; James & McIntyre, 1983) have addressed the moral dimension of family therapy in pointing out the need to attend to sex-role inequities, the consequences of unequal power, and the implicit values in family therapy theories that appear to perpetuate these problems.

These are important beginnings in making the moral bases of family therapy more explicit. However, we suggest that family therapy theory be expanded to encompass broader moral and social issues. Although the contextualist focus on fairness in interpersonal relationships includes the extended family and one's progenitors, its ethics primarily concern fairness among family members (Fowers & Wenger, 1997). The feminist perspective is broader in scope and explicitly encompasses crucial social and political issues, but it often operates within a framework that focuses on central liberal individualist values such as the promotion of individual rights, autonomy, and equality (Fox-Genovese, 1991). Most of us may agree that principles of fairness, equal power, and the like have an important place, but it would be a serious and consequential error simply to assume that these principles constitute the entire domain of ethics.

Taylor (1985b) argues that every society and its members inescapably endorse a wide "diversity of goods" concerned with what is decent, excellent, worthy, or fulfilling in human life. The modern West has typically narrowed this domain to respect for human rights, equality, and procedural justice, claiming these principles are universal while viewing other questions about the good life as matters of purely personal preference. This approach reflects modern individualism's characteristic strategy for harmonizing freedom with some sense of moral authority, namely keeping ethical principles purely formal in order to accommodate pluralism and undercut dogmatism. But it is a precarious scheme at best. It is a dissonant blend of universalism and relativism whose subjectivizing of most values constantly threatens to undermine its own moral commitments to human dignity and rights as well. Taylor suggests that it is an inherent task of human life (and therefore of families) to somehow coordinate and honor a wider and more interesting diversity of goods. Only if therapists take a broader view of the moral domain of family life will they be able to participate more actively and less cryptically in our ongoing cultural conversation about what constitutes the good life.

Given the pervasive and problematic influence of individualism in family therapy, where it might be least expected, we feel that a deeper understanding of the historical and social embeddedness of individuals and families is needed. The hermeneutic viewpoint seems to us to offer a very promising perspective in this respect. It emphasizes that every way of life is shaped at the core by a vision of the good that forms the moral framework for the participants' actions and interpretations (Taylor, 1989). The modern individualist outlook is just one such vision of what constitutes a decent or worthwhile human existence, even if it denies that fact in its somewhat tortured attempt to escape dogmatism while still providing us with some sort of moral compass.

The kinds of traditions developed and maintained in the historical evolution of communities are not so much monolithic as they are a welter of diverse elements that are meaningfully interrelated, never perfectly harmonized, and always being sifted and reinterpreted in the light of evolving ideas, practices, and circumstances. This view does imply, however, that we are more historically embedded and have less easy access to absolutes than either traditionalist dogmatism or a modern faith in reason would suggest.

If we recognize the moral dimension of family therapy, we come to see that family therapy is the process of helping families to develop and actuate a view of what constitutes a good family. From this point of view, family therapy is a multifaceted dialogue about the good life that is always guided by the traditions and commitments of both the therapist and the family. It calls on all participants to examine, contrast, and reinterpret the values that animate their lives, in an open and respectful manner.

4

THE CHALLENGE OF PSYCHOTHERAPY INTEGRATION

IN RECENT YEARS, a number of creative theorists have tackled the problem of integrating diverse psychotherapy theories (Norcross, 1986). As mentioned in Chapter Two, some kind of therapy integration, in theory and practice, appears to be needed and desirable but turns out to be very difficult to achieve. It may be that different therapy systems both incorporate partly different visions of the good life *and* uncritically assume some of the same problematic notions about human life we have discussed in this book, such as the "ontological individualism" (Bellah et al., 1985, p. 143) mentioned in the Introduction. Thus a straightforward approach to combining the best features of diverse theories is not possible.

Paul Wachtel's approach to this problem, which he calls integrative psychodynamic therapy or cyclical psychodynamics, represents the most fully developed effort to date to identify and overcome the barriers to meaningful therapy integration. For our purposes, it is most instructive to examine Wachtel's original and creative undertaking. Wachtel (1977) originally presented what he calls an interpersonal alternative to traditional psychoanalytic and behavioral therapies, which creatively reinterpreted what those approaches are all about. Subsequently, Wachtel and Wachtel (1986) extended this view to incorporate family therapy perspectives. Wachtel's most recent book (1997) includes most of his seminal 1977 book and six additional chapters applying the cyclical psychodynamic viewpoint to important new "relational" perspectives in psychoanalysis, recent developments in the behavioral and cognitive therapies, and other topics.

Wachtel's integrative theorizing does not merely fit one therapy under the conceptual umbrella of another or simply coordinate different approaches on a practical or technical level as appropriate for different disorders or populations of clients. Rather, it coherently interrelates psychodynamic, behavioral, family systems, and cognitive therapy perspectives in terms of a unique model or point of view. This model of the "interpersonal context" or "interaction system" in which both psychological processes and social relationships are caught up and more or less harmoniously integrated seems elegantly simple, freshly illuminating, and replete with practical implications. Moreover—something even more rare—Wachtel has extended and deepened the interpersonal perspective through a discussion of the vision of human fulfillment and the good life implicit in these various therapies and of their entanglement in some of the ethical dilemmas and deficiencies of modern society.

Interpersonal Context

In Wachtel's view (1997), the psychoanalytic tradition generally locates the source of difficulties in living in certain archaeologically buried forces from the past. Unconscious desires, fantasies, conflicts, defenses, and the like are portrayed as "independent variables" that are established by an early structuring of the personality and continue to cause or manifest themselves in the "dependent variables" of symptoms and maladaptive patterns of living (p. 42). These patterns are relatively unresponsive to changing life circumstances, cannot be modified by current perceptions and experiences, and persist in spite of these contemporary influences. The engine of therapy in this view is interpretation that leads to insight, namely an understanding of the origins and nature of unconscious trends and conflicts that allows an individual to relinquish or resolve them. Improvements in one's present way of living, in Karen Horney's words, "will automatically take place. . . . They are not primary changes, however, but result from less visible changes within the personality (Horney, 1942, p. 118, quoted in Wachtel, 1997, p. 65).

Contemporary behavior therapy, according to Wachtel, represents the most original and thoroughgoing challenge to psychoanalytic views and other therapies derived from them. Behavioral theorists or therapists tend to see symptoms and maladaptive patterns of living as under the control of a different set of independent variables, namely reinforcement contingencies or stimuli to which responses have become conditioned in some manner. Therapists and clients collaboratively manipulate these causes, existing in the present, to bring about desired change directly. Behavioral approaches, Wachtel feels, have illumined many important behavior-environment transactions and afford helpful new therapeutic techniques, most notably methods for anxiety reduction and social skill training such as systematic desensitization and assertive training.

Wachtel advocates a theoretical "interpersonal alternative" that he feels goes a long way toward capturing the valid insights and therapeutic stratagems of both psychoanalytic and behavioral approaches while eschewing their theoretical one-sidedness and practical limitations. At the heart of his view is the idea that the unconscious "desires or conflicts which may dominate a person's life can be understood as following from, as well as causing the way he or she lives that life" (1997, p. 43). Such motives and conflicts can be understood equally well as antecedents that have discernible effects or as outcomes that are themselves consequences of the overall pattern of one's life. Wachtel's model might be diagrammed as shown in Figure 4.1.

To summarize one of Wachtel's many fine examples, an individual who is particularly active, independent, and responsible for others may indeed be discovered, in a sense, to "unconsciously long for dependent gratification and to fear the extent of [his] passive yearnings" (1997, p. 43). His conscious attitudes and behavior need not be seen, however, simply as defenses against desires from the past. Rather, his compulsive and overly responsible way of life may be seen actually to continually create so-called overweening oral needs in the present. It denies him normal affiliation with, support from, and reliance on others in a way that keeps him

Figure 4.1. Interpersonal Context or Interaction System.

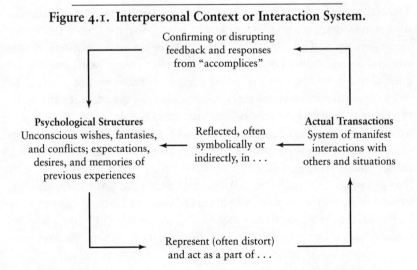

yearning for dependent gratification to an unusual degree. In a similar manner, an excessively unassertive and self-denying pattern of living can be seen as motivated by the need to cover up aggressive urges that an individual learned to fear early in life. But such a style of living can just as appropriately be viewed as *generating* that underlying, continually disavowed rage.

Wachtel's approach downplays the idea of pathogenic motives and conflicts as a "simple perpetuation of the past" and explores how they might fruitfully be seen as "brought about in the present, both by the patient's own behavior and by the behavior he evokes in others" (1997, p. 43). This model stresses the role that other people play as "accomplices," often quite unwitting, in maintaining the self-perpetuating "vicious circles" that are the essence of problems in living. Our unconscious conflicts or our perceptions and expectations (less deeply buried but still distorted) can skew our perceptions of and actions toward often ambiguous interpersonal situations. It is actually quite difficult for others *not* to react in ways that tend to perpetuate our flawed outlook and approach. For example, our excessive deference born of self-doubt engenders a subtle contempt in others, or at least a hesitancy and pulling back by them, which we take as confirmation of our poor estimate of ourselves. Indeed, it is difficult for others not to take some advantage of our unassertive, overly compliant behavior, breeding more resentment in us. Feedback or reactions from others sometimes disrupt but very often confirm our dysfunctional stances toward life.

Therapeutic Implications

Wachtel maintains that his cyclical psychodynamics has real advantages over standard approaches. For example, psychoanalytic theory can infantalize patients and has difficulty explaining the areas of emotional maturity and interpersonal competence that usually coexist with unresolved conflict and persistent, self-defeating actions. For that matter, it has difficulty explaining its own successes. Gaining insight via accurate and well-timed interpretations into the origins and unrealism of one's attitudes and actions is at best an incomplete account of personal change in therapy. Wachtel contends, for example, that becoming conscious of or gaining insight into a repressed fear of humiliation does not by itself lessen that fear of failure or humiliation! Also, the "pure gold" of interpretation, instead of being the only reliable means of deep and lasting change, may be rendered quite ineffective by experiences in everyday life that, correctly understood or not, repeatedly confirm one's worst fears. Wachtel congratulates behavior therapy for recognizing the powerful role of everyday events and consequences in helping maintain maladaptive living patterns and for zeroing in on anxiety reduction as the linchpin of therapeutic change. However, behavior therapy tends to portray the client as a victim of controlling events and stimuli, which is no improvement on portraying her as a victim of unconscious conflict. In addition, behavior therapy lacks the subtle categories of meaning needed to conceptualize the sorts of feelings or thoughts that usually evoke anxiety in all but the simplest of phobias. In Wachtel's view, behavior therapy, in its overreaction to psychoanalytic excesses, focuses in a one-sided manner on overt performances and may harmfully downplay the importance of empathic connectedness and therapeutic dialogue for ferreting out and reworking such internally generated fears.

Wachtel makes a plausible case that psychoanalytic and behavioral insights can be integrated to a large extent in the interpersonal model. Within this perspective, both the most recondite unconscious conflicts and the manifest interpersonal transactions of everyday life are conceptualized as different, overlapping phases of the holistically conceived flux of human existence. "One's hidden 'inner world' is, in this view, not a realm unto itself, but at once a product, a symbolization, and a cause of the interaction patterns in which a person engages" (Wachtel & Wachtel, 1986, p. 18).

Wachtel's model represents an improvement over both psychoanalytic drive and behavioral reinforcement theories that too sharply dichotomize subject and object and rely on reductive, pseudoscientific, unicausal explanations, which always seem to clash somewhat with both commonsense and clinical understanding. But much work remains to be done in fleshing out this interpersonal perspective and relating it to other therapy theories. The Wachtels suggest, for example, that even Horney's sensitive portrayal of how defensive efforts tend to stir up the very feelings and anxieties they were designed to ward off still underestimates the functional significance of everyday interaction sequences. And they contend that family systems approaches, despite important overlap with the interpersonal view, tend to reify the "system" that "needs" its members to act as they do. These approaches unnecessarily downplay the importance of individual motives and perceptions. They tend to portray individual agency as largely epiphenomenal, as produced by the actions (in its own way unicausally) of an hypostatized system. Instead, individual motives and perceptions, operating in concert with the activities of unwitting accomplices, are thought of as real and important parts of the process.

Wachtel stresses that it is not only possible but at times necessary to intervene at different points in the overall interaction system. Both clarifying motives and conflicts and "facilitating action in the real world" (1977, p. 211) may be needed for change. Insight may remain impotent unless the client or patient takes concrete steps through such activities as modeling and social skill training to reverse the chain of failure and negatively confirming feedback in everyday life. But the person's acquiring of subtle interpersonal skills in living often will not succeed without her also gaining some understanding of unconscious dynamics and ingrained flawed expectations of others. Perhaps most therapists are more eclectic than their avowed theories would suggest, but most are probably more sensitive to one side or the other of the interpersonal equation, in part because of the lack of a credible map of the "big picture" of personal dynamics and social context.

Social Ethics and the Image of the Human

Wachtel extends his analysis of human dynamics to incorporate broader social contexts and important cultural meanings and values. He suggests that many analytically oriented therapists are deeply attached to a value-laden understanding of humans as *autonomous* agents and see their notion of "change from within" as the only one compatible with personal responsibility and individual dignity. This view persists, paradoxically, in spite of aspects of traditional psychoanalytic theory that might be thought of as undermining human autonomy. These include its marked determinism and, as Roy Schafer (1976) and others have pointed out, its tendency to undermine responsibility by reifying psychic "actions" into "structures" that can be then be blamed inauthentically for one's choices and actions. (Or, as someone put it recently, "My inner child made me do it.") Wachtel argues that this leads such therapists dogmatically to denigrate most forms of facilitating action in the real world as intrusive and ineffective. It also leads them, he contends, to downplay the unavoidably strong influence of the therapist and therapeutic approach on the client's emotional and practical life. Thus, a client's producing increasingly regressive fantasies and inclinations in analytic treatment may not represent the emergence of causal factors unmodified from childhood so much as the *effects* of an unduly frustrating treatment approach that intensifies deficient emotional or behavioral trends by leaving the client excessively to her own faulty devices! Finally, Wachtel suggests that proponents of autonomy are attached to an "ethic of the lonely struggle" that eschews support, direct assistance, or even much in the way of mutual aid in a pointlessly "moralistic" or "puritanical" fashion, reflecting the "highly individualistic spirit that pervades our culture" (1997, p. 289).

Behavioral writers, according to Wachtel, have provided a very different view of humans as predominantly *reactive* or controlled by external or environmental forces. Wachtel does not speculate about the moral outlook underlying this view of humans. We might conjecture that this approach chooses to regard human action and personality as strictly determined just in order, ironically, to strengthen our ability to freely shape it toward desired ends! Of course, this presents a terribly confused picture of human agency as simultaneously dominated and masterful. (It would take more space than available to defend Wachtel's suggestion, with which we generally agree, that newer conceptions of so-called behavioral self-control and Bandura's inventive "reciprocal determinism" do not really clear up this confusion.) The ethical spirit of behavioral approaches is perhaps best described as another version of modern individualism with its rejection of arbitrary authority and celebration of personal autonomy. One is reminded of Messer and Winokur's interesting distinction (1980) between the "tragic" cast of psychoanalytic theory and the "comic" story line of behavioral therapy. Perhaps Wachtel's "autonomous man" is mired in that side of modern experience characterized by a sense of lonely self-responsibility cut off from larger meanings while the model of "reactive man" serves another kind of modern sensibility, one devoted to increasing control and blithe, untroubled hedonism.

Wachtel recommends a third model of human interaction that stresses the *responsive* nature of a healthy existence. Responsive individuals are not separate beings whose dynamics can be understood apart from their context and whose autonomy "is always couched in terms of autonomy *from*" (Wachtel, 1997, p. 279). They understand that genuine freedom is what Fromm called a "freedom to," distinguished from mere "freedom from," and do not confuse it with being passively shoved around or conforming to the demands of others. Autonomy without detachment, connection without conformity, seem to be what Wachtel has in mind. "Responsive man" is a possibility for two basic reasons. The first is that he "actively selects, filters, and organizes the input he receives" (p. 280). In other words, immersion in the interpersonal context of living need not mean passivity or external control unless the person's inherently active, always somewhat unique, manner of construing of her world is hampered by fear, inhibition, or lack of skills for social living. The second reason is that the most fulfilling possibilities of human life are cooperative rather than competitive. It is "just as human to be able to turn to others as it is to stand alone," even if this fact is obscured in contemporary American society, which has lost a "sense of community" due to the one-sided value "we place on individual rights and civil liberties" and our "highly problematic . . . emphasis 'on each man doing for himself.'" This distortion comes to be reflected in "the goals and methods of militantly individualistic psychodynamic and humanistic psychotherapists" (pp. 289–290). Wachtel feels that the interpersonal model could correct this imbalance. It allows us to see that there is no inherent contradiction between (1) paying attention to manifest interactions with others and to therapist influence that facilitates new action in the world and (2) engaging in genuinely inner-directed behavior that actually requires the right kind of honest, respectful feedback and assistance from others.

Wachtel stresses the practical, clinical importance of keeping both sides of the interpersonal context and their interrelationship in full view. Behavior therapy's categories of conditioning and reinforcement are far too coarse to capture the subtle meanings in terms of which human actors construe their purposes in living, often in conflicted, defensive ways. However, distorted meanings and perceptions may very well persist, increased insight notwithstanding, unless they are disconfirmed in a powerfully *experiential* way by the tangible results of new action in real-life situations (1997, p. 365).

Integrative Therapy Theory

Wachtel's interpersonal alternative portrays a "continuing interaction between cognitions and motivations on the one hand and external events on the other" (1997, p. 74). We are thus equipped, to an extent, to perceive internal psychodynamics, human relationships, the broad sociocultural contexts of action, and their interplay, all within a single, coherent framework. This does not mean, however, that we have finally arrived at the promised land of full psychotherapy integration. It is not entirely clear how other important therapy approaches might be smoothly integrated into this perspective. In addition, there appear to be important ambiguities and shortcomings in Wachtel's account of the social and ethical values underlying modern psychotherapy that cause us to doubt the final adequacy of this approach.

One's understanding of the goals of therapy depends on one's view of the goals of a mature or successful life in general. What are those goals in Wachtel's case? They seem to be captured by two terms he uses frequently, namely *mastery* and *intimacy*. These terms seem to refer to the successful, appropriately assertive pursuit of one's self-chosen goals in living and a rewarding, mutually respectful intimacy made possible, in part, by such independent and successful endeavor. The two most commonly mentioned impediments to reaching these ends are debilitating anxiety and a lack of necessary, subtle skills required to negotiate one's interpersonal world. Thus therapy focuses centrally, in this view, on the extinction or reduction of anxiety and the acquisition of new skills in living.

Wachtel makes "anxiety reduction through exposure" the centerpiece of therapeutic change. In his view, psychoanalytic conceptions of gaining insight or emotional understanding, sometimes spoken of in terms of "resolving conflict," remain quite vague. They remain limited to achieving an awareness of the idiosyncratic origins and generally unrealistic or inappropriate nature of certain feelings and fears. These conceptions therefore usually have little to say about how one's current interactions with others serve to stimulate and perpetuate these dysfunctional fears and conflicts. The interpersonal model is intended to provide a more plausible and helpful account of these pathogenic elements than viewing them as simple, unidirectional causal influences from the past. It is also intended to open up new, possibly crucial avenues of therapeutic intervention. Even more important, psychoanalytic accounts have little to say about how neurotic anxiety is actually modified. Such generalities as "actively giving up" infantile wishes and objects and subjecting conflicts to mature "reality testing" are insufficient. These formulations may *name* the phenomenon (albeit in a somewhat moralistic or judgmental way), but they do not *explain* it, claims Wachtel. They fail to articulate clearly the basic truth that "resolving neurotic conflict, very centrally, means the reduction of unrealistic anxiety" (1997, p. 89). Psychoanalytic "working through" may be profitably conceptualized as something like a series of extinction trials. Change involves gradual, repeated exposure in an appropriate therapeutic setting to fears and perceived dangers that, even in an imperfect and risk-filled world, do not warrant the inhibition or defensive avoidance they have come to provoke.

Wachtel suggests that behavior therapy's stress on the systematic desensitization of debilitating anxiety through exposure and its design of specific new methods for accomplishing this end are generally on target in a theoretical sense. Moreover, structured desensitization techniques often may be effective in undoing specific phobias. But usually, he believes, anxiety is internally generated or associated with thoughts and feelings that can only be identified and exposed to the light of day in therapeutic conversation of a more traditional sort. He also suggests that behavior therapy is not sensitive enough to the need to clarify conflicting aims and motivations as well as to reduce anxiety associated with one or another specific goal or situation. Thus Wachtel proposes the notion of anxiety reduction through exposure as an attractive third alternative both to unduly vague psychoanalytic notions of emotional understanding and to overly simplistic and mechanistic behavioral concepts of extinction or counterconditioning.

In his earlier book, Wachtel (1977) has little to say about evident parallels between his notion of anxiety reduction through exposure and cognitive therapy concepts of modifying "irrational beliefs" (Ellis) or "cognitive distortions" (Beck). He says only that he is inclined to place greater emphasis than rational-emotive therapy on unconscious conflict, defense, and resistance. Even granting that cognitive therapy fails to take full advantage of analytic wisdom in that regard, it seems that an integrative approach like Wachtel's might easily incorporate and profit somewhat from, for example, cognitive theorists' useful specification of different modes of faulty reasoning or judgment in social interaction (for example, Beck & Weishaar, 1989), such as "arbitrary inference" and "overgeneralization," or their descriptions of typical therapist interventions to modify these patterns, such as "reattribution" or "decentering." Such cognitive distortions, in this view, represent the main ways people generate a sense of exaggerated threat and undue anxiety, which prevent realistic appraisal and effective coping. It would seem that much of cognitive therapy might be integrated into the interpersonal perspective, perhaps to their mutual benefit.

In his later book, Wachtel (1997) does point out some of these parallels. Still, he tends to present cognitive therapy in a somewhat negative light as often focusing too narrowly on overly intellectual efforts to "persuade the patient that her way of thinking is 'incorrect' or 'irrational'" (p. 359). He makes it plain that he thinks behavior therapy has more to offer his integrative view than does cognitive therapy because the former adds a new dimension of the direct, experiential disconfirmation—a form of "hypothesis testing" (p. 359)—of negative and fearful perceptions of the environment, whereas the latter focuses too intellectualistically on inner beliefs and meaning structures, a territory already explored more subtly by psychoanalytic approaches. Perhaps cognitive therapy, more than Wachtel allows, discusses debilitating self-talk and distorted interpretations of events, along with constructive alternatives to them, as pivotal processes taking place in everyday contexts of living. But that issue aside, there may be some interesting theoretical reasons of a deeper sort that lead Wachtel to downplay cognitive therapy's ongoing, rather intensive struggle with "irrational" thinking in favor of behavior therapy's emphasis on changing everyday action patterns.

Wachtel does stress the active, interpretive nature of "responsive man," and he refers at times to things like the "correction of faulty assumptions" as part of therapeutic change. Nevertheless, the notion of anxiety reduction through exposure seems somewhat passive and two-dimensional when set alongside cognitive therapists' typical portrayals of the lengthy, intense, multifaceted efforts on the part of both therapist and client to rework faulty attitudes and perceptions. Something of the Sturm und Drang of reworking personal meanings and entrenched attitudes toward others, familiar to every therapist, seems missing. Of course, generally speaking, Wachtel understands this as well as anyone. Moreover, he is surely correct in pointing out that cognitive therapy downplays the role of the therapeutic relationship and tends to overlook the importance of the sort of "experiential disconfirmation" that takes place in therapy and everyday life (1997, p. 363). But the often protracted dialogue and struggle between therapist and client and within the client herself seems not to be captured well by the specific idea of anxiety reduction through exposure.

Within the strict terms of the interpersonal model, it appears that human action is rather narrowly conceived as straightforward, more or less effective instrumental performance. Little more is said, beyond such considerations as "mastery," "effectiveness," or "realism," about the nature or worth of the ends sought in this activity or about its congruence with any other personal values or social norms. Perhaps that is why, in this model, personal reorientation in therapy seems so tightly focused on undoing irrational anxiety and either cognitive or overt avoidance behavior. The simple absence or presence of such anxiety and avoidance behavior is all that would be relevant to this sort of instrumental activity aimed at pregiven ends. So the interpersonal model downplays the importance of any more extensive reconsideration of one's basic purposes or meanings in living or of the ends of one's action in the world. We can certainly question whether this characterization of human activity and personal agency is broad and rich enough to capture all that is needed for us to understand either human action or therapeutic change.

With the possible exception of certain types of behavior therapy or strategic therapy, most therapies make reference to some other dimensions of meaning or value that play an important role in reinterpreting oneself and one's world. For example, the picture of human action in cognitive therapy is largely outward-looking, calculating, and utilitarian in its overall cast. But cognitive therapists also stress that therapy usually involves the arduous reworking of beliefs and attitudes having to do with one's sense of personal worth, significance, or importance to others. In other words, they focus more on the *meaning* of feared events in quite personal terms—not just the impersonal fact that some adverse outcome relative to one's goals is more or less likely to occur. To be sure, cognitive therapy's views on this topic are largely *negative* in character, typically asserting that it is best that a sense of self-worth *not* be based on external achievement or on the evaluations of others, for example. Still, issues of personal worth, debilitating moral ties to others, and coming to terms with life's inevitable disappointments in an acceptable manner seem to receive a great deal of therapeutic attention in this approach. Wachtel (1997, p. 89) points out that the conservative Freudian viewpoint he effectively critiques often makes references to "renunciation" or the "active giving up of infantile wishes and objects." Even this intellectualized and oddly moralistic point of view paints a richer picture of human intentionality in struggle with itself than is conveyed by Wachtel's highly abstract and rather bloodless notion of anxiety reduction through exposure.

We encounter similar issues when we seek to integrate other important therapeutic perspectives into Wachtel's scheme. Existential therapies of the sort outlined by May and Yalom (1989), examined in greater detail in the next chapter, also stress both personal reevaluation of fundamental fears and conflicts and the importance of undertaking new kinds of courageous and fulfilling action in the outer world. But existential therapy theorists emphasize inward reflection that goes considerably beyond just seeing through distorted perceptions of harm and rejection. They typically underscore the need to come to terms with threats of death and meaninglessness in a concerted, philosophical manner. They also stress a more outward kind of "wholehearted engagement" or "patterning the events of one's life in some coherent fashion" by finding a way to "care about other individuals, about ideas or projects, to search, to create, to build" (May & Yalom, 1989, p. 390). Perhaps considerations of this sort could be harmonized somehow with a modified interpersonal model. As it stands, however, there are tensions between the two perspectives. Existentialists are likely to emphasize both the inauthenticity or "bad faith" built into so many normal social values and routines. They challenge our comfortable conformism and our reluctance to face up to intractable existential dilemmas in living. The interpersonal model, by contrast, tends to valorize existing social possibilities for success and fulfillment in a somewhat uncritical manner and to focus mainly on getting on with the business of achieving and enjoying them. (For reasons we go into later, we do not think Wachtel's thoughtful remarks about the shortcomings of American individualism really alter this picture.)

This is not to say, however, that existential writers have provided us with a completely acceptable alternative. It is difficult to tell from May and Yalom's remarks (1989), for example, whether the kinds of purposes and commitments mentioned are being recommended because of their inherent ethical or spiritual value or merely because they are useful psychological avenues for "wholehearted engagement." Existentialists, who commonly stress the fashioning of personal meanings in the absence of any metaphysical support, would be uncomfortable with the first approach—it would seem to compromise their understanding of existential or radical freedom. But the extreme relativism of the latter approach may be self-undermining in that it tends to undercut the credibility and staying power of one's commitments over the long run.

How would an influential therapeutic orientation like Kohut's self psychology (1977) mesh with the interpersonal viewpoint? Self psychologists might suggest that Wachtel's discussion of anxiety reduction and social skill enhancement presupposes emotional difficulties at the oedipal level of development or beyond, difficulties that afflict individuals who have already consolidated a fairly coherent sense of self and values but are plagued by various internal conflicts, guilt, and inhibitions. Self psychology's focus, instead, they might contend, is on the increasing number of narcissistic and other personality disorders representing mainly pre-oedipal difficulties. These disorders involve extreme oscillations of self-esteem, feelings of depression and emptiness, and pervasive difficulties in forming satisfying relationships with others. Self psychology presumes that at the heart of these difficulties is the lack of having formed a stable, coherent, purposeful self in the first place. Self psychology focuses on building a clear sense of identity through the ministrations of what Kohut called "therapist empathy" and "mirroring" and through providing "opportunities for idealization" that allow the "vulnerable self" to begin to lay down guiding values and ideals felt to be necessary for psychic health. Kohutians would probably find Wachtel's explanation of therapy and the therapy relationship (mainly in terms of anxiety reduction through exposure) as narrow, underdeveloped, and aimed predominantly at a restricted set of developmentally more advanced problems in living. They and adherents of other approaches might argue that much anxiety is best seen as more of a by-product of personality disorder or underdevelopment than as the central pathological element itself.

Still, there would seem to be both fruitful possibilities and sharp limitations related to integrating self psychology and the interpersonal framework. The tendency of self psychologists to characterize personality disorders as the direct, unicausal manifestation of a fragmented self whose development was delayed in childhood fairly begs to be reformulated in interpersonal terms as something that may be the effect as well as the cause of an individual's current way of living and that may coexist with very real competencies in some areas of her life. Such a reformulation might serve both to undercut the exaggerated infantalization that writers

like Wachtel and Eagle (1984) claim distorts many psychoanalytic formulations, including Kohut's, and to open up additional avenues for helpful intervention. In fact, Wachtel and Wachtel (1986) outline how an
individual's narcissistic need for specialness and a relative insensitivity to
others' needs can skew her perception of and approach to the world.
Because of this skewed perspective, interactions with others become structured such that they tend to perpetuate a style of life built around those
very narcissistic traits. Others tend to respond positively or not at all to
the person's more or less subtle efforts to be the admired center of attention. In *either* case, nothing corrective occurs, and the person's loneliness
and painful lack of ordinary human satisfactions are intensified in a way
that fuels her continuing frantic efforts to achieve or be noticed. Wachtel
helps us understand that narcissists may be able to persist and flourish to
the extent they do only in a "culture of narcissism."

Beck, Freeman, and Associates (1990), who try to integrate a number
of psychoanalytic insights into personality disorders into their cognitive
therapy perspective, report that patients with narcissistic problems are
often difficult to motivate or "hook" on qualitatively different kinds of
human relationships. It is difficult to get them to appreciate and settle for
the ordinary pleasures of an imperfect humanity. To deal with this problem, these authors stress the need for concerted efforts with such patients
to define new "schemas" for interpersonal interaction, role-play new interactions in therapy, actively cultivate new and possibly rewarding kinds of
feelings and values such schemas and interactions evoke, and experiment
deliberately with putting them into practice in everyday life. Wachtel's
interpersonal model would seem to offer support and a more developed
rationale for such methods.

Nevertheless, self psychology, the cognitive approach of Beck et al.
(1990), and other theories typically portray personal change in therapy in
more ample terms than Wachtel's exiguous theory of anxiety reduction
through exposure that fosters more effective coping in one's social world.
Why not just expand Wachtel's approach to accommodate insights from
these and other therapy approaches? It seems to us, unfortunately, that
there is no straightforward way to integrate these views. Once we get
beyond neutral-sounding language like *anxiety reduction, reality testing,*
and *more effective behavior,* it becomes more and more apparent, as discussed in Chapter Two, that different therapies incorporate different ideals
concerning what is a good or worthwhile human life. In turn, these contrasting views of the good life, which are controversial and often incommensurable, inevitably generate somewhat different explanatory accounts
of human action and personality (Taylor, 1985a). As a result, different

therapy systems may employ different, value-laden criteria of effectiveness from its point of view, and may prescribe different routes and techniques for reaching its preferred goals. An even more disturbing problem is the very real possibility that all modern therapy systems incorporate cultural or moral values that are distorted or inauthentic in some manner. In that case, an eclectic or integrative approach, as argued in Chapter Two, would actually obscure important problems.

For example, Kohut's self psychology does not just present a different or expanded account of personal change or growth in therapy. It advocates a different *kind* of growth in a partly different *direction* than Wachtel's interpersonal view and many other therapies. Kohut advocates as an ideal for therapy and human living in general the somewhat odd-sounding notion of "healthy narcissism." Kohut's theory has obviously been influenced by modern Romantic ideals of creativity and self-expression. As several writers have pointed out (Eagle, 1984; Cushman, 1990), a distinctive feature of Kohut's theory is an emphasis on the importance of "values" as well as what Kohut terms "skills" and "ambitions" in psychic health. Still, these writers point out, Kohut's stress on values is ambiguous and its merit qualified by his tendency to portray these values as personal choices or possessions that serve the goal of self-enhancement rather than as shared communal interpretations that have ethical authority for those who embrace them. Kohut's writings tend to portray therapy as focused on nurturing one's ability to pursue one's unique ambitions and creative talents, with the social world largely conceived of as an arena for self-expression or a source of companions or admirers in these creative undertakings. In contrast, the image of successful living in Wachtel's interpersonal model seems to be not self-expression but effective transactions with one's social world in order to move toward desired goals of, broadly speaking, mastery and intimacy. Self psychologists might feel that the interpersonal model portrays individuals as excessively enmeshed in the details of more or less cooperative social transactions or that it tends to mistake the means for the end of human existence. Those drawn to the interpersonal model might find self psychology excessively individualistic and dangerously inattentive to more mundane but important, even meaningful, aspects of living.

Ethics and the Good Life

It would appear that self psychology and Wachtel's interpersonal model reflect the contrasting emphases of what Bellah et al. (1985) term expressive and utilitarian individualism in modern life. As we discussed in

Chapter One, Bellah et al. outline how modern individualism views humans as decontextualized from any larger cosmic or moral order and as capable of separating themselves from their own families and traditions in order to choose the beliefs and values that will guide their lives. In fact, the exercise of that capacity—as opposed to some sort of other-directed, dependent, or ineffective kind of living—seems to define a large part of what we mean by the term *mental health* in modern psychology circles. Much of our thinking about psychological well-being thus seems grounded in individualism and offers only what Fromm and Wachtel call "freedom from," with little to say about a more substantive "freedom to." The utilitarian form of individualism, which emerged first, sees human life as "an effort to maximize self-interest" relative to given ends of security and satisfaction (Bellah et al., p. 334) and tends to depreciate other outlooks as pointlessly sentimental or superstitious. The expressive form sees each person as having a unique inner nature that requires expression for it to be realized, and regularly castigates the utilitarian approach for its exaltation of control and neglect of human feeling.

The existentialist point of view, reflected in existential, Gestalt, and a number of other therapies, represents a third variation on the modern individualist outlook. It shares the expressivist suspicion of conventional morality and ordinary social patterns as tending toward the conformist and inauthentic. But it goes further than either utilitarian or expressive individualism in emphasizing our lack of a home in the universe and the need to fashion our own values and consolations without any basis or justification for our choices whatsoever, not even utilitarian ideas of maximizing pleasurable outcomes or expressivist confidence in the deepest impulses of our inner natures.

As we have said, one of the problems facing therapy integration is that different therapy theories and methods are shaped at the core by different, controversial, and at least partly incommensurable visions of the good life. The difficulty becomes even more acute when therapeutic approaches that challenge some of the assumptions of modern individualism itself are brought into the picture. Philip Rieff (1966) reminds us that traditional forms of psychological healing were not primarily oriented toward maximizing individually defined well-being and fulfillment. They all required a certain amount of self-limitation or self-denial, which is compensated for by a sense of belonging and purpose as part of a meaningful cosmic order with which one strives to be in touch or in harmony. Alfred Adler's notion of "social interest" as a transcendent ethical goal and felt sense of the unity of all humankind was a self-conscious attempt to transcend aspects of modern individualism and reconnect with elements of a traditional sense of life. Jung's idea of individuation, or reaching a condition of balance between ego and shadow within a larger Self grounded in timeless archetypes, was another such undertaking. Adler, Jung, and Otto Rank, it is worth recalling (Progoff, 1956), felt that distinctively modern dilemmas in living could not be satisfactorily addressed without in some way reconceptualizing human life as part of a wider field of moral or spiritual significance.

In addition, newer, so-called postmodern psychological perspectives have emerged lately that are not nearly as sympathetic to traditional values as were Adler and Jung but that also roundly criticize modern, individual-centered thinking about human existence. For example, as we discussed in the Introduction, Cushman (1990) argues forcefully that modern psychology and psychotherapy have tragically obscured the historically situated nature of our discourses and practices. Therapy theorists' "decontextualized approach" (1) uncritically assumes the modern Western "concept of the self—the bounded, masterful self—as an unchangeable, transhistorical entity" and (2) treats the way of life associated with this modern self, which he calls self-contained individualism, as "an unquestioned value" (p. 599). Cushman argues that this bounded, masterful self, which is only one way human identity has or could be configured in history, is overblown and insupportable. It almost inevitably degenerates into the "empty self" so evident in the post–World War II era, manifested in familiar forms of cultural and more pathological narcissism, such as "low self-esteem . . . values confusion . . . eating disorders . . . drug abuse . . . and chronic consumerism" (p. 604). Cushman rather pointedly illustrates how psychology, advertising, and pop religion have helped form and maintain a consumption-oriented stance toward ourselves that "ministers to" the empty self by attempting to fill it up, even if only temporarily, with a hollow kind of "self-acceptance," spiritual nostrums, and emotional and physical self-improvement.

In Cushman's view, the main problem for modern psychotherapy is that it tends to perpetuate the problem in the cure. A therapy like Kohut's, for example, is clearly designed to minister to the contemporary empty self. But in its theory and practice it rearticulates and perpetuates the sort of decontextualized notion of human identity that is presumably a major source of the current malaise. Such theories are thoroughly embroiled in a central cultural paradox. On the one hand, "the self of our time is expected to function in a highly autonomous, isolated way . . . to be self-soothing, self-loving, and self-sufficient." On the other hand, most contemporary psychologies stress that to grow and flourish "one must have a nurturing early environment that provides a great deal of empathy, attention, and mirroring." But why would genuinely autonomous, ambitious, self-serving individuals ever "choose to undergo the self-sacrifice and suffering necessary to be nurturing parents?" (Cushman, 1990, pp. 604–605). We might add that if the idea that the bounded, masterful self necessarily degenerates into the hapless empty self is correct, such individuals would not be capable of executing that role anyway. They would be too emotionally needy or narcissistically wounded to make very good parents in the first place!

What would the goals of psychotherapy look like from a postmodern perspective? Cushman holds out the relatively upbeat possibility that we might effect "structural societal change" or "develop social practices that could construct a terrain in which the obsessive preoccupations of an hypertrophied self, such as self-acceptance, would not show up" (1991, p. 543). But he remains quite vague about what those practices would look like or what creditable new sorts of meaning or purpose they might offer. Loewenstein (1991) adopts a more resigned, even grim, postmodern viewpoint based on Lacanian psychoanalysis, to the effect that modern notions of a cohesive, unified, "healthy" self are harmful and unrealistic. Instead, she contends, psychoanalysis should aim to increase one's "capacity to withstand the ambiguity, contradiction, and discontinuity" that mark our experience (p. 26).

We can only conclude that pursuing the task of therapy integration beyond superficial levels means becoming embroiled in our civilization's basic struggles with questions about the place of traditional values, the shortcomings of the modern moral outlook and worldview, and the merit of emerging postmodern views, however distressed we may be about that prospect or unprepared we may feel for the challenge.

Where does Wachtel's interpersonal model fit into this spectrum of diverse visions of human living? For one thing, we are inclined to see something of Adler's ideal of "social interest" reflected in Wachtel's views. His expressed concerns about American individualism, emphasis on the social embeddedness of psychodynamics and human agency, evident concern for social justice, and frequent reminders that ordinary-seeming, everyday pleasures of belonging and connection are a large part of what life is all about may offer something of an antidote to modern trends of excessive self-preoccupation and a "culture of narcissism." They cut against the grain of the kind of modern subjectivism that Robert Coles (1987) complained about when he decried the pervasiveness in American life of a kind of psychology that fosters a "concentration, persistent, if not feverish, upon one's thoughts, feelings, wishes, worries—bordering on if not embracing, solipsism: the self as the main form of (existential) reality" (p. 189). The interpersonal model reminds us of the pressing need to do a better job of striking a balance between individual integrity and social responsibility. This strikes us as a distinctive and unusual feature of Wachtel's interpersonal therapy theory.

Nevertheless, we feel that in certain key respects, Wachtel's interpersonal model remains within the problematic confines of the kind of modern individualist outlook that he sharply criticizes. Wachtel and Wachtel (1986) discuss how the traditional view of human society as a kind of "organic unity" has been replaced by an "atomistic vision of essential separateness" that insists on the "separate responsibility of each person for himself and minimizes our interdependency." This widespread modern view happily "affirms the dignity and worth of each individual" (p. 240) but otherwise is unduly stern and alienating. Unfortunately, Wachtel says, we tend to "conceive of psychotherapy as the means of increasing that autonomy still further, of helping us to differentiate from our families and free ourselves from the pressures of society to conform" (p. 241). Wachtel feels that his interpersonal model or cyclical psychodynamics opens the door to the cure for this one-sided individualism. It affords a vision of life and living in which autonomy is balanced by a "sufficient appreciation of the fact and necessity of interdependence." Thus, we can begin to see how "new values can reintegrate our newly liberated psychological selves into a web of firm but flexible relations . . . in which the pursuit of happiness is no longer conceived of as a zero sum game" (p. 243).

It is doubtful, however, that this "appreciation of the fact and necessity of interdependence" along with a handful of unspecified "new values" will accomplish all that Wachtel hopes. There is, of course, an important element of truth in his analysis. Modern society is characterized by a historically unprecedented sharp dichotomy between the public and private spheres. The public sphere is increasingly dominated by impersonal, often competitive relations among individuals that are drained of meaning except as means to the end of survival or gain. MacIntyre (1981) points out a great paradox of modern individualism—that our becoming more "liberated" individuals goes hand in hand with the increasing bureaucratization of our social world, because impersonal bureaucratic organization tends to be the only form of association available for organizing our common life. Thus, many of us feel that only in the private sphere of subjective life, family, and friends can we find genuine emotion and real meaning. It is there we seek, with whatever therapeutic assistance we may require, well-being and happiness.

The trouble with this new arrangement of things is that both the public world of impersonal work and the private world of purely affectional ties are largely emptied of traditional linkages of custom, religious faith, or shared political purpose. Sarason (1986) discusses this loss in terms of the consequences for society in general and modern psychology in particular of our no longer having any viable concept of the "public interest." The worldview of traditional societies, according to Sarason, was characterized by a strong sense of "interconnections among the individual, the collectivity, and [a sense of the] ultimate meaning and purpose of human existence." This triad of interrelated elements has a "common center" that shapes and lends coherence to "all features of living" (p. 899). The common center establishes some sense of ethical purpose and genuine community beyond impersonal cooperation or merely sentimental bonds. In modern times, we have to a large extent lost the third element of this triad. We may have private views about life's meaning and purpose, or the lack thereof, but we certainly do not share a deeply felt sense of such matters with very many of our fellow citizens. Therefore, we lack anything like a traditional common center, which the "secular mind" has great difficulty envisioning. We also lack an acceptable modern substitute for that center, which Sarason confesses he has been unable to identify. As a result, we almost inevitably "choose the route of rampant individualism" and pay a heavy price in terms of emotional isolation and difficulty in resolving pressing ethical and social questions (p. 905).

These losses and the failure to find a credible substitute for them may help explain why instead of accomplishing the ideal of the modern family's being a secure "haven in an heartless world," the private sphere of life almost inevitably becomes invaded by the economic, purely contractual, often cruelly competitive features of public life (Lasch, 1978). An example of such incursion might be the new ideal for marriage and love relationships that Bellah et al. (1985) detect among many contemporary Americans. They term it *therapeutic contractualism*, whereby supposedly autonomous individuals reciprocally exchange a kind of love—almost an emotional commodity—that is defined by purely personal feelings, with no obligations beyond "honest communication" about how one happens to feel. There is little place for more traditional values of commitment, patience, or even sacrifice in this view, without which many deeper human needs may never be met. Of course, our real lives are usually richer than any such abstract ideal suggests, in part perhaps because we often surreptitiously draw on and adapt some values from older moral or religious traditions. But in a world neatly divided into just the two compartments of public work and private feeling, we suffer for the lack of any terms or language in which to articulate and nurture other values. Wachtel's picture of more effective coping making possible greater intimacy with others seems to fit only too well with the world of increasingly meaningless work and shallow therapeutic contractualism in private life that these various social critics call into question.

Thus, for an individual to withdraw from the public sphere of work and economic struggle—including from politics, now seen cynically, too, as just another kind of competition for personal gain—in order to find fulfillment in a private enclave may be quite self-defeating. In this situation, we all need to be reminded that we cannot escape our common fate in a thoroughly interdependent world. That reminder could be a starting point for a much-needed rethinking of some of our institutions and values (Wolfe, 1989). In Wachtel's integrative model, this rethinking has already helped correct the stress many therapies place on mainly inward shifts of attitude and feeling to the neglect of the need for an equal emphasis on facilitating action in the real world. However, the most important question concerns not just the *fact* but the nature or *quality* of our interdependent way of life. We always have been and will be considerably interdependent social animals. Even thoroughly atomized individuals in a Hobbesian state of nature are radically interdependent. That is why they cannot survive, let alone flourish, without a carefully crafted social contract and an all-powerful sovereign. The simple fact of interdependence will not prevent the stark Hobbesian vision of a barely contained war of all against all from coming partly true in many areas of modern life. We may remain disturbingly close to a precarious condition of that sort until we find or fashion a different vision of what interdependence is all about.

We might say that the twin pillars of the modern individualistic outlook are what psychologists have come to call separation and individuation and the instrumental conception of action (Sullivan, 1986, p. 38). The first pillar is the cultural fiction that, to reach maturity, we can and must break with all custom and tradition and make up our deepest beliefs in the isolation of our private selves (Bellah et al., 1985). The second pillar is the idea that human action is basically instrumental and consists of more or less effective efforts to achieve certain consequences or results. The instrumental conception of action sharply dichotomizes means and ends. It treats all values as subjective and leaves the choice of ends to personal preference. This view is intended to protect us from interference by any sort of arbitrary authority while underwriting our efforts to gain control over events for human benefit. As discussed in Chapter One, this scheme portrays human action as essentially self-interested, at the same time that it advances a commitment to human rights according to which one may only engage in pursuits that are consistent with the rights of others to do the same.

In recent decades, we have increasingly come to question many of the key elements of this liberal individualistic view. If action is basically instrumental and values are purely subjective, then we can no longer rationally evaluate the worth of ends, a situation that encourages an expansion of bureaucratic organization and technological prowess but with less and less conviction or consensus about the goals such an expansion should serve. In fact, under such conditions it becomes progressively harder to defend even minimal notions of human rights and fairness against aggressive self-interest. Why are those cherished modern liberal values, too, not finally subjective and preferential like all the others? "Separation and individuation" as a master plan for the good life begins to look less like a path to untrammeled liberation and more like a recipe for emotional isolation in a never-ending rat race. Wachtel understands many of these problems, and desires a real alternative. But he offers little to distinguish his notion of interdependence from this distressing picture of interrelated cogs in our economic and social machinery, cogs that have mainly contractual, impersonal ties to others except within a shrinking and rather escapist private realm. We can be thoroughly enmeshed with others in enterprises where we only cooperate with them or play by the social rules in order to achieve ultimately private or personal ends. We need to be told a lot more about why being "newly liberated selves" in "a web of firm but flexible human relations" is anything new or different from this problematic condition.

In subsequent chapters, we will draw on the resources of critical theory (Habermas, 1973, 1991) and philosophical hermeneutics (Gadamer, 1975; Taylor, 1985b) to outline a picture of the human situation within which we might better understand the phenomena of interdependence and the interplay of psychic realities and social context with which Wachtel is concerned. The critical theorists' noted "critique of instrumental reason" (Bernstein, 1988) could serve as the cornerstone of that effort. According to this critique, human activity is *not* primarily instrumental in character but rather what Habermas calls *communicative action*. Communicative action refers to shared practices and institutions that are not undertaken as means to an extraneous end but are considered good or worthwhile in themselves. Communicative action describes a realm of praxis, which subsumes mere techne, or instrumental action, as just one subordinate part. In this realm of praxis, our shared meanings and values are just as much "out there" in our practices and institutions as "in here" in our thoughts and feelings about outer events. This notion helps us overcome the debilitating gulf between private and public or self and world, whereas Wachtel's approach tends merely to combine the two realms in a more comprehensive scheme.

Contemporary hermeneutics offers further resources for overcoming the one-sided individualism, about which Wachtel rightly complains, that so colors modern psychology. In the hermeneutic view, we are deeply embedded in the historical flow of shared meanings and undertakings in a way that threatens many of our cherished modern illusions of separateness, uniqueness, and control but does not mean abandoning the best of a modern critical consciousness. At the center of the hermeneutic approach is a conception of dialogue (Gadamer, 1975; Guignon, 1991) in which interpreters and events mutually shape one another in a continuing search for understanding, including ethical insight, which is more fundamental than the issues of mastery, reality testing, or effectiveness that Wachtel emphasizes. We respectfully submit that Wachtel's search for a "responsive" alternative to autonomy and reactivity, and his effort to clarify a kind of influence that is not inimical to genuine freedom and responsibility on the part of the one who is influenced, are unfinished business and could be improved on within the framework of a hermeneutic ontology.

5

EXISTENTIAL PSYCHOTHERAPY: A REASSESSMENT

ALTHOUGH THE EXISTENTIAL MOVEMENT in psychotherapy no longer has the prominence it had thirty years ago, many of its core ideas continue to be central to psychotherapy theory and practice. As John Norcross (1986) observes, basic assumptions of existentialist thought have been integrated into traditional theories and newer eclectic approaches, where they are treated as so self-evident that no thought is given to their source. Thus "the existential orientation frequently underlies clinical practice without explicit recognition or awareness" (p. 42). This pervasive influence is hardly surprising when we recall the concerns that first brought existentialism to center stage in the fifties and sixties. At that time, there was the feeling that the two main "forces" in psychology—roughly, psychoanalysis and behaviorism—were excessively deterministic and dehumanizing, too much under the pall of scientific objectification to be able to address the life issues of humans living in an increasingly mechanized world. Only by introducing a "third force" (including both existentialist and humanistic approaches) would it be possible to help people deal with the harsher aspects of modern life.

Many of the insights of existentialism seem as pertinent today as they were a half-century ago. First, there is the idea that we can only really understand and help people if we get in touch with life as it is actually lived—with the concrete realities of human experience. This commitment to being true to life means we must bracket conceptualizations drawn from science and traditional theories in order to focus on the client's actual experience. The ideal of holding to an "experience-near" standpoint while fighting against a premature "hardening of the categories" is one of the enduring contributions of existentialism.

A second valuable aspect of existentialism is its uncompromising commitment to the ideal of freedom. In the face of scientific determinist conceptions of the human, which see behavior as governed by causal antecedents in such a way that personal agency becomes unintelligible, existentialists have insisted that we have free will, the ability to be the source of our own actions and lives. The belief in free will, together with the commitment to the ideal of freedom understood as the right to choose one's own life course, is central to our own modern self-understanding. Moreover, even otherwise highly deterministic theories seem to presuppose free will to the extent that therapy is seen as a process enabling a person to make changes in her life. In fact, we would argue that this existentialist conception of freedom lies at the core of most contemporary therapy theories, and this fact makes it all the more important to examine the implications of the existentialist ideal of freedom.

A third appealing feature of existentialist theory is its conception of the successful outcome of therapy. From its inception in the nineteenth century, existentialism has called attention to the baleful effects of modern secularization, technology, and mass society on the lives of individuals in the modern world. Rollo May and Irvin Yalom (1989, p. 400), for example, point out that "our present age is one of disintegration of cultural and historical mores, of love and marriage, the family, the inherited religions, and so forth. This disintegration is the reason that psychotherapy of all sorts has burgeoned in the twentieth century." As May and Yalom observe, most people who seek help today suffer not from hysteria or compulsive hand washing but from "loneliness, isolation, and alienation," and from "'character neuroses,' which is another description of existential neurosis . . . the condition of the person who feels life is meaningless" (pp. 399–400).

Existentialist thinkers have long been aware that, where social conditions are the sources of suffering, it makes little sense to think of the aim of psychotherapy as helping people to be better "adjusted" or "adapted" to the world. On the contrary, when the "normal" individual is what R. D. Laing (quoted in Bankhart, 1997, p. 333) calls "a half-crazed creature more or less adjusted to a mad world," it is better to think of the aim of therapy as liberating the individual from the stranglehold of a demented social existence in order to open the possibility of achieving personal self-fulfillment or self-realization. Given this point of view, existential approaches have tried to envision the healthy individual as one who has become *authentic,* where this is understood as being able to embrace one's being and to realize and express one's unique potentialities as an individual despite the negative pressures exerted by the social world. This notion of individual fulfillment, like the existentialist conception of freedom, has become so widely accepted today that it seems to be part of the distilled "common sense" shared by most therapy theories. Yet the very aura of self-evidence surrounding this notion makes it important to examine its roots.

Existentialist Philosophy

In this section, we briefly sketch out some of the central themes in the philosophical movement called existentialism and explore some of the ways these themes have been influential in the existential psychotherapy movement. Instead of pointing out differences among the various theorists who have formulated the existential viewpoint, we focus on their commonalities and construct a picture of a prototypical existentialist that embraces the core ideas of a variety of different theories. Our critical examination of existential therapy at the end of the chapter is aimed at typical assumptions of existentialists generally and not at any individuals in particular.

Early Existentialists: Kierkegaard and Nietzsche

Before turning to existentialist psychotherapy as such, it will be helpful to get an overview of the philosophical sources behind that approach. Existentialism is a fairly new movement in Western thought. Its origin coincides with the major shifts toward secularization, industrialization, and rapid scientific advance of the mid-nineteenth century (Guignon & Pereboom, 1995; Guignon, 1998a). The Danish philosopher Søren Kierkegaard (1813–1855) is usually seen as the seminal figure in existentialism because of his emphasis on the "existing individual" and his criticisms of both scientific system-building and the bland self-assurance of the bourgeoisie in the present age. Kierkegaard sees modern life as characterized by a tendency to level down all hierarchical oppositions and to treat all things as being of equal value. Although this leveling process has led to democratization in public life, it has also created a world in which, for most people, nothing *really* matters much any more. Where nothing seems especially worthwhile or valuable, it becomes difficult to find meaning and fulfillment in one's life, with the result that people tend simply to drift along aimlessly, doing what "one" does but living without real passion or commitment.

In Kierkegaard's view (1846/1995a), one can escape from this condition of meaninglessness and become fully human only if one comes to have an "infinite passion" in one's life, a defining relation or commitment to something that gives one's existence a content and focus. An individual who has an infinite passion of this sort is called a "knight of faith." Though Kierkegaard's primary interest is in authentic Christian experience (1843/1995b), the examples of faith he offers (for example, Abraham's relation to Isaac, and a "young swain" who falls in love with a princess) show that this ideal is not limited to any particular religious orientation. In fact, because the worthiness of one's commitment is defined through the intensity of one's subjective stance toward that object (the "subjective truth" of one's relation), what gives a life its meaning turns out to be something that is private and highly personal (Kierkegaard, 1846/1995a, 1843/1995b). To be an "existing individual," then, is to live with the intensity, focus, and purposiveness of someone who has a defining content for his or her life.

The idea that contemporary life has become flat and meaningless is also found in the writings of the German philosopher Friedrich Nietzsche (1844–1900). In his view, most people conform to the rituals and routines of the "herd," mechanically adhering to a morality that serves to domesticate them and deaden their creativity, and trusting that there is a higher order which justifies their existence so long as they follow the rules. Nietzsche's notorious claim that "God is dead" (1882/1995, p. 133) must be understood in the light of his critique of the complacent conformism of contemporary life. In speaking about the death of God, Nietzsche was not just talking about the decline in religiosity of modern society. Rather, he was referring to the breakdown of shared belief in any sort of absolute whatsoever, that is, any belief in a transcendent basis for values, whether this absolute is thought of as God, reason, history, the cosmic order, or science. By announcing the death of God, Nietzsche wants people to recognize that they can no longer turn to something outside themselves for direction or validation and that they must therefore find a meaning for their lives on their own. Thus, whereas Kierkegaard is called a religious existentialist because of his belief that fulfillment requires a relation to something outside oneself, Nietzsche is described as an atheist existentialist because of his rejection of any external source of meaning and value.

Recent Existentialists: Heidegger and Sartre

Drawing on the thought of Kierkegaard and Nietzsche, Martin Heidegger (1889–1976), in *Being and Time* (1927/1995), lays out all the great existentialist themes, including the notions of anxiety, guilt, conscience, being-in-the-world, freedom, authenticity, and being-toward-death. Like his existentialist predecessors, Heidegger refuses to simply buy into the concepts derived from traditional theories and science, and instead turns to a careful description, or *phenomenology,* of our "average everyday" existence as agents in a practical life-world. This phenomenology reveals that we are always being-in-the-world, in the sense that, as actively involved in everyday activities, our own being is inextricably tied up with a shared, meaningful life-world. Given Heidegger's description of the uni- fied, holistic phenomenon of being-in-the-world, the traditional distinc- tions of self and world, subject and object, consciousness and thing, simply have no role to play.

The phenomenology of our involvements with everyday contexts also reveals that we are meaning-endowing beings. What this means is that, in our interactions with the world, we do not directly perceive "facts" about how things are. Instead, our encounters with things are always mediated by interests, feelings, and background assumptions we bring with us to the encounter. For example, a person who is afraid of spiders will encounter a spider as a looming threat, whereas the entomologist will encounter the same spider as a fascinating object for research. In each case, the *being* of the spider is defined, to some extent at least, by the interests, point of view, and emotive orientation of the agent who encoun- ters this entity. It is of course true that our acculturation into socially stan- dardized ways of interpreting entities ensures that most of us will see things in similar ways. But it remains the case, according to phenomeno- logical analysis, that our experience of the world has the characteristics it has largely because of the meanings we impose on things in our meaning- giving activity.

Because he thinks of humans as the source of the determinate meaning things have, Heidegger characterizes human existence as a "clearing" or "opening" through which a concrete context of "worldhood" becomes possible and things come to stand out or matter in specific ways. If there are no absolutes outside us that determine the correct way of interpreting things, as Nietzsche observed, we have to recognize that we alone are the source of the interpretations entities have in our world. In this sense, real- ity is *made,* not *found*—it is a matter of invention rather than discovery. There is no way to get at anything "out there" as it is in itself that would compel us to interpret things one way rather than another.

Many of Heidegger's ideas were developed by Jean-Paul Sartre (1905–1980), the first philosopher to use the term *existentialism* to refer to his own thought. Sartre (1946/1995b, p. 270) provided the succinct definition of existentialism that is nearly universally accepted today: existentialism is the view that, for humans, "existence precedes essence." What this means is that we first exist—we are simply there one day, "thrown" into a world not of our choosing, with no essential traits that determine in advance what we ought to be or must be—and it is only afterwards, through our own choices and actions, that each of us as an individual creates and defines her own personal identity or essence. In other words (Sartre 1946/1995b, p. 271), "there is no human nature" that fixes our basic characteristics in advance. Though we might have traits that limit our possibilities (for example, being too short to play basketball), it is up to us to take over and deal with these traits, and the way each individual acts in dealing with her situation is what defines the kind of person she is. Thus, in the view of existentialists, a human "is nothing else but what he makes of himself. . . . What we mean is that man is nothing else than a series of undertakings, that he is the sum, the organization, the ensemble of the relationships which make up these undertakings" (p. 278).

This statement leads to one of the most fundamental claims of existentialist philosophy: humans are self-creating beings. If there is nothing given in advance that determines what we are or ought to be, then our identity is something we create in the course of our active lives. And this means that we *are* what we *do*. Whether we realize it or not, each of us is creating an identity for himself or herself in the course of acting in the world.

To clarify this claim, Sartre (1943/1995a) considers the case of a coward. It might be that a person has inbuilt characteristics that incline him toward being a coward—perhaps a weak physical makeup or a fearful disposition. But Sartre holds that, because we always have the ability to deal with our traits in our actions, we can transform these characteristics, or at least transform our attitude toward them. Thus, if a person is a coward—if he runs away when he is threatened or avoids frightening situations—it is because he is *choosing* to be a coward. "He has made himself a coward in his acts." But in that case, he is "responsible for his cowardice" (p. 279). Because one always has the ability to transform one's life by beginning to act differently—by choosing to stand firm in the face of frightening situations—one can reverse a lifetime of cowardly behavior and start to become a brave person. To the extent that the coward does not change his life, he is *making himself* into a coward, and he has no one to blame but himself.

The conception of humans as self-creating beings is correlated with the distinctive conception of the self found in existentialist philosophy. For existentialists, a human being should not be thought of as an object or thing of any sort but rather as an unfolding *event*—a life course or life story extending from birth to death. When we think of a human life as an event, we can distinguish two aspects or dimensions of a human being. On the one hand, there is everything that has happened up to the current moment, including the fixed characteristics of the situation in which the person now finds herself. This dimension of the past is called *facticity*, and it is something that is experienced as simply given, in the sense that it affects and limits one's choices. For example, if a person chose to marry and have children at an early age, then this is something she has to deal with in making choices for the future. It presents itself as, so to speak, a task the person has to take up or deal with in deciding what to do.

On the other hand, in all our actions we are taking a stand on what we are, and by so taking a stand, we are projecting an image of what we are into the future. This future-directed dimension of human existence is called *transcendence* or *projection*. As agents who are capable of free choice, we can surpass or transcend our facticity by seizing on specific possibilities for our lives through our actions. In this way, we shape and define the meaning of our facticity. Thus, the person who had children at an early age has a choice: she can sit around being miserable and taking it out on the children, or she might take on the task of parenting with exuberance and joy, thereby defining this facticity as something overwhelmingly positive. What this shows is that facticity is not a set of causal determinants that force us to act in a particular way; it consists rather of conditions and circumstances that open us up to choice.

Our constant ability to transcend and thereby transform our facticity leads Sartre to the conclusion that humans have unlimited free will in determining their own fate. We are, he says, "condemned to be free" (1946/1995b, p. 274). At each moment, whether we realize it or not, we are shaping our own identities as individuals in the choices we make—whether we choose to go on doing the same old thing or choose to set out on a totally new course. It is true that facticity delimits our choices, but we always have the ability to reflect on that facticity and decide what meaning it is going to have for us. Because there is no way to identify a brute, uninterpreted reality that forces us to act in one specific way—because there is no way to pick out or identify boundary conditions that cannot be reinterpreted and restructured through our choices and actions—our freedom is boundless.

Moreover, if there are no absolutes given in advance that tell us how we ought to act, we have nowhere to turn for guidance or direction in making our choices. People might feel that they are constrained by a particular moral outlook in making their decisions, but moral codes and ethical principles can seem binding on us only if we *choose* to adopt that morality. It follows that when you are faced with a painful choice in a concrete situation, all you can do is simply "leap" in one direction or another. Nothing compels you to act one way rather than another, for any criteria you turn to in making a choice are criteria you are *choosing* to accept in making this choice. Thus, every choice in the end is *radical choice*, a matter of simply plumping for one option over the other, with no basis or justification. As Sartre says (1946/1995b), "No general ethics can show you what is to be done; there are no omens in the world." Ultimately, each individual stands alone, without supports: "there is no determinism, man is free, man is freedom" (p. 276). Because it is up to us to decide how our situation and prior commitments influence us and what goals we have, we cannot assume there are values, principles, or obligations that direct our choices. "So, in the bright realm of values, we have no excuse behind us, nor justification before us. We are alone, with no excuses" (p. 274).

Sartre's conception of our freedom to choose what things mean to us and what factors will affect our decisions implies that we are totally responsible not only for what we do but also for how the world in general appears to us. The upshot of this outlook is that humans have "terrible freedom." This freedom seems terrifying, for no one wants to be held responsible for all aspects of her life. This is why we are inclined to think that what we do is something we *have* to do rather than something we choose to do when, for example, we say, "I have to go to the office to finish up some projects" instead of "I am choosing to go to the office." What this means, in Sartre's view, is that most of us live in "bad faith," the self-deception of believing that we are, in a sense, trapped into doing certain chores and routines when in fact we could always refuse to do these things and do something quite different.

If we come face-to-face with our freedom and responsibility, our lives can be radically transformed. Confronting the ultimate groundlessness of our choices and our total responsibility for our lives can lead to the experience of "existential anxiety" or "dread," the feeling that one is suspended over an abyss with no supports. But this experience is not entirely negative. A person who comes to terms with anxiety can come to embrace a more authentic way of life. Although different existentialists have different conceptions of what authenticity is (see Guignon & Pereboom, 1995, pp. xxxi–xxxv, 1–17, 85–110, 175–202, and 247–267), most agree that it is a way of life that rejects the complacent drifting and conformism of everyday social existence and instead focuses on fulfilling the potentialities of the individual. For Nietzsche (1882/1995), the authentic individual, or *Übermensch,* seems to be a free spirit who plays with all the old absolutes of the past in making his or her life into a work of art. Heidegger (1927/1995), who first explicitly used the word *authenticity*, envisions authentic existence as a matter of accepting our finitude—our "being-toward-death"—and making a resolute commitment to fulfill the deepest possibilities built into the "destiny" of our communal world. And Sartre (1943/1995a) promotes a stance of *engagement* or commitment in whatever "fundamental project" one embraces in imparting a meaning and content to one's life. What these views have in common is a profound suspicion toward the humdrum social circumstances of life and a belief that a person must fully embrace her being as an individual if she is to realize her ability to be a fulfilled human being. As we shall see, the obscurity surrounding the notion of authenticity creates a number of puzzles for those who attempt to formulate an ideal of human existence for existential psychotherapy.

Existential Psychotherapy

Early Existential Theorists: Binswanger, Boss, and May

When existentialist thought first became influential in European psychiatry, it was primarily through the influence of Heidegger on such thinkers as Ludwig Binswanger (1881–1966) and Medard Boss (1903–1991) (Halling & Nill, 1995). Drawing on Heidegger's conception of humans as being-in-the-world, Binswanger (1958) distinguishes three types of world—the surrounding environment (*Umwelt*), the "with-world" we share with others (*Mitwelt*), and (creating a concept fundamentally alien to Heidegger's thought) the individual's "own world" (*Eigenwelt*). In treating a patient, Binswanger holds, we must understand the individual's entire "world-design"—his unique way of constituting the life-world in which he lives. In this view, psychological problems arise when the individual's world "is narrowed and constricted to such a degree [that] the self, too, is constricted and prevented from maturing." Treatment therefore consists in loosening up these constrictions in order to help people recover "the *freedom* of letting 'world' occur" (p. 204; compare with p. 194).

Drawing on Heidegger's conception of a human as a "clearing," Boss (1963) characterizes human existence as a holistic "realm of world-openness" that cannot be reduced to subjectivity. In line with this interpretation of human existence, Boss rethinks some of the core concepts of psychoanalysis. For example, he sees guilt not so much as a matter of a *feeling* resulting from childhood trauma as a manifestation of a pervasive "existential guilt" that results from the individual's inability to realize all her potentialities. According to Boss (1963), existential guilt is a consequence of one's "failing to carry out the mandate to fulfill all [one's] possibilities" (p. 271). One reason why we fail to fulfill all our potentialities is that we follow "acquired moral concepts" circulating in the public world. This public morality is a "foreign and crippling mentality which [a person's] educators forced upon him" (p. 271), and it is something one needs to break with if one is to become an authentic individual. Boss defines the authentic individual as one who "accepts all his life-possibilities" and can "appropriate and assemble them to a free, authentic own self no longer caught in the narrowed-down mentality of an anonymous, inauthentic 'everybody'" (p. 47).

When the existential outlook caught on in the United States, it was strongly influenced by such European thinkers as Viktor Frankl (b. 1905) and R. D. Laing (1927–1989). Under their influence, therapy was seen as more than a matter of relieving misery or fixing people up so they could function. Existentialist theorists see the aim of therapy as enabling people to become authentic, which is understood to mean being freed from an inauthentic, constricted world-experience in order to become the individual one truly is. C. Peter Bankhart (1997, p. 324) sums up this literature when he says, "Existential therapists do not try to help their patients adapt to the social, political, and cultural realities around them. Instead, they attempt to guide patients toward discovery of the 'authentic' self." The conception of authentic existence as the ideal outcome of therapy is central to most American existential theorists. Rollo May (1909–1994), for example, holds that therapy involves "an expansion of awareness, an enlargement of self, a courageous release of potential, in spite of threat, in the context of genuine client-therapist encounter" (Halling & Nill, 1995, p. 31). This project of self-enlargement requires that we embrace and express all sides of ourselves; this is something May thinks we can achieve only by having values that provide a basis for productive and creative commitments in our lives. For May (1953, pp. 175–176), values are needed to serve "as a psychological center, a kind of core of integration which draws together [one's] powers as the core of a magnet draws the magnet's lines of force together."

Recent Existential Theorists: Bugental and Yalom

Similarly, James Bugental (b. 1915) (Bugental & Sterling, 1995) sees the aim of therapy as grasping the client's entire "self-and-world construct" in order to identify the "awareness-constricting and awareness-distorting ways of defining oneself and the world" (p. 232). The aim is to "modify those limiting and constricting patterns" (p. 237) and free the client so that she can realize her potential. To be authentic is not necessarily to be a rebel or outsider in any sense. Bugental (1981, p. 34) points out that authenticity "does not consist in the rejection of the familiar world." An individual does not deny values, activities, associates, or any other aspect of his life; rather, he relates to these social realities in a new way. As Bugental defines it, authenticity is an "ultimate state of at-oneness with the cosmos" in which "our being-in-the-world is in accord with the nature of ourselves in the world" (p. 32).

This definition of authenticity points to two key features of the healthy way of being in the world. First, it holds that the ideal relation to the world involves a "letting go" of mundane attachments and concerns as one directs oneself to higher things. In speaking of the authentic individual, Bugental says, one may employ "the frequently used phrase, 'He was *in* but not *of* the world'" (1981, p. 34). Being in but not of this world means "letting be, an acceptance of all things human, and then a finding of more encompassing ways of being in relation to all such things" (p. 35). Second, this definition of authenticity suggests that both the self and the cosmic order in which the self is embedded have fuller and more meaningful potentialities than are currently being realized or even noticed in ordinary social existence.

In Bugental's view, then, the aim of authentic existence is realizing and expressing the greater potentialities we have within us—being all you can be, as the now hackneyed phrase has it. As examples of these potentialities, Bugental (1981) lists creativity, love, and, above all, commitment. In his more recent writings, however, Bugental observes that it is not the therapist's task to lay out specific goals and ideals for the client. Therapists "are not consultants in how to live. They can be consultants in how to use one's own capacities to better guide living. . . . Change comes when fresh perspectives open up possibilities that formerly were unseen" (Bugental & Sterling, 1995, pp. 245–246). The therapist's contribution is "fostering greater client inner awareness" to aid in "enlarging and changing the client's way of being alive in the world." The fundamental aim is the "freeing and realizing (recognizing and making real) of latent human capacities for fuller, more creative, and more satisfying living" (p. 249). Which capacities to realize, and how one is to be creative, are left up to the client to decide.

Though there is a great deal of open-endedness in the definitions of authenticity found among existential theorists, there is general agreement that being authentic means embracing one's freedom and acknowledging one's responsibility for what one is and does. Irvin Yalom (b. 1931) develops this theme of existential freedom in his important book, *Existential Psychotherapy*. In Yalom's view (1980, p. 218), the authentic individual is one who is "aware of responsibility," which means being "aware of creating one's own self, destiny, life predicament, feelings and, if such be the case, one's own suffering." This conception of freedom, he notes, is derived from Sartre. "Sartre considered it his project to liberate individuals from bad faith [in most cases, the self-deception of thinking one is not free] and to help them assume responsibility. It is the psychotherapist's project as well" (p. 222). Following Sartre, Yalom holds that humans constitute the meaning of the situations they encounter, and they should recognize that they have created their own unhappiness. Thus the therapist "must continually operate within the frame of reference that a patient has created his or her own distress" (p. 231). Only by acknowledging that "one has created one's own dysphoria" can the individual "achieve autonomy and his or her full potential" (p. 268). Here Yalom agrees with Schneider and May (1995, p. 6), who say that confronting one's freedom "is enlivening and health-promoting"; it "promotes a more vibrant, invigorating life-design . . . exemplified by increased sensitivity, flexibility, and choice."

From its inception, existential psychotherapy has been concerned not so much with devising new techniques or accounts of psychic dynamics as with trying to understand the human being in the fullest way as an experiencing, desiring, and willing whole. From this standpoint, we have to understand causal processes and forces in terms of their place within the holistic fabric of meanings that make up the individual's life. The emphasis is on the concrete, *existing* human, not on abstract generalizations or high-level intellectual constructs. Like their philosophical precursors, existential psychotherapists see human existence as an *event*, something that is "always in the process of becoming, always developing in time" (May, 1958, p. 66). This unfolding event of human life is fundamentally futural: existence is "on a trajectory toward its future: a man can understand himself only as he projects himself forward." A "person is always becoming, always emerging into the future" (p. 69). This holistic view of the self as a unique "self-world construct" projected toward realizing specific ends implies that the therapist must understand the individual on his own terms, not as tailor-made to fit a set of pregiven categories.

Nevertheless, existential theorists have tried to make some general claims about the roots of psychological distress. Drawing on the existentialist conception of anxiety, Yalom (1980) argues that anxiety should be viewed not simply as a pathological condition which needs to be eradicated so that people can lead pleasant lives. Instead, anxiety is an ineradicable feature of the human condition, and it is beneficial to the extent that it brings us face-to-face with the groundlessness, fundamental loneliness, and grave responsibility built into the human condition. Existential psychotherapy therefore does not set out to eliminate anxiety: "Though the existential therapist hopes to alleviate crippling levels of anxiety, she does not hope to eliminate anxiety. Life cannot be lived nor can death be faced without anxiety. Anxiety is guide as well as enemy and can point the way to authentic existence" (p. 188).

Yalom (1980) offers an account of the sources of anxiety in terms of four basic "givens" of human existence: death, freedom, isolation, and meaninglessness. These four givens are inescapable facts that confront all humans everywhere. According to Yalom's "existential psychodynamics," the anxiety that results from our awareness of these "ultimate concerns" is a normal and healthy reaction, though in its extreme form it can become crippling neurotic anxiety and the source of pathological defense mechanisms. The role of therapy is to help people face up to these givens and learn to live with a healthy anxiety without slipping into neurotic anxiety and counterproductive defense mechanisms. *Existential Psychotherapy* provides deep and thoughtful descriptions of how therapy can help people confront the brute givens of existence. Concerning solitude, for example, Yalom speaks of the need to accept the timeless, unchanging truth that we are always ultimately alone: "No matter how close each of us becomes to another, there remains a final, unbridgeable gap; each of us enters existence alone and must depart from it alone" (p. 9). Only if we accept our fundamental aloneness will we be capable of a genuinely fulfilling relationship with another.

Similarly, Yalom claims that one must face the fact that there is no pre-given meaning to life, that "the only true absolute is that there are no absolutes" (1980, p. 423). Though Yalom thinks it is important to accept the ultimate groundlessness of life, he also recognizes that people "apparently need absolutes" (p. 422) and so "one must invent one's own meaning (rather than discover God's or nature's meaning) and then commit oneself fully to fulfilling that meaning" through "a leap into engagement." To show what sorts of meanings are available, Yalom provides a "survey [of] the secular activities that provide human beings with a sense of life purpose," identifying such "intrinsically satisfying" life meanings as altruism, dedication to a cause, creativity, self-actualization, self-transcendence, and hedonism. Therapists should encourage clients to opt for one or more of these values, because "patients who experience a deep sense of meaning in their lives appear to live more fully and to face death with less despair"

(p. 431). People should embrace values because they "not only provide the individual with a blueprint for personal action but also make it possible for individuals to exist in groups" (p. 464).

The accounts of death and freedom follow the same pattern. In each case, Yalom points to a fundamental feature of the human condition that causes anxiety and proposes ways of helping people confront that fact without being overwhelmed by anxiety. The goal of this treatment is not to make people happy but to make them more clear-sighted and courageous in dealing with the realities of their lives. In this process, Yalom (1980) says, the focus is not so much on the past—on the cause of a person's problems—as on the future, on how she can change her interpretations and actions in order to face life's realities in a way that is truly her own.

Limitations of the Existential Approach

Existentialism continues to be appealing today because it captures a number of profound truths about the human condition, truths that need to be acknowledged in any form of psychotherapy and taken into account when rethinking psychology and psychotherapy in general. But many have felt that the view of humans in existentialism is too narrow and one-sided to provide a sufficient basis for a general approach to understanding our lives (see, for example, Bernstein, 1971; Taylor, 1985a; Flax, 1988; Guignon, 1986). This section discusses criticisms of several aspects of existentialism, including its views on freedom, the self, and meaninglessness.

The Existential Concept of Freedom

Many critics have focused on the conception of human freedom presupposed by existentialists. We saw that freedom is the pivotal concept in existential psychotherapy: pathology is defined in terms of lack of freedom, therapeutic practice is described in terms of instilling a sense of freedom, and the authentic individual is characterized as a person who is genuinely free. The range of our freedom, as existentialists conceive it, is much wider than the ordinary person might suppose. For such theorists, we are even free to create our past to the extent that each of us decides the meaning the past has in our lives. As Sartre (1943/1995a, p. 333) says, "I *choose* being born"—that is, I choose the meaning my childhood and parents have for me, and if I choose to see my childhood as something that condemns me to misery, then that is my choice, and I alone am responsible for it.

Needless to say, such a view supplies a useful antidote to the focus on victimization in contemporary culture. For Sartre (1943/1995a), "There are no innocent victims." Because it is always up to us to interpret and respond to what is done to us, seeing ourselves as victims simply complies with and helps constitute the behavior of others as victimization. Thus Sartre says, "I am without excuse; for from the instant of my upsurge into being, I carry the weight of the world by myself alone" (p. 332). Although facticity limits an individual's ability to define his context, he decides how his facticity *counts* in relation to his life. It follows that a person chooses his facticity and chooses the ways it can constrain him. Even *other people* are "only *opportunities* and *chances*" (p. 333) for his free, meaning-giving activity. As May and Yalom (1989, p. 378) claim, each individual "constitutes others" and can never know other selves except as she has created them.

Existential theorists conceive of freedom as "negative liberty," that is, as the absence of constraints and the ability to do whatever one chooses. Because each of us is free to decide which criteria and standards will guide our choices, there are no guidelines independent of our choices that we can turn to in making decisions. In facing decisions or moral dilemmas, we have no basis for making our choice, with the result that all we can do is simply "leap" one way rather than another, as the diner surveying equally appetizing pastries on a dessert tray finally just grabs any one of them, with no basis for choosing it over the others. Thus, in Sartre's famous example (1946/1995b), a young man during the war tries to decide whether to stay home and care for his infirm mother or go off and fight with the Resistance. Where can he turn to for guidance? Sartre notes that, in this situation, there is no ethics the young man can turn to, because the choice is precisely between different ethical standpoints—one of filial duty, the other of civic duty. So in choosing his action he also chooses his ethics. How does he decide, then? Sartre answers that he just sets off in one direction rather than the other. He "invents," as an abstract expressionist might decide to splash a little red onto the center of a canvas. There is no pregiven rule book that determines what the "correct" or "better" choice is.

The question has been raised, however, whether such an agent of radical choice is really free at all. Concerning "a choice made without regard to anything," Charles Taylor asks, "is this still a choice?" (1985a, p. 32). If all the agent can do is throw herself one way rather than the other, then she has "no language in which the superiority of one alternative over the other can be articulated" (p. 30). But here "choice fades into non-choice" (p. 31). The agent of radical choice seems to be buffeted about by whatever momentary whims and impulses come along. Far from being an autonomous agent, such a person is no different from a leaf floating down a stream, pushed around by the changing eddies and currents. But this is clearly not an image of freedom at all; it is, if anything, an image of the most complete form of slavery, a matter of being controlled by every passing inclination, with no capacity for steadiness, self-restraint, or meaningful deliberation.

Existential theorists might reply that their vision of freedom does not sink into such paradoxes because, in their view, the agent always has a firm basis of values to depend on in making choices. Thus, as we have seen, May (1953) holds that values are necessary if a person is to achieve integrity and maturity as an individual: "The mark of the mature man is that his living is integrated around self-chosen goals"; such a person "plans and works toward a creative love relationship or toward business achievement or what not" (p. 176). Needless to say, however, the question here is precisely what this "what not" leaves open. When values and projects are seen as things we choose solely in order to gain integration and maturity, and when it is assumed at the outset that no values are intrinsically better than others, then values appear as purely adventitious, mere means to ends, and presumably dispensable in favor of other means—perhaps unbridled aggression or some sort of pill—if those would do the job just as well. If one starts from the assumption that there are no absolutes, then Sartre's claim that ethical systems are as much a matter of radical choice as actions are seems inescapable, and meaningful freedom becomes unintelligible.

The Existential Concept of the Self

The problematic notion of freedom in existentialism springs from the conception of the self in this philosophy. Sartre's view that humans are self-creating, with no essence or identity other than what they shape in the course of living out their lives, suggests that the self at its core is a dimensionless point of choice and action with no determinate characteristics given in advance. Seen in this light, the existentialist self is heir to what Charles Taylor (1989) calls the modern "punctual self" that emerged in the writings of Descartes and Locke, the self as an extensionless center of pure agency which, because it is unconstrained by prior bonds to the world, is capable of making and remaking its identity as it wishes. Taylor shows how this notion of a disengaged self crops up again and again in Western thought from Descartes and Locke to Freud's conception of the ego as a "pure steering mechanism" whose "job is to maneuver through the all-but-unnavigable obstacle course set by the id, super-ego, and external reality" (p. 174). Such a punctual self appears, for example, in Mancuso and Sarbin's distinction (1983, p. 246) between the "first-order self-concept, *I,* self-as-storyteller" and the protagonists in the tales we tell about our lives, "selves-as-objects"; and it is central to Roy Schafer's attempt (1992) to distinguish the teller and the told in self-narratives. In all these accounts, a distinction is made between the self that creates—a self that does not itself have any substantive characteristics—and the various substantive selves created by that primary self.

Despite the appeal of this conception of a totally disengaged, unencumbered self, critics have raised questions about whether such a notion makes sense (see Sandel, 1982). As our examination of the notion of radical choice revealed, it is not at all clear that such a punctual self would be capable of meaningful choice. With no defining commitments or deeply embedded values, what basis would such a self have for making choices? Even if we could answer this question, we might wonder whether this punctual self could contain the resources needed for it to be able to follow the injunction to authenticity, "To thine own self be true." For what self am I to be true *to* if my true self is a dimensionless point of pure choice?

Questions like these have led many existentialists to turn away from the image of the punctual self, which is derived from the rationalist tradition, and turn toward the image of the *substantive self* that comes to us from our Romantic heritage. The substantive self is conceived of as having a rich array of inbuilt potentialities, capacities, and possibilities that it must strive to realize and express in the course of living out its life. This, as we have seen, is how Boss and Bugental conceive of the self, and it seems to be implicit in the thinking of many other existential theorists. R. D. Laing, for example, "hoped that his patients could break through their [socially induced] madness to discover their true selves and live courageously outside the constraints of social, political, and cultural expectations" (Bankhart, 1997, p. 324), and May (1969, p. 19) decries the way that "contemporary outer-directed, organizational man" makes it impossible to actualize "the *individual's unique pattern of potentialities.*"

This substantive vision of the self makes a sharp distinction between the social circumstances of life and the inbuilt capacities and potentialities that make up the "true self." Certainly, this way of thinking of the self marks a retreat from Sartre's claim that existence precedes essence, for it assumes that individuals enter the world with inbuilt characteristics and so have a predefined identity or personal "essence" *before* they begin to express themselves in their actions. Thus even though it abandons

Sartre's antiessentialism, the Romantic image of the self, with its picture of each individual as containing a seed of possibilities that must be brought to fruition, seems worth embracing.

What is unclear about this Romantic image is whether a sharp distinction can be drawn between the potentialities that make up a person's true self, and the social self that emerges in the course of the person's acculturation into a shared life-world. Even if we assume that individuals are born with specific capacities and dispositions, it is not always possible to clearly separate the inbuilt traits from the form these take as a result of upbringing and socialization. An even more troubling worry about this Romantic view is whether it is right to assume that realizing and expressing one's inborn potentialities are necessarily good. For individuals seem to be born with many violent and brutal capacities as well as creative and loving tendencies. In the project of coming to actualize *all* our potentialities, how are we to know which are genuinely worthy of being expressed and which would be better left repressed? Note that if we try to resolve this dilemma by suggesting that social ideals are needed to show us which potentialities we should fulfill, then we can no longer sustain the sharp dichotomy between social self and authentic self presupposed by the Romantic concept of the self.

Existential Accounts of Isolation, Meaninglessness, and Value

A substantive conception of the self seems to be supported by Yalom's intriguing suggestion (1980) that there are human "constants" underlying all forms of anxiety. Thus Yalom makes a convincing case for saying that death is something all humans face (although, as Ariès, 1974, has pointed out, people's understanding of the *significance* of death has changed immensely through the centuries). But a close look at Yalom's other "constants" leads to the suspicion that, far from being human universals, they are in fact products of some fairly recent developments in Western history. Consider, for example, the claim that all humans have to come to terms with their fundamental isolation in the world. Yalom gives a moving account of how "the individual is inexorably alone" (p. 353) in life and how the "unbridgeable gulf between oneself and any other being" (p. 355) makes us aware "of our utter loneliness and helplessness" (p. 398). This description accords well with the pervasive feeling in America that each person ultimately stands alone, with no real connections to anyone else— a feeling expressed to Robert Bellah and his colleagues (1985, p. 15) by an American who said, "In the end, you're really alone and you really have to answer to yourself." Because of this all-pervasive sense of loneliness, "the individual who is flooded with isolation anxiety reaches out desperately for help through a relationship" (Yalom, p. 393).

Now we are certainly inclined to believe that isolation and neediness are universal facts. But is isolation really a human universal or constant in Yalom's sense? Bellah et al. (1985) have argued that the belief that the self is a solitary individual who can only achieve fulfillment through *a* relationship is relatively new in America, a way of seeing things that was first made possible by the rise of modern individualism and the breakdown of an older sense of familial and communal bonds. Rather than being a timeless truth about the human condition, this experience of isolation is a cultural innovation that has generated many of the problems modern therapy struggles to cure. If this is so, however, it may turn out that existential therapy, by treating isolation as an unchanging "absolute," may exacerbate some of the problems it is trying to alleviate. The idea that we are *essentially* isolated individuals who need a "mature" relationship might serve to reinforce an image of our predicament that closes off possibilities of seeing ourselves as initially and at the deepest level *participants* in the wider community of family, neighborhood, village, church, or nation.

The same sort of criticism applies to Yalom's claim that the experience of meaninglessness is a universal and unchanging fact of the human condition. Certainly, given the pervasive angst in contemporary life, there will be people who claim that there are neither aims worth pursuing nor values demanding respect. Once again, however, the evidence shows that this experience of meaninglessness is a relatively new phenomenon in Western thought, one found primarily among those who have been perhaps overly impressed by the impact of secularization and scientific advance on contemporary life. If the feeling of meaninglessness is indeed a cultural innovation, then treating it as an unchanging truth about the human condition may do more to aggravate psychological problems than it does to help resolve those problems.

Moreover, the suggestions for relieving this feeling of meaninglessness may actually have the opposite effect. Theorists like Yalom and May and especially Frankl (1963) try to come to terms with the experience of meaninglessness by proposing a set of possible meanings people could adopt and then encouraging them to "go for" one or two of them. The effect is that of a smorgasbord where people can pick and choose the values and meanings they find appealing. What is wrong with this picture, however, is that if people start thinking of values as lifestyle options on hand for their choice, they will no longer be able to experience the real pull of those values. Why, one might ask, should one latch on to one of the healthy, life-affirming meanings Yalom proposes rather than, say, self-centered cravings for power or gratuitous acts of violence? Why, after all, should one do what is socially acceptable if social norms are seen as inherently conformist and inauthentic?

The section of Yalom's book (1980) dealing with the problem of meaninglessness, titled "Engagement: The Major Therapeutic Answer to Meaninglessness," suggests that the proper response to meaninglessness is simply to glom on to some values and projects in order to endow one's life with meaning and thereby alleviate one's feelings of emptiness. As May and Yalom (1989, p. 390) put it, "Wholehearted engagement in any of the infinite array of life's activities enhances the possibility of one's patterning the events of one's life in some coherent fashion. To find a home, to care about other individuals, about ideas or projects, to build—these and all other forms of engagement are twice rewarding: they are intrinsically enriching, and they alleviate the dysphoria that stems from being bombarded with the unassembled brute data of existence."

May and Yalom are wise enough to see that making a commitment solely in order to feel better tends to be self-defeating. Citing Frankl, they note that "happiness can not be pursued, it can only ensue" (p. 390). Happiness is a felicitous consequence of having a meaning in one's life, not its motive. But we might still ask *why* one should strive to have a meaning for one's life, given the existentialist image of the human condition. If meaninglessness is the bedrock fact of life, isn't it simply a matter of bad faith to delude oneself into thinking there are meanings? It seems obvious that the only reason one would fall into such dishonesty is that life is intolerable without some meaning to help us impart coherence to the cold, brute reality of daily life. But this means that despite Yalom's disclaimers, the justification for our value commitments *is* instrumental: we adopt some meanings and values because doing so helps us feel better or function more effectively or, even more basic, get out of bed in the morning. Yet there seems to be a vicious circularity in this instrumentalist justification of values. For when we ask what existentialists mean by "feeling better" or "functioning well," we find that they usually define these notions in terms of a particular way of life: a life that is loving, creative, productive, and so forth. In other words, existentialists must *assume* the very meanings and values they have already dismissed by claiming that life is meaningless. Their reasoning therefore moves in a circle: on the one hand, they hold that values are justified by their ability to help us achieve such essentially nonmoral ends as happiness or efficacy or ability to function; on the other hand, those ends are themselves justified on the grounds that they lead to a life which is inherently valuable because it includes such things as helping others, being loving and creative, making a contribution to society, and so on.

What this circularity shows is that there is a deep inconsistency in the existential outlook on this issue. For if life really is meaningless and there are no ultimate values independent of the individual's decisions to adopt such values, then there is no basis for advocating that a person live one way of life rather than another. If one needs a meaning, one can simply opt for whatever feels good, so long as one is truly "engaged" and "committed." But this would lead us to conclude that in the end it should make no real difference whether you practice altruism or genocide, whether you create works of art or destroy them, whether you love others or abuse them. "Whatever floats your boat" seems to be the ultimate teaching of this way of thinking. But where all values are up for grabs, purely matters of free choice, they lose the traits that made them values in the first place: their exigency and normative force. The result is the modern situation that Rieff (1966, p. 93) described when he spoke of achieving "the absurdity of being freed to choose and then having no choice worth making."

When we think of values as items on hand for our free choice, and of reality as inherently meaningless and value-free, we will tend to think of ourselves as dimensionless points of raw will who are selecting among options with no basis for making our choices. In the end, the existential outlook, with its distinction between brute, meaningless stuff "out there" and the subject's "inner" leaps of meaning-giving activity, seems to be a prime specimen of what Iris Murdoch (1985, p. 26) describes as the predicament of moral philosophy today:

> Philosophy . . . has been busy dismantling the old substantial picture of the "self," and ethics has not proved itself able to rethink this concept for moral purposes. The moral agent then is pictured as an isolated principle of will, or a burrowing principle of consciousness, inside, or beside, a lump of being which has been handed over to other disciplines. . . . On the one hand a Luciferian philosophy of adventures of the will, and on the other natural science. Moral philosophy, and indeed morals, are thus undefended against an irresponsible and undirected self-assertion which easily goes hand in hand with some brand of pseudo-scientific determinism.

As Murdoch makes clear, the existentialist outlook buys into many of the assumptions that are characteristic of the modern scientific outlook it hopes to supplant. Both existentialism and scientific naturalism assume, first, that the universe consists of nothing but physical stuff that is inherently devoid of value and significance, so values and meanings must be imposed through human subjectivity. Second, they both tend to assume that the subject exists above, or at least outside, the natural order and so can engage in its quest for intellectual mastery and self-realization unaffected by what goes on in nature. Sadly, instead of providing an alternative to scientism, existentialism seems to have merely followed it through to its logical conclusion.

Integrating Existentialist Insights into a Wider Outlook

Our overview of existentialist approaches in psychotherapy suggests that this way of thinking about humans falls prey to many of the limitations and dilemmas that undermine mainstream scientistic approaches. In fact, having arisen hand in hand with the movement toward secularization and technologization of modernity, existentialism both reflects and helps to shape the ways of thinking characteristic of the modern worldview. For this reason we should not be surprised to find that even the most "avant garde" developments in social theory—for example, the social constructionist views we discuss in Chapter Eight—uncritically buy into the existentialist conception of freedom as radical choice.

But our largely critical assessment of existentialism is not meant to suggest that this theoretical framework should be discarded as worthless. For the insights of existentialism continue to provide a powerful alternative to mainstream scientistic approaches, and, as their appearance within hermeneutic theories suggests, they have an enduring value when properly modified and interpreted. For example, Charles Taylor (1978) suggests that the existentialist's respect for freedom can be preserved if it is embedded in a deeper understanding of what freedom is. It is true that the existentialist conception of freedom as negative liberty, as total *freedom from* constraints, can lead to a destructive, anything-goes attitude of doing whatever feels good. But Taylor suggests that we can also envision a more viable conception of freedom, the ideal of positive liberty or the *freedom to* do something worthwhile. This conception of freedom is found in the vision of "situated freedom" Taylor sees in the thought of Hegel. On this account of freedom, the agent is always situated in a cultural and historical context that provides the guidelines and meaningful objectives in terms of which one can deliberate about possible courses of action and make informed choices. From the standpoint of Taylor's account of situated freedom, choosing a course of action is not a matter of radical choice, whereby any course of action is as good as any other (including, as in *The Stranger* [Camus, 1946], gratuitously killing an innocent man on the beach). Instead, choice is a matter of understanding the genuine options that are available, weighing the relative merits of the different possibilities, having the strength of character to see what is best and to act on it, and, finally, doing what is best. Here freedom and being constrained by duty and context are often one; as the old saying goes, "The only meaningful freedom is doing what you ought to do because you want to do it."

It is arguable that the existentialists' emphasis on individual self-realization and authentic existence served as a helpful antidote to the uncritical conformism of postwar America. But one can also argue that this emphasis on the individual has gone too far in contemporary life. As the research done by Bellah and his colleagues (1985) suggests, the extreme ontological individualism in America today tends to undermine our capacity for commitment and helps sustain a society in which calculative, manipulative relations are the norm. Yet there are also traditions within existentialism that tend to counteract this extreme individualism and offer a deeper insight into the primacy of human relations. *I and Thou* (Buber, 1958) stands out as a classic attempt to show the priority of dialogical relations among people, and new readings of Heidegger, such as *The Fragile "We"* (Vogel, 1994), show how a strong sense of "being-with" and ethical responsibility can be central to existentialist thought. According to these more "communal" readings of our situation, individuality is an achievement rather than a given. Because we are initially and inescapably bound together with others in a historical culture, being an individual must be thought of as a *mode* of social existence rather than as an ontological "fact."

Existentialism has always been associated with radical doubts about the foundation of ethics (see Guignon, 1986). Sartre's claim (1943/1995a) that being-in-itself is a meaningless, shapeless "plenum" and that values therefore arise from the projections of individuals seems to support an extreme subjectivism about values—the view that all values are matters of personal preference and feeling, and therefore lack any foundation in objective reality. In a similar way, Nietzsche (1882/1995) and Camus (1956) have concluded that, given this conception of values, nihilism—the complete disbelief in all values—is an inescapable conclusion.

Once again, however, it would be wrong to think that nihilism is a necessary concomitant of existentialism. *Being and Time* (Heidegger, 1927/1995) devotes many pages to showing that humans are being-in-the-world, which is understood to mean that we are from the outset embedded in a shared, meaningful, norm-governed world of tools and social interactions. From this standpoint, the Sartrean picture of brute being-in-itself would appear to be the result of some fairly high-level theorizing, a manifestation of the scientistic assumptions of modernity and not an experience-near description of the everyday life-world in which we find ourselves.

It would be a mistake to underestimate the influence existentialism has had in the twentieth century. A fair assessment of the significance of existentialist thought suggests that we should not reject the approach wholesale but instead thoughtfully integrate its fruitful, albeit one-sided, ideas into current developments in therapy theory. In addition, the insights of existentialist thinkers into the cultural fragmentation of this era and the difficulty individuals have in finding an integrating sense of purpose in modern circumstances are helpful in rethinking the modern psychology enterprise. But existentialism's focus on helping individuals leap out of or beyond this cultural condition into true freedom or self-realization is probably a reflection of modern individualistic hubris, not a cure for it.

PART TWO

BEYOND SCIENTISM AND CONSTRUCTIONISM

6

COGNITIVE THEORY OF
AGGRESSION: A CASE STUDY

SUPPOSE THAT YOU ACCEPT our conclusions in previous chapters concerning the usually unacknowledged cultural and moral values that suffuse modern psychotherapy theory and practice. You might still wonder whether the moral commitments highlighted in these theories and practices are inherent in them or are vestiges of a prescientific attempt to relieve human suffering that can be rooted out through careful scientific conceptualization and investigation. In other words, you might accept that psychotherapy is shot through with contemporary values but still maintain that this evaluative dimension can be eliminated by reformulating these theories and practices along more objective, scientifically justifiable lines. The belief or faith that any such evaluative dimension can be eliminated in favor of more discrete and properly scientific accounts of human behavior and personality is perhaps the cornerstone of mainstream psychology in this century, in both the scientific and professional branches of this enterprise.

Although we have no doubt that many psychotherapeutic theories and practices can be stated with greater precision, we argue that the attempt to conduct value-neutral science is just as likely to perpetuate a "disguised ideology" as are the psychotherapeutic theories and practices we have examined (Bernstein, 1976). We will pursue this line of inquiry by highlighting some specific ideological underpinnings of psychological research, analyzing in more detail the way in which this ideology is hidden by claims to scientific neutrality, and beginning to outline a possible alternative view of human science inquiry.

This chapter presents a case analysis of the ways in which the cognitive theory of aggression presented by Huesman, Eron, and their colleagues

seems to perpetuate a disguised ideology. We have chosen to focus on specific domains of theory and research in this and the following chapter in
order to concretely examine the extent to which social scientists promote
a moral perspective in their purportedly value-neutral research. We hope
that exploring specific areas of research will clarify the subtle and often
hidden influence of cultural and moral values on psychological research. If
these in many ways admirable scientific efforts turn out to be strongly
influenced by unacknowledged moral commitments, we might begin to
doubt the ability of even the most perspicacious investigators to conduct
value-neutral social inquiry, and find ourselves motivated to rethink fundamentally what it means to seek the truth about human action.

In this chapter, we argue that the cognitive theory of aggression exemplifies the prominence of individualism in psychological theory and
research. Although efforts to understand and reduce undesirable forms of
aggression in our society are indeed worthwhile, there is reason to think
that this type of aggression theory and research embodies unacknowledged sociocultural and moral values in a way that distinctly limits its
potential for either fully understanding unwanted forms of human aggression or orienting a practical response to them.

We have chosen this body of work for scrutiny neither because it is deficient with regard to the standards of traditional social science nor because
we see it as entirely lacking in merit. Rather, as we will show, the strength
of Huesman, Eron, and their colleagues' efforts to carefully work out data-
driven, causal explanations of the compelling human problem of aggression makes their work an ideal target for analysis. Moreover, their efforts
have yielded some very valuable insights and illuminated certain regularities that, if understood in the light of a more interpretive framework, can
help us reflect on the daunting problem of aggression in our society.

Cognitive Aggression Theory

We begin with a description of the ways that Huesman, Eron, and their
colleagues attempt to carefully follow scientific canons in their research
program on aggression. First, they emphasize the importance of careful
definitions and operationism. These researchers use a peer nomination
procedure to measure aggressiveness: classmates are asked who among
their peers engages in aggressive behaviors (Walder, Abelson, Eron, Banta,
& Laulicht, 1961). This measurement of aggression has rather impressive
psychometric properties (Eron, Walder, & Lefkowitz, 1971; Huesman,
Eron, Lefkowitz, & Walder, 1984).

Second, Eron (1987) outlines how their results have required them to develop progressively more inclusive theoretical accounts, from Hull-Spence theory to their current "cognitive framework." This progression demonstrates an approach that recognizes the importance of falsifiable theory and is a good example of the dialectic of theory and observation at the heart of scientific inquiry.

Third, Eron (1987) attributes their ability to recast their results in theories that provide better explanations of the data to their use of an operational and behavioral method: "The variables have been explicitly defined, and the measures have stemmed directly from these definitions" (p. 435).

Fourth, these researchers employed a longitudinal design in order to overcome the pitfalls of cross-sectional research and provide some grounds for causal inferences and prediction. Thus, their methods are a good example of the explanatory ideal of psychological research that attempts to explain observable human behavior in terms of general causal laws.

In addition, Huesman, Eron, and their colleagues report a number of interesting and important findings regarding the development of aggression. Their initial research was conducted with eight-year-old children. They report that the following variables were associated with aggression: low nurturance and acceptance from parents, more punishment for aggression at home, more physical punishment, lack of identification with parents, and greater success with aggressive actions (Eron et al., 1971).

Data collected eleven years later show a remarkable stability in the aggressive behavior of the study participants. They report that greater aggression at age nineteen is associated with the following variables measured at age eight: greater aggression, higher degree of upward-mobility orientation of the parents, lower intelligence, watching more violent television, lack of identification with and nurturance from parents, and lower school achievement (Lefkowitz, Eron, Walder, & Huesman, 1977).

A third wave of data again confirms the stability of aggression over a time period of twenty-two years (Eron, Huesman, Dubow, Romanoff, & Yarmel, 1987). Further, the researchers report a substantial level of stability in aggression over three generations (Huesman et al., 1984). The level of aggression at age eight is related to multiple measures of aggression at age twenty-two, including a composite of Minnesota Multiphasic Personality Inventory (MMPI) scales (F, 4, and 9) that indicate overt aggression, criminal and driving convictions, and spouse ratings of aggression (Eron et al., 1987).

Cognitive Aggression Theory and Individualism

Huesman, Eron, and their colleagues identify an impressive array of regularities in human aggression. The influence of individualism emerges most clearly as they interpret these regularities within their cognitive framework. Their interpretation relies heavily on four individualistic presuppositions discussed in preceding chapters: (1) that humans ought to be seen as autonomous individuals; (2) that people are motivated primarily by self-interest; (3) that the nature of purposes and goals is essentially preferential and subjective; and (4) that human goal seeking is best understood in terms of matching the most effective means with individually chosen ends. We will examine how this largely instrumental view of human agency has far-reaching consequences for the understanding of aggressive behavior and the remedies suggested for it.

Aggression as a Problem-Solving Strategy

Throughout their writings, these authors portray human agents as autonomous, strategic actors seeking to maximize outcomes that are merely preferential or individually defined. This means that the authors tend to view aggressive behavior as one of many problem-solving strategies for reaching individual ends. As Eron (1987, p. 439) states, "it is assumed that a child will encode any problem-solving strategy he or she observes if it seems to work." Huesman and Eron (1984) elaborate further by asserting that "social behavior is controlled to a great extent by cognitive scripts, schemas and strategies that have been stored in memory and are used as guides for behavior. . . . Once a schema of strategies for social behavior has been firmly established, it would probably be very resistant to change" (p. 244).

One crucial result of this sort of instrumental focus is that it powerfully restricts these theorists' discussion of any inherent rightness or wrongness of various forms of aggressive behavior. The authors have little to say about why aggression should be studied in the first place or why it is desirable that it eventually be reduced. In discussing the impetus for their research, Eron et al. (1971) give numerous examples of individual and institutional aggression without providing any rationale for why aggression ought to be controlled.

Because Huesman and Eron provide no evaluative basis for the control of aggression, we are forced to infer from their writing what such a rationale might be. Given the strong instrumental cast of their theory of aggression, the only conceivable justification of one type of action over another would seem to be strategic effectiveness. The difficulty here is that it is easy to imagine situations in which aggressive behavior (which may, for other reasons, be undesirable) would in fact be the most effective means to a chosen end. If effectiveness is the sole evaluative criterion, we are left without a rational basis on which to proscribe violence for ourselves or others.

Subjectivity of Purposes and Goals

The proponents of the cognitive theory of aggression relegate considerations of intentionality and values to the subjective realm and do not deem such considerations worthy of or amenable to investigation. For example, Eron (1987, p. 435) defines aggression simply as "an act that injures or irritates another person." He does not address the aggressor's intentions because, according to him, "intentionality is difficult or impossible to measure" in an objective manner (p. 435). Clearly this is an unsatisfactory definition, as it fails to distinguish between, say, physical abuse and some of the activities of a physician, dentist, or psychotherapist! Even accidental injury falls under this definition of aggression. Although Eron seems to recognize this inadequacy, his commitment to a strict separation of the supposedly objective realm of facts and the ostensibly subjective domain of purposes, intentions, and meanings seems to prevent any move to address it.

Unfortunately, this definition of aggression seems to go beyond inadequacy and to lead Eron and his colleagues to misconstrue the responses of their research participants. Although the researchers' operational definition specifically neglects intentionality, participants in their studies would have a very difficult time using the peer nomination procedure without including some ideas about the identified aggressor's intentions. The peer nomination items seem at least implicitly to involve the perceived intention to harm. For example, one item asks, "Who *hits first* in a fist fight?" Another item asks, "Who *spits at* children?" (Walder et al., 1961, p. 504, italics added). Even if these researchers took pains to carefully explain the scientific necessity of disregarding the identified aggressor's intentions, it is difficult to believe that third-grade children would refrain from the commonsense belief that aggressive acts are partly defined by the actor's intentions. Thus it appears that these researchers distorted the description of their measurement in order to meet the standards of scientific objectivity as they saw them.

Taylor (1985a) argues that meaningful human action is actually *identified* by the purpose it aims to achieve, which can be read from interpretations of overt actions and a knowledge of the context. The action may need to be redescribed based on what agents believably tell us about their intentions and the meanings their context has for them. Therefore, the individual's "personal interpretation can enter into the definition of the phenomena under study" (Taylor, 1985a, p. 121). So what we *mean* by aggressive behavior must be partly defined by the actor's intentions and the meaning the action has for her. This behavior would have a different nature altogether if her aims were different.

Such personal interpretations usually involve some sort of ethical dimension. Even to speak of aggressive behavior in the first place would seem to reflect a moral evaluation. To rule out the construal of intentions with their inextricable value component forces a rather absurd equivalence on all decisions and actions. Thus, in the absence of an ethical dimension, the decision whether to compromise with someone or slug them is no different in kind from the decision whether to eat ice cream or cake. On the instrumentalist view, both are seen merely as choices between alternative means to attaining individual satisfactions. Such an approach not only dehumanizes the phenomena being studied but also belies the social and ethical concerns that appear to have originally inspired aggression research.

Individualism and Aggression

A third major consequence of viewing persons as essentially strategic actors is that it limits social relationships to (1) opportunities to obtain some kind of gratification or (2) opportunities to learn more effective means to attain one's ends. This restricted view of human relationships cripples Huesman and Eron's attempts to make sense out of the importance of meaningful social bonds in the development of aggression. In other words, they seem to assume that all human relationships, including parent-child and friendship bonds, are essentially instrumental. This assumption neglects important aspects of human relationships such as attachment, nonstrategic cooperation, and enduring commitments. It seems at least as plausible that these relationships are part of a more meaningful social matrix within which we learn our own place and value and the reciprocal valuing of others. On what basis did these researchers choose the former understanding of humans? Can they justify that choice empirically? They do not seem even to recognize that the choice was available to them: they take the instrumental nature of humans as self-evident (Huesman, 1993).

One example of how this formulation leads to difficulties is Eron's discussion (1987) of the internalization of societal standards against violence, a process that seems to result in less aggression. Guilt and confession related to transgressing these standards are negatively correlated with aggression (Eron et al., 1971; Lefkowitz et al., 1977). What is left unclear, however, is what those standards of behavior are, how they are transmitted, and on what basis these researchers prefer nonaggressive standards to the aggressive norms that are also promulgated in day-to-day living and in the media. Further, how is it that these standards carry moral weight (as indicated by guilt) for some individuals who apparently regard them as more than merely subjective or arbitrary values?

These researchers appear to be backing into a dilemma. On the one hand, they seem to be endorsing social standards against aggression that are compelling enough to reduce violence. On the other hand, the instrumental nature of their theoretical perspective undermines any such conception of moral standards by portraying such values as merely subjective and relative to one's strategic goals. Dilemmas such as these reveal the difficulties that current aggression theory has in dealing with the central issues regarding the sources of aggression and why aggression is undesirable.

One of the major findings in this body of research suggests that lack of identification with parents may be an important factor in explaining why some individuals become aggressive whereas others do not (Eron et al., 1971; Lefkowitz et al., 1977). That is, "as long as children can identify closely with one of their parents, they tend to be nonaggressive" (Eron et al., 1971, p. 123). The importance of identification was explained by Lefkowitz et al. (1977) in the following way: "Our concept of identification is most closely related to imitation by modeling as understood in its broad sense. . . . We found that children who copied their parents' values concerning unacceptable behaviors were lower in aggression than children who did not identify with their parents" (p. 194). Although this may be plausible as far as it goes, it only explains *nonaggression* through modeling. In order to be consistent, it must be shown that aggression in children is developed through identification with and imitation of aggressive parents. The research results, however, suggest that it is the combination of low identification with parents and high parental aggression that predicts aggression (Eron et al., 1971). Thus the concept of parental modeling does not provide anything like a sufficient theoretical explanation of the etiology of aggression. It could be argued, as Lefkowitz et al. (1977) do, that given a rejecting or nonnurturant parent, a child models her behavior on violent actors, as portrayed on television. They do not explain, however, why the child chooses violent rather than benign actor models. If modeling is the avenue for learning aggression, then the reason children choose particular models to emulate becomes central in understanding why some children become aggressive and others do not.

We might hazard an alternative and, we feel, more compelling explanation of this pattern of findings. Perhaps both the child's aggression and the choice of violent television programming are results of a rather non-nurturing parent-child relationship in which a child learns that it is up to her to satisfy her desires and that consideration for others is unimportant apart from self-gratification. Such a limited instantiation of this important social relationship might lead to a devaluation of both self and others, perhaps resulting in the child's viewing persons primarily as either means or obstacles to her ends. In other words, rather than encompassing human relationships in general, the exclusively instrumental understanding of human relationships may best characterize the instances in which the important relationships in an individual's life have broken down.

These authors do not rely entirely on modeling to explain aggression. They also discuss the negative relationship of parents and aggressive children as instigating aggression through the frustration of the child's need or goal to be nurtured (Eron et al., 1971). Although there is a certain similarity between the cognitive theorists' explanation and ours, the difference is that Huesman, Eron, and their colleagues focus on the importance of the parent-child relationship as an arena in which the child's internal need for nurturance is to be filled, whereas our alternative suggests that the parent-child relationship is best seen as the primary social bond within which children learn their own value and how to view and value others. Viewing others primarily as avenues for gratification is only one of the ways social relationships can be construed. A telling point here is that these authors (Eron et al., 1971) do not consider any etiological explanation of aggression that incorporates differences in the ways aggressive and nonaggressive actors regard or evaluate persons and relationships. Their individualist presuppositions apparently constrained these theorists from any consideration of noninstrumental explanations.

Alternative models of human agency and action are available for use in interpreting such phenomena as aggression. For example, from the point of view of Habermas's version of critical theory (1973), the sort of aggression theory we are discussing reflects the collapse, in modern life, of the moral or "practical" into the instrumental or "technical" dimension of human action. Habermas argues that, consequent to such a restriction of rationality, we have highlighted and enhanced our ability to produce technical recommendations but have become increasingly inarticulate and confused in our ability to constructively reflect and deliberate about moral questions. He suggests that what he calls *communicative*

action or *interaction* embodies cultural meanings and values and is governed by "binding consensual norms." Such interaction is different in kind
from instrumental activity governed by technical rules and cannot be
reduced to instrumental activity.

Clearly, Huesman, Eron, and their colleagues have collapsed the moral
dimension of aggression into purely technical concerns. In so doing, they
restrict their ability to understand aggression to narrow categories of
instrumentally oriented individual action, which makes it difficult for
them to appreciate that societal practices, such as parenting, entail views
of persons within which the nature and acceptability of aggression are
defined.

In Chapter Two, we cited the views of William Sullivan (1986) as
describing some of the essential ingredients needed for a kind of social
theory that overcomes the ontological individualism and, in Sullivan's
words, the "liberal instrumentalism" that has dominated twentieth-century social science. We concur in Sullivan's description of human beings
as "intrinsically social" and with his emphasis on how human action and
identity only develop within "a context of interaction" that is "always
and necessarily a moral order" (p. 39). Such a perspective can clarify the
essential connection between aggression and a strategic conception of
human agency. It underscores that individualism itself is a moral standpoint that may actually foster aggressive behavior due to its emphasis on
strategic effectiveness as the primary criterion for evaluating the success
and maturity of human action, a point we discuss more fully in the next
section.

A further and profound consequence of the individualism assumed in
the cognitive theory of aggression is that violence tends to be viewed as
an individual and inherently antisocial act (Lubek, 1986). As such, it
requires social control, because it otherwise interferes with other individuals' "pursuit of happiness." This view leads to two related difficulties.
The first is that aggression is seen as having fundamentally psychological
origins: it occurs because of modeling, the frustration of a child's need for
nurturance, its value as a problem-solving strategy, and so on. This diverts
attention from social conditions involving serious injustice and from social
practices embodying a strategic orientation to living that may well promote continuing violence.

The second difficulty lies in seeing how the violence that is often
involved in otherwise valued social change could be discussed within
Huesman and Eron's approach, as their perspective seems to assume that
the reduction of individual aggression is an unqualified good. This pos-
ture has significant ideological implications. It proscribes noninstitutional

aggression and thereby lends support and legitimacy to an unquestioned role for the state in controlling aggression (even when such action itself involves violence). This viewpoint would tend to preserve the status quo, replete with the social practices and conditions that may well be important factors in giving rise to aggression. Suppose, for example, one viewed the struggle against apartheid in South Africa during the last few decades through the lens of the cognitive theory of aggression. This theory's assumption of the individual and antisocial nature of aggression would significantly distort the reality of that situation and skew our evaluation of many of the steps taken to remedy it. Of course, this is probably not intended by cognitive aggression theorists. But it may be part of the price we pay when we isolate our theory and research from ongoing reflection on our communal life and its ideals.

Aggression Reduction

Many of the problems we have discussed become even clearer when aggression theorists turn their attention to the topic of practical solutions to aggression in society. Eron and his colleagues present a program of behavior modification that would replace aggressive behavior with "prosocial" behavior. They argue "that these two traits, aggression and prosocial behavior or altruism, represent opposite kinds of problem solving strategies which are learned very early in life. If a child learns one mode well, he or she does not tend to learn the other well" (Eron & Huesman, 1984, p. 202).

There are several problems with such an approach to reducing aggression. First, Eron and Huesman (1984) appear to extend their conclusions far beyond their data when they assert that prosocial behavior and aggression are "opposite ends of a single dimension of behavior" (p. 203). The actual correlations between the two variables range from $-.12$ to $-.36$. Such modest correlations offer rather weak support for the interpretation that these behaviors are opposites. Because the statistical relationship does not justify the conclusion the theorists reach, we must look elsewhere for the basis of this assertion.

The instrumental view of human action presupposed by these writers construes persons as problem solvers who restlessly employ any of a variety of means to reach their ends. From this perspective, aggression and cooperation are equivalent as means to attain one's aims and are therefore interchangeable. That is why it is easy to view prosocial and antisocial behaviors along a single dimension. It therefore appears to us that these authors' morally loaded, philosophical assumptions about human action, rather than their data, shaped their conclusion concerning the basic nature and oppositionality of prosocial and violent behavior.

Second, even if it were the case that prosocial behavior and aggression are nothing more than incompatible problem-solving strategies, it is hardly clear that they are simply interchangeable. Current aggression theory has few conceptual resources for making sense out of *why* persons adopt or discard aggressive strategies except for reasons of instrumental effectiveness in reaching pregiven ends. At a minimum, however, a change in a person's aggressive behavior often would seem to represent a profound change in how that person views and values others. These theorists largely ignore important questions as to *why* others are viewed as means to personal ends in some situations and *on what basis* they may come to be valued as people to be treated with respect in other situations. Thus, the straightforward substitution of aggression with prosocial behavior appears a dubious possibility.

Third, the recommendation that aggression ought to be replaced by some form of prosocial behavior is problematic in that this alternative lacks a clear definition. A coherent explication of prosocial behavior would seem to require some concept of what sort of individuals and society we wish to promote. What counts as prosocial depends on what we value as a social group. Eron and Huesman's measures of prosocial behavior (popularity and aggression anxiety) barely imply any such notion of a worthy individual or good society.

Fourth, the program advocated by these authors for the reduction of aggression entails a broad educational and behavior modification program involving community, educational, and parental efforts, without any discussion of the desirability of aggression reduction, of what sorts of aggression are unacceptable, or of precisely what would replace it. They write, "Throughout it has been our assumption that aggression, for the large part, is a socially learned behavior and that manipulation in certain ways of a set of social conditions will produce an aggressive individual, whereas manipulation of these conditions in another way will produce a nonaggressive individual" (Lefkowitz et al., 1977, p. 210). This emphasis on the technology of reducing aggression without any significant attention to the ethical and value issues involved indicates the degree to which Huesman, Eron, and their colleagues appear to have rather unreflectively incorporated an instrumental understanding of social issues that collapses moral questions into technical problems in a way remarkably similar to what Habermas (1973) described.

These theorists are not naïve about the wide-ranging promotion of aggression in contemporary American society. They state, "To produce a diminution in the level of violence, a broad change in values must be effected, hopefully through socioeducational means. In contemporary American society aggression and violence are glorified. . . . When violence is successful in winning a cause, the perpetrators are reinforced and a model of emulation is created. This apotheosis of violence and the implements of violence are the child's earliest fare" (Lefkowitz et al., 1977, pp. 207–208). It is quite apparent that American society encourages aggression as a means of attaining one's ends, and recognizing that fact is essential in confronting the problem.

Lefkowitz et al. (1977) acknowledge how thoroughly interwoven aggression is in American culture in stating, "The conventional view that aggression is a positive trait associated with ambition, the entrepreneurial spirit, and such events as discovery and the technological advancement of a society are actually supported by these findings" (p. 83). Further, they discuss achievement as one of the valued ends of aggression: "In fact, our longitudinal data permit us to state that the conventional view of aggression as a behavior that enhances achievement, particularly of material goods, has some validity. Upwardly mobile fathers apparently serve as salient models of striving and aggressive behavior for their sons" (p. 198).

These findings indicate how tightly intertwined aggression and the highly prized value of upward striving seem to be. But the authors fail to recognize the close connection between the notion of aggression as a means to personal and social advancement and the instrumental understanding of human action built into their own theoretical framework.

Instrumental Theory and the Perpetuation of Aggression

If the cognitive aggression theorists are correct in recognizing a connection between the instrumental focus on individual achievement and the high level of aggression in American society (and we believe they are), then it would seem that the attention of psychologists and other social theorists is misplaced. If our best understanding of unwanted aggression is that it is an outgrowth of a socially prevalent instrumental and individualistic model of persons, then perhaps our attention and efforts ought to be directed toward the illumination and critique of this problematic model of human life. Efforts along these lines would seem both more consistent and more effective than trying to intervene, individual by individual, with those whose behavior becomes (in some way that is yet to be clearly defined) unacceptable as a result of being shaped by this striving, individualistic self-understanding. The conclusion that an instrumental orientation and one-sided focus on competitive achievement contribute to undesirable aggression surely implies that we ought to focus on cultivating alternative models of what sorts of individuals and society we want to develop.

If, however, psychology continues to propagate theories and recommendations (with the social weight of science behind them) that reflect this instrumental view of human conduct, the situation is much different. Psychology will thereby help perpetuate an approach to living that incorporates the individual striving and aggressiveness that characterize current American society. Huesman and Eron's approach to the problem of aggression may actually exacerbate the roots of violence if the exclusively instrumental view of human action and the moral outlook of liberal individualism in which it is embedded really do contribute to both the current fragmentation of society and the resultant aggressive behavior. Therefore, their notion of replacing ineffective aggressive tactics with more instrumentally successful prosocial behavior appears in many ways a recipe for perpetuation of the problem and is unlikely to succeed.

The Moral Dimension of Aggression Research

Our analysis suggests several important conclusions concerning the appropriateness of the widespread, naturalistic self-understanding of the social sciences that views them as exclusively seeking knowledge of functional or causal relationships among variables, subscribes to a narrowly instrumental view of the relation between theory and practice, and assumes that scientific methods automatically protect against the encroachment of ideology into theory and research. First and foremost, we need to recognize that our very definitions of aggressive and nonaggressive behaviors occur in a field of cultural and ethical meanings and values that are not confined to a subjective sphere but help define and shape the ostensibly objective forms of human action we are investigating. The cognitive theory of aggression, for example, seems to reflect a commitment to minimizing most forms of aggression in human affairs, even though our present understanding of their sources and what might replace them is sketchy at best. The cognitive aggression theory narrows our view of unacceptable violence to an instrumental form of individual actions and neglects the influence of cultural values in aggression, thus making it difficult to criticize our current social structure intelligently. These presuppositions render these theorists stunningly inarticulate about which particular behaviors are undesirable and why, and their very definition of aggression is woefully inadequate. This supposedly value-neutral inquiry into aggression helps perpetuate a pervasive form of instrumental individualism that may itself contribute to unwanted aggression.

Second, our efforts to make sense out of aggression and other human action must include the exploration of the dynamics of social actors' intentions and purposes as they arise within a symbolically structured social realm, an exploration that takes us far beyond merely correlating objective indices of various attitudes with observed or self-reported behavior. This need points toward the usefulness of a more hermeneutic view of social inquiry as mainly an effort to understand human actions, practices, and norms in terms of the meanings, purposes, and ideals that they embody. As we will discuss in subsequent chapters, this perspective sees human behavior as constituted within historical forms of life and traditions operative in the community or society under study. This outlook recognizes that knowledge claims are adjudicated within a social order that incorporates and strives to fulfill a more or less explicit set of values, in contrast to the distortions incurred in the attempt to maintain factitious distinctions between facts and values and between objective and subjective domains. Of course, we will continue to adhere to openness and objectivity as paramount values of inquiry—by trying to characterize states of affairs in a manner as free of personal bias as possible and by self-critically trying to see the possible validity of points of view other than our own—but we would not claim access to any sort of brute data.

Finally, as we will discuss more fully in Chapters Nine and Eleven, efforts to understand forms of life seem to have an indelible *practical or moral* aim. They may be better characterized as undertakings on the part of citizens who are concerned to improve their society and better human life than as kinds of detached, value-neutral investigations of an objectively given social reality. But if we acknowledge that human practices, including social science, are imbued with defining values or moral viewpoints, our situation as social scientists is changed drastically. There may not be a "categorical distinction between empirical and normative theory" (Bernstein, 1976, p. 45). Inquiry is not detached or morally neutral but is shaped at the core by our continuing efforts to come to conclusions about what is decent and worthwhile in human living.

If the preceding examination of the unacknowledged values inherent in the cognitive theory of aggression can be replicated with other domains of psychology, then psychological theory and research can no longer remain innocent of these troubling issues concerning the role and justification of values in social science. Progress in clarifying the interlacing of the factual and the moral, the objective and the subjective, in psychological inquiry is unlikely to occur apart from explicit questioning of the disguised liberal instrumentalist ideology that seems to color much psychological theory and research. The moral outlook of liberal individualism, its virtues notwithstanding, seductively promises us that we may have our cake and eat it too. In the social science arena, that outlook suggests that we can remain comfortably value-neutral in our inquiries while supported by an ethic of individual freedom and dignity that virtually guarantees our results will contribute to, or at least not be inimical to, human welfare. Instead, our research into human action is an inherent part of current debates about the nature of the good life. The results of that inquiry may very well call into question the moral sufficiency of our individualistic credo and way of life. The enormous importance and tragic fragility of contemporary marriage described in the next chapter may help further clarify how social inquiry can help us critically reflect on our form of life.

7

INDIVIDUALISM, MARITAL RESEARCH, AND THE GOOD MARRIAGE

THE CONTEMPORARY CRUCIBLE of marriage is another illuminating domain for assessing the degree to which scientific psychology reflects and perpetuates cultural values and confusions. In Chapter Three we noted the centrality of marriage in contemporary American culture and in family therapy theory and practice. Marriage has an extremely prominent place in the scientific study of families as well. Exploring the enormous importance Americans place on marriage will make it clear why this topic provides such a rich opportunity to examine the remarkable intermingling of current popular values and aspirations with social science.

Modern American Marriage

With unfailing regularity, researchers report that marital satisfaction has a very strong correlation with overall personal happiness in contemporary America. For most people, it is more important to personal well-being than friends, jobs, religion, housing, or money. In fact, in most studies, the association of marital quality and well-being is stronger than all these other sources of well-being combined (Lee et al., 1991; Weingarten, 1985). Joseph Veroff and his colleagues are among the foremost researchers of psychological well-being in America. They began to study the early years of marriage because, "[i]n conducting research on the quality of life of the American population, time and again we came to the conclusion that for most adults the cornerstone of a solidly constructed life free from overwhelming tensions is a happy and stable marriage" (Veroff, Douvan, & Hatchett, 1995, p. xii).

Married individuals report greater general happiness than do those who are not married (Lee et al., 1991; Weingarten, 1985). When individuals are dissatisfied with their marriages, however, they are almost always unhappy with their lives as a whole. Compared to those who are not very happy with their marriages, happily married individuals are five times as likely to report that they are very happy overall. Unhappily married individuals are even less satisfied with their lives than the unmarried. This led Norval Glenn, a prominent sociologist of marriage, to conclude that "it appears that having a 'very happy' marriage is almost essential to being personally 'very happy'" (1991, p. 263).

Of course, the whole idea that personal happiness or well-being is of primary concern is part of the overweening contemporary emphasis on the individual, as we have discussed in previous chapters. Both current society and much social science seem to place individual happiness at the pinnacle of human values. Marriage plays a critical role in the nexus of individual and social worlds and is therefore a crucial aspect of our cultural accommodation to individualism. For this reason, marital research makes an especially interesting subject for scrutiny. How can social scientists who wish to maintain some sort of objective or critical detachment vis-à-vis their subject matter properly approach such a loaded topic?

Part of what makes marriage so important is that it appears to be beneficial in more tangible and consequential ways than just shoring up individuals' more or less durable sense of well-being. Married individuals tend to be better off financially. Both husbands and wives earn substantially more money than their unmarried counterparts (Ross, Mirowski, & Goldstein, 1990). Married individuals have a lower risk of illness and greater longevity. Women's mortality is 50 percent higher among the unmarried, and men's mortality is 250 percent higher (Litwack & Messeri, 1989). Married individuals are also much less likely to experience serious forms of mental illness, particularly anxiety and depression. Being married substantially reduces the risk of suicide; divorce more than doubles that risk (Ross et al., 1990; Litwack & Messeri, 1989). It is hard to imagine how we as a culture could emphasize the importance of marriage more than we do.

Given all these apparent benefits, it is hardly surprising that marriage is the most popular voluntary institution in our society. Some 96 percent of Americans indicate that they have a strong desire to marry, and this has not changed over the past thirty years (Thornton, 1989). Although there has been a slight decline in the proportion of people who marry in this country, over 90 percent of all adults do marry at least once (Schoen &

Weinick, 1993), giving the United States one of the highest rates of marriage in the world (Glick, 1988). The popularity of marriage is remarkable in the context of Americans' general dissatisfaction with social institutions and a common disinclination toward long-term personal commitments in our society.

This collection of facts about marriage is usually understood to mean that a satisfying marriage simply is good for individuals. This is a natural interpretation that has been questioned only on the grounds of whether marital quality exerts a causal influence on individual well-being or is merely correlated with it, because both good marriages and well-being are brought about by other causes (Ross et al., 1990). There are other reasonable interpretations of these facts that are rarely, if ever, considered. For example, it may be the case that individuals experience well-being when they believe that their lives fulfill the paramount ideals of their culture, in this case the aspiration toward a satisfying marriage. If these ideals were to change, many of these associations of marital quality with indices of well-being might disappear from the scene. Or it may be that personal well-being and a satisfying marriage are not independent at all, because in contemporary American culture, we define them as mutually entailing one another. That is, our current understanding of what it is to live well encompasses both personal and marital happiness, and we do not understand how we can have one without the other. Later in the chapter, we will explore these alternative accounts and why they are not given consideration.

The Good Marriage

Although simply being married appears to be beneficial in itself, in this culture we place the real emphasis and value on marital happiness or satisfaction—on how spouses *feel* about their relationship. A recent cross-sectional study of expectations for marriage among young people over a twenty-seven year period reported that experiencing love and affection in marriage is far and away the most important expectation for marriage (Barich & Bielby, 1996). In fact, the importance of companionship and emotional security increased over the course of that time span. Barich and Bielby conclude their survey of marital expectations by commenting, "Love continues to stand alone, almost as an a priori element of marriage in our culture, despite the social and cultural change of the last quarter century" (p. 162). Similarly, Bellah and his colleagues (1985, p. 98) note that "Americans tend to assume that feelings define love, and that permanent commitment can come only from having the proper clarity, honesty, and openness about one's feelings." Thus couples remain committed to each other out of desire, not obligation. Although this contemporary vision of love includes a large measure of spontaneity and natural harmony, it also includes a recognition that this kind of relationship is the result of considerable work and risk taking.

These desires are repeatedly expressed in the popular literature about marriage as well. In their recent, widely read book, *The Good Marriage,* Wallerstein and Blakeslee (1995, p. 5) rhapsodize: "We want and need erotic love, sympathetic love, passionate love, tender, nurturing love all of our adult lives. We desire friendship, compassion, encouragement, a sense of being understood and appreciated. . . . We want a partner who sees us as unique and irreplaceable. . . . Marriage provides an oasis where sex, humor, and play can flourish."

Similar examples abound: "In fact, love is what marriage is all about . . . what most people must do to strengthen their marriages is to begin to remember how to be friends, how to play together, how to love each other in ways that rekindle the romance they knew when they were newly in love" (Ruben, 1986, pp. 15–16). "The presence of the mate is indispensable to the feelings of satisfaction which [any] activity provides. . . . An activity is flat and uninteresting if the spouse is not a part of it. Other valued things are readily sacrificed in order to enhance life within the vital relationship" (Cuber & Harroff, 1966, pp. 55–56).

Robert Bellah and his colleagues (1985) highlight very similar themes in their astute study of freedom and commitment in American life. They summarize a common aspiration among their respondents to have a relationship that is "so spontaneous that it carries a powerful sense of inevitability." Such a relationship feels so natural that it promotes a deep sense of belonging, "a sense that the self has found its right place in the world" (p. 91).

Communication and Marriage

Contemporary Americans believe that communication is critical in maintaining relationships in at least two ways. First, according to the expressive strand of individualism, love is the spontaneous flowering of an initial attraction that is deepened by coming to know that person more fully. Thus, in romantic relationships, partners deepen their love and intimacy through talking and spending time together. Similarly, this ongoing open conversation is seen as the key ingredient in maintaining their feelings for each other. In this view, sharing one's thoughts and feelings is indispensable both because expression itself is important to the individual and because continuing to commune together fosters love. It provides the possibility for discovering more about each other and for growth as a couple.

Many Americans believe that being able to listen, understand, and respond to each other's needs continually replenishes a couple's bond. Wallerstein and Blakeslee (1995) highlight the contemporary centrality of nurturing communication by asserting, "The main task of every marriage from the early days of the relationship to its end is for each partner to nurture the other. The loneliness of life in cities, the long commutes, the absence of meaningful contact with people have all sharpened our emotional hungers. More than ever before, we need someone special who understands how we feel and responds with tenderness. . . . A marriage that does not provide nurturance and restorative comfort can die of emotional malnutrition" (p. 239).

Howard Markman and his colleagues (Markman, Stanley, & Blumberg, 1994) highlight the importance of communication to the married individuals they interviewed. Their respondents emphasized friendship over finances, sex, and other areas of marriage: "The major desire people have is for their partner to be a friend. When we ask, 'What is a friend?' people tell us that a friend is someone who listens, who understands, who validates" (p. 84).

This mutual expression and validation of needs and feelings brings up the second way that communication is central to relationships based on love and intimacy. Given the frequency with which the partners' needs and desires come into conflict in any relationship, the ability to communicate effectively to resolve these differences is widely seen as crucial.

As these aspirations about marriage indicate, contemporary Americans hope that marriage will help them cope with their intolerable alienation in a modern society that offers little consolation for their existential plight. Unfortunately, the lack of commitment to anything larger than individual well-being not only is a source of the creeping sickness of social alienation but also has been incorporated into the intimate cure of marriage as well. Because unequivocal commitment is not acceptable, spouses must rely on communication to preserve their marital happiness and to resolve the inevitable conflicts that arise in marriage. In the general absence of firmly held common values, partners can only ask one another to do the work of communicating their needs clearly. If spouses do not meet one another's needs, they must be willing to leave, because, in the end, that may be the only way to pursue one's individual interests (Bellah et al., 1985).

Marital Ideals and Divorce

It is in this context that marriage has become an extremely vulnerable institution in this country. The United States has one of the highest divorce rates in the world. Current estimates of the probability of divorce range from 42 percent (Schoen & Weinick, 1993) to 64 percent (Martin & Bumpass, 1989). Following divorce, a very large majority of divorced individuals remarry, half of whom do so within three years after their divorce (Cherlin, 1992). Americans place such a high premium on happy marriages that we not only marry at a high rate but also are quite willing to leave an unsatisfactory marriage and remarry, seeking a better relationship. Thus, at the same time that we have maximized our expectations for emotional fulfillment in marriage, we have minimized our sense of obligation and commitment to marriage as an institution. This cultural apotheosis of the emotional marriage means that a relationship is good only if it feels good.

One way to understand the paradoxical importance and fragility of marriage is to recognize that we have come to expect an enormous amount from it. If spouses feel that the marriage delivers these goods, they tend to report very strong satisfaction with it (Fowers, Lyons, & Montel, 1996). Individual reports of marital satisfaction are so strong and so prevalent that many investigators doubt their veracity (Fowers et al., 1996; L'Abate & Bagarrozi, 1993).

If the marriage fails to provide the expected benefits, then divorce is a very common solution. Although there is an apparent contradiction in the value placed on marriage in America and this high divorce rate, divorcing is actually one of the strongest ways people express their wish for a satisfying marriage. The more important marriage is to our personal happiness, the more likely we are to divorce if it is not conducive to our well-being. This tendency is made all the more likely considering that happiness in marriage can be somewhat ephemeral and easily lost in the humdrum of everyday life or the tumult of inevitable conflict.

The reasons that couples give for divorcing help make this even clearer. Divorced individuals explain their divorces in many different ways, but the most common reasons are that they had difficulties with communication and intimacy. In her fascinating book on divorce, Catherine Reissman (1990) recounts how divorced people talk about their marriages and divorces. She concluded, "The ideal of a 'marriage of companions' persists in the imaginations of people despite a reality that often contradicts it. . . . Individuals justify their divorces on grounds that the ideal's central components—emotional intimacy, primacy and companionship, and sexual fulfillment—were lacking" (pp. 23–24).

Marriage and Modern Individualism

Of course, this conundrum is a relatively recent one. The high frequency of divorce is unprecedented, and marriage has not been seen primarily in terms of personal fulfillment until very recently (Hareven, 1987; Mintz & Kellogg, 1988; Shorter, 1975). In the premodern era, marriages were more frequently arranged—among the aristocracy on the basis of political considerations, among the peasantry for economic reasons. Thus there was little or no expectation for romantic fulfillment. In fact, experiencing the passionate love we currently idealize was seen in earlier times as a kind of madness or loss of self-possession.

The rise of the modern aspiration toward satisfying and companionate marriages seems to be an outgrowth of the development of the modern identity (Taylor, 1985b). As the primacy of the individual has increased over the past several centuries, personal fulfillment has become central to the good life (Bellah et al., 1985; Taylor, 1989). Whereas premodern people saw the worth of their lives primarily in the fulfillment of a role or place in a meaningful cosmic order, modern agents view the fulfillment of their inner needs and desires as a primary indication of how well they are living. As we noted earlier, that fulfillment appears to be largely contingent on participating in a satisfactory marriage in contemporary America. As David Popenoe (1993, p. 533) has expressed it, "Traditionally, marriage has been understood as a social obligation—an institution designed mainly for economic security and procreation. Today marriage is understood mainly as a path to self-fulfillment. One's own self-development is seen to require a significant other, and marital partners are picked primarily to be personal companions. Put another way, marriage is being deinstitutionalized. No longer comprising a set of norms and social obligations that are widely enforced, marriage today is a voluntary relationship that individuals can make and break at will."

The idea that abiding love is the key to a lasting marriage may actually be indispensable to individuals in this society, for several reasons. The most important is that it helps preserve an essential sense of individual autonomy while allowing for a kind of ongoing commitment. As Bellah and his colleagues (1985) show so compellingly, the overriding importance of individual freedom in American life makes unconditional commitment virtually impossible. If individuals are to feel truly free to live their own lives, they must be able to alter or terminate their commitments as they see fit. Feeling bound by strong obligations would substantially curtail that freedom. If, however, one can maintain the feeling of love for and freely given attachment to one's spouse, then freedom is preserved because commitment derives from one's own desires, not through constraint. To the extent that a marriage is characterized by belonging, intimacy, and nurturance, the relationship appears to "meet the spouses' individual needs," and continued personal commitment and investment in the marriage are consistent with the freedom to pursue the spouses' individual aims. In the absence of this need fulfillment, commitment seems like an unreasonable burden that is difficult to justify. The difficulty with this cultural response to the freedom-commitment dilemma is that marriage has become increasingly fragile as commitment has become secondary to the personal gratification expected from the relationship.

Appreciating the role marriage plays in our shared understanding of the good life helps us understand why people invest so much in such a brittle institution. Our contemporary perspective on marriage has arisen as part of the development of individualism. One of the defining features of individualism is that it obscures the importance of the contextual and intersubjective aspects of experience so as to heighten the appreciation and pursuit of individual aims. From an individualistic perspective, the quality and stability of marriage are seen as a result of the desires, decisions, and skills of the individuals involved. But this leaves no conceptual space for understanding how the contemporary fragility of marriage is related to a widely shared view of the good life, one in which personal fulfillment experienced in marriage plays a central role.

The contemporary importance of companionate marriage is part of what Taylor (1989) has called "the affirmation of ordinary life." In traditional society and moral philosophy, such as Aristotle's ethics, ordinary life, including marriage, served mainly as a needed context or infrastructure for the pursuit of "higher" goods or excellences. Post-Reformation views, however, place ordinary life at the very center of the good life. Living well is now less a matter of participating in some distinctively higher or nobler activity, such as contemplation or monastic life, than a question of how this ordinary life itself is led. The initial emphasis on leading a godly life has been gradually transmuted into the contemporary concern with individual contentment or well-being. Because the Protestant reformers wanted to emphasize our unmediated access to the divine, many located our connection with that higher realm in our inner experience. Over time, the importance of God in this inner life has been effaced, and spontaneous inner feelings themselves have come to be seen as the best indicator of the quality of our lives.

The attempt by contemporary social science to abstract itself from the societal values regarding marriage was doomed from the beginning. As we shall see, the mainstream ethical vision of marriage as a crucial feature of the good life is an obvious and inherent component of marital theory and research.

Psychological Science and the Good Marriage

Through most of its history, psychology has approached such problems as the paradoxical importance and fragility of marriage through the pursuit of universal, context-free laws of human behavior, in the hopes of eventually explaining the behavior in question and rendering it controllable. There is a voluminous and rapidly growing literature on the quality and stability of marriage and a widespread therapeutic and educative effort to deal with the problems of marital dissatisfaction and dissolution. The supposed detachment and neutrality of this well-intentioned endeavor are belied by the fact that the scientific effort tends to embody the same aspirations and ideals as the popular conception of marriage. Moreover, social scientists are no less concerned about the decline of marriage than any other observers (Glenn, 1991; Glick, 1988; Popenoe, 1993). Many of these researchers see the methods of social science as the best way to understand and combat the miseries attendant to marital distress and dissolution. The concordance of popular and professional emphasis on the importance of marriage, the shared concern about marriage, and the widespread consensus about what constitutes a good marriage make this an ideal topic for exploring social science as a form of morally grounded social practice.

The Centrality of Marital Satisfaction

Marital happiness is not only of great importance to the general population but also the most frequently studied topic by marriage and family researchers (Glenn, 1990; Spanier & Lewis, 1980). There has been a great deal of debate about how best to conceptualize and measure marital quality, but virtually all of it has centered on capturing the emotional or narrowly interpersonal experiences that ultimately refer to personal satisfaction or contentment. The attention social scientists pay to theory and measurement is in the service of efforts identifying the factors that make successful marriages possible. This good-faith effort is an attempt by marital researchers to develop the kind of theory that can predict the conditions for marital quality and stability and help foster those conditions to enhance marriages and reduce the frequency of divorce.

The narrowness and consistency of the definition of a good marriage is one of the most interesting features of research on marriage. Whether social scientists are attempting to identify the "causes" of good marriages, the differences between distressed and nondistressed couples, or the effectiveness of marital therapy, they rely on essentially the same concepts to assess marital quality: almost invariably, they define good marriages in terms of individual satisfaction, individual adjustment to the marriage, or individual perceptions of intimacy in the marriage, all of which are virtually indistinguishable empirically.

In the most authoritative review of longitudinal research on marriage, Karney and Bradbury (1995, p. 16) note, "Marital researchers have rarely explored outcomes other than satisfaction or stability." Even after they point out the narrowness of social scientists' notions of a good marriage, they do not propose broadening our conception of the good marriage to consider other aspects of marriages that might be viewed as indicators of its quality, such as commitment, loyalty, the extent to which the couple has common aims, and so forth.

The most widely used measures of marital quality are the Marital Satisfaction Inventory (Snyder, 1981), ENRICH (Olson, Fournier & Druckman, 1987), and the Dyadic Adjustment Scale (Spanier, 1976). The first two contain multiple scales designed to assess how satisfied the individual is with various aspects of the relationship, such as communication, conflict resolution, leisure activities, the sexual relationship, and so forth. The Dyadic Adjustment Scale is the most commonly used measure for research with couples; it focuses on the individual's perceptions of satisfaction, cohesion (relational closeness), consensus, and "affectional expression." These domains are clearly consonant with the popular emphasis on satisfaction in marriage.

Marital quality has a second dimension that is frequently studied as well. This includes marital instability, disharmony, and other indicators of marital difficulties. Interestingly, these measures are empirically relatively independent of the positive indicators of marital quality (Fincham & Linfield, 1998; Johnson, White, Edwards, & Booth, 1986). Although these scales do not measure satisfaction, they are concerned with the likelihood of divorce (marital instability) or with marital conflict and disaffection. They also reflect the popular concern with marital distress and dissolution. Therefore, in spite of the impressive psychometric validation of these scales, their content—the ideals or understandings about marriage they reflect—is quite similar to contemporary American cultural expectations and concerns.

This overwhelming consensus in popular and professional conceptions of what is desirable in marriage (the impressive jargon of professional accounts notwithstanding) belies the pretense of value-neutrality in marital research. Social scientists identify the good marriage with individual satisfaction, thereby accepting the widely held individualistic perspective on what is valuable in marriage, which has proven to be a particularly problematic conception. This perspective has been linked by many commentators with the high rate of divorce in the United States (Bellah et al., 1985; Fowers, forthcoming; Furstenberg & Cherlin, 1991). This scientific emphasis on emotional gratification in marriage may very well heighten the already excessive popular expectations of marriage, thereby inadvertently helping to maintain or accelerate the rate of divorce.

Communication in the Scientific Account of Marriage

In studying the presumed causes of marital satisfaction, marital researchers have focused the vast majority of their attention on examining communication patterns and on devising ways to improve such communication. Numerous studies have been conducted with a focus both on observations of couples' communication (for example, Gottman, 1994) and on their self-reports of that communication (for example, Fowers & Olson, 1986; Snyder, 1981). Social scientists often advocate training in very specific communication skills as the key to perpetuating marital satisfaction and reducing the likelihood of divorce (Gottman, 1993; Markman, Resnick, Floyd, Stanley, & Clements, 1993). Teaching these skills in some form is a part of almost all approaches to divorce prevention, marital enrichment, and marital therapy (Gottman, 1994; Markman et al., 1993; Guerney, Brock, & Coufal, 1987). In general, these efforts seem to involve supporting marital stability through understanding and increasing personal satisfaction in marriage, which is deemed dependent on improving communication, enhancing intimacy, fostering an egalitarian relationship, and encouraging spouses to work to improve their marriages (Fowers, 1998). There is an undeniable logic to this viewpoint if you take happiness with the marriage as the sole or primary criterion of its quality and see the development of a satisfying relationship as a technical problem primarily dependent on the acquisition of good communication skills.

In a book designed for popular consumption, Howard Markman and his colleagues (1994) begin with a standard exhortation about the importance of good communication in resolving the inevitable conflicts of marriage. They assert that the ability to work out conflicts depends on good communication: "Contrary to popular belief, it's not how much you love each other that can best predict the future of your relationship, but how conflicts and disagreements are handled. So if you want to have a good marriage, you'd better learn to fight right" (p. 1). Similarly, John Gottman, perhaps the most prominent marriage researcher, proclaims that "a lasting marriage results from a couple's ability to resolve the conflicts that are inevitable in any relationship. . . . I believe that we grow in our relationships by reconciling our differences" (Gottman & Silver, 1994, p. 28).

This focus on communication skills reflects a technical approach to dealing with the widespread disaffection within and dissolution of marriages. Marital researchers assume the centrality of marital satisfaction and see communication skills as the means for attaining that good. One of the consequences of this degree of emphasis on a technical solution is that the goal—marital satisfaction—is seldom, if ever, questioned. In this way, the researchers sustain and strengthen the popular conviction that positive feelings about the relationship are the central good worth pursuing in marriage.

This is another example of the modern tendency to collapse the moral dimension of life into the technical realm of human action (Habermas, 1973). By emphasizing the technical, we limit our ability to more fully understand and reinterpret the goods we seek to promote. That is, within this exclusively technical framework, questions cannot even be raised about whether we wish to continue to promote the contemporary ideal of marriage. The instrumental cast of contemporary society makes it easy for marital researchers to maintain the illusion that they employ value-neutral "techniques" that are not inherently tied to one or another view of the good life. Such "techniques" are not morally neutral: they advance, reinforce, and extol one ethical outlook or way of life and discourage and undermine others. Therefore, an unexamined emphasis on technique and effectiveness constitutes a serious form of moral blindness.

To be sure, marital researchers have identified empirical links between marital communication, satisfaction, and stability. They have identified particular communicative behaviors that are implicated in marital distress, disaffection, and, in some cases, physical abuse. This is all rather impressive, and marital theory and research may contribute to a worthy public policy agenda of helping us cope with and reduce the palpable human distress resulting from marital distress and dissolution.

In fact, responses to marital communication and marital satisfaction scales have such strong empirical relationships that there is some question of whether they are really measuring distinct phenomena (Olson et al.,

1987; Snyder, 1981). Virtually no one reports that they have a happy marriage unless they feel that they have good communication, and vice versa. These research results show us how thoroughly these two concepts are intertwined in our society.

Toward an Interpretive Approach to Marital Research

All of this research and theory is premised on the notion that this enormously important and fragile form of marriage arises from a set of universal, causal laws of behavior. Following his success in predicting marital dissolution on the basis of communication difficulties, Gottman (1994) states triumphantly that "the social world appears to be quite lawful, predictable, and understandable" (p. 409). But what if, as many social commentators have suggested (Bellah et al., 1985; Lasch, 1978; Taylor, 1985a), this excessive stress on individual emotional fulfillment and instrumental action is itself the underlying problem? Standard psychological theory and research are then obviously out of their depth, because they assume the primacy of individual perceptions and desires. Psychological research on marriage assumes that marital difficulties are the result of narrowly personal or interpersonal shortcomings and recommends teaching communication skills to troubled couples.

These researchers fail to recognize that the modern understanding of marriage represents a rather unique and anomalous interpretation of this institution. They do not take into account the fact that marriage has been understood in very different terms at other times in history, primarily as an economic, social, or political alliance within which satisfaction, intimacy, and romantic love were not particularly expected. Marital researchers have assumed that our contemporary understanding and experience of marriage is a largely universal and timeless reality. They go on to develop elaborate theories and interventions to improve marital communication and satisfaction without pausing to reflect on this problematic conception of marriage. Social scientists have placed the responsibility for the well-being of both spouses and the marriage so resolutely within the narrow interpersonal world of the two partners that they have helped obscure the social conventions and practices that maintain this form of marriage. This predominant approach proceeds as if marriage does not have a sociohistorical context and assumes an instrumental perspective on relationships. In fact, the nearly exclusive focus on the couple obscures the historical and social sources of our current situation and, of course, perpetuates the need for experts to study, train, and advise couples.

It is important to realize that we have defined marriage in a particular way in this society and that we expect certain benefits from it. To some degree, marriage delivers. But the benefits of marriage for individual health and well-being are not independent of our way of looking at marriage and the burdens we place on it. In other words, we have collectively decided over the past few hundred years that marriage would be the primary source of personal well-being in our society. For that reason, we expect it to enhance our happiness and are very distressed when it does not. If we did not have these kinds of expectations, the situation would be very different.

The centrality of marriage in the good life is a social convention or agreement, not the result of natural laws of human behavior. The current state of marriage, with all of our confusion and dismay, is not a natural phenomenon, nor is it inevitable. One of the unfortunate consequences of social scientific interest in marriage has been the impression that marriage can be understood primarily as the product of causal forces rather than as a human institution shaped by human desires and imagination. Unfortunately, the emphasis on studying and therapeutically improving marital satisfaction, intimacy, and communication may actually increase the pressure on the marital relationship, as these efforts tend to raise expectations and add the presumed authority of science to the promotion of these aims. Thus, standard scientific and therapeutic approaches to the dilemmas of contemporary marriage have considerable potential for reinforcing these dilemmas rather than resolving them. This analysis suggests that for us to comprehend and respond to the dilemmas of modern marriage, we must carefully examine the cultural history of marriage and its place in our evolving framework of meaning and values. This is a task that standard social science appears singularly ill-equipped to handle.

It seems clear that contemporary marital theorists and researchers have adopted an understanding of marriage that is strikingly similar to the popular conception of it. One might wonder, Is this conjunction merely a matter of poorly conceived science, or is it an inevitable feature of the effort to work out this sort of difficult social problem? From a hermeneutic point of view, the incorporation of contemporary ideals and aims in social inquiry is to be expected. After all, social scientists are embedded in the same social world as those they study and are likely to be captivated by very similar concerns. In subsequent chapters, we will broach the thorny question of how social scientists can bring needed, genuinely critical perspectives to bear on a subject matter in which they are so intimately involved.

For the moment, let us underscore that current marriage theory and research is profoundly shaped by the same sort of liberal instrumentalism we find in cognitive aggression theory and research—an ideology according to which, ideally, individuals' expressive sensibility tunes them into unique personal desires and goals while various instrumental skills and activities permit these desires to be satisfied. Once we step back and look at it, it is strikingly evident that marital investigators are every bit as much socially and historically conditioned as those they study.

This unacknowledged adoption of individualistic ideals shows that marital research is intimately tied to a particular moral framework. In a manner strikingly similar to the cognitive theory of aggression examined in the previous chapter, this domain of social inquiry appears to have an essential moral dimension. Because marital happiness is so obviously a culturally valued and morally loaded topic of inquiry, the example of marital research drives home the impossibility, almost the absurdity, of a strictly morally neutral form of human science inquiry. Attempting to understand the way we live requires investigators to come into contact with the goals and ideals that animate a form of life and to orient their research around them. Investigators are immediately plunged into the midst of an intensely ethical and rhetorical debate just by taking up the challenge of defining or clarifying what we mean by a good, functional, satisfying, adaptive, or successful marriage. In a quite literal sense, researchers and those they study are engaged in an ongoing struggle and dialogue about what kinds of marriage and life are truly worthwhile. Although scientific approaches to understanding marriage recognize that we are not neutral about the form our marriages take, they tend to relegate this evaluative dimension to the subjective realm, failing to recognize that the contemporary conception of marital quality is a cultural convention that shapes both scientists' and spouses' approaches to marriage.

Even if we assume that social science is inescapably imbued with contemporary values, does that mean that we should abandon this enterprise? We may come to feel that the search for universal, ahistorical laws regulating marriage and other human activities is misguided. Such a proposition would seriously alter the way we understand social inquiry. If we adopted a more interpretive approach, much of the available research on marriage (and other topics) might yet retain its importance and relevance. However, the *purpose* of the inquiry would change from searching for universal laws of behavior to attempting to discern how marriage is understood and enacted in this particular time and society. And the *meaning* of many findings to date might turn out to be somewhat different than is currently thought.

The search for regularities in particular forms of life would remain an important facet of this kind of social inquiry. Marital behavior, like most important human activity, is clearly rule governed. In a hermeneutic perspective, however, we need not see these rules as either universal or as describing causal processes that bypass human agency and creativity. Rather, to a great degree, we should understand them as reflecting norms and conventions that embody a societal vision of the good and decent life.

It is indeed instructive to know that divorce rates have doubled since the early 1960s (Schoen & Weinick, 1993), that marital quality and stability can be predicted (Fowers & Olson, 1986; Gottman, 1994; Markman, 1981), that the majority of individuals who divorce remarry (Cherlin, 1992), and so on. Significant regularities of marital life can be brought to light through empirical investigation. But they are likely to remain unhelpful, relatively trivial, or even misleading without some deeper perspective on their meaning. Research does serve to confirm the prevalence and importance of our cultural beliefs about marriage, but without an appreciation of that cultural and moral background, contemporary mainstream ideologies tend to be misconstrued as general laws of marital behavior.

Given the dilemmas of modern marriage and the tendency for psychology to perpetuate them, it becomes essential to move beyond the presumed naturalistic description and explanation of marriage and to raise questions about the validity and desirability of contemporary ideals of marriage. Inquiry directed toward more fully understanding the cult of marital satisfaction and the cultural pattern that promotes it may serve as a starting point for altering the virtually unquestioned prominence of this ethic. This would involve raising such questions as, Why is personal satisfaction with the marriage the primary criterion of marital success? Why is marriage (or some similar romantic arrangement) generally seen as a requirement for a personally fulfilling life?

To begin to examine these kinds of questions, marital researchers would have to recognize the obvious narrowness of the current ambit of marital research. To think of marriage primarily in terms of personal satisfaction, marital stability, intimacy, social exchange, and so on seems appallingly thin. Unless marital researchers participate in developing or reclaiming some deeper language of marital relationships, we will continue to perpetuate the current self-defeating and brittle character of marital relations. Moreover, this misplaced attention tends to obscure other aspects of marriage that may prove more important for enduring commitment and the well-being of spouses, children, and their communities. It is not at all clear why inquiry into marriage has not included the study of questions involving loyalty, sacrifice, the place marriage has in the community, the importance of shared purposes and meanings, the bonds forged through shared suffering and pain, how ideals are collectively embodied within marriage, how being marriage shapes individuals, and so forth.

The primary point is that we must recognize that psychological research is not conducted in a moral vacuum. Rather, it appears to be a fundamentally moral enterprise designed to improve human welfare, an enterprise that will inevitably tend to promote some ideals over others. Marital research serves as an illustration of what is at stake in psychology, but it is far from unique in its tendency to reflect the moral thrust of contemporary culture. Although portraying science in culturally relative terms may be unacceptable to some, we believe that this portrayal makes the relevance and importance of social inquiry clearer and more compelling. The price of this social relevance is that we accept our accountability for the values and aims that guide our research enterprise and seriously sift and refine the ideals our work promotes. There appears to be little to lose in this kind of transformation except perhaps an illusory promise of eventual certainty and a deceptive belief that psychology could somehow remain above the ever-tumultuous cultural debate about what kind of life is truly worth pursuing. Accepting responsibility for the ethical positions we espouse as psychological theorists and researchers is the entry requirement for psychology to begin to take on its heretofore disguised and unacknowledged role as an important form of public philosophy.

8

CLASHING VIEWS
OF SOCIAL INQUIRY

MUCH ACADEMIC PSYCHOLOGY has managed to seal itself off from contemporary debates about the nature of knowledge, its own historical embeddedness or the extent to which it is socially constructed, and its entanglement with moral values and political forces. Few psychologists critically evaluate the metaphysical and moral underpinnings of their methods or theories. They are not taught how to inquire into these matters, and there is little encouragement or support for doing so. Nowadays, however, it is harder for psychological researchers or theorists to isolate themselves from the widespread questioning that has swept the academic world regarding the linkage of knowledge claims with various interests and ideologies.

In today's world, it is also increasingly difficult for psychology to avoid getting caught up in the vehement ideological strife or "culture wars" among conservatives, liberals, Marxists, postmodernists of various stripes, and others. Many of these theorists offer critiques of social science that are illuminating, but even if they identify a real problem or issue, they rarely indicate how to resolve it. Psychological researchers may often be naïve about the implicit epistemology or moral ideals that guide their activities, but they usually wish to carry out their investigations in an unbiased, scrupulously fair manner, even if it is not always entirely clear just what this means or how it is to be done. Certainly, they do not wish to abandon their self-image as neutral scientists for the role of naked partisan for one or another ideology or cause. To participate in the current discussion about the nature of knowledge and inquiry, theorists and researchers require some sort of coherent overall framework within which they can begin to evaluate the merits and drawbacks of widely divergent views about social science inquiry.

Some of the more astute critics of modern social science insist that its scientism masks a highly contentious ideology and program for living centered on individualism and the technical mastery of nature, our institutions, and ourselves (Bellah, 1983; Bernstein, 1976; Taylor, 1985a). At last, however, we may be getting to the point where we can take fuller responsibility for the ethical aims that inevitably imbue our activities, instead of slipping them in unnoticed under the cover of "science," technical expertise, or value-neutral psychotherapy. Perhaps taking such responsibility is part of the greater "mature adulthood" Michel Foucault (1987) called for in his essay "What Is Enlightenment?" Foucault encourages us to desist from being either the perpetrators or victims of what he calls *Enlightenment blackmail,* which we might freely translate as "Do you agree with my Enlightenment program of science, rationality, and progress, or are you an unenlightened dunce?"

Acknowledging that social inquiry may be indelibly linked to ethical reflection touches on some of our deepest hopes and fears and raises all sorts of difficult questions. What becomes of the mainstream social science program of value-neutral inquiry? What metatheoretical view concerning the nature of social inquiry and the role of cultural and moral values in that inquiry would we, at least in part, put in the place of the mainstream view? Does the departure from familiar "objective" social science plunge us into a chaotic or destructive relativism? What particular cultural or moral value commitments do we wish to guide our theoretical and research undertakings, and how would we justify them? No wonder we vacillate between denial and frustration in confronting these issues. Clearly we have been made the target of that fabled Chinese curse: "May you live in interesting times!"

To begin with, let us note that there does seem to be a pervasive influence of cultural and moral values on the methods and results of inquiry in the human sciences. In an influential paper published over thirty years ago, Isaiah Berlin (1961/1982) asserts that the "first step to understanding" human beings "is the bringing to consciousness of the model or models that dominate and penetrate their thought and action," and determining "the content as well as the form of beliefs and behavior." He stresses that people's "beliefs in the sphere of conduct are part of their conception of themselves and others as human beings." This conception, in turn, consciously or not, is "intrinsic to their picture of the world." Any change in our dominant models or paradigms means a change in "the ways in which the data of experience are perceived and interpreted." Moreover, the categories of this interpretation have a "direct connexion with human desires and interests" and "are shot through with evaluation." Berlin asserts that social and political theory, like all human activity, involves taking up "metaphysical and ethical positions." Therefore it must explain the "normative" notions inherent in those positions and seek some "justification of their validity" (p. 13). It is no wonder that Bernstein (1976) credits Berlin with early insights into the idea that human beings are "self-interpreting beings" whose basic beliefs, meanings, and values are not simply "subjective states in their minds" but are "constitutive of the actions, practices, and institutions that make up social and political life" (p. 61).

Nowadays it is increasingly hard to find social scientists willing to defend the complete value-neutrality of their disciplines. Many have at least heard rumors to the effect that, in a postpositivist era, it is believed that observation itself depends on theory and that the confirmation or rejection of theories is not determined by any strictly neutral algorithm but is influenced by other norms of scientific communities and traditions (Bellah, 1983; Bernstein, 1983; Spence, 1985).

There are two common ways of responding to this troubling entanglement of science with values in the human sciences. One is the familiar approach of making a sharp distinction between the so-called context of discovery and context of validation. In the context of discovery, it is said, all sorts of intuitive, speculative, or value-laden guesses as to possible explanatory hypotheses are allowed. But claims to knowledge can only be verified in the context of validation, in a strictly objective manner. The second way is more sophisticated and increasingly influential. This approach admits the indelibly value-imbued character of our accounts of human activity or the "social determination of truth" (Lukes, 1987) and goes on to embrace the thoroughgoing relativism such a view seems to imply. The philosopher Richard Rorty (1987) recommends this approach as offering an upbeat kind of "ungrounded hope" that "gives mankind an opportunity to grow up, to be free to make itself, rather than seeking direction from some imagined outside source" (pp. 253–254).

The first of these approaches is surely inadequate. It fails to do justice to Kuhn's widely accepted contention (1970a) that even in the natural sciences there is "no neutral algorithm for theory choice, no systematic decision procedure which, properly applied, must lead each individual . . . to the same decision" (p. 200). The second approach, in spite of its stress on the historical embeddedness of social inquiry, may not acknowledge fully how intimately cultural and moral values are implicated in the articulation of social knowledge. For example, Guignon and Hiley (1990) argue that even though Rorty asserts that all our constructions of social reality and our own identities are thoroughly "ungrounded" and revisable, his own thought seems still to presuppose some version of the "classical liberal belief that a society designed as a neutral matrix to promote freedom . . . will naturally lead to the public good" (p. 357). In other words, even this kind of thoroughgoing antifoundationalism may turn out to be inseparable from certain ethical commitments. So, we are left to wonder, is there any alternative to a stultifying scientism or a despairing relativism?

Mainstream Social Science

Chapter One set out our interpretation of how the modern outlook has combined an objectified picture of reality with a deeply antiauthoritarian moral outlook. Taylor (1995) describes how Descartes gave definition and momentum to this outlook by way of an historically unprecedented inward and "reflexive turn." According to Descartes, knowledge and understanding come not from authority, custom, or tradition, but consist in correct inner representations of an outer reality or independent realm of objects. They come about through the use of reliable methods that generate "well-founded confidence" in such beliefs. This confidence, understood as the progressive elimination of doubt about the accuracy of our theories, is something the mind has to generate for itself through the "examination of our own ideas in abstraction from what they 'represent.'" As a result, for many moderns "an almost boundless confidence is placed in the defining of formal relations [including objective methods in social science] as a way of achieving clarity and certainty about our thinking" (p. 5). This faith in method as the path to true knowledge shows up in the insistence in the mainstream social sciences on the use of correlational and experimental methods regardless of the subject matter being investigated. For example, it appears in the privileging of formal relations in Kohlberg's enormously influential theory of moral development (1984). For Kohlberg, the highest level of morality is the ability to apply highly abstract, formal principles to concrete situations.

Modern social science takes shape within the ambit of this outward-looking faith in method coupled with a drastic inward turn. It seeks confident knowledge of a realm of human events that is independent of the observer or the accounts of social scientists, even if in another sense observers are also part of that realm. This new "disenchanted" world of nature, including the social realm, is correlative to a new kind of "self-defining identity" (Taylor, 1975, p. 8). Winning through to this new identity "was accompanied by the sense of exhilaration and power, that the subject need no longer define his perfection or vice, his equilibrium or disharmony, in relation to an external order" (p. 9). Now the horizon of human identity is found within, not in some wider world of roles and purposes in which we participate. Achieving this new sense of identity involves "a massive shift in self-experience" (Taylor 1985b, p. 258). The modern world's intensely individualistic moral outlook encourages individuals to get in touch with their inmost inclinations and desires, ideally uncontaminated by authority, custom, or the opinions of others.

Certain naturalistic approaches to social inquiry from Hobbes to modern behaviorism regard the social and psychological realms as simply part of nature, to be analyzed by methods analogous to those of the natural sciences. Proper scientific knowledge is thought to be about facts, not about values. Values reflect only subjective attitudes or feelings about objective states of affairs (although one might also treat these subjective factors as an order of events to be linked in their own right to antecedent causes or subsequent effects). Sometimes, rather paradoxically, naturalistic approaches deny human freedom altogether.

It is important to realize that the epistemological ideal of mainstream American social science has never been the mere collection of correlations among interesting variables (Bernstein, 1976). Rather it is the achievement of "empirical theory" or lawlike correlations that are both theoretically derived and empirically confirmed. Only when we have such theory can we draw counterfactuals and the precise prediction taken to be the mark of genuine explanatory knowledge.

Let us risk oversimplification for the sake of a brief example. We might find it interesting that subjects with an "internal locus of control" (that is, they generally believe they can influence the course of events by their actions) persist longer trying to solve difficult problems in a laboratory setting. But who knows whether this belief system really causes such persistence? Perhaps both the belief and the persistence are the coeffects of other unknown factors, psychological or physiological. This matter can only be sorted out in the long run by a more rigorous experimental science that finally reaches the goal of genuine empirical theory. Ideally, from the naturalistic perspective, such theory consists of universal psychological or sociological laws that are logically derived from a few assumptions and definitions concerning the basic nature of the realm being investigated (atomic and subatomic particles and forces in physics, for example, or elementary behaviors linked to stimuli or reinforcing conditions in behavioral psychology). Moreover, these laws must have been empirically confirmed by means of carefully controlled experimentation. The resulting theory and laws generate relatively precise predictions about events that are remote in space and time and may afford us instrumental control over those events.

Serious doubts have been voiced for decades, in and out of the social science arena, about whether the ideals of empirical theory and true value-neutrality ever have or could be achieved in accounts of human activities in their real-life social and historical setting. Slife and Williams (1995), for example, point out that mainstream social science in this century is based on the idea of a sharp dichotomy between theory and method, with theory or ideas validated or rejected by the best available methods. However, they argue cogently that it is impossible to differentiate sharply between theory and method in this way. All methods presuppose a great deal of theory. They presuppose a number of things about what the world is really like, what truth about the world would resemble, and what is worth knowing in the first place—without which we could not even know we needed methods in the first place, let alone which ones would serve our needs. Therefore, methods are hardly in a position to serve as an independent test of our theories or beliefs.

As the twentieth century draws to a close, there is little disagreement among sophisticated observers that the achievements of modern social science, even when evaluated by the field's own favored standards, are paltry at best as compared to the accomplishments of the natural sciences. There is much less agreement about what this situation means. Some feel the evidence is almost overwhelming that we are significantly on the wrong track. Others draw the inference that we should stick with and refine our methods and redouble our efforts. Either way, in the absence of well-developed empirical theory we daily face the question, On what basis do we interpret our (rather voluminous) findings and correlations? The philosopher David Hoy (1986, p. 124) observes that "theory choice in the social sciences is . . . more relativistic than in the natural sciences, since the principles used to select social theories would be guided by a variety of values. Unlike a natural scientist's explanation, which relies on the pragmatic criterion of predictive success, a social scientist's evaluation of the data in terms of a commitment to a social theory would be more like taking a political stand."

In recent years, increasingly refined arguments have been mounted to the effect that the great difficulties of social science in attaining genuine empirical theory reflect a deeper inappropriateness of this epistemological ideal to its subject matter. Thus, Kenneth Gergen (1982, p. 12) asserts that a "fundamental difference exists between the bulk of the phenomena of concern to the natural as opposed to the sociobehavioral scientist." In fact, "there appears to be little justification for the immense effort devoted to the empirical substantiation of fundamental laws of human conduct. There would seem to be few patterns of human action, regardless of their durability to date, that are not subject to significant alteration." Further-more, Peter Winch (1958, 1977) argues that human action is purposive, inherently social, rule-governed activity. In his view, explaining human action means giving an account of why people do the things they do—their motives, reasons, and goals—by reference to the intersubjective rules or standards that constitute their particular "form of life." Indeed the acceptability of such an account would depend on its making sense to the social actors themselves. In this view, the elucidation of rule-following behavior is seen as different in kind from explaining nature or society via context-independent general laws. Thus, human action is deeply social and consists more in cooperative activities guided by common meanings and shared values than in radically self-interested behavior. After all, indi-viduals are socialized to see themselves as distinct individuals in our com-petitive, individualistic society. They are taught a very detailed set of rules and customs about how to live successfully within that context.

Some of Winch's otherwise sympathetic commentators have moderated his position by stressing that the explanation of an action may be more sophisticated than its subjects are able to grasp and need only be mean-ingfully connected to agents' own intentions and beliefs (Taylor, 1985a; Warnke, 1987). Others have pointed out that nothing in Winch's critique prevents us from affirming that information about correlations among factors in the social realm may help elucidate the dynamics of forms of life in various ways, including detecting erroneous beliefs, rationalizations, and self-deceptions in social actors (Bernstein, 1976). Thus, it seems point-less and harmful to insist on an either-or choice between correlational and interpretive approaches in social inquiry (Taylor, 1985b). But all these crit-ics would agree that such correlations should not be thought of as approx-imations or stepping stones to strict empirical theory and universally applicable laws of human activity. Rather, these correlations indicate reg-ularities or systematic interrelationships in the personal or social existence of particular historical communities, which evolve and ramify in varied and unpredictable ways.

"Descriptivisms"

Roy D'Andrade (1986) captures the essence of many critiques of the mainstream social science approach with his suggestion that conventional models of scientific explanation seem inadequate to capture what goes on in the "semiotic sciences." By this term, he means inquiry that studies "'imposed' order based on 'meaning' rather than on natural or physical order." This kind of imposed order "creates meaning and is created by the attempt to convey meaning." It is an "arbitrary order, which can change rapidly and varies from place to place and time to time" (p. 22). In other words, human actions and emotions, indeed our very selves, unlike events in the natural world, are symbolically structured aspects of social reality. They are constituted by their location within the practices and norms of language games, traditions, or forms of life. They would be different if these practices and norms were different. Therefore, as Taylor (1985b, p. 121) says, "personal interpretation enters into the very definition of the phenomenon under study."

Insights of this sort concerning meaningful human action have been incorporated into such views of social inquiry as phenomenological approaches (in psychology, see Valle and Halling, 1989), ethnomethodology, and a broad array of research approaches loosely termed *qualitative*. Bernstein (1976) suggests the helpful label *descriptivist* for all these approaches to social inquiry. In varied ways, they partake of the spirit of Clifford Geertz's credo (1973, p. 5): "Believing, with Max Weber, that man is an animal suspended in webs of significance he himself has spun, I take culture to be those webs, and the analysis of it to be therefore not an experimental science in search of law but an interpretive one is search of meaning." For many critics of mainstream social science in this century, some sort of descriptivist approach has seemed the only plausible alternative. We should describe meaningful human action or lived experience rather than reduce it to something less than human and seek to explain it via deterministic general laws.

How should we evaluate this approach to understanding human life? Giddens (1976) argues that social inquiry is characterized by a "double hermeneutic." In his view, postpositivist or postempiricist views of scientific inquiry like Kuhn's gain ground epistemologically by acknowledging the first half of that double hermeneutic. Namely, they acknowledge that a science's theory and findings are shaped in crucial ways by the investigators' interpretive framework of assumptions, conventions, and purposes. This is something that applies to the natural and human science alike. Descriptivist approaches to social inquiry, like Winch's, begin to take account of the other half of this double hermeneutic, which may apply only in the social disciplines, where the object of study is the same sort of activity or being that carries out the inquiry. That is, descriptivist approaches appreciate that characteristic human actions and emotions, unlike events in the natural world, are symbolically structured aspects of social reality. Moreover, social science is in every way a part of this reality, even as researchers study other parts of it. It thus appears that at the heart of social inquiry there is a mutually influencing interplay or dialogue between meaning-laden events and the interpretive framework of investigators.

However, descriptivist views of social inquiry do not take the full measure of this interplay or double hermeneutic. What does it mean to give a valid or true account of social reality from this perspective? Phenomenological and descriptivist writers either state or imply that we should try to give a thoroughly objective characterization of the lived experience or patterns of meaningful human action that are being scrutinized. However, for reasons that will be explored more fully in this chapter, that would seem to be neither possible nor desirable. We bring our cultural concerns and commitments to the work of understanding such that "our" accounts of "their" reality will always be creative, somewhat value-laden interpretations. Such accounts are not unlike translations from one language to another in which both languages or perspectives will be somewhat altered and may be enriched in the process (Gadamer, 1975). If this is true, however, descriptivist approaches do not give us any clear sense of what constraints will be placed on our interpretive activity or what standards will be used to discriminate adequate from inadequate accounts.

Nevertheless, descriptivist viewpoints make real gains. They cut against the grain of the ahistorical, self-contained individualism presupposed by so much modern psychological theory and research (Cushman, 1990; Sampson, 1985) and give us valuable insights into the inherently social and moral texture of human life. They suggest that human action is not exclusively instrumental but in large measure an enactment of what Winch calls the *form of rationality* a particular community or society pursues. In other words, baseline social reality consists of cooperative practices and institutions that embody shared understandings of what life is all about. One or another set of intrinsic values orients our instrumental activities and prereflectively shapes our experiences and practices long before we begin consciously to deliberate about such matters.

These gains notwithstanding, Bernstein (1976) argues that descriptivist approaches like Winch's seem to founder when it comes to explicating the normative dimensions of social theory. In the "investigation of a human society," Winch (1958, pp. 102–103) writes, "[i]t is not [our] business to advocate any Weltanschauung. . . . In Wittgenstein's words, 'Philosophy leaves everything as it was.'" The trouble is, just that statement of Winch's is morally loaded and self-refuting. It contains a plea for positive values of openness to and respect for the variety of forms of life and necessarily implies a condemnation of any Weltanschauung that excludes those values. Moreover, Winch remarks movingly that "the concept of *learning from* which is involved in the study of other cultures is closely linked with the concept of *wisdom*. We are confronted not just with different techniques, but with new possibilities of good and evil, in relation to which men may come to terms with life." But Bernstein (1976) observes that "such a 'wisdom' is empty unless it also provides some critical basis for evaluating these 'new possibilities of good and evil.' Certainly we can recognize that there are forms of life which are dehumanizing and alienating, and we want to understand precisely in what ways they are so; to insist that philosophy and social theory remain neutral and uncommitted undermines any rational basis for such a critique of society" (p. 74). In the descriptivist view, the social scientist seems to remain detached from the social reality in which she is in fact historically embedded and thoroughly a part, in a way that creates much epistemological confusion. Also, she remains strictly neutral and morally disinterested in a way that obfuscates the practical aims of social inquiry.

Perspectives of Critical Social Science

To make what is sometimes called the critical turn means to acknowledge that all social theory and research findings are inescapably interpretive and evaluative. Critical social scientists find both positivistic and descriptivist approaches sharply limited for two main reasons. First, those approaches deceptively (and often self-deceptively) deny the moral commitments or ideological beliefs that animate their own theory and interpretation of research findings. Second, because of their pretense to complete objectivity or value-neutrality, they are unable to come to grips with some of the most interesting features of human action, especially its revealing contradictions or inconsistencies. Consider a few examples. Someone says he or she never gets angry but has crippling headaches for weeks after a confrontation. A leader of the religious right turns out to have a sexual relationship with his stepdaughter. An educational bureaucrat claims to support academic excellence but routinely discourages innovative teaching. Ordinary citizens claim to be dedicated to democracy but usually fail to vote. A demagogue touches on people's real frustrations but offers no real solutions, only enemies to blame for their troubles. Or an environmental activist advocating living in harmony with nature turns to violent politics to advance his or her aims. Very often it is just such inconsistencies that spur us to deeper thought, illuminating research, and important refinements in our values and ideals. However, mainstream social scientists, if they stick strictly to their methods, have difficulty making sense of these inconsistencies. Their commitment to value-neutrality tends to blind them to troubling contradictions and possible serious defects in our way of life. Because they think they are only "telling it like it is," they have difficulty doing anything more than just describing these inconsistencies. To do more would involve interpreting the sources of these tensions and contradictions in social currents and human motivations—telling a story about their development or decline—in ways that inescapably reflect some evaluation about the human goods or moral evils involved.

Critical social scientists often discuss this issue as the problem of ideology (see Fox and Prilleltensky, 1997, for a recent overview of the critical viewpoint in psychology). They suggest that a particular way of life may contain apparent contradictions because the self-understanding or beliefs of the social actors involved contain systematic distortions. These distortions may reflect the kind of repressions and rationalizations Freudians and Marxists analyze. In other words, they may represent inauthentic accommodations to force or threat. Perhaps unconsciously, one ignores problems or denies injustices for fear of losing one's income, one's status, or one's very life, for the same sort of reason that an abused child often clings to and professes great love for the abusing adult. But this means that our attempt to describe things in a neutral and objective manner will likely lead to error. Our accounts are likely to portray oppressed workers as happy campers and grim workaholics as proud citizens, rationalizing the status quo and evading questions of justice and human welfare. We will reproduce the blindness and rationalizations of social actors in our supposedly objective account of what they do and why they do it.

The critical theory of the Frankfurt school (Held, 1980) and Jürgen Habermas (Habermas, 1973, 1991; McCarthy, 1978) is concerned with both familiar evils and injustices and with new forms of domination and corruption that are unique to a modern technological society. The cornerstone of critical theory is its "critique of instrumental reason." According to Habermas, modern society to a great extent is built on a damaging confusion of *praxis* with *techne*, Greek words meaning roughly "culturally meaningful activities" and "technical capacity." This kind of society tends to collapse the cultural and moral dimensions of life into merely technical and instrumental considerations. It harmfully reverses their priority, putting techne on top. As a result, according to Habermas, "the relationship of theory to praxis can now only assert itself as the purposive-rational application of techniques assured by empirical science." Unfortunately, such applications "produce technical recommendations, but they furnish no answer to practical [or moral] questions" (Habermas, 1973, p. 254). Too many spheres of life have become dominated by a calculating and instrumental viewpoint that discerns means-ends relationships, performs cost-benefit analyses, and seeks to maximize our control or mastery over events. This viewpoint may increase our instrumental prowess in some areas, but it also undermines our ability to evaluate the worth of ends on any basis other than the sheer fact that they are preferred or desired.

Habermas points out that far from being value-neutral, the positivist outlook celebrating instrumental reason actually contains a tacit value system and even a tacit "critique of ideology" of its own. In the tradition of the Enlightenment, positivism thinks of itself as doing battle with ignorance, superstition, dogmatism, and arbitrary authority. It does this in order to promote an understanding of human rights, freedom, and dignity, values most of us share in some form. The difficulty is that it does this by treating all values as merely subjective and limiting knowledge to the findings of objective science. But this rather simplistic faith in individualism, science, and progress hides its own commitments behind a facade of value-neutrality.

The critical theorist Horkheimer (1974) noted contradictions of this sort. He argued that the modern outlook which glorifies instrumental reason actually turns into its opposite or an "eclipse of reason." Scientific neutrality and the regarding of all values as merely subjective undermine our ability to reason together about the inherent quality of our way of life and about what ends we might best seek. As the means of control and influence grow, life gets more organized and complicated, but we lose the ability to set priorities and impose needed limits. In this way, critical theory sheds light on our tendency to despoil the environment, our fascination with power and control to the neglect of other important values, and our stressful, overextended lifestyles.

Habermas contends that to restore our praxis we first need to appreciate that human action or social life is not fundamentally instrumental or "purposive-rational," even if the bulk of twentieth-century social science assumes it is. Instead, what he calls *communicative action* or *interaction* is more basic (1991). For Habermas there is "an ontological reality beyond the autonomous subject [which] is communicative action, with the community and life-world it creates" (Davis, 1990, p. 170). Communicative action is not instrumental activity governed by technical rules but "symbolic interaction" that is "governed by consensual norms, which define reciprocal obligations about behavior" (Habermas, 1970, p. 92). Most often, we cooperate with one another in terms of shared cultural, ethical, aesthetic, or religious meanings. These meanings, not instrumental prowess, are what human life is basically about—even though that fact is obscured by the official ideology of our consumerist culture.

But—here is the rub—how are going to evaluate social norms and adjudicate social conflicts in a modern, pluralistic context where disagreement and conflict are rife and where we have a strong sense of how different outlooks and ways of life are socially constructed and relative to their historical origins? We have the same problem in a different form in choosing between diverse social or psychological theories. They seem shaped at the core, in part, by different value commitments or implicit views of human maturity and the good life. Critical social scientists are opposed to endorsing the social constructionist alternative discussed later in this chapter, which they see as abandoning the idea of an ethically serious social science and allowing that anything goes. For them, like Habermas, a key question for both practical life and social science is, How, in modern times, can we reach agreement about matters that are at least partly evaluative or moral without reverting to dogmatism and arbitrary authority?

For the most part, twentieth-century social scientists have believed they could avoid these kinds of troubling questions about the basis for justifying moral beliefs or social policy. They want to do science, not philosophy or ethics. They wish to discover important truths about human functioning and leave their practical application to others or to the democratic process. To put it bluntly, they would rather eat dirt than struggle with arguments weighing the pros and cons of Habermas's discourse ethics! But it now looks like they have not avoided ideology and moral advocacy, only smuggled them in through the back door. Democracy itself is based on a social and moral vision that needs much clarification and defense and is threatened in ways that ought to make it a prime target for social science inquiry (Elshtain, 1995; Etzioni, 1996; Kane, 1998).

In Habermas's earlier work, he contended that humans as a species have an inherent "interest" in or essential tendency toward "emancipation." To many critics, this designation of emancipation as the master value seemed somewhat arbitrary. (It also may reflect what Fromm called a one-sided "freedom from.") Later, Habermas outlined a more subtle approach to the problem of justifying norms and values. He argued that when current values or practices are questioned, it is possible to turn to an explicit kind of "discourse" to test the norms or the claims to rightness that are always an essential part of our praxis. We cannot, of course, appeal to standards of mere technical effectiveness. Nor should we ever rely dogmatically on an established authority or viewpoint. In fact, it seems we will have to do without fixed decision procedures or explicit criteria. Otherwise, we fall into an infinite regress of having to find criteria to evaluate our norms, and then standards by which to justify those criteria, and so on indefinitely. Instead, Habermas contends, we can and should engage in the process of argument and discussion itself, and continue it until we reach as much of a consensus as possible.

Habermas argues that this kind of discussion and argumentation should follow the pattern of a certain *ideal speech situation*. It is impossible to do complete justice to the elaborate details of his proposal in this brief chapter. Essentially, however, he claims that the pattern of such an ideal speech situation is built into our very nature as social, communicative beings in such a way that it actually defines in a general way how we should deliberate about such matters. Inherently, humans seek a consensus about issues of rightness or justice through discourse that involves such things as full accountability to one another for the quality of our reasoning, arguing as many different points of view as possible in the search for a valid consensus, and the exclusion of "all motives except that of the cooperative search for truth" (1973, p. 18). He feels that this kind of argumentation, although never achieved perfectly, can lead to a consensus that is relatively more free of deception and ideology, and therefore relatively valid, in both everyday life and the more formal enterprise of social science inquiry.

Discourse without fixed standards or established authorities might appear to be empty or circular. But Habermas's view does seem to capture something profound about the ethical search. Imagine a professor and student carrying on a friendly argument about the need to protect the environment versus the desirability of more commercial development. Suppose the teacher sensed that the student was qualifying or backing down from her environmentalist views, perhaps fearing for her grade in a course. If the professor were to follow the principles of the ideal speech situation, she might switch to another role in the dialogue and suggest, "Perhaps I am overlooking something important in your position. After all, environmental considerations are very important. I feel their importance, too. Would you go over your main point again for me?" In addition, in this kind of discourse, individuals can directly challenge one another's arguments and even motives. Thus it is possible that balance or equality might be restored and the joint search for understanding put back on track. It takes a certain amount of character or self-discipline to keep this process on track. Most of us appreciate the effort and skill it takes to engage in such dialogue or interchange and have experienced its fruitfulness. Habermas feels that restored dialogue of this sort—concerned as it is with "needs that can be communicatively shared" (1975, p. 107) and issues of rightness or justice—has the power to bring injustice to light and to counteract the distortion of our life-world by a one-sided instrumental reason.

A major difficulty with Habermas's critical theory concerns its claim that the kind of moral reasoning defined by the ideal speech situation is both universally valid and sufficient for moral purposes. In the end, his approach seems to be a rich, dialogical version of modern liberal individualism, and encounters many of the same difficulties. Taylor (1985b) calls this outlook *formalist*. He suggests that the formalist approach arose in part to avoid the strife and conflict associated with traditional moral disputes about virtue, the common good, or natural law. However, liberal individualist or formalist thinkers dearly hold values of justice and respect for human dignity and rights. As a result, they try to legislate how we ought to engage in ethical reasoning or debate and claim neutrality because they do not dictate the content of these discussions. They try to legislate the "how" but not the "what" of ethical reasoning or debate. Examples are Kant's famous categorical imperative to treat others as ends and not as means to one's own ends, Lawrence Kohlberg's theory of moral development, and Habermas's definition of the ideal speech situation. Formalist thinking also undergirds our notion of the rule of law in modern liberal democracies, which provide their citizens with a highly abstract or procedural kind of justice. It is hoped such principles will preserve a genuine moral sense while avoiding controversies about ultimate truth or the nature of the good life.

However, Taylor (1985b) argues that such ethical principles, although very general, still reflect substantive moral beliefs. They reflect our civilization's commitment to the fundamental equality and dignity of all individuals. As he points out, these principles have in fact been anything but universally recognized. In addition, Taylor doubts it is possible to step out of history and demonstrate conclusively that our moral beliefs are anchored in any sort of moral or metaphysical absolute. That would include Habermas's attempt (1971) to ground his beliefs in the nature of our species as communicative beings. Also, Taylor (1985b) argues that no society or tradition, even our own, ever strictly limits itself to formalist principles concerning moral matters or the good life. In fact, all societies are built around a "diversity of goods." They incorporate diverse and sometimes conflicting ideals of maturity, success, integrity, honor, the social good, beauty, knowledge, existential meaning, or spiritual fulfillment, making moral and political discussion both more interesting and a lot messier than the ideal speech situation.

Thus, Habermas's procedural universalism contains an element of "Enlightenment dogmatism" (Warnke, 1987, p. 174). It builds into the ideal speech situation a specifically modern bias in favor of limiting moral discussion to broad, formal issues of justice and fairness. If so, the ideal speech situation presupposes a distinctively modern ethical outlook that cannot itself become the subject of critical inquiry! However, this modern outlook is open to reasonable doubt. Many postmodern thinkers (for example, Foucault, 1980a) feel that this position is self-absolutizing and tyrannical in its own way. Hermeneutic writers and others who are sympathetic to Habermas's ethics of dialogue (for example, MacIntyre, 1981; Sullivan, 1986; Taylor, 1985b) still feel that modernity involves such things as a loss of meaning or exaggerated individualism that can be understood only from other standpoints, including older traditions of thought and practice.

These problems with the ideal speech situation are likely to have practical or social consequences. For example, Moon (1983, p. 186) points out that in his widely read book *Small Is Beautiful,* E. F. Schumacher argues that a certain "reverential conception of nature and of man's relationship to nature" is part of the good life and may be essential to accepting needed limits to exploiting the environment and finding a greater sense of meaningfulness that could make those limits stick. Our "predatory" attitude toward nature, Moon suggests, might require stiffer medicine than mere Habermasian "generalizable interests." Whether or not this is the case, Moon's point is that the ideal speech situation arbitrarily rules out even discussing such issues. Critical social scientists tend to assume that their ethical and social program of unmasking domination and striving for greater procedural and distributive justice in a modern context is entirely sound or sufficient. But they seem to embrace much of the modern formalist ethical outlook and inadvertently reinforce the one-sided individualism in our society, which views individuals as separate and self-interested to a very great extent. This outlook may fail to provide a needed sense of common purpose and healthy limits. It is reasonable to worry that our best modern ideals of justice may be unachievable unless motivated and buttressed by other serious commitments or values.

Postmodern–Social Constructionist Viewpoints

A number of thinkers loosely grouped together as postmodern theorists offer, in part, a different kind of critique of the one-sided individualism and technicism of modern times. Postmodern thinkers, somewhat like Habermas, want to restore a sense of humans as embedded or contextualized in a historical culture or praxis. But they vehemently reject Habermas's attempt to define a universal standard or procedure for critically evaluating our values and practices. They see that sort of critical theory as just another example of modern Western society's absolutizing its own way of life and arbitrarily insisting that all cultures and peoples be judged in terms of its ethnocentric point of view. They reject any sort of foundationalism that tries to reach beyond the shifting sands of history and identify metaphysical grounds, infallible methods, or universal moral standards for judging our beliefs. They feel that any claim to have found such a basis or standard amounts to a false and perhaps dishonest projecting of our particular community's viewpoint onto the universe. It is time to bite the bullet, they say, and acknowledge the fundamental truth (any irony intended) that all our beliefs and values are strictly relative.

Postmodern thinkers generally concur with the contention of the philosopher Dreyfus (1987, p. 65) that "humanity is a self-interpreting way of being whose practices have enabled it to act as if it had a whole series of different natures in the course of history." In other words, humans do not have a transhistorical or transcultural nature. Rather, culture "completes" humans by explaining and interpreting the world. Culture does not differently clothe the universal human. Rather, it infuses individuals, fundamentally shaping their natures and identities. In Cushman's words (1990, p. 599), "cultural conceptualizations and configurations of self are formed by the economies and politics of their respective eras. . . . There is no universal, transhistorical self, only local selves; no universal theory about the self, only local theories." Similarly, Rorty (1985, p. 28) writes that there is "no criterion that we have not created in the course of creating a practice, no standard of rationality that is not an appeal to such a criterion, no rigorous argumentation that is not obedience to our own conventions."

Social Constructionism

One prominent branch of postmodern thought is represented by the American philosopher Richard Rorty (1982, 1985) and the leading social constructionist theorist in contemporary psychology, Kenneth Gergen (1982, 1985, 1994). In a clear and vivid way, Gergen (1985) argues that the "terms in which the world is understood are social artifacts, products of historically situated interchanges between people." In both theory and practical life, the "process of understanding is not automatically driven by the forces of nature, but is the result of an active, cooperative enterprise of persons in relationships" (p. 267). According to Gergen (1994), Western culture has given the individual a place of "commanding importance," making individual minds the "critical locus of explanation" in psychology and the social sciences in general. But we have reached an "impasse of individual knowledge" (p. 3). Thus Gergen (1985) invites "inquiry into the historical and cultural bases of various forms of world constructions." Such inquiry makes it plain that conceptions of "psychological process differ markedly from one culture to another" (p. 267). Many of the findings and theories of empirical social science, from this perspective, are quite distorting. They pretend that the world, the self, and psychological processes are just one way, which is not the case, and that they are our way, which is ethnocentric and erroneous. The prevalence of a given form of understanding depends not "on the empirical validity of the perspective in question, but on the historical vicissitudes of social process (e.g., communication, negotiation, conflict, rhetoric)" (p. 272). To put it another way, objectivity is only a "rhetorical achievement" (Gergen, 1994, p. 165).

According to Gergen (1985), social constructionism helps us get past traditional subject-object dualism. This means that psychological inquiry is deprived of any notion of experience as a "touchstone of objectivity." So-called reports or descriptions of one's experience are really just "linguistic constructions guided and shaped by historically contingent conventions of discourse." Therefore, there is "no 'truth through method,'" no correct procedure that bestows a warrant of objectivity on our findings or theories. Moreover, social constructionism "offers no alternative truth criteria." Instead, "the success of [our] accounts depends primarily on the analyst's capacity to invite, compel, stimulate, or delight the audience, and not on criteria of veracity." We might say that constructionism brings theory and practice still closer together. We argue or "negotiate" the full range of human concerns and values (even though all are just "linguistic constructions") in everyday life and social theory alike (p. 272).

Gergen and Rorty defend their postmodern approach against charges of irrationalism or destructive relativism. First, according to Gergen (1985), because there is an "inherent dependency of knowledge systems on communities of shared intelligibility," there can be "stability of understanding without the stultification of foundationalism." Our practices and values can evolve only gradually through a coordinated effort rather than chaotically or whimsically. Second, because the "practitioner can no longer justify any socially reprehensible conclusion on the grounds of being a 'victim of the facts,' he or she must confront the pragmatic implications of such conclusions within society more generally." Not being able to hide behind a pretense of objectivity or facade of value-neutrality actually "reasserts the relevance of moral criteria for scientific practice." Because our psychology theory and practice "enter into the life of the culture, sustaining certain patterns of conduct and destroying others, such work must be evaluated in terms of good and evil" (p. 273). Finally, Rorty

(1985) even goes so far as to claim that this sort of relativism or contextualism will lead not to social fragmentation or personal directionlessness but to a deepened sense of solidarity. A sense of the pervasive contingency of life will actually tend to undermine dogmatism and yield a positive sense of connectedness and shared purpose with fellow practitioners of our particular way of life.

Michel Foucault

The penetrating analyses of Michel Foucault (1977, 1980a, 1980b) present a perhaps more realistic but much less cheery view of our embeddedness in culture than do Gergen and Rorty. Initially, Foucault termed his primary unit of analysis *discourse*. In his later writings, he discusses the same realities in terms of *relations of power*. Foucault tries to reveal sets of discursive rules that allow us to produce a field of knowledge, including all of the field's possible statements about what is true or false, good or evil. But these productive rules "operate 'behind the backs' of speakers of a discourse." Indeed, the "place, function, and character of the 'knowers,' authors and audiences of a discourse are also a function of these rules" (Philip, 1985, p. 69). As a result, there can be no overall truth or falsity of a discourse. Rather, "truth" is simply an "effect" of the rules of discourse or the power relations that create and constitute a particular form of life. Typically, power relations are not a matter of either explicit consent or violent coercion but are the myriad ways people are constrained together to act within a particular, ultimately arbitrary system of "power/knowledge." Foucault typically characterizes these relations in terms of haphazard and incessant struggle and conflict. What we might call domination or justice are simply truth effects within our cultural order. They are in no way less dominating or morally superior as compared with past or future systems of power or "regimes of truth" occurring down a directionless historical path. They are only different.

Foucault suggests that the human sciences (he calls them the "dubious sciences") aim at truth but, in fact, deceptively classify and manage people in line with the current regime. They augment "biopower," the kind of detailed surveillance and control that he feels power mainly acquires in our era, reflected in our peculiar modern obsession with the creation of a normal and healthy population. Foucault has illuminating things to say about how modern penology, psychiatry, and other human sciences contribute to this process. His views augment and enrich critical theory's critique of instrumental reason and account of the "eclipse of reason." Foucault (1980b) analyzes not only how modes of domination form the modern person but also how certain practices, usually mediated by an external authority figure like a confessor or psychoanalyst, bring individuals' active self-formative processes in line with the current system. For example, therapy clients are induced to scrutinize themselves interminably until they find (or even fabricate) certain problems or tendencies. Then they are persuaded to assume individual responsibility for suppressing or managing these desires in order to conform to current norms of health and productivity. Critical social scientists and hermeneutic thinkers would not accept this argument in its entirety; but they might feel that it sheds light on how the emotionally isolated modern individual is trained to adapt to being a cog in the social and economic machinery, to do without lasting social ties, and to criticize only herself and not the social order for problems in living (Hare-Mustin, 1991).

However, Foucault does not moralize in this way. Instead of social science or ethical discussion, he recommends the practice of "genealogy." Genealogy limits itself to uncovering the likely origins of "totalizing," or all-determining, discourses and showing how their deceptive claims to unity and truth arose from historical accidents and arbitrary machinations of power. This approach resembles an austere descriptivism. Nevertheless, Foucault often expressed support for those who "resist" or "refuse" these systems of power/knowledge in ways that open a space for the rediscovery of particular, fragmented, subjugated, local sorts of knowledge or understanding. Toward the end of his life Foucault felt pressure to articulate some more positive ethic beyond merely engaging in the detached genealogy of ultimately equally dominating regimes of truth. He hinted that from the lack of any fixed or universal human nature we could infer a practical program of ceaselessly creating and recreating ourselves "as a work of art" (Foucault, 1982, p. 236). But it is impossible to imagine how Foucault could have justified this odd reversion to Romantic individualism—why that, rather than nihilism, existentialism, or a religious leap of faith?

---
o

Both these versions of postmodern thought have the virtue of helping to unmask damaging modern pretensions to exaggerated autonomy, certainty, and control. They provide new, helpful tools for recovering diverse and possibly valuable experiences and understandings that indeed have sometimes been "subjugated" by scientistic, rationalistic, or instrumentalist ways of thinking. Also, postmodern notions of irony and play surely have something to contribute to our understanding of knowledge and ethics in a time when the permanent ambiguity and uncertainty of the human situation seems more obvious. Nevertheless, postmodern–social constructionist theory harbors serious flaws.

The postmodern outlook sets forth a paradoxical and ultimately implausible view of the human self as both radically determined by historical influences and yet radically free to reinterpret itself and social reality as it wishes for its own self-invented purposes. It is not clear where such historically embedded beings would get the leverage needed to radically reinvent themselves in this way. Moreover, doesn't this approach reproduce in another guise some key features of the modern outlook it criticizes, including a characteristically modern view of the distance between self and world, and modern pretensions to absolute freedom and indefinite control? Also, postmodernists sometimes suggest that just denying all metaphysical and moral universals will free us from tendencies toward dogmatism and domination. But where in this brave new world would we find the conviction or dedication needed to keep from abandoning our society's ideals of freedom and universal respect in favor of shallow diversions or some comforting new tyranny?

We are asked by postmodern theory to believe that when such ideals as freedom and respect for human life are taken seriously, they are dangerous illusions. Unfortunately, however, the social constructionist recommendation that we escape this danger by evaluating our moral beliefs and values in terms of their "pragmatic implications" severely clashes with what we really mean whenever we invoke these beliefs and values in everyday life. One wonders if constructionist thinkers have really thought through what it would mean, for example, to collapse the distinction entirely between feeling guilty merely from the fear of disapproval versus feeling remorse from violating one's personal moral standards. Taken literally, that would mean adopting an inhuman and quite destructive amorality. However, more likely it means we are being asked to endorse postmodern relativism as the most humane and authentic viewpoint, one that actually will help undermine irrational guilt and dogmatic beliefs. Such a viewpoint, though sincere, seems utopian and naïve. The loss of credible conviction and sense of purpose it entails would seem more likely to lead to individual apathy and social atomization (if not despair and violence) than to social peace and humane pursuits. Such thinkers seem to believe that their own hard-won character and cultivation will spring up automatically in others as a result of embracing relativism. Also, very much like liberal individualists, they are embroiled in the contradiction of treating all moral values as purely relative or subjective in order to promote certain moral values, such as human solidarity, which they do not appear to view as purely relative or optional.

Foucault, as we mentioned, clearly sides at times with those who resist or refuse totalizing discourses. But Philip (1985) argues that without a conception of the human good, Foucault cannot explain either why people should struggle at all or what they should struggle for. Similarly, Taylor (1985b) argues that Foucault's analyses of systems of power/ knowledge as dominating individuals and of truth as a kind of illusion or merely truth-effects really only make sense if some critical dimension or genuine goods are implicit in Foucault's own analysis. If there is no positively valued alternative to *domination* or *illusion,* these are emotionally loaded and quite misleading terms for describing a situation. In fact, the denial of any such positive alternative by postmodern thinkers seems belied by their writings. Most convey a strong sense of opposition to arbitrary authority and domination. And they clearly suggest that it is more enlightened, mature, or wise not to be taken in by false absolutes and ethnocentric moral beliefs, sometimes clearly recommending they be replaced by an attitude of detached irony and nonchalant play. In the end, it seems, just like the rest of us, they advocate their own brand of wisdom and certain character ideals. But postmodern thinkers' denial of any such ideals leads many critics to worry that postmodernism will end up encouraging passivity or cynicism, thereby accelerating social atomization and personal malaise.

Both the strengths and weaknesses of the postmodern approach to human science inquiry can be found in an engaging recent paper putting grief in an historical perspective (Stroebe, Gergen, Gergen, & Stroebe, 1992). In this thoughtful article, the authors compare grief experiences and bereavement practices in our society with those in the Romanticist ethos of the last century and in other cultures. They make a strong case that there is linkage between our practices of efficiently breaking bonds with the deceased, the tendency to pathologize any reluctance to do so, and contemporary pressures to return individuals to a busy, autonomous, goal-directed lifestyle. Such breaking of bonds contrasts sharply with grief in the Romantic age, when nurturing a continuing sense of communion with the deceased, in spite of a broken heart, signaled the "significance of the relationship" and the "depth of one's own spirit." To dissolve that bond would destroy one's identity and "deny . . . one's own sense of profundity and self-worth" (p. 1208). In addition, the authors find evidence that "romanticist styles of attachment remain robust in significant sectors of the adult population" today (p. 1209). They contend that much contemporary social science and professional psychology does violence to these people and practices by falsely universalizing "breaking bonds" as the "natural" or "functional" way to do things. This study concludes with a call for a "broadening of self-reflective dialogue within the field" (p. 1211) concerning how we interpret bereavement practices and guide people in situations of loss.

The main problem with this analysis concerns its notion of self-reflective dialogue. The authors speak of cultivating a "postmodern consciousness" that encourages an "expansion of responsibility," and of "educating for alternatives." Surely they are correct in insisting that social science accounts and therapy theories "harbor implicit systems of value, favoring certain ideals over others" (Stroebe et al., 1992, p. 1211). But if we reject conventional, scientific social science and descriptivist approaches as inadequate or insufficient, on what basis should we accept these authors' historical account and practical recommendations? The postmodern "education for alternatives" seems likely to confront us with such a wide-open cafeteria of options that it would be paralyzing. It would undermine the possibility of meaningful choice at the same time that it enriches our options, because it tends to deny that there are any good grounds for choosing one option over another. Postmodern theory is thus a kind of closet existentialism. Lacking an alternative, it reverts to the idea of a radical choosing of values in a highly individualistic manner. But, as with existentialism, this view may actually tend to undermine autonomy and integrity. This kind of boundless existential freedom seems hard to distinguish from a condition of being paralyzed by indefinite options or making oneself the slave of every passing impulse.

Contemporary Hermeneutics

The following chapters outline a contemporary hermeneutic view of human agency and social inquiry, and take steps toward applying this view to the task of rethinking psychotherapy and psychology. It seems to us that a hermeneutic ontology is well suited to gathering, coordinating, and extending insights from a variety of sources concerning what is problematic about the human sciences in our day and how we might improve on them. Hermeneutics finds much to admire in naturalism: healthy skepticism and iconoclasm, and commitment, in some form, to objectivity, accuracy, and reproducibility. It also prizes the sensitivity of descriptivist approaches to the richness and irreducibility of meaningful human action. Hermeneutics endorses Habermas's general critical intent and rejects the moral relativism of postmodernist–social constructionist approaches as harmful and unnecessary. But it also agrees with postmodern or constructionist thought that there is a troubling residue of modern hubris in the critical social science approach.

We wish there were space in this book to discuss in detail feminist thinkers' powerful critiques of twentieth-century social science and their rich counterproposals concerning how to elucidate the human struggle. It seems to us that the hermeneutic viewpoint and some feminist critiques overlap to a great degree. Also, we feel that hermeneutic thought might be of assistance in elaborating some key feminist insights. (Of course, the reverse is true as well.) In the next few paragraphs we indicate some of the positive resonances between hermeneutics and certain feminist notions, as a bridge to the fuller exposition of hermeneutic ideas in the chapters that follow.

Sandra Harding (1990) distinguishes three broad epistemological positions that feminist theorists in the social sciences have adopted in recent decades. Thinkers adhering to the first of these positions, "feminist empiricism," do not seriously question Enlightenment ideals of individual freedom, self-determination, and universal human dignity (Benhabib, 1992). Rather, they embrace empiricism as a liberationist strategy and have employed it to expose the many ways that the objectivity of social science inquiry has been biased by sexism and androcentrism.

What Harding refers to as "feminist standpoint" theorists take exception to the Enlightenment tradition's exaltation of rationality as the pinnacle of human achievement and virtue. They contend that the tactics of feminist empiricism leave intact what they see as male-normative schemes of human agency and knowledge production. Instead, they seek to clarify and celebrate the unique, in many ways superior, sensibilities and moral virtues women have developed—compassion, cooperation, spirituality, and so forth. They express hope that these qualities will counter the overly rationalistic, technocratic mentality that erodes families, communities, and the environment through a pursuit of unbridled control that often becomes outright exploitation (Chodorow, 1978; Gilligan, 1982; Tavris, 1991).

Those who endorse "feminism postmodernism," the third position Harding (1990) identifies, express skepticism about granting epistemic or ethical privilege to women's perspectives. They suspect that "being oppressed is no guarantee of clarity of vision" (Felski, 1989, p. 40). They argue that feminist standpoint theories express some of the same essentializing tendencies and false generalizations of the patriarchal tradition they claim to surpass. These thinkers adopt postmodern intellectual strategies such as deconstruction and Foucauldian genealogy to unmask *all* pretentious metanarratives and claims to universal truth, in science or ethics. However, leading feminist thinkers and others voice concern about a postmodern strategy which proclaims that "in order for a proliferation of voices to flourish, we must abolish all criteria for distinguishing among them" (Fox-Genovese, 1991, p. 153). They worry that by undermining the grounding of all forms of knowledge, one also undermines the emancipatory ideals of the women's movement and feminist social critique (Felski, 1989; Warnke, 1993). Moreover, Flax (1990) points out inconsistencies in the work of Foucault, Lyotard, and others who claim to dismantle modern notions of selfhood but still embrace a profoundly modern Romantic-aesthetic vision of the "constant remaking of the self." They "presuppose a socially isolated and individualistic view of the self" that seems impossible to reconcile "with, for example, the care of children or with participation in a political community. It is deeply antithetical to feminist views of self in relation to others" (pp. 216–217).

Each of these strands of feminist theory has made substantial contributions to rethinking psychology. Nevertheless, a number of contemporary thinkers are dissatisfied with any of the readily available options for feminist thought and inquiry. For example, Hare-Mustin and Marecek (1994), leading feminist thinkers in psychology, have suggested a need for feminist thought to move beyond both modernism and liberal humanism on the one hand and postmodernism on the other hand, for some of the reasons we have just discussed.

It seems to us that hermeneutic thought has much to contribute to such an effort. Georgia Warnke (1993) has already explored the possibilities of hermeneutics as a framework for feminist inquiry. One might suspect that a major concern of feminist theorists—something confirmed by our conversations with feminist colleagues in psychology—is the hermeneutic claim that all understanding is tradition-bound, which means that all the questions we ask and the standards we apply are historically conditioned ones. As Warnke (1993, p. 210) notes, many feminists agree with Okin that "history is a nightmare that I am trying to escape." Okin points out that Western traditions have systematically excluded women and so women should not expect to find equality and justice embodied in traditions. Warnke replies, however, that in a sense there is nowhere else to find them, even if they have been imperfectly realized in practice. Any attempt to start afresh to construct principles of justice and nonoppressive social relations on allegedly neutral, historically unconditioned grounds owes a enormous amount at the outset to the moral and political assumptions, categories, and vocabulary of our particular moral and political traditions. Warnke explains, "The notions of liberty and equality we hold up against a society that restricts the opportunities of minorities or women are notions that are the result of the struggles, social movements, and interpretive orientations that develop in the course of a society's and culture's experience. To this extent, understanding moves in a kind of historicized hermeneutic circle in which we reinterpret the practices, principles, and concerns of the tradition of which we are a part in terms of prejudices we have inherited from it and hold it up to the ideals tradition itself has bequeathed to us" (p. 208). In any case, a fruitful and mutually enriching conversation between feminist thought and hermeneutics seems possible and desirable.

The following chapters are a direct response to Cushman's challenge (1990, 1995) to the field of psychology to re-envision itself as a truly "historically situated" enterprise. In the hermeneutic view, we are participants in a temporal and storied existence. We sometimes follow the path of abstraction and objectification and creatively formulate a knowledge of lawfulness or of repeated patterns in events, patterns that occur regardless of the everyday meanings these events have for us. But there is a more fundamental, ultimately practical kind of understanding that humans always and everywhere thrash out together, one that does not primarily mean comprehending events mainly as "instances" of a general concept, rule, or law. In everyday life, and in a more systematic way in the human sciences, people seek to understand the changeable meanings of events, texts, works of art, social reality, and the actions of others in order to appreciate them and relate to them appropriately. A hermeneutic ontology, with its core conceptions of understanding and dialogue, seeks to describe and interpret this basic dimension of human life. It thus appears to offer a promising philosophical or metatheoretical framework for rethinking modern psychology, one that can help identify the important shortcomings of contending approaches to social inquiry while preserving the best insights of those approaches.

9

WHAT IS HERMENEUTICS?

MUCH OF THE EXCITEMENT surrounding hermeneutics today comes from the feeling that this approach to humans provides a way of rethinking some of the underlying assumptions pervading our thinking in the social sciences. Such hermeneutic theorists as Martin Heidegger, Hans-Georg Gadamer, Paul Ricoeur, Jürgen Habermas, Charles Taylor, and Hubert Dreyfus offer fresh and creative ways of thinking about our human situation, and researchers who have applied hermeneutics to specific areas of study—figures like Clifford Geertz in anthropology, Thomas Kuhn in history of science, and Michael Walzer in political theory, to mention just a few—have transformed their disciplines in important ways. Our aim in this book is to use hermeneutics to resolve some of the persistent puzzles that arise in the fields of psychology and psychotherapy.

What exactly is hermeneutics? As a first approach, we might look at the traditional way of characterizing this field. Because the term *hermeneutics* comes from the Greek word for interpretation, hermeneutics has been thought of as the theory or art of interpretation. But what this amounts to in detail is harder to work out. The discipline called hermeneutics has been thriving for more than three hundred years, and during that time the view of what it involves has shifted constantly as a result of the innovative moves made by pivotal thinkers in a changing historical context. To get a handle on what hermeneutics is, then, we need to get some sense of the different views of its role and scope that have developed over the years.

Although hermeneutics can be traced back to reflections on interpretation in the writings of the Stoics and church fathers, the term first gained currency as the name of a specific field of study during the Protestant Reformation. The Council of Trent (1545–1563) had decreed that Scripture is fundamentally unclear and that church authority and tradition are needed to determine the proper allegorical readings of God's Word. Opposing this view, the reformers Martin Luther and Philip Melancthon insisted on the literal truth and accessibility of the Bible. Luther's doctrine of *sola scriptura,* which holds that Christian faith should be based solely on the individual's own readings of the Bible, created the need for guidance in interpreting Scripture. By the seventeenth century, hermeneutics had come to be thought of as a branch of theology that offered a technique or method for biblical interpretation (Grondin, 1994, see pp. 17–44).

The transition from this earlier view of hermeneutics as an auxiliary discipline in theology to the contemporary view can be seen as taking place in two distinct stages (Ricoeur, 1981). The first, which occurred in the mid-nineteenth century, was the shift from thinking of hermeneutics as a set of "regional" forms of interpretation adapted to specialized areas (for example, judicial, theological, literary, and so forth) to the idea of a *general hermeneutics* applicable to all forms of human communication. In this universalized conception of hermeneutics, the goal is to work out a method of interpretation applicable to every form of human discourse.

The second major transformation, occurring at the start of the twentieth century, reflected the growing awareness that devising rules for interpreting humans is impossible and that the whole fascination with method is a by-product of the very scientism being called in question. The result was a shift from seeing hermeneutics as primarily epistemological or methodological, where the aim is to develop an art or technique of interpretation, to today's *ontological hermeneutics,* which aims to clarify the *being* of the entities that interpret and understand, namely, ourselves. This two-stage development is evident in the changing views of hermeneutics from Schleiermacher through Dilthey to Heidegger, Taylor, and Gadamer.

Friedrich Schleiermacher and Romantic Hermeneutics

Friedrich Schleiermacher (1768–1834) was the pivotal figure in the move toward a general or universal hermeneutics. Schleiermacher's vision of our human situation reflected the Romantic notion that the world we perceive around us is merely a veil of appearance, a purely phenomenal realm, which conceals a deeper, underlying reality, the world as it is "in-itself." This idea also lies at the root of Schleiermacher's claim that behind every "external" linguistic act—the noises we utter, the marks we make on paper—there is always something hidden, namely, the speaker's real intentions or meaning. According to this distinction between "outer sign" and "inner intentions," meanings are always concealed from us, so misunderstanding is an unavoidable problem in any communication. Understanding is therefore something we must constantly make an effort to achieve. The role of a general hermeneutics, then, is to supply procedures and techniques for recovering the inner meanings that outer expressions only obscurely reveal.

Schleiermacher distinguishes two components in interpreting the discourse of another person. The first, *grammatical* interpretation, involves deciphering the language the author uses. The second, *psychological* interpretation, tries to grasp the actual thought processes or intentions lying behind the author's words. Though there may be rules for interpreting what others say, Schleiermacher thinks that understanding others ultimately depends on a special capacity for sympathy or empathy, the ability to get into the other's mind and grasp his or her thoughts and feelings. Interpretation simply reverses the speaker's act of creation: just as the speaker raises ideas to expression in the act of speaking, the interpreter reads backward from the spoken words to the ideas from which they sprang. The goal of interpretation, then, is to reconstruct the speaker's original act of construction. It should be obvious that this form of Romantic hermeneutics based on empathy is quite similar to Carl Rogers's client-centered therapy and Heinz Kohut's self psychology.

Wilhelm Dilthey's Grounding of the Human Sciences

Wilhelm Dilthey (1833–1911), the most influential figure in the rise of contemporary hermeneutics, was also influenced by the Romantic belief in an inner mental domain distinct from outer expression, but his interests in history and social life led him to a deeper appreciation of the public dimension of meaning. Dilthey saw his task as working out a methodology for the human sciences (*Geisteswissenschaften*) in general. Given this view of the scope of hermeneutics, Dilthey was interested not just in understanding speech acts but in understanding any human phenomena whatsoever, including actions, historical events, monuments, works of art, and social institutions. Thus Dilthey moves toward an even more universal understanding of the role of hermeneutics, though his motivation is still epistemological and scientific: the question is still about how we can achieve knowledge of others.

Despite this epistemological orientation, Dilthey rejects the traditional view of knowledge derived from figures like Locke and Kant. In a famous remark, Dilthey (1976, p. 162) criticizes the traditional conception of the knowing subject: "No real blood flows in the veins of the knowing subject constructed by Locke, Hume and Kant," he writes; "only the diluted juice of reason, a mere process of thought." In his view, the traditional conception of the epistemological subject, which was part and parcel of the picture of knowing that made the natural sciences possible, is totally inappropriate for the study of humans. In the natural sciences (*Naturwissenschaften*), Dilthey claims, we view objects externally as brute material things with no inner capacity for experience and intentionality. Furthermore, the goal of the natural sciences is to *explain* events by subsuming them under general laws, and this requires the ability to treat the world as a collection of decontextualized objects that may appear in various causal interactions. Such an objectifying stance toward things presupposes a capacity for *abstraction* in which all meanings and values are removed from what is experienced so that the things we study are encountered as inherently meaningless spatiotemporal objects subsumable under covering laws. As Dilthey says, we can see the world around us as a collection of objects regulated by laws only "if the way we experience nature, our involvement in it, and the vital feeling with which we enjoy it, recede behind the abstract apprehension of the world in terms of space, time, mass and motion" (p. 172). The objectified worldview requires that we remove ourselves from the picture: "All these factors combine to make man exclude himself so that, from his impressions, he can map out this great object, nature, as an order governed by laws" (p. 172).

Delimiting the Human Sciences

It is precisely this exclusion of the human subject that leads to the "punctual self" of traditional epistemology (Taylor, 1989). Dilthey's conviction that the natural-scientific view of our epistemological situation is inappropriate for studying humans led to his "methodological dualism": the view that there are two distinct scientific methods, one for studying nature and the other for studying humans and their creations. According to this distinction, the goal of the human studies is to understand meaningful and purposive human phenomena, not to explain causally interacting objects in a space-time coordinate system. Although causal generalizations and physical laws may be helpful in understanding the context in which human actions and creations take place, the primary goal of the human sciences is not to subsume human phenomena under laws but rather to *understand* what humans do by grasping the aims and interpretations of agents in the meaningful situations in which they find themselves. For this kind of understanding, we must put into play the "full totality of life" within ourselves: our insights into what is important in life and the "know-how" we have picked up in dealing with things as feeling, desiring agents within a shared, practical life-world.

Dilthey's "descriptive and analytic psychology" therefore begins by examining the totality of life-experiences (*Erlebnisse*), the complex, meaning-filled experiences we have in the course of our involvements in the world. What defines the unity of a life-experience is not its position in a particular space and time but a unifying meaning and purpose that, in some cases, binds together a number of discrete events. Teaching one's child to drive, for example, takes place at a number of times and places, but it is nevertheless a single life-experience. According to this technical sense of the term, a life-experience presents itself as a lived reality that is prior to any distinction between self and world, mind and matter, or inner and outer. In Dilthey's view, these dualistic oppositions are derivative from and parasitic on a more original kind of experience in which we exist as a "self-world" unity. In our most familiar experiences, we are not aware of an "I" or "self" distinct from what is experienced. The subject-object opposition of traditional epistemology is, in this view, a high-level theoretical abstraction with no relevance to understanding concrete life.

Understanding Humans

In his last writings, Dilthey turned more and more to the "anthropological" task of understanding humans in terms of their sociohistorical context. His earlier descriptive psychology described the ways things show up for us in the course of our actual lived experience. According to this account, when we look at the holistic totality of life in everyday experiences, we find it is shaped by what Dilthey calls *structures,* recurring patterns that display fundamental connections and interrelationships characteristic of psychological life. Every human experience, for example, involves a dynamic interplay of cognitive, affective, and volitional elements that reflects an underlying structure of experience. These initial structures are supplemented with "acquired mental structures" as one grows up into a culture. Structures provide ways of making sense of human phenomena without recourse to standard causal explanations, for structural accounts do not assume that there is any strict necessity in structural connections; such connections display only recurring, intrinsic relations, not temporal, causal succession.

The most important structure for understanding life, according to Dilthey, is its temporal structure, the distinctive way life unfolds through time. This temporal structure determines that what we experience at any

moment always has a connection to the past and the future. This connectedness of any experience with past and future defines lived time as a
flowing, interconnected life course in which "every single experience is
related to the whole" (1976, p. 185).

Dilthey's picture of human existence as a temporal flow leads him to
identify some important "categories" he regards as crucial to understanding life. First, he holds that life is always organized and given direction by *purposiveness* (1977, p. 88). Life is fundamentally teleological: it
is a thrust forward into a realm of future possibilities, in terms of which
all the events in a life are knitted into a connected whole. A second category of life, following from life's inherent teleology, is its *development*.
Life has continuity and cumulativeness in the sense that it strives toward
increasing organization, and it takes on a distinctive shape (*Gestalt*) as it
runs its course in "striving to achieve stability" (1958, p. 347). This characteristic of development points to a third category of life, the constant
movement in life toward the formation of a *meaning* that binds together
past, present, and future into a more or less coherent whole. Dilthey com-
pares the way the unity of a life history emerges through what he calls significance relations to the way a "melody acquires its form—not from the
mere succession of notes but from the musical motifs that determine its
formal unity" (Gadamer, 1989, p. 223). Because the ultimate meaning of
a person's life is determined by what she achieves in the course of living
out her life as a whole, her understanding of her own life is subject to constant revision so long as she is alive. Only at the moment of death, Dilthey
says, can life achieve a final, closed configuration of meaning (1962). As
an ongoing flow toward a stable meaning, life involves a constant process
of *interpretation and reinterpretation*. Dilthey (1958) observes that we all
have a certain facticity in the sense that we are located in a specific
worldly milieu and have already made certain choices that limit what is
possible for the future. But we also have the ability to take up our facticity and do something with it in carrying out the goals we set for ourselves
in the future. These futural undertakings transform the meaning of the
past. The meaning of our lives is thus always subject to revision in the
light of the projects we take up at any time. One example Dilthey (1962)
examines of such a revision is the way St. Augustine's conversion retroac-
tively clarifies and defines the meaning of the events of his earlier years.
In a similar way, most of us are reshaping the meaning of our lives as we
take new directions and set out on new paths.

It follows from this view of life as an ongoing process of interpretation
and reinterpretation that there is a circularity built into life itself: a person understands what his life is all about in terms of the specific events

that occur along the way, yet those events can only be understood as having a determinate significance in terms of where his life as a whole is heading. There is a *hermeneutic circle* built into life itself: we understand the whole in terms of the parts, yet those parts have the meaning they have only in the light of the whole.

Dilthey's descriptive psychology therefore portrays human experience as a dynamic temporal flow with a determinate structure characterized by teleology, development, and meaning. This temporal flow of life is inextricably bound up with the wider context of a specific culture and history. In his later writings, Dilthey tries to account for our understanding of others in terms of three fundamental features of human existence: *life-experience, expression,* and *understanding.* The dynamic interdependence of these dimensions of life provides the basis for the human sciences.

Dilthey sees the first of these elements, life-experience, as internally related to expression. In his view, our experiences naturally and spontaneously take on a concrete form as expressions in the world: for the most part, life-experience is manifest in gestures, actions, and words. To speak of expression here, however, is not to imply that one's inner feelings and thoughts are at first clearly formulated and accessible to introspection and only later come to be vented. On the contrary, for Dilthey, one's thoughts, feelings, and desires are only defined and given a concrete form through what one *does* in speaking and acting in the world. This means that a person can only gain full access to what she feels or thinks through her expressions. Expressions first bring to realization what was initially only inchoate and partially formed. As Dilthey (1976, p. 176) says, "Only his actions, his formulated expressions of life and the effects of these actions on others, teach man about himself. Thus, he comes to know himself only by the circuitous route of understanding." Dilthey even suggests that for certain very basic feelings, the "inner" or "mental" *is nothing other than* the meaningful expression as it appears in the full context of life—as he says, "the gesture and the terror are not two separate things but a unity" (p. 221). Given this view, we can see that the Romantic distinction between inner, mental events and outer, physical behavior is a relatively high-level abstraction from "the psycho-physical unity"—the full, embodied human being—and not something that is actually found in our experience.

Dilthey calls the different kinds of expression found in the public world *objectivations of mind,* and he sees the totality of enduring human expressions as making up what he calls (following Hegel) *objective spirit (objektiver Geist).* Objective spirit or mind (the word *Geist* suggests something essentially shared and worldly, like "team spirit") includes expressions of life that have been deposited throughout history in the systems, institutions, customs, and practices of a historical culture, and it makes up the common background of intelligibility we all come to master as we are initiated into the practices of our historical community. In Dilthey's words, "The great outer reality of mind [Geist] always surrounds us. It is a manifestation of mind in the world of the senses. . . . *Every single expression represents a common feature* in the realm of this objective mind. Every word, every sentence, every gesture or polite formula, every work of art and every political deed is intelligible because the people who expressed themselves through them and those who understood them have something in common; the individual always experiences, thinks and acts in a common sphere and only there does he understand" (1976, p. 191).

As we become enculturated into these publicly accessible forms of life, we all come to have some shared grasp of how things count and where things stand for our culture. "We live in this atmosphere, it surrounds us constantly. We are immersed in it. We are at home everywhere in this historical and understood world; we understand the meaning and significance of it all; we ourselves are woven into the common sphere" (Dilthey, 1976, p. 191). For example, we all have some grasp of what is at stake in the religious sphere in America, whether we have been brought up to be religious or not. Because each individual first finds himself or herself in terms of these socially mediated possibilities of understanding, Dilthey says we are "bearers" and "representatives" of common social systems in our culture (pp. 195, 197).

The shared intelligibility of objective mind leads to the third element in Dilthey's triad: understanding. In Dilthey's view, it is because the public life-world is always already comprehensible to us as participants in this world that we always have a direct understanding of a wide range of the actions and gestures we encounter around us. Dilthey (1976) describes forms of "elementary understanding" that provide the building blocks on which more complex forms of understanding are built: "acts from which continuous activities are composed, such as picking up an object, letting a hammer drop, cutting wood with a saw," and so on. The purposes of these acts are, so to speak, written on the face of things—we are not "conscious of any inference from which this understanding could have arisen" (p. 220). As Dilthey (pp. 221–222) says, "From this world of objective mind the self receives sustenance from earliest childhood. It is the medium in which the understanding of other people and their expressions takes place. For everything in which the mind has objectivated itself contains something held in common by the I and the Thou. . . . The child grows up within the order and customs of the family which it shares with other members and its mother's orders are accepted in this context. . . . Thus the individual orientates himself in the world of objective mind."

As a rule, we immediately understand others in terms of their *place* within the familiar systems of interaction that make up our public life-world. When the behavior of others is not immediately transparent to us, however, we have to make an effort to "reconstruct" (*Nachbilden*) the mental context of that person in order to understand him or her. But such reconstructing or "reliving" has nothing to do with sympathy or empathy (Dilthey, 1976, p. 227). What is at stake is not feeling the other's psychic states but reconstructing the life structures and context from which the behavior emerges. When I watch *Hamlet,* for example, I do not want to understand the ideas in Shakespeare's mind when he wrote the play; I want to understand the lived reality that is made manifest in the actions of Hamlet.

In Dilthey's view, hermeneutics—the attempt to understand the experience of life embodied in works, and especially in written works—has the same open-endedness and defeasibility as life itself. The circularity built into life is reflected in the hermeneutic circle that characterizes all human sciences. The circularity built into all inquiry means that the human sciences can never achieve final closure in their investigations. Our changing interests and goals shape our understanding of the subject matter we are studying, while those studies themselves constantly transform our self-understanding and goals. There is no exit from this circularity to uninterpreted data or timeless truths independent of the background of understanding we bring with us to our interpretations.

Martin Heidegger: Ontological Hermeneutics

Dilthey's primary interest in hermeneutics was always epistemological. His ultimate concern throughout his life was grounding the human sciences by showing how the understanding of others is possible. Heidegger achieved the shift from epistemological to ontological hermeneutics in his greatest work, *Being and Time* (1927/1962). Where epistemological hermeneutics had asked the question, How can we understand others? Heidegger's ontological hermeneutics asks, What is the mode of being of the entity who understands? When this sort of ontological question is given priority, Heidegger believes, it becomes apparent that epistemology, far from being a neutral inquiry into justifications for belief, is in fact loaded down with ontological presuppositions about human beings and their basic relation to the world, presuppositions we would do well to set aside in order to take a fresh look at the reality we want to understand (see Guignon, 1983). Heidegger's breakthrough into ontological hermeneutics is surely the most important event in the formation of the contemporary approach to this discipline. Yet his texts are notoriously difficult to grasp, and the tightly interwoven ideas in *Being and Time* are hard to summarize succinctly. For the purposes of this book, it should be enough to sketch out some of Heidegger's main claims about the being of humans (commentators use the German word for existence, *Dasein,* to refer to human being). Because many of these claims pick up on ideas implicit in Dilthey and are developed later by Charles Taylor and Hans-Georg Gadamer, this short account should suffice for the purpose of indicating Heidegger's relevance for the social sciences.

Being-in-the-World as the Being of Humans

Like Dilthey, Heidegger (1927/1962) holds that we must start from the facticity of life, that is, from our own existence as it is "there-for-us" in the midst of our ordinary activities, prior to all abstract theorizing and scientific conceptualization. If we are to be true to the concrete realities of actual existence, we have no choice but to start out from a description of our own vague, tacit "preunderstanding" of ourselves and our world as this is made accessible in our everyday ways of being-in-the-world. What the early Heidegger called the hermeneutic of facticity, and renamed the analytic of Dasein or existential analytic in *Being and Time,* starts with a phenomenological description of our own way of being as agents dealing with equipment in a public life-world. On the basis of this description, Heidegger hopes to identify basic "essential structures" characteristic of all humans.

The method of *Being and Time* is hermeneutic: it involves an interpretation of one's own being as an entity who is engaged in the activity of interpreting. Seen in this way, *Being and Time* is an interpretation of interpreting, and its preliminary goal is to identify the structures common to any interpreting activity whatsoever. Interpretation is needed for us to get clear about our own being, Heidegger suggests, because our ordinary self-understanding is shot through with misinterpretations and distortions that are due in part to our tendency to think of ourselves in terms of the categories and concepts handed down to us by what he calls the *tradition.* This tradition leads us to think of ourselves as substances with attributes, as objects among others in a space-time coordinate system, as distinct "individuals" with no real bonds to others, as entities located in the present, and so forth. In order to free ourselves from the calcified views we absorb from the metaphysical outlook of our culture, then, we need to engage in a deep interpretation of the "text" of average everydayness to try to find its "hidden," underlying meaning—the most "primordial" and authentic interpretation of our own being beneath the misinterpretations that crop up in our so-called common sense.

Heidegger characterizes our everyday way of being—as agents "dwelling" in familiar situations—as "being-in-the-world." With this hyphenated expression he tries to undercut the idea that, at the most basic level, we are minds or subjects who happen to be in contact with an "external" world of material objects. As Heidegger describes it, being-in-the-world is a "unitary phenomenon" in which self and world are reciprocally intertwined in such a way that there is no way to drive a wedge between a "self" component and a "world" component. To clarify this unitary phenomenon, he begins by describing the way equipment shows up for us in a familiar activity such as building something in a workshop. When we are hammering boards together in our workshop and everything is running smoothly, Heidegger suggests, what we initially encounter is not a brute object, a "hammer-thing," which we then invest with properties of usability and function. Rather, what shows up for us is a holistic "totality of equipment" where the being of the equipment is determined by its possible and real uses in achieving specific ends in this specific context. Insofar as equipment "always already" presents itself as *counting* for us in some way or *mattering* to us in relation to what we do, it presents itself from the outset as significant or meaningful.

Heidegger calls the structure of significance relations we find around us the *worldhood* of the world. What is most striking about this account of the "worldhood of the world" is that Heidegger resists the temptation to treat the meaningfulness of things as mere projections of human mental "coloring" onto intrinsically meaningless and valueless objects. His goal is to get us to see that in our initial, everyday, prereflective encounter with the world, things show up for us directly as already value-laden and as having significance. Although it is certainly true that meanings cannot exist unless there are agents (humans) in the world, there is no reason to think that meanings exist only in our minds. Instead, they are as much a part of the furnishings of the world as mass, velocity, and position. In this view, then, meanings and values do not exist in out heads; they are "out there" in the dynamic life-world we encounter in our day-to-day affairs. In this view, the subjectivization of meaning and value in modern naturalism is a high-level theoretical construct, the result of a sort of breakdown in our ordinary being-in-the-world, which gives us no insight into the true nature of reality as we actually encounter it.

The Self as Agency in a Social and Historical Context

Heidegger's description of being-in-the-world shows how the being of equipment is tied up with our undertakings as agents in familiar contexts. But it is not just the case that contexts of significance depend on us for their being. Heidegger also tries to show that *our own being* is constituted by the world in which we find ourselves. His claim is that we can become human in the full sense of that word only by undertaking roles that are made possible by the familiar contexts of worldhood in which we act. My ability to *be* a home craftsman, for example, is made possible by the context of significance of the workshop, where I can be a handyman or a klutz but not a samurai paying court to a daimyo or a priest saying mass.

In Heidegger's view, the worldly contexts in which we find ourselves are themselves given their content by the wider context of practices and customs of our historical culture. Like Dilthey, Heidegger holds that the intelligible life-world is organized and given content by the ways of acting and speaking that are common within the social context in which we live, a totality of practices he calls *das Man*—the "they" or the "one" (in the sense of "anyone"). As we are initiated into the practices and forms of life of our shared world, we gain some mastery of the norms and standards regulating interpretations and actions in that context. This is what Heidegger means when he says, "From this world, it [that is, *Dasein*] takes its possibilities, and it does so first in accordance with the way things have been interpreted by the 'they.' This interpretation has already restricted the possible options of choice to what lies within the range of the familiar, the attainable, the respectable—that which is fitting and proper" (1927/1962, p. 239). As essentially social agents whose most basic way of being is to be part of a "we," humans exist as a *clearing* in which things in general (tools, quarks, mental events, selves) first come to show up *as* entities of a determinate sort.

It should be obvious, then, that our embeddedness in a wider cultural context cannot be thought of as a limitation or a burden that constricts our ability to be our "genuine selves." On the contrary, our participation in the "they" is an enabling condition that first lets us *become human* in the sense of having a substantive, meaningful identity. If such a cultural content were lacking, we would be not so much free spirits or noble savages as Roman candles going off in all directions, lacking any coherent direction or content. Thus Heidegger firmly rejects any existentialist conception of authenticity understood as shaking off the influence of the "herd" in order to get in touch with one's true, inner self. To be authentic is not to transcend the public but to realize public possibilities in a more coherent, focused, and creative way.

In trying to understand what it is to be a human being, Heidegger rejects traditional conceptions of humans as *objects* or *substances* of some sort, whether mental or physical or some combination of the two. Instead, he proposes that we think of a human being as an ongoing *happening* or *event*—the unfolding of a life course "between birth and death." This conception of Dasein as becoming and movement follows from the description of Dasein as having a hermeneutic structure. For Heidegger, humans are self-interpreting beings. What this means is that humans *care* about their own lives—their *being* (who and what they *are*) is "at stake" or "in question" for them. In Heidegger's words (1927/1962, p. 32), Dasein is "ontically distinguished by the fact that, in its very being [that is, in the process of living out its life], that being [its life] is an *issue* for it." Through our care about our own lives, things around us can be disclosed as *meaning* something to us in our undertakings.

Because our lives are at issue for us, we have always taken some *stand* on our existence by taking up some set of the possible roles, lifestyles, and personality traits made accessible in the "they." Heidegger refers to this way of taking a stand on one's being as *understanding*: Dasein is the entity that, in taking a stand, understands what it is to be. This understanding generally takes the form of a competence or "know-how" in living that never comes to be explicitly formulated. For example, taking a stand as a teacher means mastering the public world of education, which in turn means coming to have a "preunderstanding" of the equipment, other people, and modes of being a self in that world. This background of preunderstanding provides us with a "forestructure" or prior grasp of things, in terms of which we make sense of what we encounter and wend our way through the world. Such a preunderstanding first gives us a window onto the world and our own being as agents in that world.

In Heidegger's view, humans just *are* the stands they take in existing in the world: we *are* what we *make of ourselves* in living out our lives. Like the existentialists, Heidegger sees humans as "self-constituting" beings whose *being* (or identity) is shaped by what they do. But in opposition to most existentialists, Heidegger emphasizes that the interpretations we draw on in defining ourselves are always made accessible by the historical culture in which we find ourselves. This means that we are always implicated in and indebted to our cultural context. In drawing on the interpretations circulating in our public world, we compose our own autobiographies, and in the process we constitute our own "essential nature" or "personal identity." This is not to say that humans have no drives or needs, but rather that any drives and needs they have come to have a determinate form only within the framework of interpretations opened by a cultural clearing. In this sense, *"the 'essence' of Dasein lies in its existence"* (1927/1962, p. 68). Our nature or being as humans is not just something we *find* (as in deterministic theories), nor is it something we just *make* (as in existentialist and constructionist views); instead, it is *what we make of what we find.*

For Heidegger, then, Dasein just *is* what it interprets itself as being in taking over roles and realizing possibilities throughout its life. This conception of life as an ongoing, self-constituting "happening" suggests that human existence has a distinctive, tripartite temporal structure. First, Dasein is futural in the sense that it is always underway in realizing aims and projects in its ordinary existence as an agent. This thrust forward into a realm of possibilities for the future Heidegger calls *projection*. Second, Dasein always finds itself *thrown* into a specific cultural and historical setting, already caught up in the midst of things, with pregiven obligations arising from its context and the choices it has made in the past. Our thrownness into a determinate situation defines our facticity, and it defines the "hermeneutic situation" one must start out from in trying to make sense of things. Finally, Dasein is always addressing and handling the entities it finds around it in terms of the linguistic articulations made accessible in its social world. This way of being engaged in the present Heidegger calls *discursiveness*.

In human "lived time," the future has a certain priority. As agents involved in practical contexts, we are always "ahead of ourselves" to the extent that we have taken a stand on our thrownness and are already accomplishing something for our lives. This directedness toward the future means that what is happening now and what has happened before have a determinate meaning in terms of where things are heading in general—the final configuration of meaning we are shaping for our life as a whole. Because the meaning of a life is determined by its movement toward this final culmination or completion, Heidegger characterizes human existence as "being-toward-the-end" or "being-toward-death." Here, death refers not to one's demise, the event of passing away, but rather to the *finitude* of life—the fact that we constantly stand before the "possibility of having no more possibilities" and that our existence is therefore moving toward a final closure or culmination, whether we are aware of it or not. Just as the events in a story gain their meaning from the contribution they make to the outcome of the story as a whole, so the events in a person's life gain their meaning from their relation to the overarching projects that define her life as a totality, right up to the end. As Paul Ricoeur (1983) has shown, Heidegger's conception of the future-directedness of human existence implies that our lives have the form of a narrative in which past and present are woven together in the light of an anticipated completion.

Heidegger calls the temporal unfolding of life *historicity*. This term is supposed to capture the way that, as futural beings, we are constantly thrown back onto our past, the reservoir of accomplishments and commitments that we take over, in acting in the present. As a historical being, "Dasein 'is' its past in the way of *its* own being which, to put it roughly, 'happens' out of its future on each occasion" (1927/1962, p. 41). But historicity also refers to our participation in and belonging to the wider context of the "destiny" of a historical culture. What Heidegger wants us to see is that the forms of life and ways of understanding that constitute the "they" have emerged over the course of history and make up the shared "heritage" of "a people." But this means that human existence is also characterized by historicity in the sense that each of us embodies a shared legacy of interpretations drawn from history. To fully realize our humanity, then, we must seize on this shared historical context as we try to fulfill the ideals and projects definitive of our community.

Charles Taylor's Development of Heideggerian Hermeneutics

Many of the core ideas in Heidegger's ontology of human existence have been developed in illuminating ways by Charles Taylor (b. 1931), the Canadian philosopher of the social sciences. Although Taylor's ideas appear in a number of intricate and tightly argued texts, for our purposes it will suffice to concentrate on one essay in which his debt to Heidegger is made quite explicit, "Self-Interpreting Animals" (1985c). Like Heidegger, Taylor starts out from a description of our everyday experience of ourselves and the world—from the familiar sense of things we have prior to the imposition of theoretical concepts and scientific abstractions. We need to start out from such an "insider's perspective," Taylor holds, because it is this concrete experience of life that the human sciences attempt to explain, and our explanations would be pointless if we were not clear in advance about the "explanandum" of our explanations. Taylor recognizes, of course, that scientific research may contribute to our finding that our initial sense of things was mistaken. Nonetheless, it is important to get clear about what that initial experience *is* if the human sciences are going to account for what they set out to explain, namely, our actual, full-blooded experience of ourselves and our world.

Like Heidegger before him, Taylor is challenging the seemingly self-evident assumption that the world is, at the most basic level, meaningless and value-free. This is an assumption embraced by theorists who believe that the world presupposed by the classical natural sciences—the world conceived as a collection of physical objects in causal interactions—is the "real" world, whereas the world we experience in everyday life is mere appearance, the way things seem *to us*. These theorists, whom Taylor calls objectivists, assume that the values and meanings we encounter in our ordinary experience (for instance, the beauty, usefulness, goodness, and badness we find in things, as well as the smells, tastes, and felt warmth we normally experience) must be thought of as projections of the human mind, products of our responses, preferences, and inclinations, and not anything that is actually *in* the world. The idea that we need to distinguish "objective reality" from the "subjective coloring" we impose on reality has become deeply ingrained in our thinking largely because of the impact of the scientific way of thinking about things that took shape in the seventeenth century. For the early scientists, it became an article of faith that statements about qualitative and experience-relative characteristics of things (for example, color or beauty) can be eliminated in favor of statements that involve no such characteristics (for example, statements about light waves, the stimulation of the retina, and brain activity). As Taylor (1985c) notes, such an objectifying orientation creates the ideal of "a reductive explanation of human action and experience in physiological and ultimately in physical and chemical terms" (p. 47), an explanation devoid of any references to qualitative and subjective phenomena like meanings and values.

The objectifying standpoint in objectivist science, together with the trend toward subjectifying all meanings and values, has led to modern subjectivism, the view that values exist only in the minds of humans—that they are created by our needs, desires, interests, and feelings, and have no concrete existence "out there" in the real world. Thus, influential moral philosophers such as J. L. Mackie (1977) suggest that values are "queer" to the extent that we cannot observe them or touch them with our fingers. From this queerness, these thinkers conclude that values are not part of the objective order of reality, so they must be human inventions, projections of our subjective goals and responses onto reality. Subjectivism in turn has led to modern nihilism, the view that because morality has no basis other than the transient and fortuitous attitudes of individuals and cultures, it is ultimately an illusion—a sucker's game. It is this sort of nihilism that Nietzsche announced in his claim, discussed in Chapter Five, that "God is dead."

Hermeneutic philosophers generally want to call in question the distinction between "subjective" and "objective" that has dominated our thinking since the rise of modern science. First, they point out that there are numerous things that are not tangible or that exist only relative to human interests which nevertheless exist "out there" in a perfectly straightforward sense. The center of gravity of a car, for example, is not a material object we can observe and touch (even if it coincides with something material), yet no one doubts that such a thing exists *in* the world. Moreover, the view of the Grand Canyon from the south rim is something that is accessible only from a particular human point of view, but that does not mean that the south rim of the Grand Canyon is only an appearance that exists in our heads. If we use the words *subjective* and *objective* as ethical subjectivists use these words, we can say that centers of gravity and things seen from particular viewpoints are as objective as light waves and brains.

More important, if we take off the scientific spectacles that govern our ways of seeing things in high-level reflection and think about how we actually experience things in everyday life, it is obvious that values and meanings are experienced as "out there" in the world rather than as in our minds. What normal person could see a child hit by a car and not feel that something bad had happened right there in the street, not just in somebody's mind? It is only a highly specialized and profoundly questionable characterization of "reality" that could lead people to doubt the reality of badness, shamefulness, or goodness in the world. If the word *objective* is understood as the opposite of *subjective,* that is, as referring to what exists concretely "out there" in the world, then it seems that we have every reason to say, and no reason to doubt, that values are objective.

Taylor wants to liberate us from both the objectified view of reality and the subjectified view of values we get from modern science. In a number of his writings (for example, 1989, especially Part 1; 1991, pp. 43–69), he has tried to show that we would not be able to think and live as we do unless we grant that meanings, imports, significances, and values have a real existence. From Taylor's standpoint, science's objectified picture of reality makes sense only if we ignore the fact that we humans are also part of that world and that the events that befall us and the things we do, with all their intrinsic significance and "coloring," are as much a part of the external world as anything else.

The essay "Self-Interpreting Animals" raises some powerful objections to the assumption that an objectifying approach to the human sciences is appropriate or even possible. Taylor begins the essay by looking at

what goes on in our familiar, everyday "experienced motivations" in acting: our feelings, emotions, and desires. We tend to think of feelings as
blasts of raw affect or as euphoric or dysphoric "passions" that pass over
us and lack any cognitive content. In contrast, Taylor holds that we can
make sense of our feelings only if we see them as embodying a judgment
about the object they bear on: "To experience fear is to experience some
object as terrifying or dangerous; to experience shame is to experience
some object or situation as shameful or humiliating" (1985c, p. 47).
Because emotions involve a sense of our situation in this way, they are
"affective modes of awareness" of the world around us. But this means
that having an emotion involves our being aware of a situation as having a particular significance or "import": in having the emotion, we experience things as being "relevant or of importance to the desires or
purposes or aspirations or feelings of a subject" (p. 48). Thus we
encounter the situation as having a *meaning* in the sense that what we
have feelings about is experienced as *counting* for us or *mattering* to us
in some way, as when, for example, something presents itself to us as
shameful or successful or threatening.

Taylor carries this description of emotions a step further by claiming
that the meanings or situational imports we experience in the world
around us cannot be regarded as purely subjective, that is, as existing
entirely within our minds. Situational imports, in his view, are "out there"
in the world in which we live. Imports cannot be reduced to the subjective responses of the agents involved in the situation, because the import
"gives the grounds or basis of our feelings" quite independent of whether
anyone actually feels the emotion in a particular case (p. 49). For example, a disgraceful action has the characteristic of being humiliating
whether the person who performed the action has the appropriate feeling
or not, which is why we can say, "You ought to be ashamed of yourself."
Similarly, it is because situational imports are the grounds for our feelings
that emotions can be mistaken or irrational—as occurs when people feel
ashamed of something about which they have no reason to feel that way.
Because the import of the situation is not reducible to the feelings and
responses of the people involved in the situation, we must conclude that
it is "out there" *in* the situational context itself; for example, a person has
a right to feel proud of her efforts because they were successful. In Taylor's view, the success is as much a part of what is out there in the world
as the things the person has done.

So far in his argument Taylor has made two main points. First, in a full
description of our ordinary motivations, we must acknowledge the existence of imports or meanings in the world. Second, statements about these

meanings cannot be reduced to statements about our subjective feelings together with statements about objectively specifiable features of the world, because the meanings provide the basis or ground for the feelings, regardless of how people actually happen to feel in a particular situation.

This second claim will be attacked by those who are committed to the objectivist ideal of explaining all phenomena solely in terms of objective factors, where these factors are understood as excluding any features of things that exist only relative to the modes of experience of humans. Such critics will hold that statements about feelings and imports should be reducible to a physiological level of statements about stimuli and responses (behavior) or about physiological mechanisms. In reply, Taylor argues that even if such explanations are possible at the level of fairly elementary human feelings (for example, fear and the danger of damage to the organism), they do not seem to be possible in understanding higher-level feelings like shame. To condense his rich and complex argument, we might isolate three main objections he raises to the objectivist's reductionist project.

First, Taylor (1985c) argues that a purely objectivist account would make it impossible to make sense of the *object* of our feelings. There is no way to characterize a shameful situation solely in terms of its objectively specifiable features, because something can be shameful only in relation to factors—"like our sense of dignity, of worth, of how we are seen by others"—that are essentially bound up with our experience of our lives in meaning-laden and qualitative terms (p. 54). Any attempt to explicate the meaningfulness of the situation will therefore inevitably make references to other meanings defining our aspirations, situational understanding, ideals, and so on, and these features of our lives can themselves be explicated only in meaning terms. As Taylor puts it, "For emotion terms like *shame,* an explication cannot be found which does not invoke other meanings for the subject" (p. 55). Emotions only make sense in relation to meaningful situations, those situations are meaningful only in relation to our goals and aspirations, and those aspirations are given shape by our emotions and the situations in which we find ourselves. When we try to specify the objects of our concern, then, we find ourselves inextricably caught up in a web of meaning terms, a mesh of experience-relative identifications that is not reducible to statements about objectively specifiable facts: "import and goal, the language of feelings and consummations desired, form a skein of mutual referrals, from which there is no escape into objectified nature" (p. 57). The holistic nature of our experience of imports renders an objectivist account impossible, *not* because statistically significant correlations cannot be established but because it is impossible to so much as specify the *terms* of the correlation without relying on the very understanding of meanings that objectivists reject.

Taylor's second line of argument (1985c) for the irreducibility of meanings leads to one of his most central claims: that humans must be understood in irreducibly evaluative terms. Beginning from the observation that feelings embody judgments about situations, Taylor notes that feelings also incorporate insights into what really matters to us in our lives. When we examine our feelings, we find that they have a hierarchical structure. There are, of course, the various first-order feelings and desires that come over us, such as a gut-level dislike of someone or a desire for sex. We experience these basic, *de facto* reactions and urges directly, and they push us to act in particular ways. But we also recognize that we have certain second-order feelings and desires that range over and govern those first-order emotions and desires. Second-order motivations include such feelings as shame, remorse, and pride, and such desires as the concern with maintaining one's dignity or being a decent person. These second-order motivations are "higher" than our first-order desires to the extent that they play a crucial role in evaluating and regulating our first-order desires: for example, a spontaneous dislike for someone is overcome by the desire to be a kind and loving person, or a physical attraction is reined in by one's sense of marital loyalty. Second-order motivations are concerned with the qualitative worth of first-order desires and feelings, and they define what is noble or base, deep or superficial, decent or sleazy, higher or lower. Thus you might resist spiteful feelings or vengeful desires because, from the standpoint of your second-order commitments, you find such responses unworthy, despicable, base, beneath your dignity.

In Taylor's view, these second-order motivations define a person's sense of the good, and this understanding of what is worthwhile in turn defines one's *identity*, giving that person a sense of purpose and direction. In this respect, feelings "incorporate a sense of what it is to be human, that is, of what matters to us as human subjects" (1985c, p. 60). Our second-order feelings and desires form a web of imports and meanings "which resonate through our whole psychic life" (p. 60). Part of what it is to have an identity as a person, then, is to try to articulate and clarify these defining motivations in the course of living out our lives. In Taylor's words, "the sense of imports that [feelings] incorporate has been articulated into our picture of our moral predicament, according to which some goods are higher than others, while still others are false or illusory" (p. 63). These *strong evaluations* define our "moral map" (p. 67) and give us a sense of "place" and purpose in the world (see Taylor, 1989, pp. 25–52). To the extent that we care about realizing such higher aims through time, they give our lives the kind of continuity and directedness characteristic of a well-formed narrative.

It is quite difficult for objectivist approaches to provide a satisfactory account of such second-order motivations, as objectivist accounts generally distinguish only pro and con feelings—basic attractions and repulsions—and limit themselves to identifying quantitative distinctions among the relative strengths of the feelings and desires. Thus an objectivist approach will see a clash of desires as similar to the conflicting pulls one might feel between two attractive options, where whichever desire is stronger wins out in the end. On such an account, in Taylor's terminology, people are seen as "simple weighers" who in the end always realize their strongest preferences (for example, choosing the éclair over the napoleon on the dessert tray because one feels a stronger "pull" toward it). What such an approach cannot account for, it seems, are real *qualitative* differences in desires, where second-order desires are not simply stronger but are distinctive in that they embody a sense of what is good or truly worthwhile and so are definitive of one's identity.

Taylor's third line of argument against objectivist reductionism rests on the Heideggerian observation that our experience of ourselves and the meaningful life-world around us is always made accessible to us through our public language. In this view, we come to grasp feelings and situational imports through the linguistic articulations we learn as we grow up into the world. This implies that the vocabulary we use in articulating our desires, aspirations, and sense of situational significance is essentially shared. In other words, our feelings and aspirations gain their point and significance from the role they play in the "public space" of dialogical interchange with others (1985c, p. 57). Thus feelings of shame, the aspiration to dignity, our care about how we stand in relation to one another—all these meanings and values are essentially public: they are *out there* in the common life-world, part of the air we breathe in growing up into our culture. Because our sense of what is important is drawn from the pool of public possibilities deposited in our language, it follows that we are always in tune with each other to some extent in our understanding of what life is all about.

The fact that feelings and the import-ascriptions they embody are mediated by language means that we have the ability to shape and transform our feelings by articulating what we feel in language. To show how language constitutes emotions, Taylor considers a case in which a person feels a strong attraction toward another person and initially thinks she is in love. As time goes on, however, she comes to recognize that it is not so much romantic love she feels as admiration and respect. It should be obvious that this way of articulating the feeling transforms the feeling: becoming able to describe it as admiration brings it into focus and defines it *as* admiration. Moreover, both the initial articulation of the emotion as "love" and the transformed articulation are shaped and given concrete content by the structure of implications and connections embodied in our historically formed language. This example shows the reciprocal interdependence of feeling and public language: emotions always come to us in a form determined by the interpretations made accessible by our language, and our ability to redescribe what we feel forms and can transform our feelings.

In Taylor's words, "To say that language is constitutive of emotion is to say that experiencing an emotion essentially involves seeing that certain descriptions apply" (1985c, p. 71). And seeing what descriptions apply determines the quality of the feeling: "Language articulates our feelings, makes them clearer and more defined; and in this way transforms our sense of the imports involved; and hence transforms the feeling" (p. 71). But this means that feelings cannot be thought of simply as objects with determinate characteristics independent of any interpretations or meanings—say, as raw feels, or epiphenomena of physiological states. Because the interpretations we accept help constitute the emotions, there is no interpretation-free datum we can pick out and characterize independent of the fabric of interpretations that shape our shared feelings and experiences. The linguistic constitution of our experience undermines one of the most fundamental assumptions of the objectivist outlook, the assumption that an object exists and has determinate features "independent of any descriptions or interpretations offered of it by any subjects" (Taylor, 1989, p. 34) and that science can us give a correct representation of that object. Given this account of feelings as "always already" interpreted, Taylor steers a path between constructionism, which paves the way to the pop psychological idea that "thinking makes it so," and scientific objectivism, which treats feelings as just "there," whether as introspectible mental items or as side effects of physiological states.

The latter two arguments against reductionism give us a picture of humans as beings who orient their lives according to strong evaluations and who articulate their feelings and sense of meanings through linguistic reflection. With this conception of humans as beings whose very identity is shaped by self-interpretations and self-evaluations, Taylor fills out Heidegger's claim that humans are self-interpreting beings. To the extent that our articulations of feeling, import, and value define our sense of what life is all about, our interpretations *constitute* our being. In Heidegger's vocabulary, we are beings whose lives are *at issue* or *in question*, and because of this we take over (or drift into) the possibilities of self-understanding made accessible in our language. As Taylor (1985c, p. 75) puts it, "our attempted definitions of what is really important can be called interpretations, . . . and we can therefore say that the human animal not only finds himself impelled from time to time to interpret himself and his goals, but that he is always already in some interpretation, constituted as human by this fact. To be human is to be already engaged in living an answer to the question [of what is important or worthwhile], an interpretation of oneself and one's aspirations."

Because of this irreducibly interpretive and meaning-laden character of many human phenomena, only someone who is in on the forms of life and sense of meaningfulness suffusing this experiential world will be able to make sense of what such self-interpreting beings feel and do. In Taylor's view, hermeneutic social science, understood as the interpretation of self-interpreting beings, is possible because the scientists doing the interpreting are themselves self-interpreting beings, coparticipants in a shared linguistic and historical world, and so are, to some extent at least, "insiders" with a prior grasp of the meanings and evaluations they set out to interpret.

Hans-Georg Gadamer: Philosophical Hermeneutics

The project of working out an ontological hermeneutics has been carried forward by Heidegger's student, Hans-Georg Gadamer (b. 1900). In his major work, *Truth and Method* (1989; originally published in German in 1960), he makes it clear that he is not concerned with developing a method or technique for understanding others: "Fundamentally I am *not proposing a method*; I am describing *what is the case*" (p. 512). His aim in this book is to answer the Kantian question, How is understanding possible? where this asks not about rules and procedures for grasping another's meaning but rather about the conditions that make it possible for there to be such a thing as understanding at all. The proper work of hermeneutics, Gadamer says (1989, p. 263), "is not to develop a procedure of understanding, but to clarify the conditions in which understanding takes place." His attempt to "discover what is common to all modes of understanding" (p. xxxi) begins with a phenomenological description of our prereflective, pretheoretical ways of encountering things. Gadamer (1976, p. 3) suggests that, ever since the seventeenth century, the "the real task of philosophy" has been to reconcile "our natural view of the world—the experience of the world that we have as we simply live out our lives" with "the pronouncements of science." Such a task of reconciliation requires that we first become clear about our natural experience of those dimensions of the human life-world that the human sciences set out to explain. The three main parts of *Truth and Method* therefore address the question of how we come to understand humans and their creations in aesthetics, in historiography, and in the study of language.

Gadamer feels he has good reason to bypass the preoccupation with method in epistemological hermeneutics. In his view, the methods that have proven so valuable in the natural sciences tend to distort and conceal when they are applied in the human sciences. We can see why this is so by considering the presuppositions built into *methodologism*, the belief that knowledge is possible only through the application of standardized procedures or sets of rules. Methodologism assumes (1) that there are objects "out there" in the world, with determinate properties that exist independent of our ways of describing and acting and (2) that we gain knowledge of those objects by bracketing our subjective interests and presuppositions so that we can be completely objective in making observations and devising explanations. Methodologism calls for an "alienating distanciation" (*Verfremdung*) from the world, a detached, objective stance in which we set aside our ordinary, pretheoretical experience of things so that we can focus on the intersubjectively specifiable features of objects.

Gadamer is willing to grant that method plays a useful role in the human sciences, but he believes that the uncritical acceptance of methodologism can act as a distorting lens in attempting to make sense of humans and their creations. First, he suggests that the kind of abstraction characteristic of the natural sciences may conceal a great deal of what is most important to us in the study of humans. "Science always stands under definite conditions of methodological abstraction," Gadamer writes, and this means that "the successes of modern sciences rest on the fact that other possibilities for questioning are concealed by abstraction" (1976, p. 11). Such abstraction presumably does no harm in the natural sciences, where our primary interest lies solely in producing testable counterfactuals and gaining predictive control over objects. But in the human sciences, where we must start out from an understanding of what things actually *mean* to people, abstraction conceals large parts of what is experienced and therefore gives us a one-sided and bleached-out picture of what we want to understand.

Gadamer sees another difference between natural and human sciences in their assumptions about the objects they study. In the natural sciences, he claims, it makes sense to suppose that there are objects "out there" in the world, with determinate, experience-independent properties, which someday might be known as they actually are. In other words, knowledge as the correct representation of an antecedently existing object makes sense in the natural sciences. This is the source of the attempt to work out what Bernard Williams (1978) has called an "absolute conception" of the world, a conception of the way things are independent of the forms of experience of any sentient creatures. Gadamer (1989) claims, however, that we cannot speak of an object of research in the human sciences in this sense because, in these sciences, "the theme and object of research are actually constituted by the motivation of the inquiry" (p. 284). Georgia Warnke (1987) clarifies this point by considering historical accounts of the First World War. Until the 1940s, the First World War could be identified as the "Great War" or the "War to End All Wars," and the events of the war were then perceived through the lens of that interpretation. When World War II occurred, however, the earlier war came to be thought of as "World War I," and the significance of its events was transformed due to this new turn of events. In a similar way, due to the events in the second half of the twentieth century, World War II is now called "the last good war," and future events will surely lead to new interpretations of that war.

Needless to say, the point here is not that the war exists only in the minds of historians. Rather, the claim is that the interests and frame of reference of a particular community of interpreters at a particular time determine what past events *mean,* and the meaning those events have in turn determines how the events show up for the interpreters. Because there is no clear way to draw a distinction between the "facts" of the matter and the ways they are interpreted (because the interpretation determines the *selection* of what can count as a "fact"), Gadamer can say that there is no "object in itself" to be studied by historiography. "This is precisely what distinguishes the human sciences from the natural sciences. Whereas the object of the natural sciences can be described *idealiter* as what would be known in the perfect knowledge of nature, it is senseless to speak of a perfect knowledge of history, and for this reason it is not possible to speak of an 'object in itself' toward which its research is directed" (1989, p. 285). In this sense, it is right to say that the human sciences *constitute* the reality they study in a way the natural sciences do not. This is why the sharp distinction between the knowing subject and the object to be known, taken as self-evident in the natural sciences, cannot be made in the human sciences.

Gadamer (1989) is well aware that challenging the idea that there are "hard facts" and fixed criteria in the human sciences runs the risk of encouraging radical skepticism about our ability to understand others. He discusses a form of "untenable hermeneutic nihilism" that arises in textual interpretation if one supposes that because "there is no criterion of an appropriate reaction" in reading a text, the meaning of the text must be determined entirely by the reader's reception of it, and any reader's response is as good as any other (p. 95). It is in order to avoid this sort of hermeneutic nihilism that some literary theorists embrace methodologism and insist that the meaning of the text is grounded in the author's intentions or the literal meaning of words. Gadamer, in contrast, thinks we can avoid both nihilism and methodologism. In his view, the feeling that we are caught in a dilemma—that we must *either* hold fast to a hard-headed objectivism *or* sink into an intolerable relativism—is actually an illusion fostered by the pervasiveness of methodologism in modern thought (see Bernstein, 1983).

One of the central aims of *Truth and Method,* then, is to liberate us from some of the uncritical assumptions built into methodologism. Gadamer (1989) tries to show that in understanding humans and their creations, there is "an experience of truth that transcends the sphere of the control of scientific method" (p. xxii). In watching *Hamlet,* for example, we gain an insight into human nature that might be distorted and concealed through methodological abstraction. To cast light on this truth, Gadamer presents a detailed description of our original, prereflective ways of experiencing such human phenomena as art, history, and language, and he gives an account of how this initial experience is deformed when it is forced into the theoretical frameworks of aesthetics, historicism, and linguistic analysis. By recovering the initial insights we have prior to theorizing, Gadamer hopes to clarify "what the human sciences truly are, beyond their methodological self-consciousness, and what connects them with the totality of our experience of the world" (p. xxiii).

Human Phenomena as Events

This totality of our experience of the world can be grasped, however, only if we can free ourselves from the tendency to see ourselves and our world in terms of the "substance ontology," the uncritical assumption that reality must be thought of as consisting of *substances* (for example, physical or mental substance) with properties—the traditional "substance/accident" ontology. The idea that reality must be understood as consisting of something that "stands under" (sub-stance) attributes and persists through change can be traced back to Greek philosophy, and it has dominated Western thought ever since. Thus, the Middle Ages conceived of the real as "created substance," Descartes thought of it as extended or mental substance, and modern science sees reality as consisting of physical substance.

Gadamer, in contrast, suggests that the traditional substance ontology, far from being a faithful portrayal of what we normally experience, is in fact the product of some rather high-level theorizing that is quite remote from our actual experience. In our pretheoretical lives, he suggests, we generally experience humans and their creations not as static objects with properties but as events or happenings. By clarifying the event-character of human phenomena, Gadamer hopes to dispel the illusion that we are forced to choose between objectivism and relativism.

We can get a feel for the "event ontology" developed in *Truth and Method* by taking a close look at Gadamer's phenomenological account of the being of works of art. Gadamer points out that, under the influence of the distinctively modern philosophical field called aesthetics, people today tend to think of a work of art as a created object (a painting, sculpture, book, or whatever) that produces in us a special sort of experience (*aesthesis* means "sensation"). Given such a view of art, we tend to think that appreciating a work of art is a matter of "getting into the artist's mind" in order to reconstruct the initial creative experience—the artist's ideas, intentions, emotions, and so forth—that led to the creation of the work. As in Romanticism generally, the work is seen as an outer sign of something inner, and understanding is a matter of reading backward from the outer presentation to the inner creative impetus.

Gadamer undercuts this aestheticist picture of a work of art as an object that induces sensations by suggesting that such a view, far from being a "natural" way of thinking of art, in fact results from the breakdown of a more original and authentic way of experiencing art found in earlier times. In premodern societies, he holds, an artwork was experienced as an event in which a truth is made manifest. Gadamer's attempt to characterize artworks as events of truth begins, oddly enough, with a description of play (*Spiel*). When people are fully caught up in play, Gadamer suggests, they tend to lose themselves in the to-and-fro of the game—tossing a ball back and forth, perhaps, or playing parts at traditional festivals. As the play becomes more and more absorbing, it comes to seem as though the game is playing the players rather than the players playing the game. In Gadamer's words (1989, p. 103), "the players are not subjects of play; instead play merely reaches presentation through the players." According to this description, the game has a buoyancy of its own, a vitality and movement that supersedes the consciousness of the players who are absorbed in the game. The ontological character of the play is "self-presentation," an "emerging-into-being" that takes on a life of its own as it unfolds. What a game *is*, seen from this standpoint, is something that is defined only in the ongoing "happening" of its emerging-into-presence or coming-into-being; the play is not just a pale reflection of some source that exists independent of the play. As Gadamer says, "In being presented in play, *what is* emerges" (p. 112, emphasis added).

The connection between play and art becomes apparent in Gadamer's discussion (1989) of how play starts to have a stable structure or form of its own. There is a "transformation into structure" that occurs when the play comes to have "the character of a work, of an ergon [completed creation] and not only of energeia [activity of creating]" (p. 110). Just as the free-for-all of ancient Dionysian festivals evolved into the great Greek tragedies, so any form of play can begin to have a structure. Open-ended playfulness can be transformed into a play in the sense of a dramatic work that contains a unified meaning in itself. The dramatic play "is a meaningful whole which can be repeatedly presented as such" (p. 117). However, like ordinary playing, which *is* only in being played, theatrical works exist only in their productions: their *being* is fully circumscribed by their actual presentations in different contexts and different times. Because plays *are* only in their productions in this way, there is no way here to make a clear distinction between "original" and "reproduction." Instead, the play just *is* the unfolding event of its being produced over time, its emergence-into-being through ever new productions.

Gadamer's most important claim in this discussion of plays is that theatrical works do not just represent life—they do not merely "imitate" a reality that exists independent of them—but rather they *present* life in such a way that a "superior truth" emerges through the presentation. The transformation into structure "is a transformation into the true. . . . It produces and brings to light what is otherwise constantly hidden and withdrawn" (1989, p. 112). We can clarify this conception of the work as a disclosure of truth by considering the relationship between tragedy in life and tragedy on the stage. We are all aware of the tragic dimension of life through our experience, yet we also see how this tragic dimension usually remains cloudy and confused due to the open-endedness of the future. Because "'reality' always stands in a horizon of desired or feared or, at any rate, still undecided future possibilities," there is always "a superfluity of expectations" that leaves undecided the ultimate significance of events (p. 112). Our interpretation of "reality" at any given moment is always underdetermined—or, more accurately expressed, *overdetermined*—to the extent that the open-endedness of the future implies that there are no completed unities of meaning in the flow of life itself.

Nevertheless, life situations can sometimes achieve a degree of closure and finality of form, and when this happens, life begins to take the form of a dramatic narrative. "Now if, in a particular case, a context of meaning closes itself and completes itself in reality, such that no lines of meaning scatter in the void, then this reality is itself like a drama" (pp. 112–113). It is precisely this sort of closure and unity of meaning that is made manifest in great dramatic works. What is distinctive about tragedy on the stage, according to Gadamer, is that it raises to truth and fulfillment the generally inchoate and ambiguous tragedy found in life. In the work of art, a world is revealed, a world through which everyone recognizes that "this is how things really are." By giving shape to what is usually only tacit and potential in our everyday world, the work of art defines and lights up what is "constantly hidden and withdrawn" in life so that we can see it *as* what it truly is: "The world that appears in the play of presentation does not stand like a copy next to the real world, but *is that world* in the heightened truth of its being. . . . Without being imitated in the work, the world does not exist as it exists in the work" (p. 137, emphasis added).

The account of art as an ongoing "event of truth" helps clarify Gadamer's general claims about the nature of such human phenomena as texts, historical events, and discourse. First, he sees such phenomena as ongoing events which, like play, are prior to and definitive of the human "subjects" who are involved in them. Thus, a literary work is not an object with a meaning fixed by an author's intentions but rather is an event in which textual meaning (the very *being* of the text as text) comes alive and is formed through different readings over time. But this means that understanding is not just reproductive; it is also creative: "Understanding must be conceived of as a part of the event in which meaning happens, the event in which the meaning of all statements . . . is formed and actualized" (1989, pp. 164–165).

Second, our accounts of human phenomena cannot be thought of as neutral depictions of a pregiven reality. When Gadamer says that "the world that appears in the play of presentation . . . *is* [the real] world in the heightened truth of its being," he suggests that reality first becomes focused and coherent in being presented. Thus, "The concept of *mimesis* . . . [does] not mean a copy so much as the appearance of what is presented" (p. 137). In other words, our articulations of human reality define and give shape to that reality, letting it be what it is. This implies that social theories do not simply mirror a reality independent of them; they define and form that reality and therefore can transform it by leading agents to articulate their practices in different ways.

Finally, the description of an artwork as an ongoing emergence of *truth* points to a way of thinking of truth not as a static picturing of an independent reality—being *true of*—but instead as a faithful presenting of aspects of reality—a being *true to*—which is open to change. Such a conception of truth lets us see how accounts of human phenomena can be subject to revision without thereby being relativistic or "merely subjective." This transformed understanding of "truth" is one of the most suggestive ideas hermeneutics has to offer the human sciences.

The Historical Embeddedness of Understanding

Gadamer's description of textual meaning shows that the meaning of a text is inseparably bound up with the different ways the text is understood throughout history. This awareness of the historicity of textual meaning leads Gadamer to reflect on the historical nature of understanding and on historical understanding itself. In his discussion of the concept of understanding, Gadamer notes that the primary meaning of the word *understanding* in German is "reaching an understanding" or "coming to an agreement" with someone about a subject matter or topic. How is understanding in this sense possible? Gadamer begins by noting that, contrary to Schleiermacher's claims, what is usually "given" in human interactions is not misunderstanding but rather a bedrock of shared understanding that results from our enculturation into communal practices and our mastery of a common language. For the most part, we already understand one another in wide areas of our lives. It is this shared background of preunderstanding that provides us with a basis for trying to understand what at first is alien. In Gadamer's words (1976, p. 15), "Misunderstanding and strangeness are not the first factors, so that avoiding misunderstanding can be regarded as the specific task of hermeneutics. Just the reverse is the case. Only the support of familiar and common understanding makes possible the venture into the alien."

Understanding becomes a problem, then, only when this "natural life in which each means and understands the same thing is disturbed," leading to the need to overcome a misunderstanding (Gadamer, 1989, p. 180, translation modified). Even when a misunderstanding does arise in talking to another person, however, we try to resolve it not by getting into the mind of the other but by trying to reach an agreement concerning the subject matter we are discussing. In other words, ordinary attempts to reach an understanding focus on what the conversation is *about*—the matter at hand (*die Sache*)—not on the other's mental events. In Gadamer's view, it is only when the attempt to reach an agreement on the topic fails that what Schleiermacher called "psychological" understanding is needed, and even then the concern with the other's mind is only a step on the way to reaching an accord concerning the topic being discussed. What matters in understanding, according to Gadamer, is what we have between us—the concern with reaching an agreement about the subject matter—rather than what is going on in the minds of individuals.

In characterizing understanding, Gadamer notes that there are two "formal conditions of understanding"—two general "anticipations" about what is going to arise—that govern any activity of interpreting. The first of these is the "anticipation of completion" (*Vollkommenheit*), the expectation that because "only what constitutes a unity of meaning is intelligible," the text or utterance one is trying to understand will have a complete or fulfilled meaning (1989, p. 294). Needless to say, this does not imply that every bit of discourse actually *has* a unified meaning; it merely holds that any activity of interpreting which is conducted in good faith is guided by an expectation that things will come together or add up in some way. Because of this anticipation of completion, attempts to understand others operate within a hermeneutic circle: each part of what is said is understood in terms of some anticipated sense of what the whole will be, while the whole is understood in terms of its parts.

The second formal structure of understanding is the "anticipation of truth." If every attempt to understand another always aims at achieving an agreement about the subject matter, then any interpretation of a text or utterance must assume that the text really has something to say to us and that we might learn something from it if we are open to what is being said. Once again, this is not to say that all bits of discourse are in fact true or that we should listen uncritically. Instead, both these formal anticipations are similar to what Kant calls *regulative ideas:* they are assumptions that are needed for interpretation to be carried out at all. Thus, the presumption of truth—the openness to the possibility that the text has something of substantive validity to say to us—is a precondition for any attempt at reaching an agreement about a matter at hand.

The background of preunderstanding that tunes us in to others includes not just these formal anticipations but also certain "prejudgments" or "prejudices" we pick up as we are initiated into the public world of a shared culture. Gadamer's attempt to "rehabilitate" the concept of prejudice is one of the best known and most contentious components of his thought. By treating prejudice as something positive, he sets himself in opposition to what he calls the Enlightenment's "prejudice against prejudices," the view that prejudgments and authority are invariably sources of error. In Gadamer's view, interpretation and reflection are always guided by a background of prejudgments, drawn from the shared understandings deposited in our historical culture, which give us a frame of reference for identifying things, posing questions, and knowing what sorts

of answers make sense. Understood in this way, prejudices are not external impositions that constrain our ability to be free and rational subjects.
On the contrary, having a "horizon" or framework of prejudgments is
what first makes it possible for us to think and act in intelligible ways.
Like Dilthey's "objective mind," prejudices serve as enabling conditions:
they give us a window onto the world and let us *be* agents of a determinate sort.

That all thinking and action is made possible by historically mediated
prejudices leads to what Gadamer (1989) calls the principle of effective
history. In contrast to both the Enlightenment's contempt for the past and
Romanticism's mystification of it, the notion of effective history is supposed to bring out the fact that past and present are so inextricably bound
together that no sharp contrast between them is possible. On the one
hand, because our current horizon of understanding is a product of what
has come before, the past—the "variety of voices in which the echo of the
past is heard" (p. 284)—constantly influences "what seems to us worth
enquiring about and what will appear as an object of investigation"
(p. 300). On the other hand, because our current ways of appropriating
the past determine how those traditions can *count* for us, the horizon of
the present first gives the past the voice in which it can speak to us. Thus,
there is a reciprocal interaction or circular relation between the past and
the present: the past is effective as a tradition that transmits possibilities
of understanding to us, while our current interpretations of those possibilities are themselves part of the historical effectiveness of the tradition
and define how the past can make sense. Thus, the concept of effective
history refers to both (1) the effectiveness of the past on the present and
(2) the effectiveness of the present in transmitting the past.

In terms of this view of effective history, we can no longer see time as
a gulf that cuts us off from earlier epochs. Instead, time "is actually the
supportive ground of the course of events in which the present is
rooted. . . . It is not a yawning abyss, but is filled with the continuity of
custom and tradition, in the light of which everything handed down presents itself to us" (Gadamer, 1989, p. 297). It follows that understanding
a text from another time or culture cannot be thought of as a matter of
bracketing our present outlook in order to recapture the thought processes
and context of the other. Instead, understanding is achieved through a
process of "fusing horizons," an attempt at achieving agreement in which
the horizon of the present lets the voice of the other be heard as making
a truth claim, while the claim of the other transforms the horizon of the
present and compels us to rethink our prejudices.

Although Gadamer discusses the concept of horizon fusing in the context of his account of understanding texts from the past, the concept applies quite generally to understanding others. The important thing to see is that reaching an understanding is not a matter of miraculously breaking through barriers in order to empathize with another or reconstruct the other's mental processes. It is, instead, a matter of *integrating* another's horizon in such a way that one's own outlook is changed in the process. In Gadamer's view (1989), it is wrong to suppose that our situation is such that we are confronted with incommensurable perspectives or worldviews that must be *either* assimilated into one master perspective *or* treated as irreducibly opposed. For "the closed horizon that is supposed to enclose a culture is always an abstraction." Different horizons "constitute the one great horizon that moves from within and that, beyond the frontiers of the present, embraces the historical depths of our self-consciousness" (p. 304). In other words, there is a constantly unfolding horizon that is shaped and reshaped by the emerging horizons of the people who make it up.

What Gadamer brings out in his account of effective history is our deep *belongingness* in and *indebtedness* to the wider historical context in which we find ourselves. Because our very identity as humans is shaped and defined by the range of possibilities passed down by history, ontological individualism—the belief that at the deepest level we are self-contained individuals—cannot capture the truth about our being as humans. In Gadamer's view, we are historical beings through and through: "Long before we understand ourselves through the process of self-examination, we understand ourselves in a self-evident way in the family, society and state in which we live. The focus of subjectivity is a distorting mirror. The self-awareness of the individual is only a flickering in the closed circuits of historical life" (1989, p. 276). As Charles Taylor (1985b, p. 40) puts it, "we are aware of the world through a 'we' before we are through an 'I,'" so that "we always find ourselves as a we-consciousness before we can be an I-consciousness." In this view, our vaunted individuality is a construct produced by particular sorts of social practices, one interpretation of the being of humans among others, with no privileged status in telling us something about our true natures.

If we are always entangled in a web of prejudices that dictate our possibilities of interpretation and assessment, then what is at issue for trying to understand another is not escaping from all prejudices, as Enlightenment thinkers supposed, but rather separating worthy prejudices from harmful ones. This is not something that can be done from the standpoint of a tribunal of pure reason outside all historically conditioned prejudices, for, as Gadamer (1989, p. 276) observes, "the idea of an absolute reason is not a possibility for historical humanity. Reason exists for us only in concrete historical terms." Yet Gadamer also insists that we should be reflective about our own prejudices: "The important thing is to be aware of one's own bias, so that the text can present itself in all its otherness, and thus assert its own truth against one's own fore-meanings [prejudices]" (p. 269). But this element of self-critique does not imply that we have some neutral position outside all prejudices from which we may check the credentials of our prejudices. Although we can subject any of our prejudices to criticism from the standpoint of other prejudices that for the moment are taken as beyond criticism, there is no way to bracket *all* our prejudices and critically assess them, for that would leave us with no basis for reflection and critique whatsoever.

Gadamer's conception of understanding as an attempt to reach an agreement with someone leads him to envision interpretation as an ongoing dialogue structured by "the logic of question and answer." We have seen that every attempt at understanding another is guided by a framework of historically shaped prejudices that determine in advance how things can matter for us. If we are concerned to reach the truth of the subject matter being discussed, then our exchange with the other must take the form of a questioning in which we try to see the relevance of what the other says to our horizon of anticipations and prejudgments. And because we are guided by the anticipation of truth—the assumption that the other has something of substantive validity to say in relation to our interests and concerns—we experience the other's utterances as answers to our questions, answers worthy of respect because they might be true.

This ongoing to-and-fro of question and answer characterizes not just attempts to understand texts and other forms of discourse; it characterizes the unfolding "play" of tradition as well. In Gadamer's view, we are always engaged in an ongoing dialogue with the meaningful, historically shaped preunderstanding we find around us, and in this dialogue we are constantly testing our assumptions in the light of what texts and other speakers have to say. In fact, for Gadamer, as for Hölderlin and Heidegger before him, a human being just *is* an ongoing dialogue or conversation in which the voices of the past are critically appropriated in the attempt to find a truth applicable to the present. Because our horizon and the questions we ask are constantly transformed through this ongoing dialogue, Gadamer (1989) says that each attempt to understand a text or discourse will produce a different result: that is why "we understand in a *different* way, *if we understand at all*" (p. 297; compare to p. 309).

One of Gadamer's most important claims about hermeneutics is that the *application* of what is understood to one's current situation is not something secondary to the task of understanding. If every attempt to reach an agreement with a text involves making that text speak to one's current situation, then the ability to apply the text to the present is a fundamental component of all understanding. Gadamer draws on Aristotle's description of the role of practical wisdom (*phronesis*) in ethics to clarify how application is carried out. Aristotle showed us how, in applying moral insights to practical situations, we start with a general insight into what ought to be (for example, the ideal of courage) and then try to see how that insight is relevant to the current situation. In this process of applying the general to the particular situation, it often happens that the general truth itself is transformed in the light of our perception of the demands of the concrete situation. Thus, to take a familiar example, we accept the general ideal of courage, but we sometimes find that the truly courageous thing to do is to turn the other cheek or to humbly acknowledge a mistake. By being applied to particular cases, the meaning of the general ideal or insight is enriched and transformed.

In Gadamer's view, the application of texts from the past has a similar structure. We start from the assumption that the text has something true to say to our current situation, and we adopt a stance of openness toward what the text says. In this process of seeing how the text speaks to our current situation, however, we generally have to critically evaluate and revise the claim made by the text so as to adapt it to the present. An example would be the way we must transform the ideals of Greek democracy, which held only for males, to make them fit our more egalitarian and inclusive political world. The result of this process is a transformation not only in the meaning of the text but also in our own self-understanding as we integrate the claim of the text into our own lives.

This moment of application displays the *critical* dimension we must adopt toward the tradition in trying to appropriate what it says. Far from recommending an uncritical acquiescence to the past in his account of prejudice and tradition, Gadamer thinks of tradition as an ongoing dialogue or debate in which we often are compelled to revise or even repudiate ideas of the past in our attempt to apply them to our lives. And the same holds for the voices of different cultural horizons: in our encounters with others, we come to criticize our own horizon. In the ongoing play of this open-ended dialogue, both the object we are investigating and our own being as investigators are transformed. This is not something that undermines tradition; on the contrary, tradition is nothing other than this ongoing process of "transmitting."

An examination of authentic dialogue provides a picture of how the event of understanding should unfold. Gadamer distinguishes three different forms of I-Thou relation. The first way of relating to another is to try to see the other as an instance of a type—for example, as a typical case of some specific trait. This objectifying approach to the other is found in attempts to explain others by using models of understanding drawn from the natural sciences: for instance, one has certain classifications and concepts on hand, and one tries to subsume the other under them. The second form of relation is the attempt to get inside the other's head—to "get his number" by figuring out how his mind is working. In this approach to understanding, one disregards what the other says and focuses on his motivations and mental quirks: "by claiming to know him, one robs the claims of their legitimacy" (1989, p. 360). This way of relating to another, found frequently in "charitable and welfare work" (p. 360), is often motivated by a desire to control and dominate the other. In the third form of I-Thou relation, the most authentic form, I listen to what the other has to say to me in an effort to arrive at the *truth* about some topic we both care about. In this sort of relationship, I start from the assumption that what the other has to say might be true, and I therefore adopt a stance of respectful openness to what she says: I constantly strive to make her arguments stronger, and I risk my own assumptions by letting them be challenged by hers. In Gadamer's view, it is only through this sort of authentic I-Thou dialogue that understanding others is realized in its fullest sense.

General Characteristics of Hermeneutics

Our survey of hermeneutics has traced the development of this movement from the nineteenth-century preoccupation with developing a *method* for the human sciences to its contemporary focus on working out an *ontology* of the human. Gadamer's *Truth and Method* shows us that the attempt to find a distinctive method for the human sciences is pointless, for such a method is neither possible nor necessary. On the one hand, because most important human phenomena make sense only within an unfolding tradition of meaning-and value-laden interpretations, there is no way to understand humans by applying an algorithm that generates objectively valid generalizations and predictions from intersubjectively specifiable data. On the other hand, it seems that no such method is needed, for truths about humans become manifest in familiar ways without the need for methodological abstraction or rule-governed procedures. (This explains the grain of truth in the old claim that you can learn more about human nature by reading Shakespeare than by reading a psychology textbook.) The ability to recognize these truths is made possible by the shared, background sense of life we all pick up in being initiated into a historical culture, and it is something we can enrich and expand through dialogue with others and through immersing ourselves in the cultural creations of our world. There is no procedure that will guarantee skill and success in the human sciences. But given the tenuousness of so much of our lives, it is not clear why anyone should expect such guarantees.

The central claim of *Truth and Method,* as the title itself reveals, is that the assumptions of scientistic methodologism are generally out of place in the human sciences because, for the most part, we already have what we need to discover the truth about humans. In appreciating the significance of this claim, however, we must note that the term *truth* has a somewhat different sense than it has in the natural sciences. Although finding the truth is still a matter of revealing the way things really are, the truths we discover about humans generally must be treated as defeasible not simply because new data may show up but because different interpretive perspectives and interests can compel us to rethink and revise the discoveries we make. The open-endedness and inconclusiveness this defeasibility implies has led some critics to charge Gadamer with a pernicious relativism: the view that whatever anyone *thinks* is true *is* true. What such a criticism overlooks is Gadamer's emphasis on how the tradition provides guidelines and models that constrain our possible claims. (Consider, for example, how the enduring value given to freedom in our culture rules out any glorification of slavery.) Such guidelines and truths may be interpreted in different ways with the appearance of new perspectives and interests, but, barring some currently unimaginable discovery or some inconceivable cultural upheaval, they will not be cast aside.

Although we would not wish to obscure the differences among hermeneutic theorists, we might identify three fundamental ideas characteristic of all hermeneutic ontology. First, hermeneutics holds that the conception of our situation as knowers that we inherit from mainstream natural science can give us a distorted view of things when we adopt it in attempting to make sense of human phenomena. The ideal of the detached, disinterested, coolly objective researcher makes no sense in the human sciences, because we are always contextualized in a public life-world, caught up in a holistic web of practices and linguistic articulations we can never objectify or control. That is why, in trying to understand others, we must draw on our own preunderstanding of what things are all about and apply it to the other, always remaining open to the need to revise our initial background understanding through the course of our interpreting activity. The human sciences therefore have an inescapable circular structure: there is a constant shuttlecock movement between the wider background understanding and the concrete realities being interpreted.

Second, humans must be seen as self-interpreting beings whose defining traits are shaped by the stands they take in being participants in a public life-world. Because our intentions, desires, and beliefs are made possible and given concrete form by the background of self-interpretations and self-assessments circulating in a historical culture, a crucial part of understanding others will involve seeing where they stand in relation to the public meanings and projects of their community. This is the point of the slogan, "Meanings are in the world, not in our heads." The conception of humans as self-composing stories in a shared context of meaning has been the basis for trying to formulate what we might call a historical-dialogical conception of the self: a way of thinking of humans as unfolding narratives whose being is shaped through an ongoing dialogue with others in a communal context (see Taylor, 1989, especially Section 2.1; Taylor, 1991; MacIntyre, 1981; Ricoeur, 1992; Bruner, 1990; Polkinghorne, 1988; Richardson, Rogers, & McCarroll, 1998; Guignon, 1998b).

Finally, because humans just *are* what they interpret themselves as being within their social context, according to hermeneutics, it follows that social theory cannot be thought of as a neutral process of recording facts about humans. Insofar as interpretations devised by social scientists feed back into the culture and so define and alter the reality they describe, hermeneutics leads us to recognize that the practice of interpreting humans has wide-ranging ethical and political implications. Far from being a neutral, value-free form of inquiry, the human sciences always operate with culturally mediated value assumptions and always influence the cultural context they address. Hermeneutics therefore calls for a capacity for moral and political awareness that is all too easily overlooked in both mainstream scientistic and constructionist approaches to studying human phenomena.

PART THREE

TOWARD AN
INTERPRETIVE
PSYCHOLOGY

10

RETHINKING PSYCHOTHERAPY

ONE OF THE MOST COMMON criticisms made of modern therapy theories, even by those who adhere to one or more of those theories or have a favorite among them, is that there seems to be a disturbingly wide gap between formal theory and actual practice. There appears to be a gulf between, on the one hand, the "existential" realities of therapy practice and everyday life and, on the other hand, the supposedly "scientific" theories and methods that purport to explain and guide the practical side of things. This gap between theory and practice likely is a major source of the extravagant proliferation of competing schools of therapy on the American scene. By one count (Frank, 1978), there were 260 such approaches in 1978! Surely that number has more than doubled in the present day. Most of these schools claim the superiority of their own explanatory framework and techniques over the others. Yet the best research on therapy outcomes (Garfield & Bergin, 1986) suggests that most approaches work comparably well for most clients. Clearly there is disorder in the house of theory.

In recent years, a number of thoughtful critics have voiced another criticism of modern therapies. As we have discussed elsewhere, they express concern that a certain one-sided individualistic outlook is built into the very fabric of therapy theory and practice, making it likely that modern psychotherapy helps perpetuate a way of life that gives rise to many of the problems in living that therapy itself is intended to ameliorate.

In this chapter, we argue that contemporary hermeneutic thought gives us powerful tools for getting to the bottom of these concerns about modern psychotherapy. It helps us detect the origins of the much-noted gap between theory and practice and discern some of the deep, less obvious sources of a supposedly problematic individualistic coloring. First, we suggest that the critique of methodologism by Gadamer and other hermeneutic thinkers gives us crucial insights into these matters. Second, we examine the revisionary interpretations of psychoanalysis developed by Heinz Kohut and Roy Schafer. Kohut's widely influential ideas incorporate many psychoanalytic revisionist themes and many of the humanistic values that pervade the therapy field. The existentialist cast of Schafer's thought captures the core commitments of many modern therapists, except that Schafer is unusually explicit and clear about his assumptions and aims. Moreover, each of these approaches seeks consciously to remedy some of the problems we have identified. Finally, we contend that they fall short of correcting important deficiencies in therapy theorizing that they themselves identify, and make suggestions concerning how a hermeneutic ontology might contribute to a needed, more fundamental reconceptualization of the field.

Methodologism and the Goals of Psychotherapy

Gadamer's critique of methodologism, as discussed in Chapter Nine, is aimed at social scientists' widespread tendency to impose an approach which assumes that the quantifying and experimental model of procedure that has been immensely successful in the natural sciences should also be employed in studying humans. This tendency leads to what Taylor (1993) calls an ontologizing of method, which assumes that this natural-scientific model of procedure gives us an accurate characterization of the nature and structure of human experience. In other words, it assumes that human knowledge at its deepest level is a matter of collecting data and forming hypotheses in a way very similar to ideal natural-scientific investigation.

The basic outlines of the ontology resulting from methodologism are well known, as we discussed in Chapters One and Nine. Modern science was made possible by an extraordinary capacity for abstraction. By rejecting the tendency to see the world only or mainly as a cosmic dwelling suffused with meanings and purposes, the early scientists could describe the world as a vast collection of objects on hand for our theorizing and technological control. This objectifying stance toward reality carries with it a particular interpretation of the experience and capacities of humans. From this perspective, humans are seen as knowing subjects registering input from the external world, processing the data according to rational procedures, and striving to devise a correct representation of reality. Less obviously, this perspective implicitly makes human knowers responsible for the rationality (in this sense) of their picture of the world. It imposes on them a demand for lucid self-awareness and critical detachment from the supposed illusions spun out by custom, example, and authority. This ontologizing also supports the tendency we have discussed throughout this book toward ontological individualism, the view that because humans are distinct centers of experience and action, human reality in general can be understood atomistically as a collection of individual "subjects."

Taylor (1995) describes how this objectifying stance and representational outlook fits hand in glove with the widespread modern picture of the self as disengaged, disembodied, and atomistic or "punctual." This self is "distinguished . . . from [the] natural and social worlds, so that [its] identity is no longer to be defined in terms of what lies outside . . . in these worlds." The modern self is able to freely and rationally treat both itself and the outside world instrumentally and to alter both for its own benefit. The representational outlook thus begins to look like a central strand of our way of life in modern culture, a way of life that seems to purchase valuable freedoms at the price of much alienation. Indeed, Taylor suggests that the modern notion of a punctual self confronting a natural and social world to which it has no essential ties is as much a *moral* as a scientific ideal. It connects with central moral and spiritual ideas of the modern age. These include the modern ideal of "freedom as self-autonomy . . . to be self-responsible, to rely on one's [own] judgment, to find one's purpose in oneself" (p. 7). This connection, however, is usually not acknowledged by modern thinkers, including therapy theorists, who advocate some version of this representational outlook. Rather, they tend to smuggle in their preferred moral outlook under the cover of what seems to be a respectably scientific standpoint.

This modern, objectifying stance toward reality entails a sharp split between the inner self—the arena in which perception and thinking occur—and the objectified outer world that is observed and explained. This subject-object split in turn generates an interlocking set of assumptions about the self, human agency, and the ends of living. First, the self is understood as a *thing* or *object* of a somewhat paradoxical sort. Humans are seen as natural organisms, subject to causal forces arising both from within and without, and as minds or fields of consciousness capable of representing objects and manipulating inner and outer nature for their own purposes. Theories in psychology may place a primary emphasis either on human behavior as the effect of causes or on the action of an autonomous agent. But they often try to incorporate both, despite the sharp tension between the two emphases.

Second, human agency is pictured as skillful means-ends calculations aimed at achieving pregiven or preferred goals. It is indeed true that the nineteenth-century Romantic backlash to this rather mechanistic picture adds a new "expressivist" vision of agency as self-realization achieved through getting in touch with and expressing one's innermost feelings and potentialities in artistic creativity, personal growth, and intimate communion with others or nature. This Romantic vision opens valuable new ways of thinking about human possibilities, and it seems to provide an antidote to the one-sided instrumentalist outlook of Enlightenment thought. But Gadamer (1975) has shown that the Romantic reaction against Enlightenment rationalism only tended to reinforce the picture of the self as essentially an individual mind set over against an artificial social order. The Romantic image of life, according to Gadamer, preserves and reinforces the modern split between *logos,* concerned with matters of reason and objective truth, and *mythos,* concerned with a subjective realm of imagination and feeling—it merely emphasizes and places primary value on the opposite number of the pair.

The modern belief that the ends of living either are pregiven or are matters of individual preference helps explain why the goal of mainstream social science and psychotherapy theory for the most part has been to restrict itself to value-neutral explanations or descriptions of human dynamics, and why this field is so comfortable treating cultural and moral values as purely subjective. Either such meanings and values must be kept at arm's length and treated for the most part skeptically and instrumentally, or they will compromise our autonomy and integrity in a domineering manner. Perhaps the reason we cling to familiar conceptions of psychotherapy in the face of the limited success in social science and worrisome questions about the goals of psychotherapy is not so much steadfastness as a stubborn attachment to the one-sided individualism and horror of arbitrary authority that inspire the representational outlook.

The third key assumption correlated with methodologism concerns what constitutes the ends of living or the good life in general. The highest goal of life, given this understanding of self and agency, seems to be *autonomy,* understood as a lack of constraints and the ability to decide one's own fate. It is important to remember that autonomy can be understood either *instrumentally,* as enhanced efficacy in means-ends strategies and success in mastering the world, or *expressively,* as fulfilling the inbuilt potentials at the innermost core of one's identity. It also can be expressed *existentially,* as a matter of choosing one's values and ideals with the lucid awareness that they lack any sort of factual or moral justification whatsoever, a viewpoint that lies at the heart of several influential therapy theories. The value of autonomy in one of these forms is taken as self-evident and ultimate in our modern outlook. However, the glorification of autonomy in therapy theorizing generates the antinomy of freedom we have discussed several times—any needed sense of legitimate authority or "freedom to," as Fromm put it, seems to irrationally circumscribe true freedom of the sort to which we are dedicated. With no authoritative guidance, the individual has no basis for decision. Neither the individual's inner life nor the mechanistic objective world (nor an existentialist void of meaning) seems sufficient to provide a basis for substantive assessments or life-defining aspirations. The sentimental overlay of Romantic faith in a deep inner truth about the self accessible through turning inward does little to improve this situation, because it buys in to methodologism's glorification of the individual subject at odds with the social world.

The ways in which major psychotherapy theories try to come to terms with this tension between autonomy and authority are strikingly similar. First, they hold fast to the antiauthoritarian temper of our age and explicitly promote only values that seem consistent with nurturing and preserving personal freedom. These include such ideals as rigorous honesty and self-transparency in reworking inner and outer reality for one's own self-chosen purposes, or self-realization through expressing one's deepest inner potential. Should the need arise to articulate some more ultimate sense of what life is all about, given their adherence to methodologism and a modern scientific outlook, theorists seem to vacillate between a quasi-Stoic ideal of detachment from an ultimately meaningless universe and an exuberant celebration of our freedom to master ourselves and our world.

At times, however, these ideals can appear empty. The lack of other substantive values aggravates the pervasive feelings of meaninglessness and isolation that are at the root of many modern problems in living. Then it appears that theorists or therapists smuggle in a moral coloring derived from older traditions, such as ideals of social service, altruism, self-sacrifice, dedication to a higher cause, acting on principle, love of neighbor, and so forth. These ideals seem to function like what Bellah et al. (1985) call second languages, languages such as those of the civic republican and Biblical traditions that lie somewhat concealed behind our first language, individualism. Nevertheless, these richer moral vocabularies are significantly at odds with our primary commitment to autonomy. We are forced to regard them in one of two ways, neither of which is satisfactory. We can treat them as mere means to achieving some unquestioned or morally neutral end, such as enhanced freedom or happiness. But then they lack any real value in themselves, are bound to appear gratuitous and dispensable, and will be unable to meet our need for authoritative guidelines or credible ideals in today's world. Or we can admit that these ideals are arbitrary, dogmatic impositions, in which case, eventually, we will have to resist them in the name of protecting individual freedom and integrity.

Freudian Metapsychology

Before turning to the theories of Kohut and Schafer, we will sketch in a few key ideas from Freud as background. The Freudian metapsychology that inaugurated modern psychotherapy reflects Freud's unquestioning adherence to what we are calling methodologism. Freud adopts the Cartesian picture of the mind as a self-encapsulated domain with no necessary connections to the world. But he also embraces the objectifying model by viewing the "mental apparatus" as a deterministic energy system undergoing internal adjustments and discharges in order to maintain homeostasis. The final product is what Ricoeur (1970) calls the familiar "mixed discourse," which blends deterministic and purposive terminologies—languages of "force" and of "meaning." Some psychoanalytic thinkers, even today, view this as a perfect way to capture both scientific rigor and faithfulness to experience, but detractors see this approach as undermining both these virtues. At the root of most complaints by post-Freudian revisionists is the deep gulf between the metapsychology and what actually seems to go on in therapeutic dialogue and life itself. Habermas (1971) astutely noted that the Freudian structural model fails to make sense of the kinds of rational self-transformations through "self-reflection" that the model was, in part, designed to explain.

As we discussed in Chapter Two, Freud's moral or existential stance toward life seems to involve an interesting combination of opposing elements. On the one hand, there is what Rieff (1966) terms Freud's analytic attitude, with its harsh "doctrine of maturity," which rejects all moral or religious values as illusory and proposes the "acceptance of meaninglessness as the endproduct of therapeutic wisdom" (p. 43). In line with this view, Freud seems at times to advocate a kind of "presentism" that encourages freeing oneself from the pressures of the past and abandoning unrealistic hopes and expectations about the future in order to live in the here and now. On the other hand, Freud has a strong sense of the tragic dimension of life, and he promotes a Stoic ethos of lifelong constancy and rigorous honesty in the face of inevitable suffering. The trouble here, of course, is that Freud's belief in the gravity and tragic worth of life is rendered gratuitous by his own analytic attitude. The Stoic ideals of detachment and fortitude seem to be no more than products of Freud's idiosyncratic personal preferences when they are stripped from the belief in a rational and meaningful cosmic order in which they originally made sense. As a result, Freud's morally serious outlook actually helps pave the way for what Rieff (1966) calls a new therapeutic age marked by the less high-minded values of a "psychological man" who "has no higher purpose than the maintenance of a durable sense of well-being" (p. 40). Freud's thinking gives no answer to the question of why we should, with him, bravely contemplate the suffering of the human race, rather than simply escape into momentary pleasures, distractions, or illusions.

Although Freud's metapsychology is deeply dissatisfying in these respects, it has proved difficult to improve upon. Freud pictured the ego as a "poor creature" caught between three masters—the "murderous id," the "punishing conscience," and a meaningless world of *Ananke* or fate. Generations of ego psychologists, object-relations theorists, philosophically minded thinkers like Erich Fromm, and others who draw on Freud's insights have tried to brighten up the psychoanalytic perspective by upgrading the powers of the ego, emphasizing our capacity for self-awareness and rational self-transformation, and acknowledging our genuine dependence on others. The problem is that these new approaches appear to be shot through with value assumptions that are no more justified than Freud's dark but dignified Stoic outlook. Their optimistic faith in our ability to achieve high degrees of lucidity and autonomy fails to do justice to what Freud saw so well: the limitations and tendentiousness of life.

From a hermeneutic standpoint, both Freudian and post-Freudian perspectives seem in many respects to be variants of methodologism, with its effacement of the meaningful life-world and its apotheosis of individual subjectivity. In the face of this gridlock, the revisionary interpretations of psychoanalysis developed by Kohut and Schafer promise a breath of fresh air. Kohut's self psychology tries to recover a sense of the wholeness of life. It brings out the importance of goals and ideals in psychic health and acknowledges the crucial importance of empathic, caring relations with others while still keeping in view life's limitations and tragic aspect. Schafer tries to capture a sense of the temporal dynamism of life by portraying the self as a self-authored narrative that is shaped and reshaped in dialogue. Both approaches enrich our grasp of practice and take steps in the direction of a hermeneutic understanding of self and world. Nevertheless, their attempts to transform therapy theory are limited because of the extent to which they still buy into key assumptions of methodologism.

The Self Psychology of Heinz Kohut

Kohut's self psychology tries to capture a richer and more holistic sense of the self than that found in the classical metapsychology. In self psychology, the self is a dynamic continuum of ambitions, skills, and ideals that strives to realize its inbuilt potential through creative expressions in the world. This "expressivist" view of the self goes hand in hand with Kohut's rejection of an objectifying explanatory approach to understanding human phenomena. As Kohut says, psychoanalysis can only "explain what it has first understood" (1977, p. 302). *Understanding* is defined as an empathic-introspective approach to others—an "immersion of the observer into the inner life" of another. In fact, the method of understanding is *definitive* of psychoanalysis: "an undertaking is defined as analytic," Kohut writes, "if it involves persevering immersion into a set of psychological data, with the instrument of empathy and introspection, for the purpose of scientific explanation of the observed field" (p. 308). As the "defining ingredient" of depth psychology, understanding in this sense has always been present in successful analytic practice, even though classical theories have failed to account for it adequately. Its priority implies that psychoanalytic interpretation aims not at discovering causal connections but at discerning "the meaning and significance of the material under scrutiny" (p. 145).

Self psychologists feel that the need for their brand of theorizing is especially pressing now because cultural transitions have led to a change in the types of problems therapists are called on to treat. They suggest that oedipal pathologies are seen less frequently, whereas "disorders of the self," and especially narcissistic personality disorders, are seen with increasing frequency (Kohut, 1977, p. 278). Therapists today are "sought out for help with depressions, with disintegrating marriages, with incapacitating work inhibitions . . ., with empty lives lacking zest and joy and seeking escape through addiction to drugs or alcohol, . . . and even [with] frenzied life styles, whether in business or the arts" (Wolf, 1977, pp. 203–204). This decrease in classical neuroses and increase in self disorders, according to self psychologists, is due primarily to recent changes in the institution of the family. Where Freud's patients were products of an *over*stimulated family environment that formed cohesive selves but led to distressing sexual conflicts in the oedipal stage, many of today's patients come from *under*-stimulated environments, and they therefore lack a sufficient sense of self to be able to enter into the oedipal stage in a coherent way (Kohut, 1977). These individuals, though often successful in their careers, experience pervasive feelings of isolation and meaninglessness, and lead joyless lives void of any sense of fulfillment. Thus, self psychology's emphasis on empathic understanding is motivated in part by the practical need under these new conditions to provide patients with the kind of genuinely caring human relationship that is necessary to the formation of a firm and cohesive self.

Kohut portrays the self as an evolving superordinate structure, sensed in an irreducible "I-experience," with classical drives and defenses as subordinate parts. The self has an inbuilt teleological structure—a striving toward fulfillment or realization—which determines a universal "narcissistic line of development" from birth to maturity. The goal of this development is a "healthy narcissism," which includes pride, assertiveness, vitality, joyfulness, creativity, and, eventually, mature wisdom and acceptance of one's mortality. In contrast to Freud's conception of the basically encapsulated mental apparatus forced into conflictual object-cathexes by its inner drives, Kohut regards the self as essentially embedded in a communal world and as initially shaped by a meaningful interplay of family relationships.

Kohut's developmental account (1977) identifies three main stages of normal or healthy development. In the earliest stage of primary narcissism, the infant experiences the "absolute perfection" of "archaic grandiosity" and omnipotence. Under normal conditions, this primal stage is disturbed by inevitable imperfections in parental care. If the child is fortunate enough to have empathic parental *self-objects* who "mirror" the child's budding assertiveness and provide opportunities for "idealizing" parental values, he or she will move with relative ease into the second phase of being a grandiose and exhibitionistic self. A measure of autonomy and initiative is attained here, although the child still remains dependent on parental and other self-objects for such vital functions as "tension regulation," maintenance of "self-cohesiveness," and "regulation of self-esteem." Under ideal conditions, this increasingly autonomous and cohesive self will experience the oedipal rivalry as a further opportunity for self-enhancement. As time passes, the child's unrealistic grandiosity and exhibitionism are tamed as he or she comes to recognize others as separate individuals. Genuine independence is achieved through "transmuting internalizations" that form stable internal structures for action in the world. It should be noted that for Kohut, autonomy is never severed from others. Internalizations of the mirroring and idealized "parental imago," together with "twinship experiences" with close self-objects in childhood, establish a dimension of social connectedness that provides the affirmation "we need to maintain the self throughout all periods of life" (1984, p. 199).

In the final stage of this development, the mature self has what Kohut calls a bipolar structure. One pole consists of the inbuilt talents and ambitions of the primal "nuclear self" as they are shaped in earlier stages of development, and the other pole consists of values and ideals derived from the idealized parental image. The two poles are bound together by an action-promoting "tension arc" relating talents to ideals. Kohut's emphasis on "the importance of goals and guiding values as both a reflection and a maintainer of psychic health" (Eagle, 1984, p. 72) contrasts sharply with Freud's generally negative view of the superego.

This account of normal development lets Kohut explain disorders of the self as the result of early parental failures in providing adequate empathic support or in being psychologically available as idealized self-objects. Such "narcissistic traumas" lead to "structural defects" in which the grandiose self and the parental image are insufficiently integrated for personality organization. Where a cohesive self is lacking, the individual experiences the threat of isolation from or merger with self-objects, a feared break-up of the self Kohut calls disintegration anxiety. In Kohut's view (1977, p. 120), such phenomena as hostility and destructiveness are not manifestations of basic aggressive drives but are "disintegration products" resulting from narcissistic injury or threats to self-cohesion. Generally, Kohut treats drivelike phenomena as products of the immature or injured self focusing on bodily functions that have not been integrated into a core identity by positive social relations.

This account of human development gone awry leads naturally to Kohut's view that therapy consists of the restoration of an empathic and supportive milieu in which the currently inhibited growth of the self can resume. Patients with narcissistic personality disorders present the therapist with symptoms that reflect immature, defensively distorted expressions of the individual's innate striving for wholeness and integrity. Through empathy and acceptance, the therapist lends himself or herself as a benevolent self-object and fosters mirroring or idealizing transferences (or both) in order to overcome past injuries and promote autonomous self-expression. What therapy practice involves, then, is not conveying insights into drive conflicts and control issues but providing an accurate, empathic understanding of narcissistic injuries and of the individual's continued striving for self-fulfillment. The goal of treatment, Kohut says, is to lay down "the structures needed to fill the defect in the self" (1984, p. 4) so as to build a self in which "an uninterrupted flow of narcissistic strivings can proceed toward creative expression" (1977, p. 53).

Kohut's claim that psychoanalysis requires understanding rather than explanation is reminiscent of the methodological or epistemological hermeneutics formulated by Schleiermacher and Dilthey, discussed in Chapter Nine. For Kohut, empathy is a matter of "recognizing the self in the other" (1977, p. 144). "Empathic observation" lets us put ourselves in the other's shoes, and "vicarious introspection" then shows us how the other person feels. Empathy is regarded as a sort of Schleiermacherian "divination" that aims at bracketing all explanatory schemas and totally immersing oneself in the subjective richness of others' lived experience in order to gain objective knowledge of their psychic life, as solid in its own way as what the natural sciences achieve in their sphere. As a result, the therapist can claim a genuine understanding of the other person and an accurate, respectful basis for interventions.

Kohut feels that psychoanalytic practice can succeed in repairing structural defects and open the way to genuine self-transformation only if it faithfully captures the deep inner truth about the individual's actual experience. If the therapist merely supplies rationalizations instead of dealing with real trigger events, Kohut says, "the analysand would . . . soon recognize that he has been exposed to a tactical manipulation" and will perceive it as "patronizing hypocrisy" or as "tantamount to lying" (1977, pp. 107–108). But Kohut's objectivism is also dictated by his theoretical project of discovering a universally valid generalization about human nature: the universal narcissistic line of development. Because he bases this generalization on adult patients' reports of empathic failures and narcissistic injuries in their early years, Kohut can claim its validity only if these reports are taken as objectively correct evidence.

Nevertheless, the critique of epistemologically motivated hermeneutics by Gadamer and others raises questions about this claim that empathy provides solid, objective knowledge of another person's inner experience. First of all, Gadamer criticizes the faith that introspection gives us immediate access even to ourselves. As Dilthey recognized, our own self-understanding is always caught up in a hermeneutic circle: we know ourselves only by way of "life-relations" and expressions that are mediated by the public practices and language of our shared historical world. The belief that we can gain direct access to a deep truth about our own innermost selves through introspection—however much the partisans of a particular brand of psychotherapy may feel they need it to justify their practices—is an illusion.

Second, because Kohut defines empathy as "vicarious introspection," it follows that the notion of empathy itself is also suspect. Kohut's belief that his theoretical generalizations are based on undeniable objective evidence both ignores the possibility that patient reports of past events may be creative interpretations that construct as well as discover meanings, and overlooks the fact that our own understanding of these reports is shaped by the historically produced prejudgments that give us an opening onto the human world. As Eagle (1984) observes, Kohut's naïve assumptions that he has direct access to the truth about his patients' experiences allows him to read his own prior evaluative assumptions about an inevitable and universal phase of a grandiose and exhibitionistic self into his patients' reports. Moreover, this "dogma of immaculate perception" may distort practice. For if the therapist interprets individuals' life histories using unacknowledged assumptions about a universal striving for self-enhancement, he is likely to arbitrarily impose his own value-laden views onto the patients' lives. If the therapist treats this ideology as an unquestioned objective truth about the human condition, then the possibility of critically reflecting on the ends of living through dialogue is closed off in advance.

Kohut's defense of his method of understanding arises from his conviction that Freud's cold and rationalistic conception of psychoanalysis as an explanatory science will be counterproductive in dealing with disorders of the self. There may be much truth in this view. But in articulating his opposition to Freud, Kohut presents us with a stark dichotomy. *Either* psychoanalysis adopts an overly detached and objectifying approach that threatens to deform lived experience and undermine therapeutic efficacy, *or* psychoanalysis will strive to achieve a respectful involvement in the lived experience of others through empathy, in which case it must assume that there can be direct insight into others independent of any interpretation. Only this second approach, Kohut thinks, will allow the analyst to achieve a "meaningful grasp—understanding—of the psychological field" of the patient in "experience-near" rather than "experience-distant" terms (1977, p. 143). Thus Kohut assumes that psychotherapy theory must choose between *either* being a somewhat manipulative explanatory science *or* a kind of empathic fusion that is supposed to provide, paradoxically, both genuine personal contact and objective knowledge of the other's inner life.

A hermeneutic ontology offers us an alternative to Kohut's dichotomy. In a genuine dialogue, Gadamer suggests, the aim is neither to see the other as a type nor to gain knowledge of his unique inner life. The special knowledge and expertise of the therapist notwithstanding, she cannot transcend her historical embeddedness and involvements to gain timeless truths of the client's inner life or pattern of living. According to Gadamer (1975), and as we discussed in Chapter Nine, by claiming to know the client in such an objective, superior way, one disrespectfully discounts her views in advance and keeps her at a distance.

Instead, an authentic I-Thou relationship focuses on the claim to substantive validity of what the other says; that is, it focuses on the "subject matter" (*Sache*) being spoken *about* in the conversation. To "experience the [other] truly as a 'Thou,'" Gadamer says, is to be open to the other and "to listen to what he has to say to us" (p. 324). But, as we discussed in Chapter Nine, this genuine dialogue is guided by an "anticipation of truth." It aims at reaching a shared agreement about the truth of what is being discussed—not a merging of subjectivities but a "fusion of horizons" understood as a reflective and critical agreement, realized in "application" to one's current situation in living. In our view, this hermeneutic conception of dialogue is quite faithful to the reality of psychotherapeutic practice. It makes sense of the sustained, mutual effort to hammer out, in ordinary language, a credible, shared understanding of what is at issue in life. Necessary moments of reflective detachment, intervention, and reinterpretation can promote meaningful self-transformation only when they unfold against the background of this kind of authentic I-Thou relation.

Hermeneutic thought also lets us see the shortcomings of Kohut's affirmation of social relations and life-guiding values and ideals. Freudian theory tends to characterize social relationships as arenas in which other people serve as either objects for or impediments to the satisfaction of the individual's biologically based drives. Part of the enormous appeal of Kohut's self psychology is its emphasis on our genuine need for others throughout life in order for us to achieve cohesive selfhood, self-esteem, and a coherent sense of direction. Yet Kohut's portrayal of these social ties is quite ambiguous. In the early stage of an individual's development, self-objects mainly serve to mirror and confirm the individual's uniqueness and vitality and to provide idealizations that stabilize the self's bipolar structure. When the individual later achieves healthy autonomy, relations to others are still important, although it is unclear what role they play aside from being supportive toward one's project of self-realization through creative activities.

In all these developments, self-objects are portrayed primarily as inner representations within the closed sphere of the individual's experience, as mental contents that contribute to a person's quest for cohesiveness and self-realization. Kohut repeatedly celebrates an "intensification of the inner life" both as the substance of the good life and as the best solution to the problems of living in an overly competitive society. But this emphasis on the individual can lead to a glorification of subjectivity and a troubling egocentricity in which others are viewed as mere means to one's own ends. Thus, paradoxically, Kohut's attempt to overcome the feelings of isolation and emptiness that result from deficits in social relationships may actually work to efface the social life-world that first makes meaningful relations possible.

The source of these difficulties may lie in the fact that Kohut falls prey to the antinomy of freedom and authority we have encountered several times along the way in examining modern therapy theories. On the one hand, Kohut wisely recognizes the need for authoritative, life-guiding ideals for imparting a sense of direction and meaningfulness to life. His

Romanticism-tinged expressive individualism provides him with substantive values, such as benevolence, self-realization, and individual accomplishment, which are taken as definitive of the good life. On the other hand, Kohut's theoretical notion of a universal narcissistic line of development, with its master value of healthy narcissism, implies that all human behavior is in the service of promoting the naturalistic or morally neutral goals of self-maintenance and psychic health. In other words, his expressivist values are *justified instrumentally* as means to natural, pregiven ends.

But his stance is clearly incoherent. For if Kohut's particular blend of Romantic and existentialistic values are taken as *defining* the good life, they cannot be justified by claiming that they are means to attaining a good life. If these recommended ideals serve only as instruments to self-enhancement, they are always dispensable if better tools are found, and they therefore have no binding authority in shaping our ends in living. Alternatively, if we insist that these values and ideals really do define the best sort of life, our affirmation of them begins to look like an arbitrary and dogmatic imposition. Despite self psychology's goal of reconciling autonomy with genuine ideals, we seem to be left ultimately either with a shallow instrumentalism, based on transient personal interpretations of what counts as self-enhancement, or with arbitrarily tacked-on ideals no better grounded that Freud's valorization of Stoicism.

From a hermeneutic point of view, we can say that Kohut's expressivist conception of the self still fails to account for the place of values in our lives precisely because it remains trapped in ontological individualism. Kohut tries to develop a conception of the self as dynamic, ongoing agency in a value-laden and meaningful shared life-world. But this conception still betrays the tensions of the objectifying assumptions dictated by methodologism. On the one hand, as Schafer (1980b, p. 86) notes, there is a residual "mechanism" in self psychology. He criticizes the image of a self whose "development" unfolds with a drivelike propulsion on the basis of a pregiven blueprint, seeing it as one that tends to reify the self and conceal our freedom for self-creation. On the other hand, this rather naturalistic and objectifying outlook on the self is coupled with a more Romantic and existentialistic image. Kohut's suggestion that self-objects are internalized mental representations on hand for one's personal project of self-enhancement reinforces the subjectivization of the life-world and the glorification of inwardness we inherit from Descartes.

In contrast, Gadamer portrays the self as always buoyed up and carried along in the "play" of those traditions that define the practices of our historical culture. Our identity as selves is therefore shaped in advance by the possibilities of self-interpretation and self-evaluation circulating in our communal life-world. This background of shared understanding provides the horizon that makes possible any dialogical quest for insight into the good life. Individuality, with its "unique" talents, ambitions, and ideals, first emerges within this wider social context. Thus values and ideals are already given, in the sense that they constitute our identity as humans. Because the individual's life history is always, so to speak, a point of intersection of these background understandings of how things count, our so-called innermost potential and deep self cannot be understood in abstraction from the unfolding practical contexts in which we find ourselves. In order to fashion an identity, individuals have to do more than just "be themselves." They have to find a credible, somewhat coherent role to play in these contexts. Agency and meaningful self-transformation must be grasped as embedded in the wider context that gives shape to any "potential" for creativity. And here, needless to say, there is no way to think of values and ideals as mere optional "items" at one's disposal to autonomously choose or resist in the name of an antiauthoritarian dedication to freedom.

Roy Schafer: Psychoanalysis as Narrative

Roy Schafer's writings are devoted to working out a "hermeneutic version of psychoanalysis" that portrays it as "an interpretive discipline rather than a natural science" (1980a, p. 82). Borrowing Habermas's suggestion (1971) that psychoanalytic theory consists of "narrative schemas" for retelling life stories, Schafer rejects the Freudian mixed discourse of force and agency as an incoherent story line. But he is also sharply critical of the Cartesian-Romantic faith that introspection can give us privileged access to a deep truth about ourselves. Introspective tellings assume that a person is a "container of experience" whose contents can be observed by "mental eyes located outside this container." In effect, such stories picture the self as *split* into (1) a passive spectator who introspects and (2) a mental arena in which experiences just occur. "The introspective narrative tells us that far from creating our lives, we witness them," and it thereby lets us disclaim responsibility for what we do (1980c, p. 41).

In order to bypass the traditional objectifying and bifurcated conceptions of the self, Schafer (1992) recommends we think of humans as agents who constitute their own identity in what they say and do. Understood as agency, the self is not one object among others but is an ongoing life course that draws on the past to realize an anticipated future. Because our being as agents is explicitly formulated and given shape by our "tellings" about ourselves, Schafer says that human existence always has a narrative structure: events are emplotted and given some degree of coherence as we articulate our own life stories. This picture of the story-shaped self implies that we are always caught up in a hermeneutic circle. Human reality, Schafer writes, "is always mediated by narration. Far from being innocently encountered or discovered, it is created" (1980c, p. 49). In the vocabulary of hermeneutic philosophy, our sense of reality is pre-shaped by a "fore-structure of understanding" built into our tellings. Even others in the social world are encountered only through our storyizing: "Other people are constructed in the telling about them," Schafer says. "The other person, like the self, is not something one has or encounters as such but an existence one tells" (p. 35).

Because humans come to appearance as tellings, an individual's experiences must be regarded as answers to antecedently formulated questions about how things figure into her life story as a whole. This structure of question and answer in experience is drawn from what Schafer calls the authority of common sense—the background of understanding, embodied in proverbs, maxims, myths, folk wisdom, fables, jokes, and literature—which circulates in a community's ordinary language. Psychoanalytic interpretation takes place in the space between these familiar "repositories of common sense" and the stories told by analysands. The narrative schemes of psychoanalysis are "refinements" of this common sense, and they must always remain faithful to it if they are to speak meaningfully to analysands. Schafer would concur with Gadamer's famous one-liner, "Being that can be understood is language." The world, as well as our own identity as agents, is preshaped by the familiar language we absorb as we grow up into a communal world. There is no exit from this lin-guistically articulated background to uninterpreted facts or raw data that could provide a basis for explaining humans.

Given this picture of the self as a telling, Schafer portrays psychoana-lytic practice as a matter of retelling the stories told by analysands. For example, a narrative that is initially filled with gaps, contradictions, and discontinuities will come to be retold in such a way that "the past is expanded, reorganized, corrected, and told more coherently and con-vincingly" (1981, pp. 38–39). Therapeutic practice aims at producing a "jointly authored work," an "interweaving of texts," that will expand the analysand's possibilities of self-understanding and self-transformation.

What distinguishes psychoanalytic dialogue from other forms of dia-logue is that the analyst is guided by the aim of retelling the individual's life story "along psychoanalytic lines" (Schafer, 1980c, p. 35). Schafer grants that there are a number of different psychoanalytic frameworks for narrativizing life histories. In his own practice, his modes of emplotment conform to "the story lines that characterize Freudian retellings" (p. 39). This means that "events or phenomena are viewed from the standpoint of repetitive re-creation of infantile, family-centered situations bearing on sex [and] aggression," and are organized "around bodily zones . . . , particularly the mouth, anus and genitalia" (p. 50). But, consistent with his constructionist interpretation of human reality, Schafer admits that the "narrative structures" dictated by theory are "optional way[s] of telling the story of human lives" (p. 41). If what is to count as data is first constituted by the narrative structures employed in tellings, there are no pregiven "facts" that could establish the superiority of one story line over another.

   Although Schafer draws his vocabulary and story lines from Freud, his theoretical framework is different in crucial respects. Where Freud's metapsychology tends toward a somewhat deterministic reading of developmental stages and psychic phenomena, Schafer employs an "action language" that describes drives, free association, resistance, and transference as actions intentionally (if unconsciously) chosen by the analysand. This mode of emplotment has the advantage of making personal change possible. In terms of an action language, such phenomena as impotence, resistance, and repetition are shown to be "enacted rather than imposed" (1980c, p. 48); they are things one chooses to do rather than things that happen as a result of internal or external forces. The logic of question and answer is transformed in the course of analysis so that the proper questions guiding experience are no longer, Why do these things keep happening to me? but instead, Why do I keep choosing to do these things? This emphasis on action, Schafer says, makes "further change both conceivable and possible. For insofar as it is a matter of what one has been doing all along, it is a matter that is amenable to change." Analysands "become increasingly dissatisfied with regarding themselves simply as products of their backgrounds." By changing the implied questions to which their experiences are answers, they gain the "freedom to conceive of the new and the different" and to assume "responsibility where they have not done so before" (1981, p. 49).

   As analysands come to own up to previously disowned responsibility, "the effects are liberating." They experience "the joyfulness of acknowledging personal agency" and "begin to tell new or drastically revised stories of their past and present lives and . . . enact them in the present with considerable benefit" (Schafer, 1981, p. 49). Schafer's theory and his understanding of practice are clearly guided by the core ideals of modernity: an antiauthoritarian commitment to freedom from constraint, and a faith that embracing our ultimate responsibility as authors of our own existence will bring us "joyfulness," personal integrity, and lucid awareness of our own potential for self-transformation. The outcome of these psychoanalytic retellings is a "second reality" that consists of "an analytically coherent and useful account of the past" pointing to an "anticipated future" no longer "imagined fearfully and irrationally." This new reality then provides a basis for free and coherent action in the present (1980c, p. 52). As individuals learn that all modes of emplotment are "optional"—made rather than found—they "learn through analysis to become more versatile, sophisticated and relativistic historians of their own lives" (p. 43).

Schafer's characterization of the self as a text and of analysis as interpretation aimed at producing new texts makes important advances in the direction of hermeneutics. But it also appears that his thought is far from completely freed from the assumptions of methodologism. We might consider, first of all, whether his theory really succeeds in eliminating the bifurcated picture of the self he correctly criticizes in mainstream approaches. With his faith in individual autonomy, Schafer assumes that all action must be rooted solely in the intentions of the individual subject, with no necessary bonds to a wider life-world. However, characterizing the self this way seems to lead to another form of "ego-splitting." Schafer is drawing a distinction between a self who tells and a self who is told; a self who cooks up stories and a self who enacts those stories. But this split self seems to be merely a Sartrean variant of what Foucault (1970) called the empirico-transcendental doublet of modernity. Schafer's account involves just such a deep split between the transcendent source of free self-elaboration—a mere pinpoint of raw will inventing stories—distinct from the story-shaped self, plodding through the empirical world and trying to live out those stories.

The problem here, of course, is that this privileging of the intending subject seems to lead to a subjectivization of all meanings and values, with the result that there is no stable background of demands and ideals to guide choice. In the end, Schafer's exhilarating ideal of unbounded freedom appears to undermine genuine autonomy. For if choice is seen as a matter of a disengaged storyteller simply plunking for one among many optional narratives and if there is no compelling vocabulary for expressing the superiority of one story over another, the agent of this radical choice would seem to be the slave of every passing whim and caprice, lacking any basis for coherent decisions whatsoever.

Moreover, this picture of humans as dimensionless points of raw will standing before a smorgasbord of optional roles and stories, far from guaranteeing personal integrity, actually threatens to lead to dispersal, fragmentation, and impotence. Nietzsche described the dangers inherent in "the faith of Americans today," whereby the "individual becomes convinced that he can do just about anything and can manage any role, [so that] everybody experiments with himself, improvises, makes new experiments, and enjoys his experiments" (1974, p. 303). The result, Nietzsche foresees, is a world in which life is treated as mere role playing, and steadfast commitment is impossible.

From a hermeneutic standpoint, we can say that Schafer's image of the isolated subject engaged in unconstrained ways of world making fails to make sense of human agency precisely because it tends to efface the meaningful life-world that makes genuine freedom possible in the first place. As Gadamer (1975, p. 245) says, "Long before we understand ourselves through the process of self-examination, we understand ourselves in a self-evident way in the family, society and state in which we live." In other words, it is through our "belongingness" (*Zugehorigkeit*) to a background of concrete bonds to others that we come to be agents at the outset. And so, in MacIntyre's words (1981, p. 207), "the history of our own lives is . . . embedded in and made intelligible in terms of the larger and longer histories of a number of traditions" that define our identity as agents.

Schafer tries to capture this sense of embeddedness in his discussion of the repositories of common sense that provide the backdrop for all interpretation. But to the extent that he treats this common sense as something merely at our disposal for refinement and reinterpretation, he cannot make sense of its authoritative pull in guiding our lives. For Gadamer (1975, p. 245), in contrast, "history does not belong to us, but we belong to it." If history constitutes our individuality, the issue is not picking a story that feels right but recovering and making manifest the background stories that already inform our lives, albeit frequently in a concealed or distorted form. Thus, there is no vantage point from which we can treat all those stories as optional items on hand for our picking and choosing.

Schafer can regard all narratives as "optional" only because he uncritically buys into the "archetypal story" of modernity: the tale of the detached, self-defining subject remaking all that is, according to his or her desires. But this comic saga of omnipotence and assured dominion closes out such alternative story lines as the Freudian tragic mode of heroic courage in the face of almost certain defeat. It also conceals its own role as a story, and it masks that concealment by treating the values it creates as timeless, self-evident truths that justify accepting the story, rather than as components of a tradition that are open to discussion and critical reflection.

More important, the implied doctrine of "thinking makes it so" runs the risk of deforming therapeutic practice. Schafer seems to endorse the line taken by Michael Sherwood (1969) that psychoanalytic narratives provide "rationalizations" that may be useful regardless of whether they are true or not. In Sherwood's words, psychoanalytic narratives satisfy a "very basic 'rationalizing drive' in human experience." The "therapeutic efficacy" of a narrative therefore "depend[s] solely upon the ability of the analyst to persuade the patient . . . to accept his narrative as being true" (quoted in Roth, 1991, p. 188). Nevertheless, when the sophisticated analysand comes to perceive the analyst's construction of a "second reality" as mere persuasion, he may well experience these rationalizations as a dogmatic imposition of the very sort she is being taught to resist. Ultimately, Schafer's image of constructing stories "along psychoanalytic lines" might begin to look like a kind of indoctrination into the analyst's styles of telling—a gratuitous imposition of a narrative structure—that could defeat Schafer's overarching goal of promoting autonomy. It does not help to be told that these rationalizations may have "therapeutic efficacy" when it is also part of Schafer's doctrine that what counts as effectiveness or success is defined by the narrative and so can hardly be used to justify it.

Gadamer gives us a way of seeing that Schafer has misconstrued the role of narrative in our lives. Schafer's description of the free construction of stories, with no point of contact with anything outside the stories themselves, yields a picture of the free-play of textuality reminiscent of Derrida's famous statement, "There is nothing outside the text." But Gadamer (1975) develops a very different view of narrative in his description of the relation between drama presented on the stage and the drama in life itself. As described in Chapter Nine, Gadamer holds that the ongoing flow of everyday life already embodies strands of narrativity, but ordinary existence generally lacks closure and a transparent meaning. Our lives stand out into a "horizon of . . . still undecided possibilities," and so they tend to be amorphous and inchoate. In the flux of experience, "mutually exclusive expectations are aroused, not all of which can be fulfilled." A dramatic narrative fulfills the "anticipation of completion" that guides experience, by transforming this diffuse and inchoate flow of events into a form or structure (*Gebilde*). Through the narrative presentation, life is raised to "a meaningful whole [that] completes and fulfills itself in reality, such that no lines of meaning scatter into the void" (pp. 101–102).

Understood in this way, narratives emerge out of and make manifest what was previously only tacit and inarticulate in life itself. By means of the narrative, Gadamer (1975, p. 101) says, "what is emerges. In it is produced and brought to light what otherwise is constantly hidden and withdrawn." It is a mistake, then, to suppose that narrativizing is just a matter of substituting optional psychoanalytic stories for other, equally optional story lines. Rather, dramatic narratives articulate and bring to realization the potential coherence already embodied in our life context. Thus, the "transformation into form" is an "emergence of truth," according to Gadamer; through it, the tacit significance of life is "raised up into its truth," and "everyone recognizes that this is how things are" (p. 102). Such recognition is possible only if, in Kohut's terms, the narrative is experience-near. Yet, at the same time, Gadamer grants that what counts as experience is only defined and realized in the presentation. Perhaps for this reason he says in another context that the moment of recognition is always accompanied by a recognition of our own finitude. Narrative closures can be superseded in the ongoing flow of life, and consequently the knowledge we attain includes the discovery of "the limits of the power and the self-knowledge of planning reason. . . . 'To recognize what is' does not mean to recognize what is just at this moment there, but . . . , even more fundamentally, [to recognize] that all the expectation and planning of finite beings is finite and limited. Thus true experience is that of one's historicality" (p. 321).

By treating agency as a free-play of tellings, Schafer is unable to account for the moment of recognition genuine narratives can produce. He fails to appreciate how the integrity of an individual's life history is inseparable from the larger life context in which agency unfolds. His restricted view of narrativity is reflected in his vision of the temporality of the analytic dialogue. Schafer (1980c, p. 49) correctly observes that human reality "is always mediated by narration" and that narrations emerge in the present of the analytic setting. But from this he incorrectly concludes that the second-order narratives developed in analysis can be about nothing other than the tellings, transferences, and resistances that take place in the present of the psychoanalytic dialogue. Schafer tells us that the analysand's history "is situated in the present: it is always and necessarily a present account of the meanings and uses of the dialogue to date" (p. 53). But a "presentism" of this kind contracts the individual's life history into the somewhat secluded and artificial present moment of the therapeutic dialogue. What presentism fails to account for is how the current exchange grows out of, mirrors, and feeds back into the concrete settings and demands of the agent's wider life course as a whole.

From a hermeneutic perspective, Schafer's theorizing runs the risk of fostering a kind of dialogue that could be experienced as manipulative and dehumanizing. There is the danger that the analyst, bent on making the analysand's tellings conform to the psychoanalytic narrative schema, will concentrate on the individual's bits of verbal behavior and treat them as mere instances of a type. In contrast, we saw that Gadamer regards genuine dialogue as directed toward the actual content (*Sachlichkeit*) of what is said. The aim of genuine dialogue is to reach an agreement about the truth of the subject matter being discussed. This kind of conversation is possible only when both partners are open to change and are guided mainly by the play of question and answer opened by the realities at stake in the dialogue. Only if there is this focus on the substantive issues can there be the kind of "fusing of horizons" hinted at in Schafer's notion of a "jointly authored text."

---
o

Kohut and Schafer each reflect a different strand of the modern outlook, each offering insightful gains while falling prey to deep limitations. Kohut's expressivist vision of the self opens the way to understanding life's teleological drive to wholeness—its "anticipation of completion"—and the possibility of self-realization through meaningful bonds to others and commitments to ideals. Yet the subjectivization of the life-world that follows from his Cartesian-Romantic emphasis on inwardness bleaches out the very sense of belongingness and embeddedness that could give content to one's agency. In contrast, Schafer's vision of humans as self-constituting narratives formed through dialogue enriches our sense of the temporal dynamism and the "linguisticality" of our being as agents. Yet what Schafer fails to see is what Kohut sensed: that a life dedicated solely to deploying means to reach the ends of freedom and flexibility is self-defeating if it is severed from overarching ideals and bonds to others in a shared life context. Both Kohut and Schafer try to overcome the somewhat dreary Freudian vision of life by playing down the role of inner and outer forces and by offering a more upbeat story of human potentialities. But they both do so at the cost of masking the resources for discovering compelling values and ideals in our shared life-world. And they both do so, paradoxically, by uncritically imposing their own preferred ideals and assumptions—their own versions of what we earlier referred to as expressive and existential individualism—rather than by opening the possibility of furthering the search for the human good through dialogue.

Toward a Hermeneutic Reconceptualization of Psychotherapy

If this hermeneutic critique of modern therapy theory is correct, there is much work to be done regarding reinterpreting what psychotherapy is all about and determining its peculiar virtues and limitations as a contribution to human welfare. We have explored how methodologism, ontological individualism, and a profound commitment to the modern ideal of freedom as autonomy have shaped modern therapy theories at their core. Hermeneutic thought offers a penetrating analysis of how this assemblage of assumptions and ideals is the source of such troubling features of the modern therapy enterprise as a wide gap between therapy theory and actual practice and a one-sided individualism that may be somewhat self-defeating. Hermeneutics helps illumine how creative reformulations of therapy theory like those of Kohut and Schafer, and even the more radical proposals of contemporary social constructionist thinkers discussed in Chapter Eight, turn out to be halfway measures that fail to get to the root of the problems.

We have argued that therapy theories generally try to make sense of their subject matter by combining a naturalistic and objectifying outlook on human behavior with a quite different view of the self as a separate, radically autonomous agent of an instrumental, expressivist, or existential sort. This bifurcated modern self is one moment searching for a role in a world of objects in which its freedom and its prospects for a sense of meaning or purpose constantly threaten to evaporate, the next moment submerged in a sphere of inwardness from which making contact with the human past or social world seems almost impossible. Hermeneutic ontology offers a clear alternative to this confused view of the self. What are some of the first steps we might take toward a hermeneutic reconceptualization of psychotherapy?

Our analysis of Kohut's and Schafer's theories yields a striking awareness of how they efface the background of shared understanding that alone makes therapeutic dialogue possible, of how they bleach out the shared life-world that gives needed content and direction to our agency and our search for a better life. A second finding concerns the extent to which both Kohut's and Schafer's approaches are at risk of subtly but dogmatically imposing on clients their preferred version of the modern story concerning what life is all about. Kohut's claim that empathy allows the therapist to objectively determine the reality and genesis of patients' ills masks the fact that he is leading them through a kind and gentle sort of persuasive dialogue toward the view of "healthy narcissism" as the best kind of life—and pity the poor devil for whom this is just not appropriate. Schafer appreciates this problem to some degree, but his recommended alternative is a bit peculiar, to say the least. He seems to combine a kind of existentialist message that possible story lines for living are entirely optional and up for grabs, a message that might undermine any genuine conviction, with a rather arbitrary insistence on Freudian retellings of a person's life and difficulties. There may be a way to combine freedom and commitment in modern circumstances, but that is probably not it.

Of course, the actual practice of therapists of these persuasions is often richer and more flexible that their explicit theories suggest. They, their clients, or both may bring to bear more substantive values or virtues of the kind Jerome Frank (1978, pp. 6–7) points out are largely ignored by modern psychology, such values as "the redemptive power of suffering, acceptance of one's lot in life, adherence to tradition, self-restraint and moderation." But such ideals are almost entirely ignored by these theories; in fact, these theories actually undermine them by their deep reliance on the story of a self-defining subject making his or her way as a stranger in a strange land.

Cushman (1990) points out that a great deal of "psychotherapy discourse advocates the objective, scientistic uncovering and 'working through' of genetic roots and traumatic causation within the self-contained individual." As a result, the therapist's influence on how the patient or client thinks, feels, and believes is considerably downplayed in most therapy theories. We have seen how this is still true to a significant degree in the revisionist views of Kohut and Schafer. Nevertheless, Cushman argues, actual psychotherapy practice, "without the therapist being aware of it," commonly "deviates from normative discourse" and the accepted "theoretical stance." It does this by "providing corrective emotional experiences of care, respect, and understanding, and by allowing the patient to 'take in' the therapist's ideas, values, and personal style." In fact, some theories "do explicitly refer to this as the patients' modeling themselves after, temporarily merging with, or introjecting the therapist." Thus Cushman is concerned that psychotherapy is at risk of becoming a shallow "life-style solution" that only serves to temporarily "fill up" the kind of empty selves who are all too often fashioned by our current way of life (p. 606). Is there an alternative to deluded scientism or mindless consumerism?

We might be able to bring about some improvement by reconceptualizing psychotherapy as a form of hermeneutic dialogue, which would make it unnecessary to choose between the ideas of re-engineering problems within individuals or filling them up temporarily with some currently fashionable therapeutic doctrine. Instead, we could conceive of therapy as a specialized form of mutually respectful dialogue between fellow citizens concerning how better to understand and actualize the good life. Such conversation, personal development, and acquisition of new skills in living take place within the context of the wider society and an historical culture (which today, of course, means a pluralistic and multicultural

society influenced by diverse cultural and moral traditions). Thus therapist and client both share and differ on background understandings and
values concerning what life is all about. Both are confronted with the challenges of actualizing these ideals, refining them in the face of new and
unforeseen circumstances, coping with contemporary pluralism, and at
times rethinking goals and ideals in basic ways.

In this view, the focus of such therapeutic conversation really is centered on what Gadamer calls the *subject matter* (*Sache*) being considered—something that should be more fully appreciated in therapy theory.
This kind of shared search for understanding provides a credible alternative to views of us either as modern punctual selves or decentered postmodern selves. It suggests that we are fundamentally "dialogical selves"
(Taylor, 1991; Richardson, Rogers, & McCarroll, 1998) who care about
the quality of our motivations and the worth of the ends we seek. Ultimately, the subject matter of therapeutic conversation is how best to live
our lives in concrete situations where we already are defined by some serious commitments and identifications but have a measure of freedom to
work out how they might best be reinterpreted. Schafer is right that the
stories of our lives are not innocently discovered but mediated by narration and reinterpreted by us in therapy and everyday life, even when the
story we adopt is one of being the victim of forces beyond our control. In
the hermeneutic view, however, our storied selves already include moral
obligations and ties to others that cannot be dispensed with, even if they
can and should be honestly reconsidered. And we certainly are under no
obligation to view human life as essentially a free-play of tellings, as in
Schafer's highly questionable metanarrative of human life—nor are we
obviously unenlightened dupes if we fail to do so.

That the therapist is a socially sanctioned healer who has more power
and influence than the client does not detract from the idea of therapy as
hermeneutic dialogue; nor does the fact that the relationship is time-
limited and exists mainly to benefit the client. Many important human
relationships have those qualities. In fact, a hermeneutic approach may
be able to explain this kind of therapeutic leverage and influence in a more
satisfactory manner than standard theories do. Take, for example, the very
high degree of influence on an individual's identity and character exerted
in the relationship between parent and child. According to Dunne (1996,
p. 145), the young child is highly dependent and impressionable, but confronts others and the world "in an active mode" and with an "open inter-
rogative stance." In turn, the child is drawn into language and practices
that shape its experiences and self-understanding from the ground up.
From the beginning, this experience and understanding take the form of

becoming a participant in "scenarios of dialogical action" (Taylor, 1991, p. 314). For example, encouragement draws the child into a culture's particular way of balancing off initiative and fear; discipline draws them into its way of interweaving gratification and restraint. Thus, the self "arises within conversation" (p. 312). A sense of self arises not so much through what many theories and textbooks term *separation and individuation* but through assimilating and becoming a participant in current cultural practices and conversations.

If this is so, the mature human self is not essentially a center of monological consciousness, conceived of as an inner space or mind that contains representations of things outside or inside this container self, including "depictions of ends desired or feared" (Taylor, 1991, p. 307). Rather the self is a scene or locus of dialogue. In this view, what I centrally *am* is an interplay or conversation among various voices, commitments, identifications, or points of view. Mikhail Bakhtin (1981) imagines this self as a conversation or struggle among multiple voices, speaking from different positions and invested with different kinds and degrees of authority. Becoming a self means internalizing the ongoing conversations or dialogues from the world around us. Some of these voices are what Bakhtin calls "authoritative" in an uncontested way. They are not in dialogue with other voices or positions but are blindly accepted or compulsively rejected. Other voices are "innerly persuasive." They have been tested, assimilated, retold in our own words. Picturesquely, Bakhtin says that they are "half-ours and half-someone else's" (p. 385).

For Bakhtin and Taylor, this kind of dialogue between and within individuals always involves matters that Bakhtin terms *ethical* or Taylor calls *strong evaluations,* which concern the moral quality of our motivations and aims. We seek conclusions that seem valid or right, even if we are aware, as we should be, that from our limited perspectives we can never attain a final or certain understanding of these issues.

In this dialogical view, through interaction with others, different aspects of a person's own experience emerge, "converse" with one another, and struggle toward some kind of accommodation. It is always an attitudinal or conversational *stance toward* diverse meanings or perspectives, not one single standpoint or another, that becomes part of the individual's identity. Most theories of personality or psychotherapy discuss how personality is formed through internalizing the perspective or evaluations of others as part of the self. But such theories take great pains to describe how a central "I," modeled after the modern punctual self, relates to these introjected elements. Such a central "I," however, can only relate to the internalized evaluations, representations, "objects," or the like either by arbitrarily submitting to their influence or by keeping them at a distance and treating them merely instrumentally.

The dialogical notion of internalizing the "whole conversation" and becoming a part of it opens up the possibility of an alternative to this stark dichotomy between dominating and being dominated in both human relationships and the affairs of the inner life. A hermeneutic-dialogical view of this sort helps explain how commitment—which involves deep, defining ties to a history and to others—can be harmonized with freedom—which includes openness to new insights concerning human possibilities and the good life—in our kind of society. It helps us better conceive how *both* profound social influence *and* individual freedom and personal responsibility can coexist relatively harmoniously in the same human situation—including the therapy relationship.

A hermeneutic critique also helps address other significant blind spots and confusions in the modern therapy enterprise. For example, Adler and Jung; critics like Perry London (1964) and C. Marshall Lowe (1969) early in the post–World War II boom in the field of psychology; Jerome Frank over the years; and more recently Cushman (1990), Doherty (1994), Hoffman (1996), and Stern (1996) have all argued that many of the questions and choices faced by therapy clients are partly or essentially moral issues. For example, Lowe (1969) offered the opinion that many modern people experience a severe crisis of values. At the same time that the authority of traditional morals and customs is waning, the uncertainty and flux of modern life tend to prevent the crystallization of any new beliefs and values to serve as a basis for living. As a result, increasing numbers of people are turning to therapists and counselors as "new moral authorities" or "secular priests." They view them as guides to living who, in effect, are asked to "make moral pronouncements in the name of science in the way the clergy was called upon for religious directives" (pp. 16–17). Therapists and clients, in part, work out the basis for decisions about marriage and divorce, how people are to be treated in many important life situations, whether and why to live for oneself or for others in all sorts of different ways, how to connect or disconnect with events and struggles in the wider society, and what larger meanings one will rely on to make sense of one's life in general and to come to terms with life's uncertainties and tragedies.

It is not at all clear, however, that mental health professionals are equipped by their scientific training to fulfill such expectations. Doherty (1994) gives the example of a young divorced father whose personal convenience and happiness would be better served by moving away from the city where his children live with their mother, thereby depriving the children of much-needed fathering. Doherty illustrates how only in a tortured and unconvincing manner—perhaps by encouraging reflection about what is the really "healthy" thing to do—does conventional therapeutic language speak to the man's dilemma concerning how to pursue his own goals and yet meet his responsibilities to his children. The liberal individualist moral outlook, which we have argued pervades modern therapy theory, provides some conceptual resources for making sense of such dilemmas, namely, the language of individual rights and entitlements. But these resources are distinctly limited. We might talk about the children in this situation having a "right" to an involved father and about the father possessing a "right" to autonomy and happiness. But how is this clash of rights to be resolved without one side or the other suffering a senseless loss of something they seem desperately to need for a fulfilling life?

A hermeneutic-dialogical view of psychotherapy might help ameliorate this situation in several ways. First, a hermeneutic ontology makes it clear that lasting social ties and obligations, such as those between parent and child, are a natural and inescapable part of the human situation. These ties and obligations are a condition of being fully human, not a regrettable or irrational constraint on it. Second, the notion of hermeneutic dialogue clarifies how the full exercise of critical thought, including the unmasking of domination and dogmatism in human affairs and psychic life, is entirely consistent with our being shaped by and carried along in the "play" of an historical culture. The hermeneutic view thus removes any impediments to the exploration of such moral issues and dilemmas when it seems helpful or appropriate to do so in a therapy context. We need no longer have a guilty conscience about doing so, as if it almost certainly meant compromising the client's autonomy. Regrettably, it appears that much therapy shies away from dealing with these important questions and that counselors and therapists are not well trained to conceptualize and explore them.

However, both the conflicted father and his therapist in our example have bigger problems. We may suppose that this client lacks a wider conception of life and the good life that would define his fulfillment in terms of carrying out the responsibilities of a father in today's world or that would lend real meaning to the sacrifices he must make to serve his children's welfare, or both. He needs more than just assistance in facing up to and clarifying a tough moral decision in terms of currently accepted values. He needs to deal with a serious absence of cultural pathways and guiding moral ideals, without which his own life and that of his family may be thrown into considerable disarray. Sandel (1996, p. 3) contends that the "anxiety of the age" concerns the "fear that, individually and collectively, we are losing control of the forces that govern our lives" and the sense that, "from family to neighborhood to nation, the moral fabric of community is unraveling around us." Our experience in teaching and talking with people in a number of contexts suggests that many individuals quickly and strongly identify with Sandel's observation. Our current political system and public discourse about the good life (apart from some of the value emphases of the religious right) are largely oriented toward guaranteeing fundamental individual rights and free choice. This discourse claims to be neutral toward competing conceptions of the good life, leaving them to individual choice. This conception of neutrality is deceptive, however, because it presupposes and privileges the model of autonomous, rights-bearing individuals in its defense of individuals' freedom to choose among different substantive goals or directions in living. Unfortunately, modern therapy theories and discourse are poorly equipped to speak to this situation. They are of little help in articulating our guiding assumptions or exploring partial alternatives to them.

At this juncture, it is helpful to recall the critiques of modern liberal individualism or philosophic liberalism briefly reviewed in earlier chapters. For example, Sandel (1996) argues that the dominant moral and political outlook of our society is that of a "procedural republic." This kind of society seeks to bracket all ideals concerning the substance of the good life, such as traditional virtues of courage or humility, and to provide its citizens with a strictly neutral framework of rights within which "free and independent selves" may choose their own ends in living, consistent with a similar liberty for others. In other words, liberal individualism advances its own blueprint or vision of the decent society and the good life but masks that fact behind a pretense of neutrality, claiming that it is only maximizing the opportunities for free individuals to do as they wish within certain broad limits. There are clear parallels between this neutralist presumption and the aspirations to value-neutrality of mainstream social science and modern therapy theories.

Presumably, a post–liberal individualist culture would be one in which we would not expect a neutral framework of rights and liberties, by itself, to ensure the social peace and maximize human flourishing. We would give up somewhat childish fantasies that either big government or big market can save us, and take on more of the job ourselves. For many of us, liberal individualism advances certain absolutely indispensable ideals of human rights and dignity, even if we may feel that it does not explain perfectly or fully what those values are all about. However, it also seems to have serious flaws or limitations. Its vision of freedom "cannot inspire the sense of community and civic engagement that liberty requires" (Sandel, 1996, p. 6). Its rather narrow conception of self-interested living will not motivate individuals to pay attention and get involved to the extent necessary to maintain a social order in which liberal autonomy itself would be actively safeguarded. Moreover, the individualist vision, by itself, seems to encourage a shallow, consumerist way of life in which our much-celebrated freedom of choice gets watered down to choosing which thirty-second political ad to be persuaded by or whether to have pizza or hamburgers at the mall. In Beiner's words (1992, p. 37), it is "not that liberal autonomy is a bad thing, but that without the 'thick' attachments provided by the kind of ethos that builds meaningful character, free choice . . . hardly seems worth the bother."

In order to address these problems, we do not need to hand over our intellects to the religious right or appoint a ministry of culture to define the quality of life for us. Rather, we need to discuss and debate these matters in a more honest, mature, and sustained manner, seeking a morally and culturally excellent way of life. And we need to accept the idea (Elshtain, 1995) that continued debate and compromise about such excellence in and between our various communities is both a responsibility and itself a significant part of a fulfilled human life. Accepting this idea would mean admitting that the liberal individualist outlook—which we have argued undergirds much of psychology—is not a purely neutral stance toward life. Rather, that outlook reflects a tradition and an understanding of the good life that we citizens need to put into serious conversation with other views of human obligation and fulfillment.

We can be strengthened and deepened by such conversation, often in unpredictable ways. In our working version of hermeneutics, there are three main, overlapping dimensions to this sort of conversation. The first dimension concerns the fact that all conversation partners live a certain understanding and set of convictions about the good life that mean a great deal to them and define, in part, who they are and what their lives are all about. The second dimension involves honoring and respecting difference among individuals and cultures, including putting up with a great deal of inevitable human pettiness and perversity. This respect is based not just on acknowledging the rights of separate individuals in the abstract but on a recognition that we all share in the human struggle and actually *need* the insight and correction of sometimes petty or perverse others to escape our own blind spots and wrongheadedness. The third dimension concerns the fact that we are caught up together in the play of historical meanings and forces. We can participate in this process in artful, responsible, sometimes highly individualized ways. But modern aims and ideals that give primacy to the mastery of events and ourselves are not very helpful in guiding this participation. There is order and causality in the human life-world, to be sure, but it *operates through* rather than bypasses our every-day dialogue and interpretive activity. Important outcomes of mutual influence and dialogue among us are generally not predictable and usually not under our direct control. To borrow the title of a recent film, we lead "an unexpected life."

The modern ideals that imbue so much psychology and psychotherapy orient us toward the mastery of outward events, including much human behavior, and toward a realm of apartness and inwardness in which we hope to find meaning and fulfillment. There is no need to deny the benefits of much technology and many modern forms of social organization or to reject entirely our sense of privacy and inward depths. We could not abandon these things, in any case, because they are so much a part of us. But we might consider shifting our understanding of the good life in a direction that takes fuller account of the basic fact that we are profoundly interdependent participants in shared cultural and moral undertakings, and we might encourage or allow psychotherapy theory and practice to be reconfigured in the wake of that shift.

In this venture, we might take a clue from contemporary theorists who encourage us in facing current dilemmas to make use of insights from Aristotle and the long tradition of civic republican political theory. For example, Sandel (1996) distinguishes between two notions of freedom or liberty. One is the liberal individualist notion of freedom, thought to consist in the capacity of ideally separate selves to "act with an autonomous will" or choose their own ends "independent of the desires and ends [they] may have at any moment." This self is "[f]reed from the sanctions of custom and tradition" and "unbound by moral ties antecedent to choice" (p. 12). Sandel contrasts this notion with the civic republican idea of liberty, which he feels is "not by itself inconsistent with liberal freedom." Such liberty consists, in part, in "sharing in self-rule" or self-government. It involves such things as a "sense of belonging," "deliberating with fellow citizens about the common good," and "helping to shape the destiny of the political community" (p. 5). It includes the "disposition to see and bear one's life circumstances as a reflectively situated being—claimed by the history that implicates [one] in a particular life, but self-conscious of its particularity, and so alive to other ways, wider horizons" (p. 16).

The idea of sharing in self-rule can be broadened to refer to myriad ways in which fellow citizens—in line with their diverse backgrounds, dispositions, and talents—might take responsibility for fashioning and maintaining a better society and culture in present-day circumstances. As mentioned in Chapter One, Wolfe (1989) describes our situation in sociological terms as ones in which we have difficulty making daily decisions partly because ties to family and locality are loosened at the same time that we are dependent on and have obligations to others in an increasingly global society. In Wolfe's view, we can't avoid this situation by retreating into a private sphere or relying on large, impersonal structures like the market or state to take care of our business for us. Rather, we need to reinterpret our traditions and take greater responsibility for the norms and practices of a common world.

If the ideas of sharing in self-rule and an outward turn toward shared responsibilities in civil society make sense in the face of our ethical and political challenges today, then they are likely to have something important to offer a re-envisioning of modern psychology as well. It seems to us that these notions might serve as the cornerstone of a modified ideal of personal development and maturity for the fields of psychology and psychotherapy. The core of this ideal would be the disposition and ability to engage others, converse with them, compromise with them, and take shared responsibility with them for parts of our social and cultural existence. Such an ideal is quite general and flexible and therefore is able to accommodate very different traditions, communities, and individual makeups; at the same time, it has real ethical bite. As Sandel suggests (1996), by virtue of the very fact that it makes us acutely conscious of our historical particularity, it encourages us to be open to and learn from other perspectives and traditions.

It is true that this ideal entails living less for oneself and more for others—with a greater sense of indebtedness to our forebears and greater dedication to the well-being, both material and spiritual, of our descendants—than we have encouraged ourselves to do in the age of individualism. But we have discussed at length in this book how badly modern individuals may need to acquire a sense of purpose beyond narrow self-fulfillment if they are to avoid many of the forms of psychological malaise and emotional isolation that modern psychology itself has often described well. Moreover, the obligations and the acceptance of limitations involved in this idea of shared responsibility and dialogue as an essential part of the good life should be seen more as opportunities than as constraints. Such obligations have nothing to do with the kind of arbitrary authority or irrational constraints that our modern sensibility is rightly concerned to condemn. Rather, accepting them, even if we often reinterpret them, requires a much fuller exercise of our human capacities and powers than do contemporary ideals of personal autonomy and self-actualization. Cultivating the skills and virtues—courage, patience, humility, and the like—needed to sustain moral bonds and cooperative ties with others can yield a more varied and interesting life than one that follows the conventional ideal of successful competitive work coupled with a satisfying private life of leisure and consumption (Bellah et al., p. 72). The path of dialogue and shared responsibility is full of dangers and risks, but so is any life worth living. That path can produce richer satisfactions and a more resilient sense of identity, of a kind that may be needed to come to terms with the ineradicable evils and tragic aspects of the human situation, than do other paths. At the very least, it is high time for psychology to acknowledge its own underlying social and ethical ideals, critically examine them, and seriously consider reasonable alternatives.

A sharper perspective of this sort on current cultural dilemmas and deficits may help therapy clients by giving them a plausible explanation and therefore a better handle on the forces at work in their lives. Rather than encouraging them to blame circumstances for their difficulties, this perspective may help them more clearly see important social realities with which they have to cope in making lasting changes, in addition to or as part of overcoming flawed internal attitudes, maladaptive personality trends, and faulty relationship patterns. Without such understanding, clients will find it difficult not to feel victimized by continuing circumstances and pressures or to try to stave off that feeling with a cynical and embittered attitude toward the wider society.

Over the years, Jerome Frank has contended that most therapy clients share a common problem, namely "demoralization" (Frank & Frank, 1991). Cognizance of the problems and challenges of the common world and the role they may play in one's own difficulties might shed fresh light on those difficulties and foster a restored sense of purpose and morale. A sense of purpose and morale may actually be undermined by the tendency in modern therapeutic thinking both to portray clients' difficulties as the result of inimical past or environmental influences and to make clients solely responsible for personal change (except, ironically, that they may require the help of a therapist to assume that responsibility). Perhaps clients would benefit from less emphasis on individual mastery over circumstances and more on a sense of shared purpose with others in meeting social, intellectual, and moral challenges, which certainly abound.

Relinquishing an orientation of excessive mastery, whether greedy or defensive, will surely not come easily. Indeed, psychotherapists certainly appreciate that lasting personal change is usually an arduous undertaking. However, the major barrier to infusing therapy with such presumed wisdom may be our deep-seated difficulty in imagining the sort of self-forgetfulness in the service of shared values or wider purposes that is not necessarily an arbitrary circumscription of individual autonomy. We may finally be making some progress on that front. For example, Etzioni (1996) notes that although the "distance between ego's preferred course" and the "right course of action" is part of an ongoing "social and personal struggle" that "cannot be eliminated," still that distance can be somewhat reduced. He suggests that the familiar golden rule, which appears in different forms in many cultural traditions, is somewhat too narrowly interpersonal in its formulation. Etzioni suggests what he calls a "new golden rule": "Respect and uphold society's moral order as you would have society respect and uphold your autonomy" (p. xviii). Such a notion fully acknowledges our dependence on others and society at the same time that it encourages individuals to cultivate excellence and develop their unique powers to the fullest extent possible.

It may be possible to broaden therapeutic conversation to deal with wider social and moral dimensions of problems in living. Doherty encourages us to move in this direction, and Cushman (1995) explores in much greater detail the possibility of rethinking psychotherapy as a kind of "moral discourse." This is a worthwhile undertaking but also has definite limitations we need to consider.

Cushman provides rich insights into ways that psychotherapy theory and practice unintentionally reproduce the cultural status quo that contains the seeds of many of the emotional difficulties it addresses. For example, he argues that self psychology adopts the romantic notion of the "organicistic growth of the nuclear self" as a purely "*natural* occurrence" in a way that makes the building of the masterful, bounded self of modern culture in childhood or therapy very difficult to question (p. 284). Also, he contends that by distinguishing between a true and false self, the healing technologies of Donald Winnicott (1965) and James Masterson (1988) "present themselves as effectively removed from the realm of moral considerations and the larger world of history and politics" (Cushman, 1995, p. 286) but fail to realize that "by labeling certain behaviors and sensations as 'true,' therapists are making a political move" (p. 298). They are as much prescribing as describing a certain mode of living. However, their prescribing is done surreptitiously, in a way that "draws attention away from the sociohistorical forces that shaped the masterful, bounded twentieth-century self, which is caught between isolation and engulfment, terrified of being unnoticed and yet determined to be independent" (p. 286).

Cushman goes further, seeking to "apply hermeneutics and social constructionism to the practice of psychotherapy" in order to help therapists and patients realize the extent to which they can, when appropriate, "think critically" and "oppose the status quo" (p. 292). They are not limited to finding a place in our kind of society, one that Cushman finds lacking because of many injustices, shallow consumerism, excessive competitiveness, and alienation. Indeed, it is the "job of the psychotherapist to demonstrate the existence of a world constituted by different rules and to encourage patients to be aware of available moral traditions that oppose the moral frame by which they presently shape their lives" (p. 295). Moreover, Cushman suggests that it would be desirable if both our culture and our schools of psychotherapy "attempted to develop a way of being that was more communal and less self-contained" and allowed us to "think of ourselves as essential parts of a . . . community of persons with whom we share certain moral understandings, obligations, and responsibilities." Then the "self could show up as being constituted by the qualities of consideration and cooperation" (p. 298).

This attempt to reformulate psychotherapy in hermeneutic terms seems to us quite valuable, in that it opens therapeutic conversation to a questioning of many problematic assumptions and beliefs that almost certainly contribute to contemporary problems in living. But Cushman's approach doesn't deal fully with other important issues we have raised in this book. It doesn't address the question we discussed at length in earlier chapters of on what *basis* modern individuals, including therapists and their clients, should weight the merits of different ways of being once they have had their consciousness raised about those alternatives. It isn't clear *why* we should reject the cultural status quo in many respects or *how* we can find our way to a credible alternative. As it stands, Cushman's approach is hard to distinguish from the existentialist or social constructionist view of our situation, as being faced with a completely wide open cafeteria of options, a situation we have argued would lead to paralysis and actually undermine meaningful choice. We must question why this kind of hermeneutic and constructionist approach, too, does not fall prey to what Rieff (1966, p. 93) characterized as the modern therapy patient's dilemma of "being freed to choose and then having no choice worth making." It is true that Cushman indicates his own view that we ought to craft a more communal, less consumerist way of being. But this vision of an alternative is quite general and vague. It consists mostly of the rejection of certain features of our current society. And some reasonable people, in any case, would not completely agree with his sentiments. This suggests to us that the main order of business is not to concentrate on either social reform or refurbishing the practice of psychotherapy but to engage more fully the debate about a better society or a less shallow culture.

It seems to us that Cushman's insights point in the direction of the sort of hermeneutic viewpoint outlined in Chapters Eight and Nine. In this view, we are always dealing with life situations that *matter* to us, and we reinterpret them, through dialogue with others and the past, partly in terms of what Taylor (1989) calls crucial and inescapable strong evaluations or qualitative distinctions about what constitutes a good or worthwhile life, for us and society. We think this approach helps explain why it is so difficult to clarify the moral and political dimensions of the modern therapy enterprise. We tend to view therapy as taking place in a cultural vacuum. As Cushman (1995) puts it, most therapists "think of psychotherapy as a private activity, most often involving the fewest number of people possible." They see it as "less an influencing than a sorting out, less a persuading than an allowing, less an offering of opinion than a pointing out of obvious scientific truth" (p. 282). But the hermeneutic view makes it clear that we are much more comprehensively embedded in history and culture than the conventional wisdom of modern psychology allows.

Assuming a hermeneutic perspective of this kind, the next step seems to be to acknowledge that counseling and psychology as we know them are terminally weak medicine for much of what ails individuals and communities in the present situation. In late modern times, we have adopted a rather paradoxical attitude toward the fate of individuals in the social realm. On the one hand, we try to keep the world and other people at arm's length, treating the world with indifference or trusting it to somewhat utopian schemes while we turn to private matters. On the other hand, we place almost boundless confidence and trust in therapists and therapy—who are, in part, representatives of the wider society—to set individuals aright and on the path to a fulfilling life. Where is this path to be found, however? First and foremost, meaning is found, convictions arrived at, courage and a sense of adventure cultivated, and sustaining social ties created on the open plain of historical life. These things happen in contexts full of possibility and risk, where fateful, often irreversible decisions are made, between life and death, hope and despair, adherence to principle and the evasion of responsibility, honesty and deceit, courage and pusillanimity, or caring and indifference. Some of this goes on in therapeutic relationships, of course. But such relationships are, quite appropriately, time-limited and one-sided, and they take place between people who remain strangers to one another in most respects. We can hardly rely on them to be the main crucible in which fundamental human affections and values can be nurtured in a frequently rootless and emotionally isolating world.

In a modern, pluralistic society that is humane and relatively free, it is hard to imagine individuals' not having available to them counseling and psychotherapy of various kinds, with therapists or advisers who are not a part of or accountable to their immediate family or community. But therapy works best in a cultural or community context where there are some shared meanings and commonly recognized pathways for finding meaning beyond just "doing your own thing" or learning to tolerate life in a depersonalized or hostile social universe. In the absence of such meanings and pathways, clients or patients will lack many of the emotional resources they need to take full advantage of therapeutic assistance, and the character and motivation of therapists who have chosen to concentrate on this kind of social service will be increasingly suspect. The tail cannot wag the dog.

What would happen if we focused our attention and energies mainly on underlying cultural deficits rather than on individual and family afflictions? Would the cultural prominence of psychotherapy and of ideologies of personal growth and self-actualization decline significantly? Probably so. Would the many insights gained by a century of psychotherapy be modified and redeployed in different kinds of educational and preventive efforts, or would they simply become part of the background understanding and store of practical wisdom we draw on in conducting our affairs? Either or both of these developments seem likely as well, although it is difficult to imagine what such a world would look like. Would therapeutic services be represented less as "scientifically" grounded or based on universally valid, value-neutral theory about the causes of human behavior and emotional problems? Would these services be admitted by their   advocates to consist, in part, of a recommended ethical outlook and philosophy of life, with therapy meaning somewhat different things and aiming at somewhat different ends, depending on who offers them or what community provides them for its members? If this occurred, it would at least amount to greater truth in advertising. Again, something of this sort seems likely, but it is difficult to imagine how the rhetoric in which these therapies would be couched and conducted would change, as it would have to, if such a basic shift in the self-understanding of the field took place. We are thoroughly indoctrinated in a view of psychotherapy as neutral theory applied to individuals or groups of individuals with more or less "effective" results. But that view is in large measure an illusion, or so we have argued. We need to begin to reconceptualize psychotherapy as a specialized form of hermeneutic dialogue, one that is shaped at its core by the current cultural conversation and struggle and, in turn, contributes its own voice and influence to that conversation and struggle.

11

SOCIAL THEORY AS PRACTICE

IN THIS BOOK, WE HAVE argued that psychological science, when conceived mainly along the lines of a natural science, is untenable. We have discussed troubling questions about three of the central premises of naturalistic psychology. First, we found that it relies on an unnecessary and ultimately implausible division of the world into objective facts ordered by causal laws that are what they are independent of our interpretations, and subjective experiences that are either epiphenomena of this "objective reality" or the results of objectively specifiable causal processes. Second, we saw that its attempt to treat humans as natural objects and to use the methods of the natural sciences to study them is dehumanizing and distortive. Third, we found that the effort to maintain a sharp distinction between fact and value has been entirely unsuccessful, resulting in an ostensibly objective scientific endeavor that in fact perpetuates a disguised ideology. These notable failures of the naturalistic aspirations for psychology cut to the very core of the attempt to fully objectify psychology, and any remedies that are offered must be similarly thoroughgoing.

The predominant definition of psychology that emerged from its extended founding debate was that humans are part of nature and can be studied just as other natural entities are. That is, the dominant naturalistic approach to psychology asserts that human psychology and behavior can be studied as objects that are what they are independent of how we as actors or observers interpret them. In Chapter Nine we argued that this interpretation-free approach to understanding the full complexity of human action is inadequate because humans are self-interpreting or self-constituting beings. In this chapter, we will outline how psychology might reorient itself as a more interpretive form of inquiry to encompass this self-interpreting aspect of human experience and thereby move beyond the problematic distinctions at the heart of the naturalistic approach.

It is important to note that psychology comprises at least two broad disciplines. There are areas of psychological investigation that may be best served by naturalistic, straightforwardly scientific methods, such as neuropsychology or basic sensory psychology. These domains of study are not as likely to be influenced by the interpretive capacity of humans as, say, applied social or clinical psychology. Because the disciplinary boundaries have been traditionally drawn in such a way that both the physical and interpretive aspects of humans are included under the rubric of psychology, it is important to acknowledge that the naturalistic model is appropriate to studies of the physical infrastructure of human action. Hermeneutic inquiry would have a very limited role in these domains. Our primary claim here is that the naturalistic model has only limited value in studying the full range of human action. Yet there are also undoubtedly domains of study in which both physical and interpretive approaches can be illuminating.

Even where the subject matter is most appropriate to the hermeneutic approach we outline here, there is generally an empirical aspect to such questions. Identifying regularities in beliefs or behavior can be quite illuminating to the extent that these regularities are understood in a broader interpretive perspective. Nevertheless, except in the case of the most basic physical aspects of psychology, there is always more to human conduct than what is strictly quantifiable. The difficulty, of course, is that there is no clear demarcation between these two extremes. The interrelationship of these two approaches is a rather complex affair that goes beyond the scope of this book. In any case, discussion of the interface of naturalistic and interpretive approaches is moot until the value of both is accepted. Therefore, we address ourselves to the question of the place of an interpretive approach in psychological inquiry.

Self-Interpreting Beings

On the naturalistic view, observations of psychological experience and behavior are simply more or less accurate descriptions of what is in fact occurring. Yet it is far from clear that human behavior and experience can be characterized as objects that have a reality independent of and prior to interpretation. In Chapter Nine, we outlined a view of humans as self-interpreting beings whose conduct is symbolically structured and is not reducible to objective facts, because the meaning of a tract of behavior or experience is not unambiguously given either for actors or observers. In real-life situations, human behavior is finely nuanced and amenable to multiple interpretations. When a mother wraps her arms around her young child, is she expressing affection, restraining the child, or both? When a supervisor puts his arm around a female underling, is he offering support, being condescending, or engaging in sexual harassment? In these commonplace situations, the actor's intentions are crucial to understanding the behavior. The actor's and other participants' interpretations of such behaviors go a long way toward constituting them as affectionate or harassing. Indeed, sexual harassment occurs only when the behavior is characterized as sexual in nature and is unwelcome or undesired by one of the participants. Behavior qualifies as sexual harassment only when it has these meanings for the participants, and this harassment cannot exist independent of these interpretations. Of course, there are blatantly obvious instances of harassment in which there is little chance of misinterpretation, but no one seriously proposes limiting sexual harassment to such cases.

Taylor (1985a, p. 36) reminds us that self-understanding is rather complex because "[m]uch of our motivation—our desires, aspirations, evaluations—is not simply given. We give it a formulation in words or images . . . [and] these articulations are not simply descriptions . . . [because] this kind of formulation or reformulation does not leave its object unchanged. To give a certain articulation is to shape our sense of what we desire or what we hold important in a certain way." That is, the supervisor might initially interpret his touching a supervisee as an offer of genuine support or encouragement, and express shock at being accused of harassment. Yet on further reflection, he may realize that he does harbor an attraction to this woman and that he was pursuing it, albeit without acknowledging that to himself. Changing his self-perception in this way is not merely a redescription of his behavior; it alters his basic sense of who he is and what he is doing. The shift from seeing a behavior as supportive to characterizing it as harassment is more than redescription— it makes it a different behavior.

Our ordinary way of thinking about such situations assumes that there is some fundamental fact of the matter about human behavior or experience and that our characterizations of these behaviors merely describe specific, independent referents without changing the behaviors in any way. Even in the course of our everyday lives, we have been enormously influenced by the scientific viewpoint that assumes there is an independent reality that exists to be discovered. So the question is, do our descriptions simply capture some underlying reality, or do the formulations help bring the psychological objects or events into being?

The naturalistic attempt to describe human behavior in terms similar to those used to describe physical events and objects breaks down on closer examination. For example, a description of an office chair as firm but flexible may be more or less accurate, but it does not in any way alter the chair. If, however, one characterizes one's stance toward teaching or child rearing as firm but flexible, one is describing not only the behavior but also one's intentions as a teacher or parent, or what counts as good teaching or parenting. This description evokes a broad modern understanding of child rearing and instruction designed to foster the abilities and independence of children. From the authoritarian perspective on child rearing of an earlier time, parental or teaching behavior considered firm but flexible today might be seen as fundamentally misguided because it does not inculcate the appropriate obedience to authority and respect for tradition. If one accepted and internalized the more authoritarian viewpoint, then what was previously seen as firm and flexible parenting would be transformed into a foolish attempt to befriend or coddle a child. Thus, depending on which of these two interpretations one accepts, being a good parent is fundamentally different.

Taylor (1985a) clarifies that this connection between self-interpretation and action is not causal in nature: "it is not to say that we change our interpretations and then *as a result* our experience of our predicament alters. Rather it is that certain modes of experience are not possible without certain self-descriptions" (p. 37). Every interpretation calls forth a skein of meanings and ideals that provides the framework for the intelligibility of the behavior or experience. These shared background meanings define the possibilities open to us and provide the vocabulary for describing our experience and behavior. Our descriptions of our actions are not just neutral depictions but part of what constitutes those actions. To say that our behavior and identity are *constituted* by the interpretations we adopt is to say that these interpretations shape and define the reality of our beliefs, feelings, and actions.

Therapy with those who have experienced sexual assault provides another powerful example of the constitutive nature of self-interpretation. Following a sexual assault, survivors frequently feel profoundly hurt, powerless, and vulnerable, often blaming themselves for the violation. One of the most unfortunate consequences of sexual assaults is that the survivor's resulting sense of powerlessness and uncertainty are evident in her behavior and can be recognized by other victimizers, leaving her vulnerable to further exploitation. In this way, her understandable self-interpretation as a victim contributes in a tragic way to constituting her as a victim.

Although therapists have somewhat different perspectives and approaches, most focus a good deal of effort on changing this constellation of self-interpretation, behavior, and experience. The aim generally takes the form of transferring the responsibility for the assault to the victimizer and characterizing the assault as an abusive violation that was immoral and unacceptable. The survivor's experienced sense of powerlessness is reinterpreted as a consequence of the victimizer's unconscionable misuse of power, whether that power was gained through physical strength, authority, or trust. In this way, the survivor comes to see that she did not deserve to be assaulted, and the characterization of the assault helps to transform her powerlessness into justified anger about it, thereby moving her from a victim stance to a position of greater strength.

None of this redescription alters the fact that the assault occurred, but, if it is successful, it profoundly changes the survivor's self-understanding, affective experience, behavior, and, indeed, identity as a survivor. To the therapeutic community, this redescription seems to be a truer account of sexual assault, and we generally claim that such a redescription helps the survivor move from a false understanding of the assault to a true interpretation. But this is unlike correcting erroneous descriptions in the natural sciences, for even the "false" description of the violation, when accepted, helps to constitute the survivor's experience and behavior just as much as the "true" description does. Human interpretation is frequently misguided, yet the accuracy of our self-understanding is not the primary consideration in its power to shape our experience and actions. Indeed, errors of self-understanding are a very fruitful area for investigation in an interpretive psychology, as we shall discuss later.

According to Taylor (1985b) there are two inadequate models for describing psychological experience and the meanings it has for us. The first is to see our psychological vocabulary as simply describing pre-existing experience—merely as a neutral representation of behavior or an inner reality. This model assumes that behaviors and experiences are independent of our descriptions or interpretations and that their accuracy is a matter of correspondence with the "real" behavior or inner state. This will not do, because achieving a more sophisticated vocabulary tends to enrich our experience; it helps create a different kind of psychic life and opens up new possibilities of behavior and expression. Indeed, this is one of the central premises of talk therapy—that verbalizing and reinterpreting one's experience can change it. For example, attaining a wider emotional vocabulary does not simply allow one to describe one's pre-existing feelings more accurately—it helps bring about a richer sense of one's inner life and creates different relationships among one's affect, self-understanding, and behavior. If these kinds of transformations are possible, then a simple correspondence model is insufficient.

The second inadequate mode for interpreting our experience is the other side of the realist-idealist coin: that thinking makes it so. Recognizing that our interpretations of our experience can transform it may prompt a leap to thinking that we can arbitrarily give our experience any label we choose and thereby change it at will. From this perspective, any talk of the truth, falsity, or erroneousness of interpretations is simply misguided. Yet taking this position overlooks the numerous constraints on the intelligibility and acceptability of interpretations. It discounts the possibility that we can misconstrue ourselves or our situation. We cannot force just any descriptor on our experience—some formulations will seem inauthentic, distortive, or alien. Our self-interpretations must have some intelligible relationship with previous self-descriptions, important facts about ourselves, our current context as we understand it, and with others' interpretations of our actions.

It seems that we face something of a paradox. On the one hand, our attempts to formulate descriptions must strive to be faithful to something. On the other hand, the difficulty is that these accounts are not entirely distinct from the behavior or experience in question. It is clearly possible to gain some degree of accurate knowledge about human behavior and this possibility suggests that a correspondence between our knowledge and social reality is attainable. Yet the achievement of lucidity about our own or others' behavior often redefines that behavior or experience. The comforting simplicity of seeking a correspondence between description and reality is insufficient, and the liberating hope of the thinking makes it so viewpoint is misguided. Understanding the human condition requires us to remain true to our best perception of the facts of the matter even while we recognize that any description is, at the same time, an articulation of those facts. Because we cannot access any ultimate realities or truths, we must also live with the possibility that any of our interpretations may be unintentionally erroneous or characterized by inauthenticity, illusion, or false consciousness. As we try to describe our own or others' behavior and experience, our descriptions actively shape those phenomena and help to bring them into being. Because our interpretations help make our experience and behavior what it is, we can say that these interpretations represent an important constitutive element of that experience and behavior.

The Constitutive Context

Characterizing human behavior or experience in a particular way can only be done through a language of interpretation that one has accepted. This prosaic fact illuminates a second constitutive element of human action—

its social embeddedness. Language is necessarily shared; it can only have an ongoing existence in a language community. Moreover, as Heidegger reminds us, we are "thrown" at birth into a fully formed life-world in which we must find a place. We are born into a full-blown, pregiven life-world that is shot through with meanings and commitments. It forms the background and basis of all our actions and thought. We are always already operating in and through the shared meanings of this life-world before we can even begin to reflect on our own self-understandings and actions or those of others.

Another way to put this is that the norms, conventions, and shared understandings of our social context help to constitute our behavior. Taylor (1985b) clarifies this in his discussion of the practice of voting, which to be meaningful requires a significant set of inherently social conventions. It has to be clear that someone is to be elected or a decision is to be made, that some measure of preponderance is to be used (for example, a simple majority), and that the choices are freely made. "If there is not some such significance attached to our behavior, no amount of marking and counting pieces of paper, raising hands, or walking out into lobbies amounts to voting" (p. 35). We would only call it voting in a sense recognizably ours if it satisfied these or similar criteria.

This means that we are not dealing here with just subjective meanings or interpretations, although actors may have a variety of attitudes and beliefs that represent variations of these shared understandings. Indeed, the overweening emphasis on having individually affirmed views in contemporary America is closely tied to our shared individualistic outlook and its practices. The hermeneutic perspective emphasizes that social norms and conventions help constitute much of the behavior that psychology studies, in contrast to the naturalistic contention that behavior is the result of a set of universal causal laws that represent some deeper reality. Just as with voting, certain mutual understandings and coordinations form the basis for practices as diverse as negotiation, exchange, showing affection, and scholarly writing. Although everyone who participates in these practices brings certain attitudes and beliefs to them, they do not bring the norms and conventions that constitute the practice as negotiation or scholarship. These must be held in common, or there is no possibility of entering into the practice at all, which means that these kinds of meanings are intersubjective rather than subjective. As Taylor (1985b, p. 36) puts it, "The meanings and norms implicit in these practices are not just in the minds of the actors, but are out there in the practices themselves, practices which cannot be conceived as a set of individual actions, but which are essentially modes of social relation, of mutual action."

Recognizing and studying the intersubjective meanings that help constitute so much of our behavior could enrich psychological inquiry
immensely.

It is important to clarify that these social practices are not static. When
an individual engages in a practice, he or she does not simply follow a formalized script but interprets the practice anew, in the context of a particular situation and in the service of specific purposes. This means that there
are continual opportunities for innovation and evolution of these social
practices.

This dynamism is an example of the hermeneutic circle, in which the
part and the whole are inseparably related and mutually define one
another. The historically given conventions frame the practices in which
individuals engage, but each instance of the practice represents a unique
interpretation of what it means to vote, negotiate, or show affection that
in some measure redefines the practice and potentially modifies the relevant social norms. These social norms define the practices and create the
context of intelligibility for the action, but the practices and norms would
cease to exist were it not for the individuals participating in them.

Taylor (1985b, p. 23) illustrates the hermeneutic circle with the example of feelings of shame: "An emotion term like 'shame,' for instance,
essentially refers us to a certain kind of situation, the 'shameful,' or
'humiliating,' and a certain mode of response, that of hiding oneself, or
covering up, or else 'wiping out' the blot. That is, it is essential to this feeling's being identified as shame that it be related to this situation and give
rise to this type of disposition. But this situation in its turn can only be
identified in relation to the feelings it provokes." The part-whole dynamic
does not end with the individual in the situation, but extends further,
according to Taylor: "To understand these concepts we have to be in on
a certain experience, we have to understand a certain language, not just
of words, but also a certain language of mutual action and communication, by which we blame, exhort, admire, esteem each other. In the end,
we are in on this because we grow up in the ambit of certain common
meanings" (p. 24). That is, we come to understand what is shameful
according to the shared understandings of a particular form of life and
experience shame in relation to that social context.

The Constitutive Future

According to Heidegger (1927/1962), the historicity of thrownness is com-
plemented by the priority of the future, by the ways that all our actions
aim toward some end-states or culminations. He emphasizes that the

shape of our lives matters to us and that we take a stand on our lives by "projecting" particular possibilities toward the future. Our day-to-day activities take their sense and purpose from the projects we seek to realize (whether or not we explicitly recognize or formulate these undertakings). Because these projects define and shape our current activities, they play a constitutive role in what those activities are. For example, carefully checking one's facts and comparing one's views with others' ideas is part of the project of being a scholar rather than merely amounting to the fidgeting of an anxious or fussy person.

A key aspect of projection is that it involves what matters; because we are beings who care about what our lives amount to, we seek to realize certain possibilities and ideals. But the projects we take on do not have merely personal significance, for the concerns and commitments of our historical communities help define what is of value and what our possibilities are.

Taylor (1989) elaborates on the interpenetration of our social embeddedness and the significance our lives have for us, by emphasizing the inherent moral dimension of human life. He argues that all human activity takes place in one or more inescapable moral frameworks. Such a framework "incorporates a crucial set of qualitative distinctions. To think, feel, judge within such a framework is to function with the sense that some action, or mode of life, or mode of feeling is incomparably higher than the others which are more readily available to us" (p. 19). Each framework is made up of qualitative distinctions that differentiate what is noble and base, significant and shallow, admirable and despicable. It defines the modes of thinking, feeling, and action that are worthy of struggle and sacrifice to pursue. Moreover, as we described in Chapter Nine, these distinctions amount to second-order evaluations that are superordinate to our basic desires and function as standards against which we evaluate our emotions, thoughts, and actions.

For example, virtually all modern versions of self-understanding place value on ideals such as self-responsibility, dignity, inherent rights, individual fulfillment, and some form of depth. These are clearly not simply factual statements; they are claims about the moral aims deemed worthy in our time. Modes of living that incorporate certain ideals are thus deemed higher, fuller, or richer than stances that slough off responsibility, disregard human dignity, or decline to seek out avenues for fulfillment.

Taylor (1989) argues that living within some moral framework is inescapable because the framework forms the basis for identity and direction in life. He sees the human agent as existing in a space of questions about who one is and what one's life is about. Our frameworks provide answers to these questions, as well as the horizon that helps us know where we stand and what is worth striving for. These frameworks are inescapable in the sense that we become human only by being inducted into some shared language of meaning and worth. Taylor points out that "the portrait of an agent free from all frameworks . . . spells for us a person in the grip of an appalling identity crisis. Such a person wouldn't know where he stood on issues of fundamental importance, would have no orientation in these issues whatever, wouldn't be able to answer for himself on them" (p. 31). That is not to say that there is only one framework that commands allegiance from all. Indeed, many of the ongoing debates and controversies in a society concern which framework is best or how to interpret a given framework. This is particularly true in a society as pluralistic as our own.

Taylor (1989) clarifies that these frameworks provide the background, whether explicitly or implicitly, for our moral judgments, beliefs, and intuitions. They clarify for us where we stand on what is good, worthwhile, or admirable. These shared moral frameworks therefore partly constitute our way of life because they define what is worth seeking. From this point of view, human life is ineluctably moral; we are always concerned with the significance of things for us, and our lives are shaped by our attempts to embody our visions of the good in the projects we undertake.

Interpretation and Psychological Science

If everyday human activity is partly constituted by the actors' interpretations, then social science may be similarly shaped by the interpretations that guide that enterprise. Of course, naturalistically inclined psychologists do not generally rule out studying the personal interpretations, emotions, or values of their subjects. However, they do insist that such investigations be carried out from a disengaged scientific standpoint. We will argue that this fundamental premise of naturalistic psychology—the claim that scientists can maintain a detached, objective standpoint beyond personal interpretation—misconstrues and thereby distorts the fact that social science is a human endeavor that is profoundly shaped by the interpretations and ideals of scientists.

Let us begin by noting that most social scientists would endorse the following characterization of science offered by Charles Sanders Pierce: "To satisfy our doubts, . . . it is necessary that a method should be found by which our beliefs may be determined by nothing human, but by some external permanency—by something on which our thinking has no effect. . . . Such is the method of science. Its fundamental hypothesis . . .

is this: There are real things, whose characters are entirely independent of our opinions of them" (Buchler, 1955, p. 18). Even though Pierce refers to the natural sciences, this interpretation-free ideal is also central to most traditional understandings of objectivity in psychology (Kerlinger, 1986).

Let us examine this claim in more detail. How have psychological researchers claimed objectivity through interpretation-free data? Lord Kelvin is widely quoted as formulating the fundamental axiom that "science begins with measurement." Following this logic, psychology made a case for itself as a distinct discipline on the basis of a quantification of phenomena previously found in the domain of philosophy (by no means the only available option). By the 1920s, the discipline's initial introspection-based investigations of consciousness, will, and mental associations had been almost entirely displaced by more quantifiable objects of study, such as intelligence and learning. This alternative is now widely taken for granted as the only reasonable option.

The unfortunate fact about quantification in psychology is that the numbers that give the impression of precision do not, in any way, naturally inhere in the objects of study. They are, at best, indirect indicators of the properties we wish to study. S. S. Stevens, one of the founders of modern psychological measurement, expressed this problem clearly when he said, "Measurement is the assignment of numerals to objects or events according to rules" (Stevens, 1951, p. 1). Thus it is the rules of numeral assignment that are at issue in the validation of psychological measurement.

Because quantifying psychological phenomena is anything but straightforward, researchers direct ever more sophisticated and assiduous effort toward the validation of psychological measures. This extensive validation is necessary because of the inescapable indirectness of our measurement, a circumstance that has bedeviled social science from the beginning. Therefore, psychological and behavioral scales and rating systems must be evaluated with respect to various indicators of the phenomenon of interest, to see if a pattern of results emerges that arguably confirms the validity of the measure.

What are the rules by which we assign numerals to objects or events of interest? How can any kind of rule or social convention form the foundation of a claim to interpretation-free data? The rule or procedure by which the numeral is assigned to the object or event is *itself* an interpretation.

Psychology has attempted to escape the observer's reliance on personal interpretation through the use of standardized measures. Of these, observational ratings of publicly observable behavior are generally taken as the best form of evidence. Observational ratings are seen as helpful in three ways: (1) by providing rules whereby overt behavior can be quantified,

(2) by relying on rating systems that are consistent across raters (that is, they are nonsubjective), and (3) by allowing the subjective and private experience of the actor to be correlated with what is publicly observable. Better rating systems are characterized by a great deal of precision about what is to be counted as a behavior of interest and involve elaborate instruction manuals and assiduous training. For example, the prominence of John Gottman's research with married couples is largely due to his use of an array of observational rating systems to assess dyadic communication. A closer look at this rating system will clarify the degree to which it is interpretation-free.

One of these systems, called the Rapid Couples Interaction Scoring System, assesses sixty-five speaker or listener acts, ratings of which are divided into fourteen scales. One of the most interesting and consequential listener behaviors discussed by Gottman (1994) is called *stonewalling*. He and his colleagues have meticulously defined this behavior as the failure to provide cues that tell the speaker that the listener is tracking (for example, head nods). The neck tends to be quite rigid, and the listener does not look at the speaker much and shows little facial movement, but she occasionally indicates displeasure with the speaker. Speakers in Gottman's studies tend to find this behavior very aversive. Males engage in stonewalling more frequently and, consequently, husbands' stonewalling reliably predicts subsequent marital separation and divorce.

The question is, Is stonewalling a set of behaviors that are specifiable independent of interpretation? Does stonewalling exist whether or not it is interpreted as such? It is true that the behaviors identified by Gottman are publicly observable and identifiable, as shown by the fact that he and his colleagues have developed a consensually effective set of rules for coding this behavior. But does this constellation of behaviors stand up and identify itself, as it were? It does not, of course. Instead it is differentiated by the speaker, the observer, and possibly the listener, as salient in a particular context.

The *Oxford English Dictionary* (Simpson & Weiner, 1989) notes the recent origin of this term (circa 1862 in reference to Stonewall Jackson) and defines it as "an epithet for one who seeks to confound by dogged resistance" (p. 765). That is, stonewalling is identified as an act of resistance to some project or aim. Moreover, although it is a wonderfully descriptive term, it is an epithet frequently used pejoratively by those whose aims are being frustrated. Thus its importance derives not so much from its independent instantiation but from how it figures in frustrating the purposes of the marital interaction from the points of view of the speaker and the marital researcher in this particular sociohistorical context.

What is the project that stonewalling obstructs? In the past 150 years or so, a unique set of marital ideals has emerged that places a premium on marital satisfaction that is to be attained through free and open communication and emotional intimacy between spouses (Mintz & Kellogg, 1988). Stonewalling takes its significance from the contemporary social expectations, conventions, and practices that place a premium on effective, reciprocal communication in marriage. In Chapter Seven we saw that this perspective on marriage is so pervasive in contemporary America that it is unreflectively shared by married couples and marital researchers alike. Stonewalling is a powerful violation of contemporary expectations about marital interaction. It is these social conventions that give stonewalling its relevance and predictive capacity, rather than some independent truth or causal law of marital interaction. Similar behaviors would be unlikely to have the same import in more traditional marriages, where they may represent a husband's assertion of his patriarchal authority rather than a breach of mutuality in communication.

The problem here is not that sets of behaviors such as stonewalling cannot be identified nor that they do not predict divorce. Gottman has clearly shown that this behavior can be reliably specified and that it is predictive of subsequent divorce. The problem is that the scientific identification and interpretation of these behaviors are embedded in a particular form of life, one creative interpretation of the human condition among many; any correlations within that constellation are quite probably entirely contingent on participation in that form of life. As Richard Bernstein (1976, p. 106) puts it, "The issue is not whether it is possible to employ empirical and quantitative techniques, but rather how to interpret the results. There has been an overwhelming tendency in mainstream social science toward reification, toward mistaking historically conditioned social and political patterns for an unchangeable brute reality which is simply 'out there' to be confronted."

Thus the contemporary understanding of marriage and the meticulous definitions of behaviors such as stonewalling turn out to be constitutive of these behaviors. That is, without these social expectations and this or a similar definition of stonewalling, it would be virtually impossible to identify this set of behaviors as significant or as problematic. This dependence on shared meanings for the intelligibility of behavior is exactly what we described earlier as a constitutive interpretation, for those "behaviors" can be called stonewalling only by virtue of the violation of the widely held expectation of egalitarian, two-way communication. That is not to say that the researcher creates it out of nothing but that these or a similar set of culturally embedded interpretations help bring the behaviors into being. Without the contemporary situational import of mutuality in marital communication, stonewalling simply does not exist. The behaviors identified by Gottman simply would not emerge at all from the myriad of other simultaneous movements and sounds. Without these interpretations, they would have no significance for the actors or observers.

What this means is that even in the most rigorous instances of psychological measurement, we cannot see our data as existing independent of our interpretations. The data do not exist separately from the interpretation, because our identification and discrimination of psychological phenomena actually give shape to them and alter them in crucial ways. The inescapability of interpretation is a severe blow to the traditional concept of scientific objectivity in psychology and other social sciences, for it means that no matter how carefully we specify and measure the phenomena of interest, these descriptions are dependent on a background of meanings that are not being measured, and the descriptions help bring the phenomena into being.

The centrality of interpretation in psychological science does not mean that we cannot be objective in any sense, only that it is unreasonable to aspire to objectivity in terms of observation free of personal interpretation. In an interpretive approach to psychology, one values objectivity in the sense of employing the best available intersubjective norms of rational inquiry, getting one's facts as clear as possible, minimizing the effects of personal interest or bias, and remaining open to the flaws and shortcomings of one's work and to the valuable insights offered by others.

Scientism and Ideology

Noting the inescapability of interpretation in social research does not tell the whole story, however. Taylor (1985b) points out that the supposed neutrality of objective social science actually weights the dice in favor of certain kinds of theories over others. The naturalistic perspective is not neutral about understanding humans, because it prescribes a certain stance on the part of the investigator toward the people that are to be understood. The scientist is to stand apart from them, to resist the temptation to see the social world as a locus of meanings through which she herself can be understood. Human life is to be understood as a neutral domain of facts, of causal relations or contingent correlations, the mapping of which will enable greater and greater explanatory capability and instrumental control.

The natural sciences have been overwhelmingly successful in demonstrating this kind of knowledge and in pointing the way to innumerable technologies that have dramatically altered modern life. These achievements partly inspired the attempts by early psychologists to emulate the naturalistic form of inquiry.

The lack of neutrality in the naturalistic model becomes clearer when we recall its aims. Bacon's dictum that knowledge is power (because the only sure demonstration of knowledge is control) has remained at the center of psychology. The experiment has held a privileged position in psychology since Wundt's followers imported it to the United States. Psychologists favor experimentation, because it seems to offer the possibility of demonstrating knowledge through the effects of experimental manipulation of independent variables on dependent variables. Experiments are prized because they offer the possibility of unambiguous demonstrations of the causal efficacy of an independent variable. The ability to effect such changes is, following Bacon, the power that confirms knowledge.

Few question the validity of some version of this model for the natural sciences, but its appropriateness for the human realm is less secure. Taylor (1985a) argues that this naturalistic view of knowledge is not just an epistemological position but also an interpretation of what it means to be fully human and of the nature of our relationships to the world and to one another, particularly when this approach is applied to studying humans. The cool, rational detachment of the naturalistic scientist serves the aim of demonstrating and eventually exercising control over certain aspects of the world and ourselves. Therefore, within this perspective, the highest form of rationality is found in relating to the world as neutral matter, to be shaped according to the individual's purposes. In other words, naturalism is ultimately inseparable from the instrumental, utilitarian bent of modern civilization we discussed in earlier chapters. This utilitarian individualism amounts to a disguised ideology that suffuses psychology and belies its purported value-neutrality.

Interpretation and Error

For many psychologists, this portrait of the centrality of interpretation in human action and its study will appear intolerable. Interpretation was eschewed in the scientific approach to psychological inquiry because it was thought to introduce error and bias and to reduce psychology to a babel of conflicting interpretations among which it would be impossible to adjudicate. Clarifying how to recognize and address the inevitable errors in interpretation in their several forms is therefore crucial. First of all, such errors can simply be mistaken perceptions or misreadings of a situation. Such human error is possible in any enterprise, including even the most rigorous scientific practices conceivable. This type of error is relatively unproblematic. It is usually identified as a mistake in argument or procedure or by its inconsistency with the results of other inquiries in the normal course of investigations by a community of scholars. What are of interest here, however, are other, more subtle forms of error.

Illusions

Errors of interpretation may go beyond individual or random mistakes by being systematic and held in common by a significant number of people. This kind of error has greater substance and has the appearance of an adequate representation of reality to those who share it. We can consider these systematic, shared errors to be illusions because they are misreadings that frequently offer a more comforting or self-affirming understanding of our situation, or they portray us as closer to our ideals than may be justifiably claimed. The study of illusions is potentially an extremely fruitful area of inquiry and may be one of the more interesting and enlightening ways for psychologists to reflect on our life-world.

Of course, providing convincing evidence or argumentation that a particular belief or interpretation is illusory is no simple matter, especially if we accept the hermeneutic premise that there is no hard social reality against which illusions can be tested. Any attempt to demonstrate the presence of an illusion can only be based on other entirely defeasible interpretations of our circumstances and practices, and cannot be seen as certain or final any more than what is identified as illusory. Nevertheless, within the limits of our interpretive situation, it is possible to identify commonly held illusions by clarifying the anomalies or self-contradictions that arise in the modes of life informed by such illusions.

For example, Taylor and Brown (1988) cite a great deal of quantitative evidence that ordinary human cognition (at least in the contemporary United States) is characterized by what they term the self-enhancing illusions of unrealistic optimism, an exaggeration of personal control, and an excessively positive perception of oneself. They make a compelling case for the widespread presence of normal illusions by citing a broad pattern of regularities that are anomalous with the traditional notion that mental health is characterized by accurate perceptions of reality. Taylor and Brown see their creative interpretation of these facts as a simple matter of better theory-to-data fit than can be attained from the perspective that mental health is attained through accurate perceptions of reality. Yet the presence of these particular illusions raises some very interesting questions about our way of life.

Their perspective of "mental health founded on self-enhancing illusions" is reminiscent of the ideal of the "bounded, masterful self" (Cushman, 1990). The illusions view suggests that mastery occurs internally, as individuals devise ways to interpret themselves and their endeavors in an unrealistically positive light vis á vis a separate, hard reality. From an observer's perspective, the discrepancy between this external reality and the illusions shows this inner "mastery" up as illusory (even though Taylor and Brown acknowledge that this external reality cannot be directly assessed).

Although the positive illusions perspective is illuminating, it is limited by the canons of traditional social science and accepts the same ontological individualism that leads individuals in this culture to employ illusions to gain psychological mastery over the "cold, hard facts of life." The illusions perspective takes one step toward exploring cultural illusions, but it shrinks from exploring the ways in which these specific self-enhancing positive illusions (control, self-esteem, and optimism) embody particularly American ambitions and ideals. When we see it as part of the individualistic tradition, the illusions perspective becomes both more compelling and a more valuable reflection on the lengths to which individuals must go to live up to the aspirations of individualism.

Another interesting contemporary illusion has come to light in the study of marital quality. Across decades of research, married individuals overwhelmingly report that they are satisfied with their marriages and that their marriages are better than average (for example, Fowers et al., 1996; Terman, 1938). There are several sets of observations that suggest that this satisfaction may be at least partly illusory. Spouses routinely endorse statements about their partners and their marriage that seem impossibly positive (Fowers et al., 1996). They see their partners as better than other people (Hall & Taylor, 1976; Pomerantz, 1995) and better than the partners see themselves (Fincham & Bradbury, 1989). Finally, spouses dramatically underestimate their own chances of divorce, seeing others' likelihood of divorce as five times greater than their own (Fowers et al., 1996).

These authors interpret these positive perceptions of marriage as illusory because they seem inconsistent with what is possible (for example, most people cannot logically have above-average marriages, and everyone's spouse cannot possibly be better than the average person) and because they are empirically highly improbable (everyone's probability of divorce cannot be five times lower than the population likelihood). Of course, neither these intriguing empirical regularities nor what these authors take to be factually likely (against which they compare the spouses' perceptions and infer that they are illusory) is founded in the kind of objective data that represent some ultimate reality. Therefore, this interpretation of marital perceptions, however plausible, should not be assumed to be a mirror of reality but must be judged by whether it helps us better understand a confusing situation in contemporary marriage.

The case for interpreting spouses' perceptions as positive marital illusions becomes more persuasive when we consider why spouses might deceive themselves in this way. These illusions may have arisen, in part, because marriage is at once extraordinarily important and very fragile in contemporary society. As we discussed in Chapter Seven, virtually everyone (96 percent) plans to be married (Thornton, 1989). Being happily married is strongly related to psychological well-being, physical health, and longevity in contemporary America (Ross et al., 1990; Weingarten, 1985). At the same time, estimates of the likelihood of divorce range from 43 percent to 64 percent (Martin & Bumpass, 1989; Schoen & Weinick, 1993). The decision to marry and remain married is partly determined by relationship satisfaction, but this satisfaction is, in turn, strongly associated with seeing the marriage in an unrealistically positive manner (Fowers et al., 1996).

These apparently widespread illusions may reflect the pressures marriage partners are experiencing in our culture. In particular, marriage has been seized on almost as a last-ditch avenue to fulfillment in a social universe where other lasting social ties and sources of community or connectedness are greatly lacking. This deeply felt but fragile wish for connection recalls Ernst Becker's notion of "cosmologies of two" (1973) in which we pin our aspirations for meaningful lives primarily on our romantic attachments. It may reflect an overweening and somewhat desperate hope for connection and meaning in life that may make such an inflated view of marriage inevitable. Or it may represent a kind of all-or-nothing thinking—my marriage is either impossibly good or not worth maintaining—because so much rides on the situation.

If spouses do exaggerate their marital happiness, it is very problematic for social scientists, because they cannot rely on self-reports as an accurate source of information on marriages. Social desirability is the most widely accepted explanation of these distortions, although it is now being challenged by the positive illusions perspective (Fowers et al., 1996). Investigators generally claim that spouses see their marriages in unrealistically positive ways because it is socially desirable to do so, which amounts to conformity to social expectations. One of the attractive features of the social desirability explanation of these positive perceptions of marriage is its apparent sufficiency. It seems to neatly explain a troubling lack of objectivity in spouses' evaluations of their marriages in terms of an identifiable force: social conformity.

Social scientists are rightly concerned to try to get the most accurate measurement they can of social phenomena. However, it seems that the social desirability response bias is the *least* interesting explanation of the widespread tendency for spouses to see their marriages in an unrealistically positive way. From the social desirability point of view, excessively positive perceptions of marriage do not say anything about marriage itself or about the sociohistorical context that gives rise to the desirability of the marital ideals discussed in Chapter Seven. Thus the social desirability conception explains these unrealistic perceptions away as an artifact of a universal, ahistorical bias in self-report measurement; it does not increase our understanding of this apparent distortion.

The apparent presence of these positive distortions of marriage offer a glaring invitation to reevaluate our understanding of contemporary marriage. If this kind of pervasive, deeply ingrained self-deception reflects our approach to marriage, it indicates a significant cultural blind spot. Thus the attempt to account for this distortion of the marriage in causal terms actually obscures more than it illumines. It fails to see the source of these illusions in the contemporary social consensus that marriages *should* be unreasonably good. At the same time, the investigation of this illusion illustrates the value of quantitative social inquiry even if we do not view its data as a representation of an independent reality. The responses and correlations discussed by these investigators are potentially very illuminating, but these regularities are little more than intriguing anomalies unless they are part of some richer, more encompassing understanding of the subject matter.

This extended example helps illuminate three aspects of how a more interpretive form of inquiry can expand psychology. First, it illustrates the kind of error that an illusion comprises. An illusion is systematic, shared, and appears to those who participate in it as an adequate representation of reality. Second, the example suggests that inquiry into such illusions might be very fruitful and illuminating. Studying this and other commonly held illusions can help us gain a better self-understanding and recognize important cultural blind spots and their often unfortunate sequelae.

Third, and most important, this example illustrates how naturalistic psychology traditionally has not only been unable to examine these illusions fruitfully but has actually become caught up in them. Psychologists studying marriage have taken marital happiness, marital satisfaction, and related concepts for granted as defining good marriages. Yet these marital ideals are historically and culturally unique (Mintz & Kellogg, 1988). Thus, the deeply felt contemporary aspiration to having a happy marriage is at once the most likely source of positive illusions about marriage and the keystone of professional research on marriage. In theory and research psychology is unwittingly suffused by these kinds of cultural assumptions, because its scientistic self-understanding precludes the investigation of this sort of intersubjective interpretation. Thus social scientists tend to be blind to the degree to which they share a particular view of social reality with the people they study. Without a more self-reflective and interpretive stance, psychology will continue to take the cultural status quo for granted and will be unable to help us sort through many of the crucial social and moral difficulties that arise in our collective lives.

Ideological Distortion

A third general type of error in interpretation has been widely discussed under the rubric of ideology. Ideologies are another sort of systematic, shared interpretive distortion, but they differ from illusions in that ideologies slant our perceptions in ways that tend to benefit one individual or group at the expense of others and hide or rationalize that endeavor. There are two important features of such ideologies: (1) they powerfully justify and legitimize this kind of injustice, and (2) they are generally taken not only to represent the truth but also to be self-evident. The classic example of ideology identified by Marxists is an economic false consciousness that benefits the capitalist class and works to the detriment of labor by portraying the marketplace as driven by natural and impersonal laws. Critical psychologists use a similar argument to criticize ways that they see psychological theory, research, and practice perpetuating economic and social injustice (Fox & Prilleltensky, 1997). Similarly, feminists castigate patriarchy as an ideology that benefits men at the expense of women. Although relatively few feminists use the term *ideology*, it does seem to capture the systematic and widespread gender-based injustice they seek to abolish.

Although critical and feminist psychologists attend to the ideological distortions in society at large, they are particularly concerned with the ways that psychology participates in false consciousness. For example, Hare-Mustin and Marecek (1997) discuss how diagnostic categories often stigmatize women, locate pathology in individuals, exonerate the social and institutional status quo, and serve the interests of the privileged classes. In this way, critical and feminist psychologists point the way to including ideological critique as an important dimension of psychological inquiry.

We find many valuable insights in these thinkers' work, but we worry that they tend to rely rather uncritically on notions of power, justice, and individual rights that are themselves modern moral interpretations shot through with tensions and difficulties. We cannot go into these difficulties in detail here, but we can mention one problem to illustrate the point. The misuse of power and authority is among the foremost concerns of both critical psychologists and feminists. In spite of the importance of power in their theorizing, they rarely discuss the legitimate or beneficial exercise of authority (see Miller, 1986, for an exception). In the absence of a clear idea of the legitimate use of power, we lose a crucial contrast, and all power becomes problematic. This one-sidedness can lead us to wonder whether these thinkers believe that parents, teachers, and supervisors can ever use power legitimately or to their charges' benefit. This blanket denunciation of power and authority is part of the potent cultural preoccupation with illegitimate authority and emancipation that dates from the Enlightenment.

The rather unreflective adoption of this historical campaign on the part of these otherwise insightful and trenchant commentators suggests the importance of a broader interpretive stance that can incorporate their valuable insights about ideological influences but is not limited to ideological critique (Prilleltensky, 1997; Richardson & Fowers, 1997). Although this critical social science standpoint deepens psychological inquiry in a number of ways, it seems to reflect the one-sided antiauthoritarian or liberationist moral outlook of modern times and to remain largely within the ambit of modern individualism. It is important to identify and combat distortive ideologies, but the moral resources of these approaches appear to be limited to emphasizing individual rights and a purely procedural understanding of the kind of justice we might seek. Thus they are confined to advocating what Fromm termed a dangerous "freedom from" arbitrary authority and lack any richer, more substantive understanding of the social good or the good life. We need to incorporate the valuable insights into ideological influence offered by critical psychologists and feminists into a "thicker" view of our social existence and the social good that can, at the same time, do justice to those insights. The false consciousness of ideological positions can better be shown by identifying the basic beliefs and interpretations that inform the ideology and exposing its internal self-contradictions and self-undermining character.

Evaluating Interpretations

If we cannot have an interpretation-free science of psychology, and if our interpretations are prone both to mistaken readings and to systematic error, how can we have any confidence in the results of a more interpretively oriented psychology? Naturalistically inclined psychologists will be quick to raise this question. They fear that if we cannot ground our theory and research in objective data, then we are in for interminable argument, because it will be next to impossible to choose one viewpoint over others. Richard Bernstein (1983) coined the term *Cartesian Anxiety* to refer to this dichotomizing along objectivism-relativism lines. Those who favor an objective, naturalistic account of human behavior have been acting as though Descartes's grand Either/Or were an accurate portrayal of our situation: either there is some firm, fixed, discoverable set of laws underlying human being and self-understanding that can be confidently known, or we cannot escape intellectual and moral chaos in a situation where nothing is firmly established. From a hermeneutic viewpoint, our situation appears both much more complex and less dire than the either-or portrayal.

Even if we were to accept the either-or perspective, the use of objective data as the arbiter between theoretical positions has always been more an aspiration than a reality in psychology, for there are precious few examples of the abandonment of theories due to inconsistency with research results. After all is said and done, there are simply too many ways for opposing viewpoints to assert that their counterparts' factual claims are based on faulty design or measurement procedures or that they do not adequately test the theory. That is, the research in question does not count as evidence weighing against the theory.

The contemporary fragmentation and disagreement about what constitutes acceptable evidence in psychology already reflects the situation the naturalists fear. That is, a chaotic situation in which we cannot arbitrate between interpretations on the basis of objective data is not just a possibility; it seems to be the best description of both the history (Koch, 1993) and the current state of the discipline (Staats, 1991). Moreover, although there are some proposals for overcoming this fragmentation (Slife, 1997; Staats, 1991; Yanchar & Slife, 1997), there is no foreseeable resolution of this babel of theory and dissension about evidence.

From the hermeneutic perspective, our interpretations of human behavior are always partial, subject to errors or illusion, and never final or certain. This means that there is always room for reinterpretation. Seen from this point of view, the fragmentation and theoretical diversity of psychology represents a variety of partial interpretations. The dismal lack of success in the empiricist project of evaluating these different interpretations by testing their accuracy against brute data (which is inherently impossible) or their success in generating powerful predictive theory (which is generally lacking) may well be the logical conclusion of a misguided effort. Because any data an investigator might gather are partly constituted by the investigator and those she studies, there are no simple "facts of the matter" that can arbitrate between the higher-order interpretations of different theories. The diversity of opinion in psychological science about how to understand human behavior may not be so much a failure or a sign of its extended youth as a discipline as it is an inevitable feature of the study of self-interpreting beings. If our self-understanding helps make us who we are, then the truth about us may be too malleable and multifaceted to be amenable to a single, overarching, consensual scientific account, now or at any time in the future. If that is the case, then we may profit far more from focusing our attention on how best to choose among competing, defeasible interpretations than from continuing to wish upon the star of empirical salvation.

Does this mean that any interpretation is acceptable? Certainly not. It is still necessary that our interpretations, hypotheses, and theories be consistent with our clearest apprehension of the facts. Moreover, objectivity remains important in the sense that we do our level best to avoid unnecessary bias, personal agendas, and premature foreclosure of our interpretive options.

How can we sort out better and worse interpretations? There are several ways to approach this without relying on the assumption that our interpretations can be grounded in some kind of foundational knowledge. It is clear that we need some criteria for identifying better and worse interpretations. We will offer several nonfoundational suggestions, recognizing that none of these admits of complete formalization, nor do they constitute, individually or collectively, sufficient conditions for adopting one interpretation over another. Rather, they amount to an initial attempt to formulate reasonable standards, used singly or in combination, for the exercise of good judgment in sifting the many ways that human action can be understood.

One obvious criterion is continuous with naturalistic psychology—that a given reading of behavior must be consistent with the facts as we know them. An interpretation that flies in the face of what we ordinarily take to be factual would be immediately suspect. It follows that continued efforts to observe and document human behavior remain important. Even if we give up on the idea of interpretation-free data, efforts to ascertain regularities in human action remain very useful. There are many questions that we can address empirically, although with three caveats: (1) whatever data we gather are always partly brought into being by the interpretative framework of the investigator; (2) these data and their interpretations are always defeasible; and (3) there are important questions that cannot be decided in any straightforward way with empirical data.

In some cases, a new interpretation may present a way to reinterpret what we have taken to be factual in such a way that we see those facts in a new light or even reverse ourselves and recognize that our best previous understanding of the case was mistaken. In this situation, we would be examining competing interpretations and would need some way of adjudicating between them. In the simplest case, both viewpoints may make use of the same observations but construe the import of the data in different ways. Or competing interpretations may rely on some overlapping observations but also make knowledge claims that are denied by their counterparts. In the worst case, the viewpoints may appear to be largely or completely incommensurable.

A second criterion of interpretation, also continuous with naturalistic psychology is Occam's razor. When all things are equal, simpler accounts are still to be preferred. It is important to emphasize that a simpler interpretation is only better if it illuminates as much as a more complex interpretation. We do not, after all, merely want to simplify our accounts of human action, but to do it full justice. In the example about unrealistic perceptions of marriage discussed above, the social desirability explanation is certainly simpler, but it leaves the most interesting questions unexamined, many of which are central in the somewhat more complex positive illusions viewpoint.

One of the ways that simpler depictions are frequently inadequate in psychology is that they focus very narrowly on a topic that the investigator tries to isolate from everything else. This emphasis on isolation is characteristic of abstraction in naturalistic science, but hermeneutics suggests that it will almost always be misleading. Therefore, a third principle of interpretation is that portrayals of a phenomenon that capture its essential embeddedness in a historical lifeworld, while inherently more complex, are superior to narrow characterizations. As we saw with the example of marital interaction research, superior interpretations increase our understanding of psychological phenomena by illuminating their embeddedness and meaning in a rich, historical life-world.

A fourth criterion requires that our interpretations go beyond good observation and admirable elegance and capture the meaning of the behavior to the actor. This requirement follows our discussion of three constitutive elements of an action: (1) the self-interpreting or self-constituting aspect of human beings; (2) the meanings, purposes, and projects for the sake of which the action is undertaken; and (3) the relevant social norms that make the action intelligible. If an observer disregards these constitutive elements in favor of a causal, mechanistic account, the observer is, in effect, treating the action as "colorless movement" (Taylor, 1985b), ruling out the very features of the action that make it what it is for the actor and for others in the social context. Such accounts drastically restrict and distort the grounds for the intelligibility of human action. Thus, in most cases, interpretations should make sense of the shared meanings embodied in the actor's behavior that are consistent with the actor's self-understanding or should be easily translatable to that point of view.

Although this fourth criterion is important, it is clearly insufficient in some situations, for individual and collective action are at times illusory, characterized by false consciousness, or even self-contradictory or irrational. This situation calls for a reinterpretation that begins with the claim that the actor's account is in some way crucially insufficient, misguided, consciously or unconsciously self-deluding, mystifying, or inconsistent with the action. The flawed self-understanding of the actor necessitates a better account that renders the action more fully intelligible. In the case of apparently irrational behavior, we can make sense of action by elucidating the coherence between the action and the meaning it has for the actor(s). As Taylor (1985b) clarifies, the coherence we recognize "in no way implies that the action is rational: the meaning of a situation for an agent may be full of confusion and contradiction; but the adequate depiction of this contradiction makes sense of it" (p. 24).

This can be stated in a more general way as a fifth principle of good interpretation. An interpretation can be judged superior to another reading when it makes sense of observations that did not fit within previously available accounts (whether these accounts are offered by the actor or the observer). It clarifies what was previously obscure, mystifying, or contradictory, and explains how these anomalies are intelligible after all. In cases where the actor seems inappropriate, confused, or irrational, such accounts amount to rational reconstructions of the reasons that informed the experience or behavior. For example, a colleague's inappropriate jocularity in an important meeting can be understood on learning more about the insecurity she feels about her job. Similarly, the sudden, apparently irrational bursts of anger that create significant difficulties for an individual begin to make sense when seen as part of a posttraumatic response that neither the individual nor her associates had previously recognized as related to the angry outbursts.

A sixth criterion is that better interpretations will be able not only to account for a set of actions more comprehensively than its predecessor but also to explain why the rival reading went awry. Accounting for its opposite number would include explaining why the other interpretation makes sense, in what ways it is inadequate, and *why* the other account adopts this problematic stance. That is, the better interpretation can not only indicate where the other viewpoint goes wrong but also explain why its rival's faulty moves were made. In this way, the superior interpretation makes better sense of its counterpart than the counterpart can of itself.

A seventh guideline is that better interpretations will open up fruitful new aspects of ongoing inquiry or illuminate previously unrecognized domains of investigation. One of the reasons we suggested that the positive illusions account of unrealistically positive views of marriage was superior to the social desirability explanation is that it opens up a whole series of interesting questions that the social desirability account ignores.

The criteria we present here cannot be fully formalized. We must bite the bullet and acknowledge that they require a certain degree of discernment and judgment that cannot be encompassed in an explicit list of rules or procedures. It is also clear that the principles of interpretation we articulate here are not seamlessly consistent with one another and that conflicts among them must be sorted out in the specific case. What counts as good judgment in these matters is worked out over time in a community of inquirers. It is taught through examples of how one account supplants another and of what counts as good argument or evidence within that community. New investigators absorb these norms through long apprenticeship and through the process of peer review and feedback.

This viewpoint is directly at odds with the kind of naturalistic approach in which formalization is seen as the keystone of objectivity. Once we recognize that interpretations are central to all human activities, including scientific observation, then it becomes clear that the aspiration to complete formalization is unattainable. As we acknowledge the presence of illusions and ideological influences in human action and observation, we can see how the ideal of formalization can also be distortive in disguising illusions and ideologies behind the veil of formal procedures.

Our emphasis on cultivated discernment may sound less well defined than contemporary quantitative methods, but, as any psychological researcher knows, every decision in the course of a research project requires exercising judgment. All these decisions require justification and can be (and often are) criticized, and it is notoriously possible for reasonable people to disagree on the basis of well-articulated positions and principles, none of which can be held to be absolutely true.

It follows that the criteria we have outlined here for good interpretation are not the final word. These formulations are fully susceptible to being supplanted by more clearly or comprehensively stated precepts.

The Hermeneutic Circle

If we accept that there is no ultimate appeal to surefire methods or indubitably objective data or to any final truth of the matter, what do we do if our interlocutors simply do not accept our interpretation? We can only appeal to further readings of behaviors, experiences, or the context that corroborate our point of view (Taylor, 1985b). Such appeals are an attempt to develop a common understanding or language for characterizing human action. Persuading our interlocutor depends not only on our ability to communicate the specific interpretation we are making but also on our conveying with clarity and in a compelling manner the "language" in which that interpretation is expressed. We are trying to establish a certain reading of a psychological phenomenon, but we can only appeal to other readings and to the overall language or perspective within which these readings make sense.

This is another instance of the hermeneutic circle. In trying to establish some overall interpretation of human action, we appeal to readings of specific actions. Because we are dealing with meanings, which only make sense in their relations with other meanings, the interpretations are only intelligible within an interrelated whole. The acceptance of a partial interpretation is always dependent on some more global perspective, and the overall interpretation can only be made sense of through a series of partial readings. The naturalistic approach was one attempt to break through this circle, but, as we have argued, it fails, because every observation is an interpretation—there are no brute data that can help us break out of the circle.

A common fear of this kind of dialectical reasoning is that it represents a vicious circle, in which we are entrapped. The hermeneutic circle is not vicious, because the relationship between part and whole are not entirely determinate. The part-whole dialectic is dynamic; it always includes the possibility that additional readings of specific examples of the subject of interest will require shifts in the overall interpretation or that a better articulation of the global perspective will lead to alterations and improvements in the partial readings.

Social Science as Practice

We can perhaps best summarize the implications of the hermeneutic perspective for psychological science by reformulating the role of the social scientist in studying human life. As we have argued throughout this book, the attempt to investigate behavior as "colorless movement" is distortive of that behavior, because it fails to account for the constitutive nature of self-interpretation, intersubjective meanings and norms, and the moral dimension of human life. We can take an additional step and recognize that if moral frameworks are inescapable, then social scientists themselves are also operating from within some shared frame of meaning and worth. After all, how could they abstract themselves from this aspect of the human condition, to stand outside all human meaning and context? We conclude from our discussion of interpretation that such a "view from nowhere" is simply inaccessible, that all observation is interpretation. We can now add that every interpretation has some standpoint, a perspective from which it is made, even when the interpreting is done in the name of a would-be value-free science.

From the naturalistic point of view, this is a scandalous conclusion; naturalistically oriented psychologists fear that such a formulation would entirely undermine the validity of psychological science by contaminating research with personal or moral biases. We have argued that psychological science is deeply shaped by various moral standpoints and that this is a *necessary* aspect of social science, just as it is with any human endeavor.

Does this invalidate psychology as a science? We think not. Rather, it invalidates only the factitious attempt to sharply divide fact from value in social science. Moreover, by recognizing the inherent moral dimension of psychology, we can begin to explicitly acknowledge the genuine moral impulses that guide our inquiry. For this reason, we see psychological theory and research as a social practice, a coordinated, ongoing activity that instantiates some aspect of a moral framework. Psychological inquiry is better characterized as the morally motivated activity of concerned citizens who want to improve the life of their community and nation, rather than as the austere work of disengaged, neutral observers.

For example, although the aggression theorists we discussed in Chapter Six claim to be representing social reality as they find it, they also assert that their theoretical viewpoint goes beyond the implicit self-understanding of the aggressive actor. They see aggressors as straightforwardly seeking to attain their goals through aggression, but suggest that these aims can often be better achieved through prosocial behavior. They see the aggressor as mistaken in the belief that aggression is the best way to attain his or her desires and implicitly claim that our society would be significantly improved by a reduction in aggression. Thus these theorists want not just to scientifically represent the actor's self-understanding and mode of living but also to criticize, challenge, and alter them for the better. We have argued that the instrumental individualism at the heart of these researchers' endeavor restricts their ethical comprehension of aggression, but this does not make their work any the less morally motivated. They clearly want to reduce human aggression and believe that an individualist perspective is helpful in pursuing their goal.

We identified a number of critical flaws in the individualism at the heart of aggression and marital quality research. This kind of critique could be repeated with virtually any area of psychology. If we recognize psychological theory as a form of committed social practice, we enlarge our horizons by legitimizing the use of theory and research to offer deeper challenges to prevailing values and practices. If such new interpretations are really more insightful and convincing than the previously accepted accounts, they will actually tend to alter the outlook and action of ordinary human agents as this new view eventually comes to be internalized as part of the agents' self-understanding. In this way, an interpretive psychology that achieves its goal would, with some frequency, lead to changes in individual and collective action. The new interpretation would alter the self-understanding of those it describes in such a way that it would undermine the shared understanding that makes the old way of doing things possible (Taylor, 1985b). This is another way of saying that social science theories do not just describe or explain events that are independent of them but help constitute the objects of study.

For example, feminists criticize the portrayal of the ideal woman as a lofty, virtuous, nurturing mother as one aspect of a patriarchal ideology that encourages the domination of women rather than true admiration of them. This feminist critique has helped undermine the traditional understanding of women in the family. The critique shows that this understanding and the practices that place women on this "pedestal" are, in part, an instance of false consciousness that often actually helps subjugate and exploit women and is therefore insupportable. As Taylor (1985b) points out, this kind of critique does not succeed simply as a psychological effect of having more information. "The disruptive consequences of the theory flow from the nature of the practice, in that one of its constitutive props has been knocked away. This is because the practice requires certain descriptions to make sense, and it is these that the theory undermines" (p. 98).

Our theory and research can also lead us to the opposite result. A compelling interpretation can highlight the relevance or significance of some practice. Research on attachment processes between caregivers and infants is a good example; it affirms the value of certain parenting practices such as turn taking and attunement in child-centered families. Many nurturing parents do not need this theory or research to tell them to match their infants' alternating capacity for stimulation and need for a respite, but the research shows that there is more to the process than even the most perceptive parent would have noticed. In addition, it reinforces those practices by suggesting that they embody the important ideal of nurturing the child's capacities in these families.

The interpretive perspective thus helps us see that our theories are not neutral with regard to the actions and practices they describe. Psychology has always been burdened with an awkward disjointedness in its insistence on pursuing a neutral form of inquiry and its coveted role as an advocate for improving human welfare. Acknowledging that our theory and research are forms of social practice puts us in a position to more fully integrate our scientific and social policy agendas. Our theory and research are certainly not neutral; by challenging, altering, reinforcing, or enriching our self-understandings and actions, they are in fact potentially transformative. Recognizing the transformative aspect of psychological theory and research is crucial, for otherwise the power of theory to support or alter our practices operates blindly and unconsciously. The naturalistic approach is unable to answer the question of whether a given theory is the best transforming account, because the possibility that theory can transform practice is seen as an extrascientific question.

Recognizing the link between theory and social practice in this way also illuminates another way to evaluate our theories. Theories can be tested by examining the quality of the practice they encourage. Good theory clarifies, enriches, and increases the productivity or lucidity of practice, and it can challenge or undermine questionable practices. Our recognition that social science is a social practice highlights our accountability for the ways in which we study psychological phenomena. For we now see that social theory and research are not simply disinterested, neutral accounts of how things operate. Rather, we are inescapably involved in expressing, challenging, strengthening, and shaping contemporary perspectives concerning what is worthy or admirable in human life (Taylor, 1985b). We must recognize that we are continually engaged in an ethical activity that grows out of and helps shape our current conceptions of the good life. In what more worthwhile endeavor could we hope to participate?

REFERENCES

Adler, M. (1985). *Ten philosophical mistakes.* New York: Macmillan.

American Psychological Association. (1986). *Accreditation handbook.* Washington, DC: Author.

Antonovsky, A. (1979). *Health, stress, and coping: New perspectives on mental and physical well-being.* San Francisco: Jossey-Bass.

Ariès, P. (1974). *Western attitudes toward death: From the middle ages to the present* (P. Ranum, Trans.). Baltimore: Johns Hopkins University Press.

Bakhtin, M. M. (1981). *The dialogical imagination: Four essays by M. Bakhtin* (M. Holquist, Ed.). Austin: University of Texas Press.

Balcom, D. A., & Healey, D. (1990). The context for couples treatment of wife abuse. In M. Mirkin (Ed.), *The social and political contexts of family therapy* (pp. 121–137). Needham Heights, MA: Allyn & Bacon.

Bankhart, C. P. (1997). *Talking cures: A history of Western and Eastern psychologies.* Pacific Grove, CA: Brooks/Cole.

Barich, R. R., & Bielby, D. D. (1996). Rethinking marriage: Change and stability in expectations, 1967–1994. *Journal of Family Issues, 17,* 139–169.

Beck, A., Freeman, A., & Associates. (1990). *Cognitive therapy of personality disorders.* New York: Guilford Press.

Beck, A., & Weishaar, M. (1989). Cognitive therapy. In R. Corsini & D. Wedding (Eds.), *Current psychotherapies* (pp. 285–322). Itasca, IL: Peacock.

Becker, E. (1973). *The denial of death.* New York: Free Press.

Beiner, R. (1992). *What's the matter with liberalism?* Berkeley: University of California Press.

Bell, D. (1978). *The cultural contradictions of capitalism.* New York: Basic Books.

Bellah, R. (1983). The ethical aims of social inquiry. In N. Haan, R. Bellah, P. Rabinow, & W. Sullivan (Eds.), *Social science as moral inquiry* (pp. 300–381). New York: Columbia University Press.

Bellah, R., Madsen, R., Sullivan, W., Swindler, A., & Tipton, S. (1985). *Habits of the heart: Individualism and commitment in American life.* Berkeley: University of California Press.

Benhabib, S. (1992). *Situating the self: Gender, community, and postmodernism in contemporary ethics.* New York: Routledge.

Berger, P. (1973). *The homeless mind: Modernization and consciousness.* New York: Vintage.

Berger, P. (1977). *Facing up to modernity.* New York: Basic Books.

Berger, P. (1979). *The heretical imperative.* New York: Anchor Books.

Bergin, A. (1980). Psychotherapy and religious values. *Journal of Consulting and Clinical Psychology, 48,* 642–655.

Berlin, I. (1982). Does political theory still exist? In H. Hardy (Ed.), *Concepts and categories: Philosophical essays by Isaiah Berlin* (pp. 143–172). New York: Penguin Books. (Original work published 1961)

Bernal, G., & Ysern, E. (1986). Family therapy and ideology. *Journal of Marital and Family Therapy, 12,* 129–135.

Bernstein, R. J. (1971). *Praxis and action: Contemporary philosophies of human activity.* Philadelphia: University of Pennsylvania Press.

Bernstein, R. J. (1976). *The restructuring of social and political theory.* Philadelphia: University of Pennsylvania Press.

Bernstein, R. J. (1983). *Beyond objectivism and relativism.* Philadelphia: University of Pennsylvania Press.

Bernstein, R. J. (1988). The rage against reason. In E. McMullin (Ed.), *Construction and constraint* (pp. 189–221). Notre Dame, IN: University of Notre Dame Press.

Binswanger, L. (1958). The existential analysis school of thought. In R. May, E. Angel, & H. F. Ellenberger (Eds.), *Existence: A new dimension in psychiatry and psychology.* New York: Basic Books.

Bograd, M. (1990). Scapegoating mothers: Conceptual errors in systems formulations. In M. Mirkin (Ed.), *The social and political contexts of family therapy* (pp. 69–88). Needham Heights, MA: Allyn & Bacon.

Boss, M. (1963). *Psychoanalysis and Daseinsanalysis* (L. B. Lefebre, Trans.). New York: Basic Books.

Boszormenyi-Nagy, I., & Krasner, B. R. (1986). *Between give and take.* New York: Brunner/Mazel.

Bowen, M. (1978). *Family therapy in clinical practice.* Northvale, NJ: Aronson.

Bruner, J. (1990). *Acts of meaning.* Cambridge, MA: Harvard University Press.

Buber, M. (1958). *I and thou* (2nd ed., R. G. Smith, Trans.). New York: Scribner.

Buchler, J. (Ed.). (1955). *Philosophical writings of Pierce.* New York: Dover.

Bugental, J. (1981). *The search for authenticity: An existential-analytic approach to psychotherapy.* New York: Irvington. (Original work published 1965)

Bugental, J., & Sterling, M. (1995). Existential-humanistic psychotherapy: New perspectives. In A. S. Gurman & S. B. Messer (Eds.), *Essential psychotherapies: Theory and practice* (pp. 226–260). New York: Guilford Press.

Camus, A. (1946). *The stranger* (G. Stuart, Trans.). New York: Knopf.

Camus, A. (1956). *The rebel: An essay on man in revolt* (A. Bower, Trans.). New York: Vintage.

Cherlin, A. J. (1992). *Marriage, divorce, remarriage* (Rev. ed.). Cambridge, MA: Harvard University Press.

Chodorow, N. (1978). *The reproduction of mothering: Psychoanalysis and the sociology of gender.* Berkeley: University of California Press.

Colapinto, J. (1991). Structural family therapy. In A. S. Gurman & D. P. Kniskern (Eds.), *Handbook of family therapy* (Vol. 2, pp. 417–443). New York: Brunner/Mazel.

Coles, R. (1987). Civility and psychology. In R. Bellah, R. Madsen, W. Sullivan, A. Swindler, & S. Tipton (Eds.), *Individualism and commitment in American life.* New York: HarperCollins.

Cuber, J., & Harroff, P. (1966). *Sex and the significant Americans: A study of sexual behavior among the affluent.* New York: Penguin Books.

Cushman, P. (1990). Why the self is empty. *American Psychologist, 45,* 599–611.

Cushman, P. (1991). Ideology obscured. *American Psychologist, 46,* 206–219.

Cushman, P. (1995). *Constructing the self, constructing America: A cultural history of psychotherapy.* Reading, MA: Addison-Wesley.

Damon, W. (1995). *Greater expectations: Overcoming the culture of indulgence in America's homes and schools.* New York: Free Press.

D'Andrade, R. (1986). Three scientific world views. In D. Fiske & R. Shweder (Eds.), *Metatheory in social science* (pp. 19–41). Chicago: University of Chicago Press.

Davis, C. (1990). Our modern identity: The formation of the self. *Modern Theology, 6,* 160–171.

Dewey, J. (1960). *The quest for certainty: A study of the relations of knowledge and action.* New York: Putnam.

Dilthey, W. (1958). *Der aufbau der geschichtlichen welt in den geisteswissenschaften: Vol. 7. Gesammelte schriften* [The construction of the historical world in the human sciences: Vol. 7. Collected writings]. Stuttgart: Teubner.

Dilthey, W. (1962). *Pattern and meaning in history* (H. Rickman, Ed. and Trans.). New York: HarperCollins.

Dilthey, W. (1976). *W. Dilthey: Selected writings* (H. P. Rickman, Ed. and Trans.). Cambridge, England: Cambridge University Press.

Dilthey, W. (1977). *Descriptive psychology and historical understanding* (R. Zaner & K. Heiges, Trans.). The Hague: Nijhoff.

Doherty, W. (1994, Winter). Bridging psychotherapy and moral responsibility. *Responsive Community, 4,* 41–52.

Doherty, W., & Boss, P. (1991). Values and ethics in family therapy. In A. Gurman & D. Kniskern (Eds.), *Handbook of family therapy* (Vol. 2, pp. 606–637). New York: Brunner/Mazel.

Donzelot, J. (1977). *The policing of families.* New York: Pantheon.

Dreyfus, H. (1987). Foucault's therapy. *PsychCritique, 2*(1), 65–83.

Dunne, J. (1996). Beyond sovereignty and deconstruction: The storied self. *Philosophy and Social Criticism, 21,* 137–157.

Eagle, M. (1984). *Recent developments in psychoanalysis.* New York: McGraw-Hill.

Elizur, J., & Minuchin, S. (1989). *Institutionalizing madness.* New York: Basic Books.

Ellis, A. (1962). *Reason and emotion in psychotherapy.* New York: Stuart.

Ellis, A. (1973). *Humanistic psychotherapy.* New York: McGraw-Hill.

Ellis, A. (1977). The basic clinical theory of rational-emotive psychotherapy. In A. Ellis & R. Grieger (Eds.), *Handbook of rational-emotive psychotherapy.* New York: Springer.

Elshtain, J. (1995). *Democracy on trial.* New York: Basic Books.

Eron, L. D. (1987). The development of aggressive behavior from the perspective of a developing behaviorism. *American Psychologist, 42,* 435–442.

Eron, L. D., & Huesman, L. R. (1984). The relation of prosocial behavior to the development of aggression and psychopathology. *Aggressive Behavior, 10,* 201–211.

Eron, L. D., Huesman, L. R., Dubow, E., Romanoff, R., & Yarmel, P. W. (1987). Aggression and its correlates over twenty-two years. In D. H. Crowell, I. M. Evans, & C. R. O'Donnell (Eds.), *Childhood aggression and violence* (pp. 249–262). New York: Plenum.

Eron, L. D., Walder, L. O., & Lefkowitz, M. M. (1971). *Learning of aggression in children.* New York: Little, Brown.

Etzioni, A. (1996). *The new golden rule: Community and morality in a democratic society.* New York: Basic Books.

Fancher, R. (1995). *Cultures of healing: Correcting the image of American mental health care.* New York: Freeman.

Felski, R. (1989, Fall). Feminism, postmodernism, and the critique of modernity. *Cultural Critique, 13,* 33–56.

Fincham, F., & Bradbury, T. (1989). Perceived responsibility for marital events: Egocentric or partner-centric bias? *Journal of Marriage and the Family, 51,* 27–35.

Fincham, F., & Linfield, K. (1998). A new look at marital quality: Can spouses feel positive and negative about their marriage? *Journal of Family Psychology, 11,* 489–502.

Fineman, H. (1994, June 13). Virtuecrats. *Newsweek,* pp. 30–36.

Flax, J. (1988). Existentialism and human development: Commentary on Salvatore R. Maddi. In S. Messer, L. Sass, & R. Woolfolk (Eds.), *Hermeneutics and psychological theory: Interpretive perspectives on personality, psychotherapy, and psychopathology* (pp. 210–215). New Brunswick, NJ: Rutgers University Press.

Flax, J. (1990). *Thinking fragments: Psychoanalysis, feminism, and postmodernism in the contemporary west.* Berkeley: University of California Press.

Foucault, M. (1970). *The order of things: An archaeology of the human sciences.* New York: Pantheon Books.

Foucault, M. (1977). *Discipline and punishment: The birth of the prison.* New York: Pantheon.

Foucault, M. (1980a). *Power/knowledge: Selected interviews and other writings* (C. Gordon, Ed.). New York: Pantheon.

Foucault, M. (1980b). *The history of sexuality. Vol. 1: An introduction* (R. Hurley, Trans.). New York: Vintage/Random House.

Foucault, M. (1982). On the genealogy of ethics: An overview of work in progress. In H. Dreyfus & P. Rabinow, *Michel Foucault: Beyond structuralism and hermeneutics* (pp. 229–252). Chicago: University of Chicago Press.

Foucault, M. (1987). What is enlightenment? In P. Rabinow & W. Sullivan (Eds.), *Interpretive social science: A second look* (pp. 157–174). Berkeley: University of California Press.

Fowers, B. (forthcoming). *The myth of marital happiness.* San Francisco: Jossey-Bass.

Fowers, B. (1998). Psychology and the good marriage: Social theory as practice. *American Behavioral Scientist, 41,* 516–541.

Fowers, B., & Olson, D. (1986). Predicting marital success with PREPARE: A predictive validity study. *Journal of Marital and Family Therapy, 12,* 403–413.

Fowers, B., Lyons, E., & Montel, K. (1996). Positive illusions about marriage: Self enhancement or relationship enhancement? *Journal of Family Psychology, 10,* 192–208.

Fowers, B., & Wenger, A. (1997). Are trustworthiness and fairness enough? Contextual family therapy and the good family. *Journal of Marital and Family Therapy, 23,* 153–169.

Fox, D., & Prilleltensky, I. (1997). *Critical psychology: An introduction.* Thousand Oaks, CA: Sage.

Fox-Genovese, E. (1991). *Feminism without illusions: A critique of individualism.* Chapel Hill: University of North Carolina Press.

Framo, J. (1965). Rationale and techniques of intensive family therapy. In I. Boszormenyi-Nagy & J. Framo (Eds.), *Intensive family therapy* (pp. 143–212). New York: HarperCollins.

Frank, J. D. (1978). *Psychotherapy and the human predicament.* New York: Schocken.

Frank, J. D., & Frank, J. B. (1991). *Persuasion and healing: A comparative study of psychotherapy.* Baltimore: Johns Hopkins University Press.

Frankl, V. (1963). *Man's search for meaning: An introduction to logotherapy.* New York: Pocket Books.

Freud, S. (1933). *New introductory lectures on psychoanalysis.* New York: Norton.

Friedman, M. (1984). *To deny our nothingness: Contemporary images of man.* Chicago: Chicago University Press.

Fromm, E. (1965). *Escape from freedom.* New York: Avon. (Original work published 1941)

Fromm, E. (1975). *Man for himself.* New York: Fawcett Premier. (Original work published 1947)

Furstenberg, F., & Cherlin, A. (1991). *Divided families: What happens to children when parents part.* Cambridge, MA: Harvard University Press.

Gadamer, H.-G. (1975). *Truth and method.* New York: Crossroad.

Gadamer, H.-G. (1976). The universality of the hermeneutical problem. In *Philosophical hermeneutics* (D. Linge, Trans.). Berkeley: University of California Press.

Gadamer, H.-G. (1981). *Reason in the age of science.* Cambridge, MA: MIT Press.

Gadamer, H.-G. (1987). Hermeneutics as practical philosophy. In K. Baynes, J. Bohman, & T. McCarthy (Eds.), *After philosophy* (pp. 325–338). Cambridge, MA: MIT Press.

Gadamer, H.-G. (1989). *Truth and method* (2nd ed., J. Weinsheimer & D. Marshall, Trans.). New York: Crossroad. (Original work published 1960)

Garfield, S., & Bergin, A. (1986). *Handbook of psychotherapy and behavior change* (3rd ed.). New York: Wiley.

Geertz, C. (1973). *The interpretation of cultures.* New York: Basic Books.

Gergen, K. (1982). *Toward transformation in social knowledge.* New York: Springer-Verlag.

Gergen, K. (1985). The social constructionist movement in modern psychology. *American Psychologist, 40,* 266–275.

Gergen, K. (1994). *Realities and relationships: Soundings in social construction-ism.* Cambridge, MA: Harvard University Press.

Giddens, A. (1976). *New rules of sociological method.* New York: Basic Books.

Gilligan, C. (1982). *In a different voice: Psychological theory and women's development.* Cambridge, MA: Harvard University Press.

Glenn, N. (1990). Quantitative research on marital quality in the 1980s: A critical review. *Journal of Marriage and the Family, 52,* 818–831.

Glenn, N. (1991). The recent trend in marital success in the United States. *Journal of Marriage and the Family, 53,* 261–270.

Glick, P. (1988). Fifty years of family demography: A record of social change. *Journal of Marriage and the Family, 50,* 861–873.

Gottman, J. (1993). The roles of conflict engagement, escalation, or avoidance in marital interaction: A longitudinal view of five types of couples. *Journal of Consulting and Clinical Psychology, 61,* 6–15.

Gottman, J. (1994). *What predicts divorce: The relationship between marital processes and marital outcomes.* Mahwah, NJ: Erlbaum.

Gottman, J., & Silver, N. (1994). *Why marriages succeed or fail.* New York: Simon & Schuster.

Grondin, J. (1994). *Introduction to philosophical hermeneutics* (J. Weinsheimer, Trans.). New Haven, CT: Yale University Press.

Guerney, B., Brock, G., & Coufal, J. (1987). Integrating marital therapy and enrichment: The relationship enhancement approach. In N. Jacobson & A. Gurman (Eds.), *Clinical handbook of marital therapy* (pp. 151–172). New York: Guilford Press.

Guignon, C. (1983). *Heidegger and the problem of knowledge.* Indianapolis, IN: Hackett.

Guignon, C. (1986). Existentialist ethics. In J. P. DeMarco & R. M. Fox (Eds.), *New directions in ethics: The challenge of applied ethics* (pp. 73–91). New York: Routledge.

Guignon, C. (1991). Pragmatism or hermeneutics? Epistemology after foundationalism. In J. Bohman, D. Hiley, & R. Schusterman (Eds.), *The interpretive turn* (pp. 81–101). Ithaca, NY: Cornell University Press.

Guignon, C. (1998a). Existentialism. In *Encyclopedia of Philosophy.* New York: Routledge.

Guignon, C. (1998b). Narrative explanation in psychotherapy. *American Behavioral Scientist, 41,* 558–577.

Guignon, C., & Hiley, D. (1990). Biting the bullet: Rorty on private and public morality. In A. Malachowski (Ed.), *Reading Rorty* (pp. 339–364). Cambridge, MA: Blackwell.

Guignon, C., & Pereboom, D. (1995). Introduction: The legacy of existentialism. In C. Guignon & D. Pereboom (Eds.), *Existentialism: Basic writings* (pp. xiii–xxxviii). Indianapolis, IN: Hackett.

Habermas, J. (1970). *Toward a rational society.* Boston: Beacon Press.

Habermas, J. (1971). *Knowledge and human interests.* Boston: Beacon Press.

Habermas, J. (1973). *Theory and practice.* Boston: Beacon Press.

Habermas, J. (1975). *Legitimation crisis.* Boston: Beacon Press.

Habermas, J. (1991). *The philosophical discourse of modernity.* Cambridge, MA: MIT Press.

Haley, J. (1976). *Problem solving therapy.* New York: HarperCollins.

Hall, J., & Taylor, S. E. (1976). When love is blind. *Human Relations, 29,* 751–761.

Halling, S., & Nill J. (1995). A brief history of existential-phenomenological psychiatry and psychotherapy. *Journal of Phenomenological Psychology, 26,* 1–45.

Harding, S. (1990). Feminism, science, and the anti-Enlightenment critiques. In L. Nicholson (Ed.), *Feminism/postmodernism* (pp. 83–106). New York: Routledge.

Hare-Mustin, R. (1986). The problem of gender in family therapy theory. *Family Process, 26,* 15–27.

Hare-Mustin, R. (1991). Sex, lies, and headaches: The problem is power. In T. Goodrich (Ed.), *Women and power: Perspectives for therapy* (pp. 63–85). New York: Norton.

Hare-Mustin, R., & Marecek, J. (1994). *Feminism and postmodernism: Dilemmas and points of difference.* Paper presented at the 1994 annual meeting of the American Psychological Association, Los Angeles, CA.

Hare-Mustin, R., & Marecek, J. (1997). Abnormal and clinical psychology: The politics of madness. In D. Fox & I. Prilleltensky (Eds.), *Critical psychology: An introduction* (pp. 104–120). Thousand Oaks, CA: Sage.

Hareven, T. (1987). Historical analysis of the family. In M. Sussman & S. Steinmetz (Eds.), *Handbook of marriage and the family* (pp. 37–57). New York: Plenum.

Havel, V. (1995, March). Forgetting we are not God. *First Things,* pp. 47–50.

Heidegger, M. (1962). *Being and time.* (J. Macquarrie & E. Robinson, Trans.). New York: HarperCollins. (Original work published 1927)

Heidegger, M. (1977). The question concerning technology. In M. Heidegger, *The question concerning technology and other essays* (W. Lovitt, Trans.). New York: Harper Colophon Books.

Heidegger, M. (1995). *Being and time.* In C. Guignon & D. Pereboom (Eds.), *Existentialism: Basic writings* (pp. 203–246). Indianapolis, IN: Hackett. (Original work published 1927)

Held, D. (1980). *Introduction to critical theory: Horkheimer to Habermas.* Berkeley: University of California Press.

Hillman, J., & Ventura, M. (1992). *We've had a hundred years of psychotherapy and the world's getting worse.* San Francisco: Harper San Francisco.

Hoffman, I. (1996). The intimate and ironic authority of the psychoanalyst's presence. *Psychoanalytic Quarterly, 65,* 102–136.

Hoffman, L. (1981). *Foundations of family therapy.* New York: Basic Books.

Horkheimer, M. (1974). *Eclipse of reason.* New York: Continuum.

Horney, K. (1942). *Self analysis.* New York: Norton.

Hoy, D. (1986). Power, repression, progress. In D. Hoy (Ed.), *Foucault: A critical reader* (pp. 123–147). Cambridge, MA: Blackwell.

Huesman, L. (1993). Cognition and aggression: A reply to Fowers and Richardson. *Theory and Psychology, 3,* 375–379.

Huesman, L., & Eron, L. (1984). Cognitive processes and the persistence of aggressive behavior. *Aggressive Behavior, 10,* 243–251.

Huesman, L., Eron, L., Lefkowitz, M., & Walder, L. (1984). Stability of aggression over time and generations. *Developmental Psychology, 20,* 1120–1134.

Imber-Black, E. (1988). *Families and larger systems: A family therapist's guide through the labyrinth.* New York: Guilford Press.

James, K., & McIntyre, D. (1983). The reproduction of families: The social role of family therapy? *Journal of Marital and Family Therapy, 9,* 119–129.

Johnson, D., White, L., Edwards, J., & Booth, A. (1986). Dimensions of marital quality: Toward methodological and conceptual refinement. *Journal of Family Issues, 7,* 31–49.

Jung, C. (1954). The development of personality. In *The development of personality: Papers on child psychology, education, and related subjects.* Bollingen Series. Princeton, NJ: Princeton University Press.

Jung, C. (1966). *Two essays on analytical psychology.* Bollingen Series. Princeton, NJ: Princeton University Press.

Kane, R. (1994). *Through the moral maze: Searching for absolute values in a pluralistic age.* New York: Paragon House.

Kane, R. (1998). Dimensions of value and the aims of social inquiry. *American Behavioral Scientist, 41,* 578–597.

Karney, B., & Bradbury, T. (1995). The longitudinal course of marital quality and stability: A review of theory, method, and research. *Psychological Bulletin, 18,* 3–34.

Kempler, W. (1981). *Experiential psychotherapy within families.* New York: Brunner/Mazel.

Kerlinger, F. (1986). *Foundations of behavioral research* (3rd ed.). Austin, TX: Holt, Rinehart and Winston.

Kierkegaard, S. (1995a). Concluding unscientific postscript. In C. Guignon & D. Pereboom (Eds.), *Existentialism: Basic writings* (pp. 77–84). Indianapolis, IN: Hackett. (Original work published 1846)

Kierkegaard, S. (1995b). Fear and trembling. In C. Guignon & D. Pereboom (Eds.), *Existentialism: Basic writings* (pp. 18–69). Indianapolis, IN: Hackett. (Original work published 1843)

Koch, S. (1993). The nature and limits of psychological knowledge: Lessons of a quarter century qua science. *American Psychologist, 36,* 257–269.

Kohlberg, L. (1984). *Essays on moral development.* New York: HarperCollins.

Kohut, H. (1977). *The restoration of the self.* New York: International Universities Press.

Kohut, H. (1984). *How does analysis cure?* New York: Norton.

Kolakowski, L. (1986, June 16). The idolatry of politics. *The New Republic,* pp. 29–36.

Kuhn, T. (1970a). Reflections on my critics. In I. Lakatos & A. Musgrove (Eds.), *Criticism and the growth of knowledge.* Cambridge, England: Cambridge University Press.

Kuhn, T. (1970b). *The structure of scientific revolutions* (2nd ed.). Chicago: University of Chicago Press.

L'Abate, L., & Bagarozzi, D. (1993). *Sourcebook of marriage and family evaluation.* New York: Brunner/Mazel.

Lasch, C. (1977). *Haven in a heartless world: The family beseiged.* New York: Basic Books.

Lasch, C. (1978). *The culture of narcissism.* New York: Norton.

Lee, G., Seccombe, K., & Sheehan, C. (1991). Marital status and personal happiness: An analysis of trend data. *Journal of Marriage and the Family, 53,* 839–844.

Lefkowitz, M., Eron, L., Walder, L., & Huesman, L. (1977). *Growing up to be violent.* New York: Pergamon Press.

Lewis, M. (1992). *Shame: The exposed self.* New York: Free Press.

Litwack, E., & Messeri, P. (1989). Organizational theory, social supports, and mortality rates: A theoretical convergence. *American Sociological Review, 54,* 49–66.

London, P. (1964). *The modes and morals of psychotherapy.* Austin, TX: Holt, Rinehart and Winston.

Lowe, C. (1969). *Value orientations in counseling and psychotherapy: The meanings of mental health.* Cranston, RI: Carroll Press.

Loewenstein, Era. (1991). Psychoanalytic life history: Is coherence, continuity, and aesthetic appeal necessary? *Psychoanalysis and Contemporary Thought, 14,* 3–28.

Lubek, I. (1986). Fifty years of frustration and aggression: Some historical notes on a long-lived hypothesis. In K. S. Larsen (Ed.), *Dialectics and ideology in psychology* (pp. 30–84). Norwood, NJ: Ablex.

Lukes, S. (1987). On the social determination of truth. In M. Gibbons (Ed.), *Interpreting politics* (pp. 64–81). New York: New York University Press.

MacIntyre, A. (1981). *After virtue.* Notre Dame, IN: University of Notre Dame Press.

Mackie, J. (1977). *Ethics: Inventing right and wrong.* New York: Penguin Books.

Madanes, C. (1991). Strategic family therapy. In A. S. Gurman and D. P. Kniskern (Eds.), *Handbook of family therapy* (Vol. 2, pp. 396–416). New York: Brunner/Mazel.

Mancuso, J., & Sarbin, T. (1983). The self-narrative in the enactment of roles. In T. Sarbin & K. Scheibe (Eds.), *Studies in social identity* (pp. 233–253). New York: Praeger.

Markman, H. (1981). The prediction of marital success: A five-year follow-up. *Journal of Consulting and Clinical Psychology, 49,* 760–762.

Markman, H., Resnick, M., Floyd, F., Stanley, S., & Clements, M. (1993). Preventing marital distress through communication and conflict management training: A four-and five-year follow-up. *Journal of Consulting and Clinical Psychology, 61,* 70–77.

Markman, H., Stanley, S., & Blumberg, S. (1994). *Fighting for your marriage: Positive steps for preventing divorce and preserving a lasting love.* San Francisco: Jossey-Bass.

Martin, T., & Bumpass, L. (1989). Recent trends in marital disruption. *Demography, 26,* 37–52.

Masterson, J. (1988). *The search for the real self: Unmasking the personality disorders of our age.* New York: Free Press.

May, R (1953). *Man's search for himself.* New York: Dell.

May, R. (1958). Contributions of existential psychotherapy. In R. May, E. Angel, & H. F. Ellenberger (Eds.), *Existence: A new dimension in psychiatry and psychology.* New York: Basic Books.

May, R. (1969). *Love and will.* New York: Norton.

May, R., & Yalom, I. (1989). Existential psychotherapy. In R. Corsini & D. Wedding (Eds.), *Current psychotherapies* (pp. 363–404). Itasca, IL: Peacock.

McCarthy, T. (1978). *The critical theory of Jürgen Habermas.* Cambridge, MA: MIT Press.

McGoldrick, M., Preto, N., Hines, P., & Lee, E. (1991). Ethnicity and family therapy. In A. Gurman & D. P. Kniskern (Eds.), *Handbook of family therapy* (Vol. 2, pp. 546–582). New York: Brunner/Mazel.

Mellman, M., Lazarus, E., & Rivlin, A. (1990). Family time, family values. In D. Blankenhorn, S. Bayme, & J. B. Elshtain (Eds.), *Rebuilding the nest: A new commitment to the American family* (pp. 73–92). Milwaukee: Family Services America.

Messer, S. (1986). Eclecticism in psychotherapy: Underlying assumptions, problems, and trade-offs. In J. Norcross (Ed.), *Handbook of eclectic psychotherapy.* New York: Brunner/Mazel.

Messer, S. B., & Winokur, M. (1980). Some limits to the integration of psychoanalytic and behavior therapy. *American Psychologist, 35,* 818–827.

Mill, J. S. (1956). *On liberty.* Indianapolis, IN: Bobbs-Merrill. (Original work published 1860)

Miller, J. B. (1986). *Toward a new psychology of women.* Boston: Beacon Press.

Mintz, S., & Kellogg, S. (1988). *Domestic revolutions: A social history of American family life.* New York: Free Press.

Minuchin, S. (1974). *Families and family therapy.* Cambridge, MA: Harvard University Press.

Minuchin, S., & Fishman, H. C. (1981). *Family therapy techniques.* Cambridge, MA: Harvard University Press.

Mirkin, M. (1990). Eating disorders: A feminist family therapy perspective. In M. Mirkin (Ed.), *The social and political contexts of family therapy* (pp. 89–119). Needham Heights, MA: Allyn & Bacon.

Moon, J. (1983). Political ethics and critical theory. In D. Sabia & J. Wallulis (Eds.), *Changing social science* (pp. 171–188). Albany: State University of New York Press.

Murdoch, I. (1985). *The sovereignty of the good.* London: Ark.

Neal, P. (1990). Justice as fairness. *Political Theory, 18,* 24–50.

Nietzsche, F. (1995). *The gay science.* In C. Guignon & D. Pereboom (Eds.), *Existentialism: Basic writings* (pp. 115–163). Indianapolis, IN: Hackett. (Original work published 1882)

Norcross, J. (1986). *Handbook of eclectic psychotherapy.* New York: Brunner/Mazel.

Norman, R. (1983). *The moral philosophers.* Oxford: Clarendon Press.

Okin, S. (1989). *Justice, gender, and the family.* New York: Basic Books.

Olson, D., Fournier, D., & Druckman, J. (1987). *Counselor's manual for PREPARE/ENRICH* (Rev. ed.). Minneapolis, MN: PREPARE/ENRICH.

Papero, D. (1990). *Bowen family systems theory.* Needham Heights, MA: Allyn & Bacon.

Philip, M. (1985). Michel Foucault. In Q. Skinner (Ed.), *The return of grand theory in the human sciences* (pp. 65–82). Cambridge, England: Cambridge University Press.

Polkinghorne, D. (1988). *Narrative knowing and the human sciences.* Albany: State University of New York Press.

Pomerantz, B. (1995). *Positive illusions: An examination of the unrealistically positive views individuals hold of themselves and their spouses as an explanation for the marital conventionalization bias.* Unpublished doctoral dissertation, University of Miami.

Popenoe, D. (1993). American family decline, 1960–1990: A review and appraisal. *Journal of Marriage and the Family, 55,* 527–555.

Popenoe, D. (1990). Family decline in America. In D. Blankenhorn, S. Bayme, & J. B. Elshtain (Eds.), *Rebuilding the nest: A new commitment to the American family* (pp. 39–51). Milwaukee, WI: Family Services America.

Prilleltensky, I. (1997). Values, assumptions, and practices: Assessing the moral implications of psychological discourse and action. *American Psychologist, 5,* 517–535.

Progoff, I. (1956). *The death and rebirth of psychology.* New York: McGraw-Hill.

Rawls, J. (1971). *A theory of justice.* Cambridge, MA: Harvard University Press.

Reissman, C. (1990). *Divorce talk: Women and men make sense of personal relationships.* New Brunswick, NJ: Rutgers University Press.

Richardson, F., & Christopher, J. (1993). Social theory as practice: Metatheoretical frameworks for social inquiry. *Journal of Theoretical and Philosophical Psychology, 13,* 137–153.

Richardson, F., & Fowers, B. (1997). Critical theory, postmodernism, and hermeneutics: Insights for critical psychology. In D. Fox & I. Prilleltensky (Eds.), *Critical psychology: An introduction* (pp. 265–283). Thousand Oaks, CA: Sage.

Richardson, F., Rogers, A., & McCarroll, J. (1998). Toward a dialogical self. *American Behavioral Scientist, 41,* 496–515.

Ricoeur, P. (1970). *Freud and philosophy.* New Haven: Yale University Press.

Ricoeur, P. (1973, Spring). Ethics and culture. *Philosophy Today,* pp. 153–165.

Ricoeur, P. (1974). Psychiatry and moral values. In S. Arieti (Ed.), *The foundations of psychiatry* (Vol. 1). New York: Basic Books.

Ricoeur, P. (1981). *Hermeneutics and the human sciences* (J. B. Thompson, Ed.). Cambridge, England: Cambridge University Press.

Ricoeur, P. (1983). *Time and narrative* (Vol. 1., K. McLaughlin & D. Pellauer, Trans.). Chicago: University of Chicago Press.

Ricoeur, P. (1992). *Oneself as another.* Chicago: University of Chicago Press.

Rieff, P. (1959). *Freud: The mind of a moralist.* Chicago: University of Chicago Press.

Rieff, P. (1966). *The triumph of the therapeutic.* New York: HarperCollins.

Roberto, L. G. (1991). Symbolic-experiential family therapy. In A. S. Gurman & D. P. Kniskern (Eds.), *The handbook of family therapy* (Vol. 2, pp. 444–476). New York: Brunner/Mazel.

Rogers, C. (1951). *Client-centered therapy: Its current practice, implications, and theory.* Boston: Houghton Mifflin.

Rorty, R. (1979). *Philosophy and the mirror of nature.* Princeton, NJ: Princeton University Press.

Rorty, R. (1982). *Consequences of pragmatism.* Minneapolis: University of Minnesota Press.

Rorty, R. (1985). Solidarity or objectivity? In J. Rajchman & C. West (Eds.), *Post-analytic philosophy.* New York: Columbia University Press.

Rorty, R. (1987) Method, social science and social hope. In M. Gibbons (Ed.), *Interpreting politics* (pp. 241–260). New York: New York University Press.

Ross, C., Mirowski, J., & Goldstein, K. (1990). The impact of the family on health: A decade in review. *Journal of Marriage and the Family, 52,* 1059–1078.

Roth, P. (1991). Interpretation as explanation. In D. Hiley, J. Bohman, and R. Schusterman (Eds.), *The interpretive turn* (pp. 179–196). Ithaca, NY: Cornell University Press.

Ruben, H. (1986). *Supermarriage: Overcoming the predictable crises of married life.* New York: Bantam.

Sampson, E. (1985). The decentralization of identity: Toward a revised concept of personal and social order. *American Psychologist, 40,* 1203–1211.

Sandel, M. (1982). *Liberalism and the limits of justice.* Cambridge, England: Cambridge University Press.

Sandel, M. (1996). *Democracy's discontent: America in search of a public philosophy.* Cambridge, MA: Belknap/Harvard.

Sarason, S. (1986). And what is the public interest? *American Psychologist, 41,* 899–905.

Sartre, J.-P. (1995a). *Being and nothingness.* In C. Guignon & D. Pereboom (Eds.), *Existentialism: Basic writings* (pp. 287–340). Indianapolis, IN: Hackett. (Original work published 1943)

Sartre, J.-P. (1995b). The humanism of existentialism. In C. Guignon & D. Pereboom (Eds.), *Existentialism: Basic writings* (pp. 268–286). Indianapolis, IN: Hackett. (Original work published 1946)

Schafer, R. (1976). *A new language for psychoanalysis.* New Haven, CT: Yale University Press.

Schafer, R. (1980a). Action and narration in psychoanalysis. *New Literary History, 12,* 61–85.

Schafer, R. (1980b). Action language and the psychology of the self. *Annual of Psychoanalysis, 8.*

Schafer, R. (1980c). Narration in the psychoanalytic dialogue. In W. Mitchell (Ed.), *On narrative.* Chicago: University of Chicago Press.

Schafer, R. (1981). *Narrative actions in psychoanalysis.* Worcester, MA: Clark University Press.

Schafer, R. (1992). *Retelling a life: Narration and dialogue in psychoanalysis.* New York: Basic Books.

Schneider, K., & May, R. (1995). *The psychology of existence: An integrative, clinical perspective.* New York: McGraw-Hill.

Schoen, R., Urton, W., Woodrow, K., & Baj, J. (1985). Marriage and divorce in twentieth century American cohorts. *Demography, 22,* 101–114.

Schoen, R., & Weinick, R. (1993). The slowing metabolism of marriages: Figures from 1988 U.S. Marital Status Life Tables. *Demography, 30,* 737–746.

Schwartzman, J. (Ed.). (1985). *Families and other systems: The macrosystemic context of therapy.* New York: Guilford Press.

Schwartzman, J., & Kneifel, A. (1985). Familiar institutions: How the child care system replicates family patterns. In J. Schwartzman (Ed.), *Families and other systems: The macrosystemic context of family therapy* (pp. 87–107). New York: Guilford Press.

Scott, C. (1977). Archetypes and consciousness. *Idealistic Studies, 7,* 28–49.

Selvini-Palazzoli, M., Cirillo, S., Selvini, M., & Sorrentino, A. M. (1989). *Family games: General models of psychotic processes in the family.* New York: Norton.

Selznick, P. (1992). *The moral commonwealth.* Berkeley: University of California Press.

Sherwood, M. (1969). *The logic of explanation in psychoanalysis.* New York: Academic Press.

Shorter, E. (1975). *The making of the modern family.* New York: Basic Books.

Simpson, J., & Weiner, E. (Eds.). (1989). *Oxford English dictionary* (2nd ed.). Oxford: Clarendon Press.

Slife, B. (1997, August). *Are knowledge communities incommensurable in a fragmented psychology?* Paper presented at the annual meeting of the American Psychological Association, Chicago.

Slife, B., & Williams, R. (1995). *What's behind the research? Discovering hidden assumptions in the behavioral sciences.* Thousand Oaks, CA: Sage.

Slife, B., & Williams, R. (1997). Toward a theoretical psychology: Should a subdiscipline be formally recognized? *American Psychologist, 52,* 117–129.

Snyder, D. (1981). *Marital satisfaction inventory manual.* Los Angeles: Western Psychological Services.

Solomon, R. (1973). Nietzsche, nihilism, and morality. In R. Solomon (Ed.), *Nietzsche: A collection of critical essays* (pp. 202–225). Notre Dame, IN: University of Notre Dame Press.

Solomon, R. (1985). *Introducing philosophy.* Orlando, FL: Harcourt Brace.

Spanier, G. (1976). Measuring dyadic adjustment: New scales for assessing the quality of marriage and similar dyads. *Journal of Marriage and the Family, 38,* 15–38.

Spanier, G., & Lewis, R. (1980). Marital quality: A review of the seventies. *Journal of Marriage and the Family, 42,* 96–110.

Spence, J. (1985). Achievement American style. *American Psychologist, 40,* 1285–1295.

Staats, A. W. (1991). Unified positivism and unification psychology: Fad or new field? *American Psychologist, 46,* 899–912.

Stern, D. (1996). The social construction of therapeutic action. *Psychoanalytic Inquiry, 16,* 265–293.

Stevens, S. (1951). Mathematics, measurement, and psychophysics. In S. Stevens (Ed.), *Handbook of experimental psychology* (pp. 1–49). New York: Wiley.

Stroebe, M., Gergen, M., Gergen, K., & Stroebe, W. (1992). Broken hearts or broken bonds: Love and death in historical perspective. *American Psychologist, 47,* 1205–1212.

Sullivan, W. (1986). *Reconstructing public philosophy.* Berkeley: University of California Press.

Tavris, C. (1991). The mismeasure of woman: Paradoxes and perspectives in the study of gender. In J. D. Goodchilds (Ed.), *Psychological perspectives on human diversity in America* (pp. 91–128). Washington, DC: American Psychological Association.

Taylor, C. (1975). *Hegel.* Cambridge, England: Cambridge University Press.

Taylor, C. (1978). *Hegel and modern society.* Cambridge, England: Cambridge University Press.

Taylor, C. (1985a). *Philosophical papers: Vol. 1. Human agency and language.* Cambridge, England: Cambridge University Press.

Taylor, C. (1985b). *Philosophical papers: Vol. 2. Philosophy and the human sciences.* Cambridge, England: Cambridge University Press.

Taylor, C. (1985c). Self-interpreting animals. In *Philosophical papers: Vol. 1. Human agency and language* (pp. 45–76). Cambridge, England: Cambridge University Press.

Taylor, C. (1989). *Sources of the self.* Cambridge, MA: Harvard University Press.

Taylor, C. (1991). The dialogical self. In D. Hiley, J. Bohman, & R. Schusterman (Eds.), *The interpretive turn: Philosophy, science, culture* (pp. 304–314). Ithaca, NY: Cornell University Press.

Taylor, C. (1993). Engaged agency and background in Heidegger. In C. Guignon (Ed.), *The Cambridge companion to Heidegger* (pp. 317–336). Cambridge, England: Cambridge University Press.

Taylor, C. (1995). *Philosophical arguments.* Cambridge, MA: Harvard University Press.

Taylor, S., & Brown, J. (1988). Illusion and well-being: A social psychological perspective on mental health. *Psychological Bulletin, 103,* 193–210.

Terman, L. (1938). *Psychological factors in marital happiness.* New York: McGraw-Hill.

Thornton, A. (1989). Changing attitudes toward family issues in the United States. *Journal of Marriage and the Family, 51,* 873–893.

Tocqueville, A. de (1969). *Democracy in America.* New York: Anchor Books. (Original work published 1835)

REFERENCES

323

Trilling, L. (1971). *Sincerity and authenticity*. Cambridge, MA: Harvard University Press.

Valle, R., & Halling, S. (1989). *Existential-phenomenological perspectives in psychology*. New York: Plenum.

Veroff, J., Douvan, E., & Hatchett, S. (1995). *Marital instability: A social and behavioral study of the early years*. New York: Praeger.

Vogel, L. (1994). *The fragile "we": Ethical implications of Heidegger's* Being and Time. Evanston, IL: Northwestern University Press.

Wachtel, E., & Wachtel, P. (1986). *Family dynamics in individual psychotherapy*. New York: Guilford Press.

Wachtel, P. (1977). *Psychoanalysis and behavior therapy*. New York: Basic Books.

Wachtel, P. (1997). *Psychoanalysis, behavior therapy, and the relational world*. Washington, DC: American Psychological Association.

Walder, L., Abelson, R., Eron, L., Banta, T. & Laulicht, J. (1961). Development of a peer-rating measure of aggression. *Psychological Reports, 9,* 497–556.

Wallerstein, J., & Blakeslee, S. (1995). *The good marriage*. Boston: Houghton Mifflin.

Warnke, G. (1987). *Gadamer: Hermeneutics, tradition, and reason*. Stanford, CA: Stanford University Press.

Warnke, G. (1993). Hermeneutics, tradition and the standpoint of women. In B. Wachterhauser (Ed.), *Hermeneutics and truth*. Evanston, IL: Northwestern University Press.

Weingarten, H. (1985). Marital status and well-being: A national study comparing first-married, currently divorced, and remarried adults. *Journal of Marriage and the Family, 47,* 653–661.

Weinrach, S. (1980, Spring). Unconventional therapist: Albert Ellis. *Personnel and Guidance Journal,* pp. 152–159.

Westerman, M. (1986). Meaning and psychotherapy: A hermeneutic reconceptualization of insight-oriented, behavioral, and strategic approaches. *International Journal of Eclectic Psychotherapy, 5,* 47–68.

Whitaker, C. A., & Blumberry, W. M. (1988). *Dancing with the family*. New York: Brunner/Mazel.

Williams, B. (1978). *Descartes: The project of pure inquiry*. Harmondsworth, England: Penguin Books.

Williams, B. (1986). A critique of utilitarianism. In C. Sommers (Ed.), *Right and wrong: Basic readings in ethics* (pp. 93–101). Orlando, FL: Harcourt Brace.

Williams, R. (1994). The modern, the post-modern, and the question of truth: Perspectives on the problem of agency. *Journal of Theoretical and Philosophical Psychology, 14,* 25–39.

Winch, P. (1958). *The idea of social science and its relation to philosophy*. New York: Routledge.

Winch, P. (1977). Understanding a primitive society. In F. Dallmayr &
     T. McCarthy (Eds.), *Understanding and social inquiry* (pp. 159–188).
     Notre Dame, IN: University of Notre Dame Press.

Winnicott, D. (1965). The maturational process and the facilitating environ-
     ment. New York: International Universities Press.

Wolf, E. (1977). "Irrationality" in a psychoanalytic psychology of the self. In
     T. Mischel (Ed.), *The self* (pp. 203–223). Oxford, England: Blackwell.

Wolfe, A. (1989). *Whose keeper? Social science and moral obligation.* Berkeley:
     University of California Press.

Wolfe, T. (1983). *The purple decades: A reader.* New York: Berkley.

Yanchar, S., & Slife, B. (1997). Pursuing unity in a fragmented psychology:
     Problems and prospects. *Review of General Psychology, 1,* 235–255.

Yalom, I. (1980). *Existential psychotherapy.* New York: Basic Books.

About the Authors

FRANK C. RICHARDSON is professor of educational psychology at the University of Texas at Austin. He is coauthor, with Robert Woolfolk, of *Stress, Sanity, and Survival*. His research has focused on cognitive-behavioral approaches to the treatment of anxiety and stress. Currently, his scholarly interests include psychotherapy theory, topics in theoretical and philosophical psychology, and the philosophy of social science.

BLAINE J. FOWERS is associate professor in the Department of Educational and Psychological Studies at the University of Miami. His research has focused on marital satisfaction and stability and positive illusions in marriage. His primary scholarly interests include the philosophy of psychology, especially the role of cultural and moral values in family therapy, and the philosophy of social science.

CHARLES B. GUIGNON is professor of philosophy at the University of Vermont. He has published widely in the area of hermeneutics, especially concerning the work of Heidegger and Gadamer. His other interests include historiography, literary theory, existentialism, and psychotherapy theory. He has published several books, including *Heidegger and the Problem of Knowledge, The Cambridge Companion to Heidegger, Dostoevsky's The Grand Inquisitor,* and *The Good Life.*

NAME INDEX

A

Abelson, R., 142
Adler, A., 106–107, 108, 265
Adler, M., 45
Antonovsky, A., 30
Ariès, P., 131
Aristotle, 62, 233, 269
Augustine, Saint, 204

B

Bacon, F., 291
Bagarrozi, D., 161
Baj, J., 77
Bakhtin, M. M., 264
Balcom, D. A., 81
Bandura, A., 97
Bankhart, C. P., 115, 123, 130
Banta, T., 142
Barich, R. R., 158
Baudelaire, C., 26
Beck, A., 100, 104
Becker, E., 294
Beiner, R., 268
Bell, D., 51
Bellah, R., 7, 11, 34, 37–38, 41, 49,
    70–71, 73, 75, 77, 87, 91,
    105–106, 110, 111, 131, 132, 136,
    158–159, 160, 162–163, 166, 168,
    174, 175, 243, 271
Benhabib, S., 196
Bentham, J., 44
Berger, P., 25–27, 29, 30
Bergin, A., 70, 239
Berlin, I., 174–175

Bernal, G., 78
Bernstein, R. J., 13, 88, 112, 127,
    141, 154, 174, 175, 177, 179, 180,
    181, 182, 224, 289, 298
Bielby, D. D., 158
Binswanger, L., 122
Blakeslee, S., 159, 160
Blumberg, S., 160
Blumberry, W. M., 83, 84, 85, 86
Bograd, M., 81, 89
Booth, A., 165
Boss, M., 122–123, 130
Boss, P., 73, 80
Boszormenyi-Nagy, I., 87, 88
Bowen, M., 81, 84
Bradbury, T., 165, 293
Brock, G., 166
Brown, J., 292–293
Bruner, J., 19–20, 236
Buber, M., 136
Buchler, J., 287
Bugental, J., 123–124, 130
Bumpass, L., 161, 294

C

Camus, A., 135–136
Chaplin, C., 6
Cherlin, A., 161, 166, 171
Chodorow, N., 196
Christopher, J., 13
Cicero, 31
Cirillo, S., 81
Clements, M., 166–167
Colapinto, J., 80

SUBJECT INDEX

A

Abstraction: as dilemma of modern culture, 26; harmful consequences of, 35–36; objectification and, 202, 240–241

Accomplices, 94

Adaptability, family, 85–86

Aesthetics, 225–228

Affirmation of ordinary life, 163

After Virtue (MacIntyre), 40

Aggression: cognitive theory of, 141–155, 304–305; development of, 143, 146–148; individualism and, 146–150, 305; instrumental theory and perpetuation of, 152–153; intention and, 145–146, 154; measurement of, 142, 143; modeling of, 147–148; as problem-solving strategy, 144–145; reduction of, 150–152; replacing, with prosocial behavior, 150–152; research, moral dimension of, 153–155, 304–305; self psychology view of, 248; stability of, 143; state control of, 149–150

Alienation, 6; marriage for coping with, 160; in modern market-oriented society, 63–64

"Analytic attitude," 54–57, 68

Ancestors, 7

Anomie, 6, 38

Anticipation of completion, 229

Anticipation of truth, 229

Antinomy of value, 40

Anxiety: Cartesian, 298; disintegration, 248; existential view of, 121–122, 125–126, 127, 131–134; of modern life, 267

Anxiety reduction: behavior therapy for, 93, 99–100; in integrative psychotherapy, 99–101, 103, 104

Application, and understanding, 233–234

Arbitrary inference, 100

Archetypes (Jungian), 58–61, 107

Articulation of emotions, 219–220

Artwork as events of truth, 225–228

Assertiveness training, 93

Attachment research, 305–306

Authenticity: in existential psychotherapy, 115–116, 123, 124–125; in existentialism, 121–122, 130–131, 136; in Gadamer's hermeneutics, 234, 250–251; in Heidegger's hermeneutics, 210–211

Authority (problem of): critical and feminist concerns with, 297; dilemmas of freedom and responsibility and, 69–72; Freudian psychoanalytic theory and, 56, 57; Fromm's theory and, 61–62, 65–67; Jungian psychoanalytic theory and, 60, 61; psychotherapy theories and, 54, 69–72, 242–243; self psychology and, 251–252

Autonomous self, 4–5

Autonomy, 15, 25; in hermeneutic-dialogue psychotherapy, 263–268;

Therapist empathy, 95, 103, 248–251, 261–262

Therapy relationship: hermeneutic-dialogue approach to, 262–276; in integrative psychotherapy *versus* self psychology, 103; moral decision making in, 265–268; therapist influence in, 262, 263–268

Time, in modern culture, 26

Tradition, in Heidegger's hermeneutic approach, 208–209

Transcendence, existential, 120

Transcendental democracy, 31–32

Truth and Method (Gadamer), 221–235

U

Übermensch, 121–122

Unconscious, collective, 58–59

Understanding: anticipations of, 229; application of, 233–234; in Dilthey's hermeneutics, 206–207; in Gadamer's hermeneutics, 228–234; in Heidegger's hermeneutics, 211; in Kohut's self psychology, 246, 248–251; in Schafer's narrative approach, 253–260; self-interpreting beings and, 213–221, 278–282, 300–301. *See also* Interpretations; Meaning

Universal intellectuals, 21

Utilitarian individualism, 49, 291; in family life, 73–74, 77–78; in psychotherapies, 105–106. *See also* Individualism

Utilitarian moral theory, 42, 44–46, 47

V

Value-neutral approach, 1, 11, 13, 17; critical social science critique of, 182–184; disguised ideology of, 141–142, 173–176, 182–185, 290–291; disguised ideology of, in aggression research, 141–155; disguised ideology of, in mainstream social science, 176–179; disguised ideology of, in marital research, 164–172; of family therapy techniques, 88; theory-and-practice approach *versus*, 303–306

Values: dilemma of objective *versus* subjective, 36–40; in existential psychotherapy, 123, 126–127, 128–129, 132–134, 136–137; and research, 16; in self psychology, 105; in social science inquiry, 173–176; underpinning family therapy, 73–74, 80–90; underpinning modern psychotherapy, 3–9, 53–72. *See also* Moral values

Vicious circles, 94, 303

Victimization: existential view of, 128; interpretive view of, 280–281

Voluntarism, in marriage and family life, 75, 78

W

Weltanschauung, 181–182

We've Had a Hundred Years of Psychotherapy and the World's Getting Worse (Hillman and Ventura), 2

"What Is Enlightenment" (Foucault), 174

Wholehearted engagement, 102, 103

Wholeness, as goal of individuation, 58, 59, 60–61

Work: impersonalism of, 109–110; meaninglessness of, 36

World Wars I and II, 223

World-design, 122

Worldhood of the world, 209

World-openness, 122–123